Jeremiah's New Covenant:
An Augustinian Reading

Journal of Theological Interpretation Supplements
MURRAY RAE
University of Otago, New Zealand
Editor-in-Chief

1. Thomas Holsinger-Friesen, *Irenaeus and Genesis: A Study of Competition in Early Christian Hermeneutics*
2. Douglas S. Earl, *Reading Joshua as Christian Scripture*
3. Joshua N. Moon, *Jeremiah's New Covenant: An Augustinian Reading*

Jeremiah's New Covenant:
An Augustinian Reading

JOSHUA N. MOON

Winona Lake, Indiana
EISENBRAUNS
2011

Copyright © 2011 Eisenbrauns
All rights reserved.

Printed in the United States of America

www.eisenbrauns.com

Library of Congress Cataloging-in-Publication Data

Moon, Joshua N.
  Jeremiah's new covenant : an Augustinian reading / Joshua Moon.
    p. cm. — (Journal of theological interpretation supplements ; 3)
  Includes bibliographical references and indexes.
  ISBN 978-1-57506-702-5 (pbk. : alk. paper)
  1. Bible. O.T. Jeremiah XXXI, 31–34—Criticism, interpretation, etc.—History. 2. Augustine, Saint, Bishop of Hippo. I. Title.
  BS1525.52.M66 2011
  224′.20609—dc22
                                                                2010047935

The paper used in this publication meets the minimum requirements of the American National Standard for Information Sciences—Permanence of Paper for Printed Library Materials, ANSI Z39.48-1984.♾™

This work is dedicated to the memory of Ebenezer and Hannah Moon

(April 4, 2009)

Amicis chara,
Parentibus charior
Deo charissima

Table of Contents

	Acknowledgments	ix
I.	**Introduction**	**1**
	1. The 'Augustinian' Contrast	3
	2. The 'New Covenant': A First Approximation	4
II.	**Jeremiah's New Covenant in Jerome and Augustine**	**5**
	1. Jerome and the New Covenant	6
	2. Augustine and the New Covenant as Mutatio Sacramentorum	11
	3. Augustine and the 'Salvific' Contrast	14
	4. Conclusions	28
III.	**Jeremiah's New Covenant in High Medieval Theology**	**30**
	1. Thomas and the Mutatio Sacramentorum	33
	2. Locating the Discussion in the Summa	39
	3. 'Law' in Thomas: Natural, Human, and Divine	41
	4. The 'New Law' in Thomas	47
	5. Elsewhere in the High Medieval Tradition	53
	6. Conclusions	57
IV.	**The Early Modern Reformed Tradition**	**58**
	1. An Augustinian Start: Philip Melanchthon	59
	2. A Contrast of Accidents: Heinrich Bullinger	67
	3. From Complexity to Simplicity: Oecolampadius	75
	4. Augustinian Remnants (a): John Calvin	82
	5. Augustinian Remnants (b): Peter Martyr Vermigli	97
	6. Conclusions	101
V.	**17th Century Reformed: The Continued Struggle**	**103**
	1. Caspar Olevianus	104
	2. John Ball	110
	3. Herman Witsius	123
	4. Widening the Struggle	132
	5. Conclusions	137

VI.	**The New Covenant in Modern Discourse**	**140**
	1. Bernard Duhm	142
	2. The New Covenant in the Life Experience of the Prophet	148
	3. The New Covenant in the Prophetic Traditions	151
	4. The New Covenant and the Deuteronomists	160
	5. A Renewed Covenant?	168
	6. An Augustinian Heritage	175
	7. Conclusions	179
VII.	**The Context of the New Covenant**	**180**
	1. The Oracle in the Book	180
	2. The Broken Covenant	184
	a. Jer 11:1-13	186
	b. Jer 7:21-28	197
	3. The Oracles of Restoration: chs. 30-31	202
	a. Jer 30:12-17	204
	b. Jer 30:4-11	208
	c. Jer 30:18-22	214
	d. Jer 31	217
	e. The Wider Book	220
	4. Conclusions	223
VIII.	**Jeremiah's New Covenant: *Restitutio ad Integrum***	**225**
	1. The Broken Covenant: 31:31-32	226
	2. The 'New' Covenant: 31:33-34	229
	3. Conclusions	243
IX.	**Conclusions and Theological Directions**	**245**
	1. Unity of the Covenant	247
	a. The New and Eternal Covenant (of Grace)	247
	b. Qumran and the New Covenant	250
	c. The Climax of the Covenant	253
	2. Unity of the People of God	258
	Works Cited	**261**
	Indexes	**285**

Acknowledgments

> At best, out theology is *theologia viatorum*. But it also stands under the promise of this best: that it really can be *theologia viatorum*. It is as such that it can and will be true.
> (Karl Barth, *Church Dogmatics*, II.1, p.209)

I take great comfort that this work has no need for higher aspirations than being written by one 'on the way' to others on the way, dim and brief as the way might be—and written surrounded by fellow pilgrims. I thank my supervisors Dr. Mark Elliott and Dr. Nathan MacDonald for their encouragements and close readings. Prof. Bruce Gordon and Dr. David Reimer likewise read the work and offered helpful comments from their spheres of expertise. Prof. Gordon McConville and Prof. Chris Seitz also were involved in this work at various stages, and I am grateful to them. Bob Stulac had the unenviable task of proof-reading my Latin translations, and I thank him for it. I had the benefit of many friends at two institutions who made this research a joy: Heath Thomas, Aubrey Spear, Ryan O'Dowd and Chad Steiner deserve special mention from Cheltenham; and Aaron Kuecker, Kevin Diller, Seth Tarrer, Gerry Wheaton, Luke Tallon, and R.J. Matava (among many others) at St. Andrews. Such good and gifted friends is a humbling grace. Unfortunately, however, none of the above have agreed to accept responsibility for the remaining flaws in this work.

My parents, David and Cyndy Moon, and my parents-in-law, Robert and Florence Rayburn, have been supportive in every way imagineable. Dr. Rayburn especially deserves my thanks—my intellectual debt to him is immense. Our friends Jim and Paige Price have also shown immense kindness to us. I also thank Alisdair Macleod for his faithful ministry at the St Andrews Free Church, and of course my new home and church family at Good Shepherd. Gregory of Nazianzus is said to have believed theology to be an act of worship. I, at least, cannot imagine doing this work of theology without the faithful worship of these two dear churches.

My wife Bryonie has been everything and more to me, my joy and crown.

> Of all that I have looked on with these eyes
> Thy goodness and thy power have fitted me
> The holiness and grace to recognize.
> (Dante, *Paradiso*, XXXI.82-84; tr. D. Sayers)

Thank you, my Beatrice.

1

Introduction

'Can anything new be said about [Jeremiah] 31:31-34?'[1]

Few texts in the prophetic literature have received as much Christian theological interest as the promise of a 'new covenant' in Jer 31:31-34. To examine the theological uses of the text in Christian tradition is to move along such central dogmatic *loci* as justification, human free will, the sacraments, the relationship between the two parts of Christian Scripture—and that ancient dispute between Judaism and Christianity, where the text finds its chief role today. Yet for all the apparent awareness that the text has a lengthy legacy in Christian interpretation very little has been done to examine this legacy, much less to bridge contemporary exegetical concerns to the readings of the text from the time between the 4th-17th centuries.[2] In what follows I will make an argument for a particular reading of Jeremiah's 'new covenant' oracle that is well-represented (if often inconsistently) in that seeming abyss that stretches from the 4th-17th centuries in the Christian tradition, only to fall almost entirely from view in most discussions of the modern period.

The central thread of the argument lies with what I have labeled an 'Augustinian' reading of Jeremiah's new covenant. My interest in the end is not 'historical' in a descriptive sense, either a history of interpretation, history of ideas, or historical reading of Jer 31:31-34 (though all these play a role). My in-

---

1. G.L. Keown et al., *Jeremiah 26-52* (WBC; Dallas: Word, 1995), 130.
2. The potential recent exceptions tend more to prove the need than satisfy it: Petrus Gräbe offers an interesting discussion of the 4th c. Syriac theologian Aphrahat, but offers just two pages on 'early federal theology', without a single independent reference to a primary source (at the end of which the tradition is summarily dismissed), and then three pages on Karl Barth. Even less helpful is the 'history of interpretation' by Fẹmi Adeyẹmi: within 8 pages he attempts to treat Augustine, Thomas Aquinas, Luther, Calvin, and the post-Reformation Reformed, with very little success in each case. Petrus J. Gräbe, *New Covenant, New Community: The Significance of Biblical and Patristic Covenant Theology for Contemporary Understanding* (Carlisle: Paternoster, 2006), 198-203; Fẹmi Adeyẹmi, *The New Covenant Torah in Jeremiah and the Law of Christ in Paul* (New York: Peter Lang, 2007), 28-35.

terest is the construction of a viable reading of the text, given today's exegetical standards, that stands deliberately as a part of a lengthy tradition of Christian theological reflection. As will be painfully clear, I offer neither a reception-history of the text nor a history of interpretation. The gaps between the chapters in the history of interpretation (and even within those chapters), like the concerns with 'patterns' of reading in the 17th century Reformed, are ample evidence that my interest is not to tell the story of the text's interpretation. Rather the selected moments of interpretation are given to provide a pedigree and a glimpse at the journey for a particular reading—and, I hope, to make it harder to dismiss the proposed reading as 'novel'.

My own story in coming to this reading follows the main lines of this work. I had already begun exegetical work and interest in Jeremiah when I was introduced to what appeared a new way of reading Jeremiah's new covenant through one recent work (Rayburn). This work pointed me back to some theologians from previous generations—first the American Presbyterian Robert Dabney. Dabney led me further back to Herman Witsius; Witsius led me to Calvin; and Calvin pointed me back to Augustine. And if a reading is found in Augustine (so I thought), then surely it must emerge more often and have more support than is often assumed. And so I began to work on two fronts: reading Jer 31:31-34 in dialogue with modern and contemporary approaches to the book, and exploring the theological and historical reasons for Augustine's reading as it is represented (or not) throughout the Christian West. In short, I found myself reading Jeremiah's new covenant in dialogue with the church of the living and the dead. This personal narrative should also explain somewhat my selection of interlocutors. I do not mean that I have only included those sources who have agreed with my reading: the selection of the early modern Reformed tradition, for instance, stems chiefly because of the confusion that appears in discussions of the text at the time. But since my goal is a constructive reading of Jeremiah's new covenant, I have engaged those sources from who seem to be most helpful for framing a reading today in the light of the past traditions. One could easily have chosen the Lutheran, Roman Catholic, or Eastern traditions to focus some of the theological questions and perhaps have emerged with different nuances in the questions asked of the text. But I have worked chiefly with the Reformed tradition, my own tradition and one in which Jeremiah's new covenant oracle has played a significant role.

The end of this work is exegetical: to read the promise of a 'new covenant' in Jer 31:31-34 better. In some ways, then, the final exegetical section must be able to stand on its own merits as able to answer questions of how best to read the text. But for all the philosophical and contextual shifts in the history of theology, the basic text of Jer 31:31-34 (especially in the West) has remained stable. And many of the theological and exegetical issues are given focus by the wrestling with the text that has occurred through the centuries. We can learn something of what 'reading better' means with respect to the text by reading the debates and ideas of older days. In this regard, the work is an unapolegetic attempt at theological exegesis: exegesis done in dialogue with, informed by, and interested in Christian theology.

1. *The 'Augustinian' Contrast*

I refer throughout the study to an 'Augustinian' reading (or family of readings) of Jer 31:31-34, in spite of the slipperiness of the adjective. W.J. Courtenay once wryly remarked that if one uses 'Augustinian' to indicate influence by Augustine, then nearly everything in Western theology could be given the modifier.[3] Further justification for my use of the term will appear, but throughout the study I use the phrase 'Augustinian reading' to describe a reading of Jer 31:31-34 that shares its main contours with the reading of that oracle put forward by Augustine in his later works. Generally this is simple enough to show since many figures in this line of thought explicitly cite Augustine on the subject. The central crux of this reading lies in the point of contrast at stake in Jer 31:31-34. Rather than seeing the contrast to be one of degree, quality, or development (such as a contrast within redemptive-history, from Old Testament to New Testament eras), Augustinian readings see the contrast as absolute: a contrast between apostasy or infidelity and faithfulness, or two mutually exclusive ways of standing before God. And because Augustine was the most significant and earliest (post-apostolic) figure to expound this form of the contrast explicitly in Christian thought, I have labeled it 'Augustinian.'

I enter into Christian interpretation rather late, offering only passing mention to the opening centuries and excluding almost entirely the uses of the text in the New Testament. The most basic reason for this is economy. In my view, and as reiterated in the conclusions, the uses of Jer 31:31-34 in the New Testament need to be reevaluated. Too often contemporary interpreters have been content with a particular (redemptive-historical) contrast of Jer 31:31-34 and taken that as the assumption for seeing what is done with the text in Paul, Hebrews, or even Qumran.[4] But to address these issues adequately would be im-

---

3. See W.J. Courtenay, *Schools and Scholars in Fourteenth Century England* (Princeton: Princeton Univ, 1987), 307-27.

4. E.g. the two pages devoted to the 'original meaning' of the oracle by Susanne Lehne, *The New Covenant in Hebrews* (JSNTSup 44; Sheffield: Sheffield Academic Press, 1990).

possible within the scope of this work. In these points the study can be seen as opening new (or re-opening old) possibilities of reading.

From beginning with Augustine and moving through the tradition up until the 17th century Reformed, I turn in chapter 6 to a lengthy engagement with modern discussions since Bernhard Duhm's seminal commentary in 1901. Though the gap between the Reformed orthodox and Bernhard Duhm is jarring and complex, in each case we are dealing with the same text and the same struggle to read the text responsibly. Modern readings are just one further part of the history of interpretation and I have found it fruitful and interesting to read the literature in the light of what is being rejected or furthered from earlier generations—wittingly or not—as a part of the same struggle even in the midst of shifting philosophical currents, theological convictions, or methods of exegesis.

2. *The 'New Covenant': A First Approximation*

My constructive exegetical argument for reading the 'new covenant' can be summarized briefly to give a first approximation that will be more fully defended and expanded in chapters 7 and 8. If our interest lies (as I think it should) in the role that 31:31-34 is given to play in the edited book of Jeremiah, we find two important points: (1) that the contrast for the 'new covenant' is the 'broken covenant' described throughout the book as the near-universal and near-absolute apostasy of the people against Yhwh; and (2) the restoration oracles throughout the book—and in chs. 30-31 in particular—play the role of overturning the oracles of judgment and establishing the way things always ought to have been. By supporting these points, then putting them together, I will argue that the oracle of the 'new covenant' oveturns the divine judgment as described in Jeremiah, and restores an ideal state in which we see everything the way it always ought to have been between Yhwh and his people. The contrast, then, lies between the universal apostasy of the broken covenant and the idyllic faithfulness of the new. In other words, the contrast is between apostasy and fidelity; the contrast between the 'old' and 'new' covenant is absolute, concerned with two mutually exclusive standings before Yhwh.

So *can* anything new be said about Jer 31:31-34, as asked by the commentators at the outset? Perhaps: since the time of that question a large number of authors seem to have thought so. But the aim of this work is to say something 'old' about it, and say it anew—to offer a 'renewed' rather than a 'new' reading, bringing into dialogue theological history and modern exegesis to ask how we might better read Jeremiah's oracle of the new covenant today.

2

Jeremiah's New Covenant in Jerome and Augustine

Our story begins with two men: one, a scholarly monk living and writing his sharp polemics in a small monastery outside of Bethlehem, and the other a younger contemporary from North Africa who would very quickly become a significant social and political figure as bishop of Hippo. These men were nearly as far apart as scholars can be, with numerous differences of personality and outlook. Jerome lived with a (wavering) disdain for the 'wisdom of the age', while Augustine made no attempt to hide philosophical learning from use within Christian theology. So while Jerome would dream of being damned a Ciceronian rather than saved a Christian, Augustine reportedly consoled himself with Plotinus while on his death bed during Hippo's siege.[1] Jerome was a gifted linguist who fought his battles in the garb of a monk, while Augustine was a systematician with more than sufficient political acumen. But the shadows cast by these two figures on the development of Western Christian theology were immense. If one cuts into any commentary on Jeremiah (up to ch.32) throughout the medieval and into the early modern period, it bleeds Jerome.[2] And the influence of Augustine is too well-known to need repeating.[3]

---

1. See Jerome, "Letter 22," in *The Principal Works of St. Jerome* (NPNF, II.6; Grand Rapids, MI: Eerdmans, 1996), §30; or "Letter 14," §11; Possidius, "Life of Augustine," in *Early Christian Biographies* (Washington DC: CUA Press, 1952), §28, 31. A recent, very helpful work on Jerome is Megan Hale Williams, *The Monk and the Book: Jerome and the Making of Christian Scholarship* (Chicago/London: Univ. of Chicago, 2006). Dated, but still helpful is J.N.D. Kelly, *Jerome: His Life, Writings, and Controversies* (London: Duckworth, 1975). With Augustine, the discussions are more diverse: see the classic work by Peter Brown, *Augustine of Hippo: A Biography* (Rev. ed. University of California Press, 2000). Brown's moderately power-centred portrait is taken to a further extreme by James J. O'Donnell, *Augustine, Sinner and Saint: A New Biography* (London: Profile Books, 2005). See the more balanced work of Serge Lancel, *St. Augustine* (Tr. by Antonia Nevill. London: SCM Press, 2002).

2. E.g. the Carolingian commentary of Rabanus Maurus (d.856): *Expositionis super Jeremiam prophetam, libri viginti* (PL 111; Paris: n.d.).

3. Cf. e.g., Irena Backus, *Historical Method and Confessional Identity in the Era of the Reformation (1378-1615)* (Leiden: Brill, 2003), 6ff.

Jerome and Augustine had many things in common as well: both skilled writers, both devoted churchmen, both engaged in polemics against many of the same heresies and arguments. But they had, as it were, a 'parting of the ways' regarding the contrast at stake in Jer 31:31-34. And so, given their influence for the later tradition, they will stand in this thesis as the representatives of two distinct approaches to reading Jeremiah's new covenant: one, represented by Jerome, in which the 'old' and 'new' covenants are two successive eras and two ways in which God deals with his people; the other, represented by Augustine, in which the 'old' and 'new' covenants contrast two absolute states before God—belief and unbelief—in any era.

1. *Jerome and the New Covenant*

Jerome's unfinished commentary on Jeremiah, which runs only through ch. 32, was the last commentary he composed before his death in 419-20.[4] Jerome had already spent significant time in the book of Jeremiah, having early in his career translated Origen's homilies on the book – though by this point in his career Jerome had publicly distanced himself from his hero-turned-heretic.[5] Modern scholars praise this commentary as one of the more 'literal' of Jerome's commentaries—though this may simply have been a matter of economy in generally excluding the 'second step' of spiritual exegesis.[6] Jerome's polemical concerns when reading Jer 31:31-34, and his merging of the 'literal' and 'spiritual' readings in this case, is made clear in Jerome's introduction to chs. 30-31:

> [These chapters] will contain mystical promises, which the Jews and our Judaizers think will be completed in the consummation of the world, be-

---

4. It was begun around 414-15: see the discussion in Kelly, *Jerome*, 316.

5. In English as Origen, *Homilies on Jeremiah* (FC 97; Tr. by John Clark Smith. Washington DC: CUA Press, 1998). Unfortunately we do not have extant a homily by Origen addressing Jer 31:31-34. Jerome remarks disparagingly of Origen throughout this commentary: e.g., 'He is delirious in this place, always the allegorical interpreter...'' Jerome, *In Hieremiam Prophetam libri VI* (CCL 74; Tournholt: Brepols, 1960), V.2.16. For Jerome's wavering relationship with Origen, see Dennis Brown, *Vir Trilinguis: A study in the biblical exegesis of Saint Jerome* (Kampen: Kok Pharos, 1992), 153-65.

6. Thus, based on its 'literalness' René Kieffer calls it the 'most satisfactory' of all his commentaries: René Kieffer, "Jerome: His Exegesis and Hermeneutics," in *Hebrew Bible/Old Testament: The History of its Interpretation* (ed. Magne Saebo; 1.1; Göttingen: Vandenhoeck & Ruprecht, 1996), 680. Cf. Kelly, *Jerome*, 316; Brown, *Vir Trilinguis*, 131. I take the suggestion of economy from the comments of Williams, *Monk*, 120-21. For discussion of what 'literal' and 'spiritual' senses mean throughout Jerome's writings see Brown, *Vir Trilinguis*, 121-65.

cause they are not yet able to prove their fulfilment under Zerubbabel. We however – following the authority of the apostles and evangelists, and especially of the apostle Paul – point out that whatever is promised to the people of Israel according to the flesh [*carnaliter*], has been spiritually [*spiritaliter*] completed in us and is fulfilled today. Nor is there any other dispute between Jews and Christians except this: that, since they and we believe Christ is the promised son of God, so those things which are to be under Christ, having been fulfilled by us, are said to need to be fulfilled by them.[7]

This principle of promises to carnal Israel fulfilled to the spiritual church operates as a kind of maxim or determining hermeneutic for Jerome and was in practice and use already in his early commentary on Hosea:

> What we have often said is to be noted: the salvation of Israel and their restoration to God, and their redemption from captivity, are not to be interpreted according to the flesh [*carnaliter*], as the Jews think, but spiritually [*spiritaliter*], as is most truly acknowledged.[8]

Given such a hermeneutic and division of promises made to Israel *carnaliter* and their fulfilment for the church *spiritaliter* (taken from 2 Cor 3:6), we are not surprised to find an interpretation of Jer 31:31-34 along the lines of a contrast of two successive (temporal) eras of God's dealings, one with Israel and the other with the church. Jerome introduces his reading of 31:31-34 by appeal to the testimony of 'Paul (or whomever wrote the epistle)' to the Hebrews and then 'all churchmen' following, who, we are told, taught:

> everything [in 31:31-34] was completed in the first coming of the Saviour, and that the New Testament—which is the Gospel—has succeeded the Old Testament, by which the law of the letter is replaced by the law of the spirit.[9]

The two successive eras—of the letter and of the spirit—are then spelled out:

> When Israel was led out of the land of Egypt, there was in that people so great an intimacy with God that he says they clung by the hand and gave the covenant [*pactum*], which they made useless; and therefore the Lord disregarded them.[10] But now he promises in the Gospel, after the cross,

---

7. Jerome, *In Hieremiam*, §VI.1.1-2. Translations throughout this work are my own, unless indicated; though I have felt free to make use, with respect to Augustine and Jerome, of earlier translations (e.g. those in the NPNF), changed or updated as necessary. Likewise, spellings of older texts throughout the work have often been updated.

8. Jerome, *Commentarium in Osee prophetam* (CCL 76; Turnhout: Brepols, 1969), §III.14.5/9.

9. Jerome, *In Hieremiam*, §VI.26.4.

10. This is from the LXX rendering of 31:32 (cf. below, ch.8), followed also in

resurrection and ascension, is given a *pactum* not in tablets of stone, but in the fleshly tablets of the heart. And when the *testamentum* of the Lord has been written in the mind of the faithful, he himself is their God and they are his people.[11]

Jerome closes his comments by addressing the concern his readers might feel (or at least that *he* felt) that the text states the new covenant is to be made 'with the house of Israel and the house of Judah.' But, Jerome states, we must remember that 'the church of Christ is from the Jews and to them has come the Lord, the Saviour'.[12] So the new covenant developed and was born out of Israel and Judah: what was promised to 'them' is fulfilled by 'us'. Jerome then reminds the reader of the turn from the Jews to the Gentiles that he sees as a mark of the New Testament, appealing to Matt 15:24 ('I did not come for the lost sheep of the house of Israel') and to Paul's words when he turned from the Jews to the Gentiles in Acts 13:46.

For Jerome, then, the promise of the new covenant is clearly read as prediction of a turning from Israel to the Church in redemptive history: a religio-historical contrast of God's dealings with his people. Such a reading, broadly construed, is by no means novel to Jerome and can be found already in Justin Martyr,[13] likely in Origen,[14] then in Cyprian.[15] It is found most profoundly and

---

the Old Latin (cf. Augustine, below).

11. Ibid., §VI.26.5-6. For his view of the relationship between *pactum* and *testamentum* see Jerome, *Commentariorum in Malachiam prophetam* (CCL 76a; Tournholt: Brepols, 1970), II.3-4: 'It is to be noted that the Hebrew word *brth*, in Aquila συνθήκην, is here interpreted as *pactum*. The LXX always uses διαθήκην, that is *testamentum*, and in most places of the Scriptures *testamentum* does not express the will of one deceased but the *pactum* of one living.' Cf. Jerome, *In Hieremiam*, VI.26.4.

12. Ibid., VI.26.5-6.

13. Justin (Martyr), *Dialogue with Trypho, a Jew* (ANF 1; Tr. by Alexander Roberts and James Donaldson. Grand Rapids, MI: Wm. B. Eerdmans, 1996), §11. Craig Allert claims that for Justin the 'two most important concepts with which he deals' – in fact the 'hermeneutical key to Justin's interpretation of OT scripture in the *Dialogue*' – are the 'new law' and the two advents of the Messiah, the arguments for both of which begin with Justin's citation of Jer 31:31-34 (and Isa 51:4-5). Craig D Allert, *Revelation, Truth, Canon, and Interpretation: Studies in Justin Martyr's Dialogue with Trypho* (VCSup 64; Leiden: Brill, 2002), 223.

14. See, e.g., Origen, *Commentaire sur Saint Jean I* (SC 120; Paris: Les Éditions du Cerf, 1996), 1.35-37. Similarly his reading of Deut 18:15: 'Thus there was an expectation of some prophet having a likeness to Moses, mediating between God and men, and receiving a new covenant from God to give to his disciples.' Origen, *Commentaire sur Saint Jean II* (SC 157; Paris: Les Éditions du Cerf, 1970), §VI.90.

15. Cyprian, *Ad Quirinum* (CCL 3; Tournholt: Brepols, 1972), §1.11. The text

influentially in John Chrysostom's homilies on Hebrews,[16] and can be identified more or less with a number of others.[17] Henri de Lubac's summary of what he sees as the patristic and medieval view of the matter (whose monolithic nature I will challenge) captures Jerome's reading well:

> For the Christian there exist two successive 'Testaments,' which are not primarily or even essentially two books, but two 'Economies,' two 'Dispensations,' two 'Covenants,' which have given birth to two peoples, to two orders, established by God one after the other in order to regulate man's relationship with him. The goal of the one that is prior in time is to prepare the way for the second.[18]

Variations of the above comments by Jerome could be coordinated within the general scheme of his thought and other writings.[19] But my interest lies in the point of contrast it creates with Augustine's reading. And we can enter that contrast through the famous correspondence between the two figures – a correspondence deemed by one scholar to be 'from the psychological, intellectual, and religious points of view, one of the most fascinating in antiquity.'[20] Augustine's initial letter to Jerome, penned somewhere around 395, unfortunately did not reach its destination for another 8 years.[21] And the initial broaching of

---

is cited under the title, 'Quod dispositio alia et testamentum novum dari haberet', and is placed between the assertion of a 'new law' (*lex nova*) being established and the claim that the 'old baptism' was to cease. The citation of the text in §3.20 is in conjunction with Jer 32:27f, testifying that, 'The foundation and support of hope and faith is fear' – a very un-Augustinian notion (whatever its truth)!

16. See throughout his John Chrysostom, *Homilies on Hebrews* (NPNF I.14; Tr. by F. Gardiner. Grand Rapids, MI: Eerdmans, 1996), (e.g. Hom. 14, §2). Cf. also the reference (with comment on the 'two laws' promised) in his John Chrysostom, *Commentaire sur Isaïe* (SC 304; Paris: Les Éditions du Cerf, 1983), §2.4.

17. The most thorough treatment of the pre-4th century interpretations of the text is in Domenico Marafioti, *Sant'Agostino e la Nuova Alleanze: L'Interpetazione agostiniana di Geremia 31,31-34 nell'ambito dell'esegesi patristica* (Rome: Gregorian Univ. Press, 1995), 81-142. See also Knut Backhaus, "Das Bundesmotiv in der frühchristlichen Schwellenzeit: Hebräerbrief, Barnabasbrief, Dialogus cum Tryphone," in *Der ungekündigte Bund? Antworten des Neuen Testaments* (ed. Hubert Frankenmölle; Freiburg: Herder, 1998).

18. Henri de Lubac, *Medieval Exegesis* (2 vols.; Tr. by Mark Sebanc. Edinburgh: T&T Clark, 1998), 1.227. My emphasis.

19. E.g., Jerome, *Against Jovinianus* (NPNF II.6; Tr. by W.H. Fremantle. Grand Rapids, MI: Eerdmans, 1996), 2.27.

20. Kelly, *Jerome*, 217.

21. For the dates, I have followed the arguments of Ralph Hennings, *Der Briefwechsel zwischen Augustinus und Hieronymus und ihr Streit um den Kanon des*

our concerns occurs by Jerome's reading of the argument between Peter and Paul put forward in his commentary on Galatians. Jerome followed the (Origenist) view that the argument between Peter and Paul was merely staged for the benefit of those around.[22] For Augustine such a reading was untenable, for once you allow such a strategy of reading then no part of the biblical text would be safe from dismissal as dissimulation.[23] Augustine expands on this in Letter 40, written sometime between 397-99 (and again long delayed in arriving) where he brings up Paul becoming 'a Jew to the Jews', and so taking part in the 'sacraments of the *vetus testamentum*'.[24] Paul did not rebuke Peter's taking part in these sacraments *per se* – for Paul took part in them as well and they 'were not hurtful to one who had been accustomed to them.' Paul simply rebuked Peter's forcing Gentiles to participate in them as though salvation rested upon their keeping.

Jerome's response to these letters finally comes in 404, where Jerome states the issue in his own inimitable style:

> Paul, even when he was an apostle of Christ, observed Jewish ceremonies; and you affirm that they are in no wise hurtful to those who wish to retain them as they had received them from their fathers by the law. I, on the contrary, shall maintain, and though the world were to protest against my view, I may boldly declare that the Jewish ceremonies are to Christians both hurtful and fatal; and that whoever observes them, whether he be Jew or Gentile originally, is cast into the pit of perdition.[25]

Alten Testaments und die Auslegung von Gal. 2,11-14 (VCSup 21; Leiden: E.J. Brill, 1994).

22. Jerome admits to following Origen in "Letter 75," in *The Confessions and Letters of St. Augustine* (NPNF, I.1; Grand Rapids, MI: Eerdmans, 1994). The admission is polemical, as he calls Augustine's reading 'novel'. Hennings points out that Jerome's is a widespread interpretation in the Greek church, with such adherents as Eusebius of Emesa and John Chrysostom. Another interpretation, put forward by Clement of Alexandria, held that the 'Cephas' in the debate was another apostle by that name. But, contrary to Jerome's accusation of novelty, Hennings believes Augustine's reading is seen 'certainly' in Cyprian of Carthage ('...daß Petrus in Antiochia falsch gehandelt hat und zurecht von Paulus deswegen getadelt worden ist'), and is known elsewhere also in the West. Cf. Hennings, *Briefwechsel*, 220ff (citation from 249).

23. Augustine, "Letter 28," in *The Confessions and Letters of St. Augustine* (NPNF, 1.1; Grand Rapids, MI: Eerdmans, 1994), §2-4.

24. Idem, "Letter 40," §4-5.

25. Jerome, "Letter 75," §4.14.

To support this he cites Paul, for whom 'Christ is the end of the Law', as well as John's statement that 'the law was given to Moses, but grace and truth through Jesus Christ', to which he appends Jer 31:31-34:

> Instead of the grace of the law which has passed away, we have received the grace of the gospel which is abiding; and instead of the shadows and types of the old dispensation, the truth has come by Jesus Christ. Jeremiah also prophesied thus in God's name... [*full citation of 31:31-34*]. Observe what the prophet says, not to Gentiles, who had not been partakers in any former covenant, but to the Jewish nation. He who has given them the law by Moses, promises in place of it the new covenant of the gospel, that they might no longer live in the oldness of the letter, but in the newness of the spirit.

Jerome here simply exemplifies what he will detail in his commentary some twelve years later: Jeremiah's prophecy contrasts two successive eras of 'letter' and 'spirit', the time and law of Moses and the time of the spirit and the gospel. So at the least, we can say that Augustine's differences with Jerome on this matter, when they come, do not emerge because Augustine was unfamiliar with other uses of the text.

2. *Augustine and the New Covenant as Mutatio Sacramentorum*

An analysis of Augustine's use of the text is rather more complicated than Jerome's consistently one-sided reading. Augustine, at least up to 412, generally followed a reading of the text as a prophecy of the change of sacraments (*mutatio sacramentorum*) from the old to the new.[26] In these texts he differs little from Cyprian or Justin—or Jerome. He posits the contrast of the old and new covenants as between two eras, centered in the change of sacraments. But in the two most important texts for understanding his reading (*De spiritu et littera* and *Contra duas epistolas Pelegianorum*) Augustine offers a reading that eliminates almost entirely the contrast of eras with respect to Jer 31:31-34.[27] There are at least two plausible answers to this diversity in Augustine. First, it may be that

---

26. 'It is about to be accomplished, that change of sacraments of the old and new testament which had already been foretold by the prophetic voice...' Augustine, "Epistula 138," in *S. Aurelii Augustini Opera Omnia* (ed. J.-P. Migne; PL, 33; Paris: 1861), §7. Cf. Augustine, *Contra Faustum Manichaeum* (CSEL 25; Vienna: 1891), §18.4, §32.8-9 (composed 397-98).

27. A.-M. La Bonnardière rightly calls the *De spiritu* 'Le commentaire le plus important, continu et intégral' for Jer 31:31-34: A.-M. La Bonnardière, *Le Livre de Jérémie* (Biblia Augustiniana; Paris: Études Augustiniennes, 1972), 65.

this is an illustration of Augustine's principle of finding multiple meanings in a text:

> Sometimes not just one meaning but two or more meanings are perceived in the same words of scripture. Even if the writer's meaning is obscure, there is no danger here, provided that it can be shown from other passages of the holy scriptures that each of these interpretations is consistent with the truth.[28]

In this case Augustine may see two readings of the text, one clearly associated with the writer's meaning (that given below), and another which – though not precisely the 'intention of the writer' – is consistent with the truth and so is fine to use.[29]

The second solution stems from Marafioti's suggestion that there is a development in Augustine's exegesis from this notion of *mutatio sacramentorum* to an emphasis on the 'interior dimension of the new salvific disposition and of the grace that is opened for man' – the reading addressed below.[30] Such development is a possibility, since we have no instance of the text read as *mutatio sacramentorum* in any work clearly dated after *De spiritu*.[31] But the dates would

---

28. He adds, 'The person examining the divine utterances must of course do his best to arrive at the intention of the writer through whom the Holy Spirit produced that part of Scripture... [But] Perhaps the author too saw that very meaning in the words which we are trying to understand. Certainly the spirit of God who worked through the author foresaw without any doubt that it would present itself to a reader or listener, or rather planned that it should present itself, because it too is based on the truth.' Augustine, *On Christian Teaching* (Tr. by R.P.H. Green. Oxford Univ. Press, 1997), §3.84-85.

29. See Marafioti, *Sant'Agostino*, ch.7.

30. Ibid., 191. Marafioti also posits a third stage in Augustine's reading, where he adds the notion of the new covenant as washing away hereditary original sin. This seems to me already present in the second stage, even if nascent. If original sin is taken away by regeneration (see point (3) against the Pelagians below), and if the new covenant is identified with regeneration (below), then it is simply left for Augustine to spell out the deduction in his later works. At no point should this be construed as arguing that Augustine changed his view of the sacraments themselves, however; merely the relation of Jer 31:31-34 with respect to the sacraments.

31. That is, if we follow an early dating for *Tractatus adversus Iudaeos*, transl. as "In Answer to the Jews," in *Treatises on Marriage and other Subjects* (FC; Washington DC: CUA Press, 1955), (cf. §6.8). If a late date is claimed, then perhaps one can explain the inconsistency by the context: in the polemics against the Jews, Augustine is willing to draw the text to his aid to confront their desire to remain in the 'vetustate supervacanea' (ibid.). But when he reads the text with his eye on the Pelagian debates, a different reading emerges. Marafioti places the date of the *Tract. adv. Iud.* in 412, but his

be impressively close to one another, both *De spiritu* and Letter 138 (and possibly the *Tract. adv. Iud.*) coming in the year 412. The shift would then have been made within a single year's time. But the reason for entertaining this solution in the face of the closeness of the dates comes from Augustine's own comments in *De spiritu*:

> When the prophet promised a *novum testamentum* not according to the *testamentum* formerly made with the people of Israel… he said nothing about the change of sacrifices or other sacraments – though such change was without doubt going to follow just as we see happened, which in many other places the same prophetic Scriptures testify. But he only pointed out this difference: that God would place his laws in their minds who belong to this *testamentum*, and would write it on their hearts.[32]

Augustine explicitly distances himself from the reading of Jer 31:31-34 as concerned with the change of sacraments, justifying the second suggestion of a development of view over the first suggestion of a multiplicity of readings. These two solutions are not mutually exclusive, of course. Perhaps the best solution sees Augustine's study of the text in the context of the Pelagian controversy as driving him to posit that it does not address the 'change of sacraments'; yet he can still use the text in that sense since that change is testified in other places and is consistent with the truth.

Perhaps important (though perhaps not) is the fact that Pelagius appears to use the text in line with Jerome's general use as a contrast of eras. Commenting on Rom 3:31 ('Do we then tear down the law through faith? By no means! Rather, we uphold the law'), Pelagius states:

> we enable it [i.e. the law] to stand firm when we show that what it said is true, namely that law would follow after law, testament after testament, circumcision after circumcision (Jer 4:4, 31:31-34).[33]

So perhaps Augustine, aware of this, was unwilling any longer to grant the reading now that Pelagius had asserted it. In any case, Augustine's chief contribution to the history of interpretation of Jer 31:31-34 does not lie in his (perhaps only

---

dependence on exact language for biblical citation is precarious; more often it is placed significantly later. I see no reason to deny an early date, anticipating further development in (rather than depending on) the *City of God*. For discussion of dating, see Bernhard Blumenkranz, *Die Judenpredigt Augustins: ein Beitrag zur Geschichte der jüdisch-christlichen Beziehungen in den ersten Jahrhunderten* (Basel: Helbing & Lichtenhahn, 1946), 198-209; Marafioti, *Sant'Agostino*, 182-90.

    32. Augustine, *De spiritu et littera* (CSEL 60; Vienna: 1913), §42.

    33. Theodore De Bruyn, *Pelagius's Commentary on St. Paul's Epistle to the Romans* (Oxford: Clarendon, 1993), 84.

early) appeal to the *mutatio sacramentorum*, but in his later reading invoked to combat Pelagius and his heir, Julian of Aeclanum.

3. *Augustine and the 'Salvific' Contrast*

Augustine's detailed treatment of Jer 31:31-34 was born in the polemics against Pelagianism. Both of the main texts where Augustine develops his view of the contrast of covenants – the *De spiritu* (412) and *Contra epp. Pel.* (against Julain of Aeclanum, between 420-23) – are polemical treatises against the Pelagian threat. The controversy appears to have started out sluggishly with Augustine addressing Pelagius in generally friendly terms, and for some time refusing to believe (perhaps only rhetorically) that Pelagius himself was the instigator of the new teachings.[34] Nonetheless by the time Augustine penned the *De spiritu* the polemics were in full force.[35] Augustine saw three main points to be upheld against Pelagian thought: (1) grace is a gift rather than something merited; (2) sinless perfection while still in the body is impossible; and (3) original sin renders everyone stained at birth, only to be taken away by regeneration.[36] Whatever one thinks of these points as adequate for discussing 'Pelagianism', Augustine's reading of Jer 31:31-34 plays its role as an argument against one particular implication of this pattern of thought as he saw it.[37]

---

34. The story of the controversy has been told many times. For recent studies, cf. Lancel, *Augustine*, 413-48; Gerald Bonner, *St Augustine of Hippo: Life and Controversies* (Rev. ed. Norwich: Canterbury Press, 1986), 312-93; Jaroslav Pelikan, *The Emergence of the Catholic Tradition (100-600)* (Chicago: Univ. of Chicago Press, 1971), 278-331. For a strongly critical view of Augustine in this context, see O'Donnell, *Augustine*, 261-85. For open sympathy towards Pelagius, see B.R. Rees, *Pelagius: A Reluctant Heretic* (Woodbridge: Boydell Press, 1988). Other helpful studies include Brown, *Augustine*, 340ff, and the dated but useful study by Friedrich Loofs, "Pelagius und der pelagianische Streit," in *Realencyklopädie für protestantische Theologie und Kirche* (ed. Albert Haurk; vol. 15; Leipzig: 1904). Cf. also the thorough study, with the history of interpretation regarding Pelagianism, by Josef Lössl, *Julian von Aeclanum: Studien zu seinem Leben, seinem Werk, seiner Lehre und ihrer Überlieferung* (VCSup 60; Leiden: E.J. Brill, 2001).

35. Jerome's Jeremiah commentary also plays a part in this controversy: he characterises Pelagius as a 'huge, bloated, Alpine dog, weighed down with Scottish oats... able to rage more effectively with his heels than with his teeth.' Jerome, *In Hieremiam*, §III.1.3-4. As translated (albeit loosely) by Rees, *Pelagius*, 7.

36. Augustine outlines these in Augustine, *De dono perseverantiae* (Œuv. de S.Aug. 24; Paris: Desclée de Brouwer, 1962), §2.4. Cf. the interaction with these points as defining Pelagianism in Loofs, "Pelagius," 755f.

37. Lössl makes a compelling case for the centrality of a (continually) good

The theological point at issue in both *De spiritu* and *Contra epp. Pel.* is the Pelagian notion that the human will can, of its own power, do that which is right, so long as the grace of instruction is provided.[38] Augustine, unhappy with such a view, uses Jer 31:31-34 to prove the necessity of the grace of the Holy Spirit as the 'assister of virtue' for Christian life. In the *Contra epp. Pel.*, the contrast of the covenants and Jer 31 emerges out of an argument Augustine places in (presumably) Julian's mouth:

> For what catholic says what they accuse us as saying—'The Holy Spirit was not the assister of virtue in the *vetus testamentum*'—except when we understand *vetus testamentum* in the way in which the apostle spoke: as 'bringing forth from Mount Sinai to slavery'?[39]

We can reconstruct Julian's argument without much difficulty: (a) if the Holy Spirit is the assister of virtue, and (b) the Holy Spirit is given only in the *novum testamentum*, then (c) the Holy Spirit is not the assister of virtue in the *vetus testamentum*. Therefore—here would be the payoff—we have instances of virtuous living apart from the assistance of the Holy Spirit (e.g. Abraham, Moses, or David). Augustine wants to affirm both premises—(a) and (b)—but deny (c). So he makes a critical distinction regarding the term *vetus testamentum*:[40]

> And so in one way, by a custom of speech already prevailing, the law and all the prophets who prophesied until John are called the *vetus testamentum* – which is more precisely called the *vetus instrumentum* than the

---

creation in the thought of Julian (even granted his asceticism), which would account for his accusations of Manichaeism in Augustine as well as his differences at least in points (2) and (3) above: 'Die zentralen Begriffe der Philosophie Julians, Seele, Natur, Freiheit und Willen, sind nur aus dem Kontext eines von Julian genau umrissenen Schöpfungsbegriffs, nämlich des Begriffs eines allzeit simultan aktiven, guten und gerechten Schöpfergottes und einer dementsprechend in sämtlichen ihrer individuellen Einzelheiten („Naturen") gut sowie nach einer eigenen Gestzlichkeit, d.h. unter der Bedingung, daß sie geschaffen wurde, *notwendig* so – und nicht anders – geschaffenen Schöpfung heraus angemessen zu verstehen.' Lössl, *Julian*, 126.

38. 'But this is to be resisted fiercely and vehemently resisted, that they believe one is able, without the assistance of God, through one's own power of human will is able either able to procure righteousness [*iustitiam*] or to strive to procure it.' Augustine, *De spiritu*, §2.4.

39. Idem, *Contra duas epistulas Pelegianorum* (Œuv. de S.Aug., 23; Paris: Desclée de Brouwer, 1974), §3.6.

40. Missing this distinction and that below regarding letter/spirit lies at the outset of Preus's otherwise helpful work, resulting in a skewed portrayal of the history of the view of the Old Testament. James Samuel Preus, *From Shadow to Promise: Old Testament Interpretation from Augustine to the Young Luther* (Cambridge, MA: Harvard Univ. Press, 1969), 16-20.

vetus testamentum – but it is in another way that this name is used by apostolic authority, whether expressly or by suggestion.[41]

Augustine makes the same distinction when reviewing Pelagius's heresy trial at Diospolis in 415—a review marked by the conviction that Pelagius was deliberately and repeatedly equivocating. So Pelagius reportedly states that, 'the kingdom of heaven is promised in the *vetus testamentum*.' But Augustine replies:

> But the name *vetus testamentum* is normally used in two ways: one according to the authority of the divine Scriptures, and another according to a very vulgar (*vulgatissimam*) habit of speech.[42]

Thus Pelagius' statement could be taken in one of two ways: in one (according to common habit) Pelagius would exclude the whole people of God before Christ in his statement since the common habit refers *vetus testamentum* to the canonical literature or to the era before Christ's incarnation. Such would be an error (and Augustine would have us assume that Pelagius always meant the sense that is in error). But if one means *vetus testamentum* in the sense approved by Scripture itself, then we are *not* speaking of a contrast of eras at all.

Augustine in both places makes an exegetical claim: when the contrast of *vetus* and *novum testamentum* emerges in Scripture, the issue is one's standing before God and not the eras or canonical literature commonly referred to by those names. Marafioti, pointing this out, refers to the contrast as 'salvific'—a term that captures the contrast very well.[43] Hence, the contrast of the old and new covenants, exegetically speaking, is not between two eras in the history of salvation (as Jerome) but rather has to do with salvation. As Lössl styles Augustine's reading, the contrast between the *vetus* and *novum testamentum* is a contrast between 'salvation and non-salvation (judgment)'.[44] The *vetus testa-*

---

41. Augustine, *Contra epp. Pel*, §3.12.

42. Augustine, *De gestis Pelagii* (Œuv. de S.Aug 21; Paris: Desclée de Brouwer, 1994), §5.14.

43. '[E]gli pone l'accento sulla dimensione interiore della nuova disposizione salvifica e della grazia che essa porta all'uomo.' Or, in the language of 'fidelity' which is even closer to what I will propose: 'Ci presenta [in *De sp.*]... un'esegesi nuova del testo di Geremia. Esso viene sempre utilizzato come profezia del Nuovo Testamento, ma con la differenza che la *novitas* di cui si parla non è più la *mutatio sacramentorum*, quanto piuttosto la grazia, che dà all'uomo la capacità di compiere il bene, e la vita eterna come ricompensa della fedeltà al Testamento stesso.' Marafioti, *Sant'Agostino*, 191, 212-13. This terminology is substantially the same to what Hagen calls 'soteriological' regarding Augustine: Kenneth Hagen, *A Theology of Testament in the Young Luther: The Lectures on Hebrews* (Leiden: E.J. Brill, 1974), 118, et passim.

44. 'Wichtig ist, daß der entscheidende Unterschied nicht zwischen den verschiedenen Formen des Heils zu suchen ist, sondern zwischen Heil und Nicht-Heil

mentum is the covenant with Hagar, a covenant of 'bondage', or of holding to the 'letter' or 'sign' without moving to the realities of faith:

> But those belong to the *vetus testamentum*, 'which brings forth from Mount Sinai to slavery, which is Hagar', who, after receiving the holy and just and good law, think that the letter can suffice for their life, and therefore, insofar as they become observers of the law, they do not inquire after divine mercy. Rather, 'ignoring the righteousness of God and wanting to establish their own righteousness, they are not subjects of the righteousness of God.' Of this kind were that multitude who murmured against God in the wilderness and made idols, and those who even in the promised land itself fornicated after foreign gods.[45]

Augustine singles out for inclusion in the membership of the *vetus testamentum* those who seek only after the 'earthly' things of the law, without faith in what the law signifies if understood 'spiritually' (according to the Spirit). And it is this group against which Paul argues in Galatians by invoking the terminology of old and new covenant.[46] But, central for our purposes, this means that not all members of the 'Old Testament' considered as an era were members of the *vetus testamentum*. The faithful were members of the *novum*:

> These [who follow the Law in faith and the Spirit] belong to the *novum testamentum*, are the children of promise, and are regenerated by God the Father and a free mother. Of this kind were all the righteous ones of old – even Moses himself, minister of the *vetus testamentum*, heir of the *novum*. Because the faith by which we live is one and the same as they lived – believing the incarnation, passion, and resurrection of Christ as future, which we believe as already accomplished.[47]

(Unheil).' Josef Lössl, *Intellectus Gratiae: Die erkenntnistheoretische und hermeneutische Dimension der Gnadenlehre Augustins von Hippo* (Leiden: E.J. Brill, 1997), 192.

45. Augustine, *Contra epp. Pel*, §3.9.

46. 'Furthermore, they, whoever was there, who only followed after those earthly promises alone which God promised, and who were ignorant of that which they signify regarding the *novum testamentum*, and who observed God's precepts from the love of gaining and fear of losing them – rather they did not observe them, but only seemed to themselves to observe them, *for there was no faith in them that worked by love*, but earthly lust and carnal fear – but whoever thus carries out the commandments without a doubt carries them out reluctantly, and so does not carry them out in the heart.... Such were the children of the earthly Jerusalem, of which the apostle says, "She is enslaved with her children," belonging to the *vetus testamentum*...' Ibid. My emphasis.

47. Ibid., §3.11. The requirement of the same *notitia* within faith (*knowledge* of the incarnation, passion and resurrection) is disputed rather strongly by Hugh of St. Victor (below).

Likewise:

> Or will we deny that he truly belongs to the *novum testamentum* who says, "Create in me a clean heart, O God; and renew a right spirit within me"?...[48]

Or:

> Whether, then, Abraham or the righteous ones before him or after him – up to Moses himself, through whom was given the *testamentum* from Mt. Sinai giving birth to bondage, or the rest of the prophets after him, and the holy men of God until John the Baptist, they are sons of the promise and of grace according to Isaac the son of the freewoman – not of the law but of the promise, heirs of God and co-heirs with Christ.[49]

Quite clearly, Augustine designates the faithful saints of the ancient era as members of the *novum testamentum*, the 'new covenant'. Augustine makes the same point elsewhere in a similar discussion:

> The children of the flesh belong to the earthly Jerusalem, which is enslaved with her children, but children of the promise belong to [the Jerusalem] which is above, our free eternal mother in heaven. Thus we can distinguish who belongs to the earthly kingdom and who to the heavenly kingdom. Thus we see that those who lived in that earlier era, who by the grace of God were made to understand this distinction, are in fact sons of the promise, and they are counted as heirs of the *novum testamentum* by the secret council of God...[50]

Membership in the 'old' or 'new' covenant is thus entirely grounded in one's relationship by faith to God, regardless of era: it is 'salvific'. So just as some were members of the new covenant in the era before Christ, others are members of the old covenant after Christ – both Jews who continue to refuse the

---

48. Ibid., §3.6.
49. Ibid., §3.8.
50. Augustine, *De gest. Pel*, §5.14. That these 'new covenant' Israelites were a minority in Augustine's mind simply affirms the point that the contrast cannot be baldly chronological: 'Therefore revealing the *novum testamentum* of our eternal inheritance, in which one who is renewed by the grace of God might live a new life (that is a spiritual life), that he might show the first [testament] to be old—in which a carnal people urging the old men (*excepting a few understanding patriarchs and prophets, and certain concealed saints*) living according to the flesh desired carnal rewards from the Lord God, and received them as a figure of spiritual goods, therefore the Lord Christ, being made man, despised all the earthly goods to show us that they are to be despised, and endured all the earthly evils that he calls us to endure, that neither happiness might be sought in the one nor unhappiness feared in the other.' Augustine, *De catechizandis rudibus* (Œuv. de S.Aug. 11/1; Paris: Desclée de Brouwer, 1991), §22.40.

realities of what was prophesied and (as seen below) Christians who fail to see the spiritual aspect of the sacraments:

> Hence there are still their children among the great multitude of the Jews, although now the *novum testamentum*, just as it was prophesied, is revealed and confirmed by the blood of Christ.[51]

We must not lose sight of the polemics. On Augustine's reading, Julian thinks that the Law can suffice for life. The Law provides all that is needed to live a virtuous life given the state of human nature, without need to seek divine mercy. Augustine retorts that the Law in itself was never sufficient. Having the Law alone condemns one to the *vetus testamentum*, regardless of era. Just so, Julian remains in the *vetus testamentum* that kills, rather than entering the *novum* which gives life through the Spirit.

Augustine thus appeals to an exegetical standard to escape Julian's argument above regarding the Holy Spirit's absence in the *vetus testamentum*. Augustine can agree that the Spirit is tied to the *novum testamentum*, but also that the Spirit was present in the lives of the faithful prior to Christ: for those faithful were in fact members of the *novum testamentum*. The distinction of 'old' and 'new' covenants, exegetically speaking, has nothing to do with two successive eras. So unconcerned is Augustine with eras in redemptive history for this point that he is implicitly accusing Julian himself of being a member of the *vetus testamentum*!

Much of this view was already given shape in Augustine's anti-Donatist writings, particularly his *De baptismo*, though the clear distinction between divergent uses of the terminology is not yet formulated. Those who refuse to see or taste the spiritual goods from God, content with the temporal or carnal signs or blessings, are members of the *vetus testamentum* in any age in which they live—if they receive baptism without receiving the things of the Spirit of God, for instance, they are members of the *vetus testamentum*. But in any era, includ-

---

51. Augustine, *Contra epp. Pel*, §9. This section can be linked to his comments in *Christian Teaching*, §3.30-31: 'Someone who attends to and worships a thing which is meaningful but remains unaware of its meaning is a slave to a sign. But the person who attends to or worships a useful sign, one divinely instituted, and does realize its force and significance, does not worship a thing which is only apparent and transitory but rather the thing in which all such things are to be related. Such a person is spiritual and free – and this was true even in the era of slavery when the time was not ripe for carnal minds to receive the clarification of the signs by which they had to be discipled. Among such spiritual people were the patriarchs and prophets and all those in the people of Israel through whom the Holy Spirit provided us with the support and comfort of the Scriptures.'

ing that before Christ, those who desire and possess the spiritual goods are members of the *novum testamentum*:

> The Apostle says that all who persevere in this animal sensation belong to the *vetus testamentum*, that is, to the desire of earthly promises which are, in fact, the type of the spiritual... At whatever time, therefore, men might start this life, though they have partaken of such divine sacraments as were appointed for the age in which they live, if they taste carnal things and hope for and desire carnal things from God—whether in this life or after—they are still carnal. But the church, which is the people of God, is an ancient institution even in the pilgrimage of this life, having some with a carnal interest and some with a spiritual interest. To the carnal belongs the *vetus testamentum*; to the spiritual belongs the *novum*... By Moses the *vetus testamentum* was revealed and in it was hidden the *novum testamentum*, for it was typified in a hidden manner. But just when the Lord came in the flesh the *novum testamentum* was revealed.
>
> Yet, though the sacraments of the *vetus testamentum* passed away, the dispositions peculiar to it did not pass away. For they still exist in those whom the Apostle declares to be already born indeed by the sacrament of the *novum testamentum* [i.e. baptism], but yet incapable as being natural of receiving the things of the Spirit of God. Just as in the sacraments of the *vetus testamentum* some were living spiritually, certainly belonging secretly to the *novum testamentum* which then was concealed, so also now in the sacrament of the *novum testamentum* which is already revealed, some live as animals. And if they are unwilling to advance to receive the things which are of the Spirit of God... they belong to the *vetus testamentum*.[52]

Augustine treats Jer 31:31-34 most thoroughly in his *De spiritu et littera*. The issue here, once again, is whether the grace of the Holy Spirit is necessary beyond an instructive role for living a virtuous life. Augustine argues that the law in and of itself is ineffective for salvation and, apart from the life-giving Spirit, only has the power to condemn. To follow Augustine's argument here we must make a second distinction in terminology, this time between what we might call the interpretive contrast of letter/spirit, and the contrast being drawn here, which (for the sake of uniformity) will be called 'salvific'.[53]

---

52. Augustine, *De baptismo* (Œuv. de S.Aug. 29; Paris: Desclée de Brouwer, 1964), §1.15.24.

53. This is the same general distinction made famous under the typology of 'Origenist' and 'Augustinian' interpretations of the maxim in Rom 7 by Gerhard Ebeling, "Die Anfänge von Luthers Hermeneutik," *ZTK* 48 (1951), 172-230. Ebeling has rightly been critiqued for the use he makes of the distinction as a grid for the history of interpretation, but *abusus non usum tollet*. See M. Kunz, "Sending Words into Battle:

Augustine often uses the language of 'letter' and 'spirit' as an interpretive rule, sometimes even to praise the 'letter'.[54] Yet this is not the way in which he urges us to consider the language as used in Paul. Again Augustine makes the issue exegetical:

> For I wish, if possible, to demonstrate that what the Apostle said, 'the letter kills, but the spirit gives life', does not refer to a figurative speaking – though also in that it may be agreeably understood – but rather plainly to the law prohibiting what is evil.[55]

And again:

> 'The letter kills, but the spirit gives life' must be understood in the sense we said above: that the letter of the law, which teaches us not to commit sin, kills, if the life-giving spirit be absent.[56]

Given Julian's close connection with Antiochene exegesis, it may be that Augustine is here trying to gain a victory on Julian's own ground.[57] So he distances the discussion from the allegorical interpretations he is elsewhere happy to commend. But understanding letter/spirit as a salvific contrast also finds voice in *De doctrina christiana* under the third rule of Tyconius. Here the rule of Tyconius is 'On the promises and the law', which Augustine says can also be called '"On the spirit and the letter", as I myself called it when writing on the subject. It could also be called "On grace and commandment".'[58]

There is no doubt some room for bringing the two uses of 'letter' together. If one refuses to move from the symbol or sign to the thing signified (interpretive rule) then clearly the Spirit is absent and thus the letter or sign can only kill (salvific contrast).[59] But bringing them together in this way only establ-

---

Reformation Understandings and Uses of Letter and Spirit" (Ph.D, Univ. of Chicago, 2002), 292-98.

54. Cf. David F. Wright, "Augustine: His Exegesis and Hermeneutics," in *Hebrew Bible/Old Testament: The History of its Interpretation* (ed. Magne Saebo; 1.1; Göttingen: Vandenhoeck and Ruprecht, 1996), 705; Lubac, *Medieval Exegesis*, 1.123-32. For a brief discussion of the varied uses of 'literal' or 'letter' in this respect, see Karla Pollmann, "Augustine's Hermeneutics as a Universal Principle!," in *Augustine and the Disciplines: From Cassiacum to Confessions* (Oxford Univ. Press, 2005), 210-12.

55. Augustine, *De spiritu*, §7.
56. Ibid., §8; cf. §6.
57. For Julian's relationship to Antiochene exegesis, see Lössl, *Julian*, 147ff.
58. Augustine, *Christian Teaching*, §3.103.
59. Ibid., §3.30f. Incidentally this entire discussion would fit in well with the emphasis throughout Augustine on salvation as tied to the growth of the intellect in or by grace, which Lössl has suggested is the central aspect of Augustine's theological system,

ishes further the point that the contrast between letter/spirit concerns more than mere interpretive rules.

Augustine defines the 'letter' in *De spiritu* as the law (embodied in the Decalogue) considered *apart* from faith and *apart* from the Spirit's enabling.[60] Hence, if one remains content with the letter (law) without the Spirit and grace, nothing remains but condemnation: the letter kills, but the spirit gives life. One must leave the 'oldness' of the letter and cling to the 'newness' of the spirit.[61] All this leads to the argument that the gift of the Spirit, which is the grace of God or the writing of the law on the heart, is the true essence of the *novum testamentum*—in any era. As Marafioti argues: 'The Law written on the heart, the presence of the Holy Spirit, and grace are the same thing.'[62]

We can sketch Augustine's chief argument easily. First, Augustine posits that 'there is no good fruit which does not grow from the root of love (*caritas*).'[63] So even partial fulfilment of the law from any other source (e.g. fear, as instilled in threatenings at Sinai) would be inadequate. Second, the Holy Spirit is the 'finger of God' through whom 'love (*caritas*) is shed abroad in our hearts' (Rom 5:5). This is explained by a contrast between the finger of God as active at Sinai, where on the one hand the law is written (merely) on tablets of stone, and on the other hand, the finger of God is the Spirit given at Pentecost which sheds *caritas* in our hearts.[64] The bare law, given to Moses, cannot of itself instill *caritas,* but can only command obedience through fear. And since '*caritas* is the fulfilment of the law', we can say that 'the law of God is love'—and so the law is written or placed in the hearts of those who believe by the Spirit who gives life.[65] The consequences for the polemic are clear: the law in itself is insufficient for life; we must have the law—*caritas*—written on our hearts by the Spirit.[66] Or, once more, the letter kills but the Spirit gives life.

---

though I am not entirely convinced of any single central point of Augustine's thought. Lössl, *Intellectus Gratiae*, see esp. 187-98 for discussion of *De spir.* and *De doctrina*.

60. Augustine, *De spiritu*, §23-24.
61. E.g., 'the oldness of the letter, if lacking the newness of the Spirit, prepares the sinner to acquire a knowledge of sin rather than to free from sin.' Ibid., §26.
62. Marafioti, *Sant'Agostino*, 215. This is a near repetition of La Bonnardière: 'Loi de Dieu écrite dans le cœur, grace de Dieu, presence de l'Esprit-Saint, trios aspects d'une même réalité.' La Bonnardière, *Jérémie*, 66.
63. Augustine, *De spiritu*, §26.
64. Ibid., §28-29.
65. Ibid., §29.
66. Thus Blumenkranz: 'Entsprechend all diesen Unterscheidungen ist auch das Alte Testament dem Menschen von aussen auferlegt, das Neue jedoch in seinem Innern

Augustine corroborates his interpretation of Paul in the contrast of letter/spirit with the testimony of Jer 31:31-34 and the same salvific contrast: a holding to the law by itself (letter or *vetus testamentum*), and the law with faith and the Spirit, and therefore life (*novum testamentum*). For Augustine the law itself is good, for 'it is that same law that Christ came to fulfill'. But in itself the law has no power to effect a virtuous life (as already demonstrated). The law stands in need of grace for fulfillment. Hence Augustine's familiar formula: 'The law is therefore given that grace might be sought; grace is given that the law might be fulfilled.'[67] But if the law is the same, then why is it that Jeremiah speaks of one as 'old' and the other 'new'?

> Why, therefore, is that one old, this one new, when the same law is fulfilled through the *novum testamentum* which said in the *vetus testamentum*, 'You shall not covet'? 'Because,' he says, 'they did not persevere in my *testamentum*, I have also rejected them, says the Lord.'[68] Therefore it is because of the crime of the old man – which through the letter, commanding and threatening, insufficiently healed – that it is called the *vetus testamentum*. But this one is called 'new' because of the newness of the spirit, which heals the new man of the sin of the old.[69]

Jeremiah confronts those who would hold to the 'letter' – the law in and of itself, without the Spirit, and thus unable to heal the wounds of the people.[70] And this is overturned by the new covenant which heals the new man. So, as Blumenkranz rightly states: 'The relationship of the two testaments corresponds to the difference between the old and new person'.[71] For Augustine this imagery of the 'new man' is directly tied to that of conversion, re-emphasising the contrast again as standing before God.[72] The 'law' is the same, but the *testamentum* is new because of the work of the Spirit in making the 'old man' new.

---

eingepflanzt. Jenes ist auf steinernen Tafeln aufgeschrieben, dieses im Herzen des Menschen.' Blumenkranz, *Judenpredigt*, 128.

67. 'Lex ergo data est, ut gratia quaereretur, gratia data est, ut lex impleretur.' Augustine, *De spiritu*, §34.

68. See note on Jerome's translation, above.

69. Ibid. A similar answer is given in *Contra epp. Pel*, §3.13. There it is combined with the further reason that 'their revelation is considered in the names, not their institution.' Cp. the citation from *De baptismo*, above.

70. For a similar strategy, this time directed to the Jews of his present day, see the use of Jer 31 in Augustine, "Answer to Jews," §8. The fittingness of the imagery of 'healing' to Jeremiah's rhetoric is noteworthy (e.g., Jer 30:17).

71. Blumenkranz, *Judenpredigt*, 128.

72. See José Oroz Reta, "L'homme nouveau selon saint Augustin," *Augustinian Studies* 17 (1986).

Moving through the passage in Jeremiah, Augustine next turns to the promise that 'all' will know the Lord:

> What, therefore is the 'all, from the least to the greatest of them,' except the 'all' who belong spiritually to the house of Israel and to the house of Judah – that is, to the children of Isaac, to the seed of Abraham?... This is the house of the children of promise; not by reason of their own merits, but of the kindness of God.[73]

Again the contrast is between membership in the true Israel and those who are members only in the flesh. Membership in the new covenant is determined primarily by being a member of the spiritual house of Israel – by being among the 'children of promise' by the mercy of God. As in *De baptismo*, the old covenant is then explained as that which belongs only to this world, its exact counterpart being the new covenant:

> Therefore, as the law of works, written on tablets of stone and its reward—the land of promise which the carnal house of Israel received after their liberation from Egypt—belongs to the *vetus testamentum*, so the law of faith, written on the heart, and its reward—the beatific vision which the spiritual house of Israel will perceive when delivered from the present world—belong to the *novum testamentum*.[74]

Apart from context this sounds similar to Jerome, who would apply this directly to the two distinct eras pre- and post-Incarnation. But for Augustine the issue is the distinction between the sign and the thing signified: the *vetus testamentum* is a remaining content with the 'letter'. The contrast of 'carnal' and 'spiritual' fits Augustine's theme traceable from *De baptismo*—and perhaps earlier—all the way through, now applied to Jer 31:31-34. We find here the context for Augustine's contrast between the Lord writing on tablets of stone (old covenant) and on the heart (new covenant) – a contrast that in recent literature is taken to entail a contrast of eras, which is emphatically not Augustine's concern.[75] For Augustine, at least by the *De spiritu*, the contrast of old and new covenant in Jeremiah is a contrast between the non-working of the Spirit (the law on stone) and the working of the Spirit (the law on the heart). Thus his conclusion on Jer 31:31-34:

> [T]here is, further, agreement of this testimony of the apostle with the words of the prophet so that to belong to the *novum testamentum* is to have

---

73. Augustine, *De spiritu*, §40.
74. Ibid., §41.
75. So also his Augustine, *Quaestionum in Heptateuchum* (CCL 33; Tournholt: Brepols, 1963), Bk. 5, §11. Here again, though the reference is very succinct, the same (salvific) contrast appears to be meant.

the law of God written not on tablets, but on the heart, that is, embracing the righteousness of the law with innermost affection, whereby faith works through love. Because it is on account of faith that God justifies the Gentiles.[76]

Augustine's polemical concerns now begin to flourish: to establish (contra Pelagius) that the law and knowledge of the law is insufficient for a virtuous life. This, he argues, is precisely the point of Paul's discussion of the letter/spirit contrast, which stands in full agreement with Jeremiah's prophecy of the new covenant. The *vetus testamentum* in Jer 31 is the 'letter', a state of unbelief and a holding to the law as a means of life; the *novum* is the Spirit who writes the law of God (i.e. *caritas*) on our hearts. Augustine has moved beyond the view of the contrast in Jeremiah being that of the *mutatio sacramentorum*, and his explicit distance from that view is worth citing again, now in its proper context:

> When the prophet promised a *novum testamentum* not according to the *testamentum* formerly made with the people of Israel... he said nothing about the change of sacrifices or other sacraments – though such change was without doubt going to follow just as we see happened, which in many other places the same prophetic Scriptures testify. But he only pointed out this difference: that God would place his laws in their minds who belong to this *testamentum*, and would write it on their hearts.[77]

Thus one commentator rightly concludes:

> The difference between the old covenant and the new is not a difference between different types of law. It is the difference between "the sickness of the old man," not healed by the threats and commands of the law, and the new human person who possesses "the new condition of the Spirit..."[78]

Augustine puts forward a salvific contrast over against a contrast of two successive eras. The salvific contrast regards regeneration, faith, and grace (new covenant) standing over against unbelief and death (old covenant).

The pattern established in the *Contra epp. Pel.* and *De spiritu* can be seen in other treatments of the 'new covenant' in Augustine's writings. The link between regeneration and the new covenant is made explicit in the *Enchiridion*:

> For the divine judgment, 'I will visit the sins of the fathers upon the children', certainly applies to them before they shall begin to belong to the *novum testamentum* through regeneration. That *testamentum* was proph-

---

76. Augustine, *De spiritu*, §46.
77. Ibid., §42.
78. M. Kunz, "Sending Words," 269. See also Augustine's comments on Psalm 70 (71) regarding this salvific contrast of letter/spirit, expounded in Kunz (ibid), 274f.

esied about when it was said through Ezekiel that the sons should not bear the iniquity of the fathers.[79]

The grace of the *novum testamentum* was entered by regeneration even for the ancients, by which alone they were able to escape the consequences of divine judgment. Similarly in his *Unfinished Work in Answer to Julian* the same idea emerges, and again with citation of Jer 31:21-30 and 31:31-34. All are born into the *vetus testamentum*, in which they are held responsible for the sins of the parents (the context is a defense of inheriting original sin). But the faithful are reborn and redeemed into the *novum testamentum*: 'Birth belongs to that former *testamentum*, but rebirth to this latter.'[80]

In a lengthy letter to Honoratus penned at the outset of the Pelagian controversy—in fact likely composed in early 412—we find the same arguments. Augustine repeatedly emphasizes the 'grace of the *novum testamentum*' as that which alone brings life and redemption, and to which he presses Honoratus.[81] The *vetus testamentum* represents a satisfaction or contentment with temporal blessings alone, carried out under fear of judgment. But then, what are we to say of the 'saints' in the era of what is popularly called the *vetus testamentum*? They 'dispensed' the old covenant, but by looking beyond the temporal to the eternal happiness they were in fact true members of the new covenant:

> Therefore God, wanting to show that even earthly and temporal happiness is his gift, nor ought it to be hoped for from any other, decided that in the earlier times of the world he would dispense the *vetus testamentum*, which belongs to the old man [*quod pertineret ad hominem veterem*], from which this life necessarily begins. But those happy things of the fathers, we are taught, were granted by the kindness of God even though they pertain to this transitory life.... Therefore those saints dispensed the *vetus testamentum* as it was fitting for the time, but they truly belonged [*pertinebant vero*] to the *novum testamentum*. For, even when enjoying temporal happiness, they understood eternal happiness was true and preferable...[82]

---

79. Augustine, *Enchiridion de fide spe et caritate* (Œuv. de S.Aug. 9; Paris: Desclée de Brouwer, 1988), §46.

80. Augustine, *Unfinished Work in Answer to Julian* (Works of St. Augustine; Tr. by Roland J. Teske. New City Press: NY, 1999), §3.84.3. Cf. §3.61-63 for discussion of original sin.

81. 'Why, then, does the Apostle say to the faithful—who belong to the *novum testamentum*—what I cited above...?' Or, 'And those who, as living from faith are the heirs of the *novum testamentum*...' Augustine, *De Gratia novi testamenti liber (Epistola 140)* (PL 33; Paris: 1861), §21.52; cf. §7.19; §30,73: 'This righteousness by which those who believe in him are righteous... is the grace of the *novum testamentum*.'

82. Ibid., §2.5; cf. §7.20.

Those who serve God from *caritas* (the work of the Spirit) rather than fear of punishment are heirs of the *novum testamentum*. Once again, one may speak of the temporal 'revelation' of the *novum*, but properly the contrast of the *vetus* and *novum testamentum*, once more, is 'salvific': a contrast of faith and unbelief, of life and of judgment.

This pattern also makes clear why Augustine in *The City of God* views the promise of Jeremiah's new covenant as addressed to the 'heavenly Jerusalem'. The two cities famously contrasted here have nothing to do with temporal designations, at least as far as the era prior to and after the Incarnation. One can be a member of either city in any era, membership in which is determined solely by relationship to God.[83] Thus, when explaining the three possible references for prophetic utterances – the 'earthly Jerusalem', the 'Heavenly City', or both at once – he places Jeremiah's promise of the new covenant as his prime example of the second, 'prophecy concerning Jerusalem on high, whose reward is God Himself.'[84]

All of this leads to the conclusion that Augustine presents a reading of Jeremiah's new covenant that stands at odds with the reading represented in Jerome. Instead of presenting a contrast between two eras or dispensations considered as such, Augustine views the contrast in terms of standing before God: 'salvation or non-salvation' (Lössl). The old covenant is the covenant of the letter, which is bondage, insufficient for healing, and thus can only kill. It is the 'old man', the law without faith – the new covenant is the life governed by the Spirit. One is a member of the new covenant by virtue of joining faith to the law, knowing and trusting in the redemptive provisions of God – and all without regard for the era in which one lives.[85]

---

83. E.g., 'I divide the human race into two orders. The one consists of those who live according to man, and the other of those who live according to God. Speaking allegorically, I also call these two orders two Cities: that is, two societies of men, one of which is predestined to reign in eternity with God, and the other of which will undergo eternal punishment with the devil.' Augustine, *The City of God* (Tr. by R.W. Dyson. Cambridge Univ. Press, 1998), §15.1. Or, §14.9: 'Hence, it is now clear what kind of life the citizens of the City of God must lead during this pilgrimage: they must live according to the spirit and not according to the flesh... On the other hand, the city, that is, the fellowship, of the ungodly consists of those who live not according to God, but according to man.' Also §14.28.

84. Ibid., §17.3.

85. The study by Kenneth Hagen, focusing mainly on Augustine's writings on the Psalms, comes to similar conclusions: 'The instrument of providence is *sermo dei verax*, a two-edged sword, present in both Testaments [considered as eras] and always present to separate *spiritualia* from *temporalia*. The *sermo* is *velatum* in circumcision, the

4. Conclusions

James O'Donnell has written (not entirely enthusiastically) of the way in which the narrative of Augustine's life in his *Confessions* 'is made to revolve around a defining moment of conversion, localized to a specific place and time and dramatized in a particular way.'[86] Such a two-part understanding of his life is unsurprising if for Augustine the fundamental contrast in all of life is between belief and unbelief – the contrast which finally gives shape to his great work on the *City of God*. And it is in this city of God that Augustine places all the believers, the members of the *novum testamentum*, from Abel and Seth through Moses, David, and down to himself. The contrast of membership in the old and new covenants is nothing less than the contrast of membership between the city of man and the city of God: unfaithfulness with the law opposed to grace and faith, the work of the Spirit.

Thus with Augustine we see a particular form or family of readings given their shape, and the center is the point of contrast to the 'new covenant'. Augustine directly confronts the theological difficulty with the standard religio-historical contrast of the two covenants—such as that seen in Jerome (and the early Augustine)—which renders problematic any discussion of the experience and faith of the believers in the Old Testament, a problem brought to the fore by the Pelagian disputes. Augustine does not doubt that the righteous of the ancient era had the law on their heart (i.e. possessed the Spirit), were the people of God, knew God, and had the forgiveness of sins—each part of Jeremiah's 'new covenant' was known by the faithful. Hence something else must be at stake when Jeremiah and Paul contrast the *vetus* and *novum testamentum*. Jeremiah and Paul put forward the absolute contrast of infidelity and true faithfulness. Of course, Augustine throughout his career contrasts the various eras that govern the post-

---

Temple, and other *temporalia, revelatum* in Christ. Those (men of faith) who separate *spiritualia* from *animalia* "belong" (grow up) to the New, those who regard the *lex bona* to be sufficient as letter "belong" to the Old... "At any time" the *testamentum iustificationis* is at work. Those who "understand" are *re* Christians by the one Holy Spirit.' Hagen, *Theology of Testament*, 42-43.

86. James J. O'Donnell, "Augustine: his time and lives," in *Cambridge Companion to Augustine* (eds. Eleanore Stump and Norman Kretzmann; Cambridge Univ. Press, 2001), 9. A similar point is made (more sympathetically) regarding Augustine's theological interpretation of his conversion experience and its impact on his life and work by Y. Miyatami, "Theologia conversionis in St. Augustine," *Congresso Internazionale su S. Agostino Nel XVI Centenario della Conversione* 1 (1987).

fall world.[87] But the 'new covenant' of Jer 31:31-34 does not play its role as a hinge between two of those eras, at least not for the later Augustine. The characteristics of the members of the 'new covenant' in Jeremiah are nothing other than the characteristics of a faithful believer in any era. Augustine posits a reading of Jeremiah's 'new covenant' in which the fundamental contrast lies between one's membership in an unfaithful (old) covenant, or in a faithful (new) covenant. The contrast is absolute: infidelity before God standing over against fidelity by grace and the Spirit. And while much of Augustine's form of this contrast will be left behind, this 'salvific' contrast (rather than a temporal one) is the definitive aspect of what I will call, and eventually defend, as the 'Augustinian' reading of Jeremiah's new covenant.

---

87. Stated summarily: 'the resurrection of the Lord was upon the third day, because with it the third epoch of the world began. The first Epoch was before the Law, the second under the Law, the third under Grace, in which there is now the manifestation of the mystery (*sacramentum*).' Augustine, "Letter 55," in *The Confessions and Letters of St. Augustine* (NPNF, 1.1; Grand Rapids, MI: Eerdmans, 1994), §5. Cf. *Contra epp. Pel*, §3.9; *Contra Faustum*, §4.2; *City of God*, §16.26, etc.

3

Jeremiah's New Covenant in High Medieval Theology

The high medieval period represents the tension between the two broad families of reading Jeremiah's new covenant outlined above: in one, represented by Jerome, the contrast is between two religio-historical eras ('Old Testament' era vs. 'New Testament' era) and largely centered on the change of sacraments. But Augustine offers another reading explicitly standing over against this religio-historical contrast. For the later Augustine, at least, Jeremiah's new covenant ought to be read as a contrast to the possession of the law without the Spirit, or law without grace. The contrast is 'salvific', between two states before God: the state of condemnation or judgment (death) and that of salvation or faith. Thus membership in the old or the new covenants depends not on location in history but on standing before God at any point in history. These two readings persist in the medieval period often side by side, and often in the same author. In this chapter I will focus on Thomas Aquinas as the chief illustration of this tension, but the struggle and tension in Thomas is by no means unique to him.

In fact, the tension or willingness to make use of both readings already appears in the writings of Fulgentius (c.467-c.532), the bishop of Ruspe in North Africa ('the greatest North African theologian after the time of Augustine').[1] Fulgentius lived during the tumultuous reign of the Arian King Thrasimund, and was a devout follower of Augustine's thought over against the semi-pelagianism of his day.[2] As becomes somewhat of a pattern, Fulgentius makes use of Jer 31:31-34 on one occasion to support the *mutatio sacramentorum*, the change of

---

1. Robert B. Eno, in his "Introduction" to Fulgentius, *Selected Works* (FC; Washington, D.C.: CUA Press, 1997). For Fulgentius' role in the semi-pelagian debates, see Rebecca Harden Weaver, *Divine Grace and Human Agency: A Study of the Semi-Pelagian Controversy* (Patristic Monograph Series; Macon: Mercer Univ. Press, 1996), 182-98.

2. Augustine's comments on Psalm 36 were the means of Fulgentius' movement into the priesthood: see the early hagiography tentatively ascribed to Ferrandus, "The Life of the Blessed Bishop Fulgentius," in *Fulgentius: Selected Works*. For his role in the semi-pelagian debates, see Weaver, *Divine Grace*, 182-98.

sacraments.[3] Yet in a later writing he makes use of the same text in a way concerned with justification by faith:

> [B]ecause he grants to them the grace of faith, he writes the work of his law in their hearts given in justification. This is in order that by a renewed nature he might have the work of the law—apart from the letter of the *vetus testamentum,* through the grace of the *novum testamentum*—which had remained written until that time. Thus one might begin to belong to the people of God, not by the merit of preceding works but by the gracious gift of justification—which teaching is deemed worthy of being common by the prophetic mouth from the heavens, by holy Jeremiah saying 'Behold the days are coming...' [cites 31:31, 33-34].[4]

So the Augustinian contrast of the covenants may be preserved after a form in Fulgentius, but (in my findings) is relatively sparse in the Carolingian period (at least as a direct reading of Jer 31:31-34).[5] One can much more easily find a pure religio-historical contrast of eras such as we find in Jerome or John Chrysostom. This especially occurs, unsurprisingly perhaps, in Christian-Jewish polemics.[6] But other examples of the tension of the two readings and perhaps at-

---

3. The context is an allegorical reading of the 'two cups' in Luke's narrative of the Last Supper, which represent the two covenants. The apostles 'receive the Scriptures of the old covenant with reverence but in such a way that they, having received the spirit of discernment, might know what was to be observed and what omitted among those commandments (§43).' Thus, we find Jer 31:31-34 employed: 'The divine word announcing in advance this unlikeness which is in the mysteries of each covenant says through the holy Jeremiah: "The days are surely coming..." In this way there comes the *novum testamentum,* not like the *vetus testamentum,* brought to an end by the Lord, that one in which the Lord gave the fulfillment of the commandments and, with the old mysteries taken away, instituted the different mysteries of revealed truth; and so what he promised in the *vetus,* he perfected in the *novum.*' Fulgentius, "Letter 14 to Ferrandus," in *Selected Works* (FC,. Washington, D.C.: CUA Press, 1997), §46.

4. Fulgentius, "Epistula 17," in *Fulgentius Ruspensis: Opera* (ed. J. Fraipont; CCL, 91A; Tournhout: Brepols, 1968), §49. So, later: 'This is the law which God writes in all of their hearts, not through their natural condition but through the abundance of grace; not through one's free will but through the ministry of the proclamation of the Gospel; not in stone through the letter of the *vetus testamentum,* but in the heart by the living Spirit of God... And so he writes the law of faith, through which God justifies the Gentiles, that giving grace he might renew nature.' Ibid., §55. Cp. Augustine, *De spiritu,* §46 (above).

5. The dubitable attribution of a brief summary of the Augustinian position to Julian of Toledo (c.642-90) at least shows the persistence of the position, even if the authorship is unknown: Julian of Toledo (?), *Responsio* (PL 96; Paris: 1862).

6. See, e.g., the 8th c. convert from Judaism, Paul Alvarez of Cordoba: Paulus Alvarus Cordubensis, *Epistle 18: Epistola Alvari transgressori directa* (PL 121; Paris:

tempts at synthesizing them exist as well, such as in the commentary on Hebrews by Alcuin of York (c.735-804), the influential court master of Charlemagne.[7] Alcuin proposes a distinction between the Mosaic covenant referred to in Jer 31:31-32 and the covenant made with Abraham 'according to the generation of the Spirit.'[8] Then he states:

> And here [31:33-34] is the great distance between law and law, between Scripture and Scripture, between letter and grace. For the letter of the law is written on tablets of stone, which Moses himself shattered when he saw the people playing before the calf: but grace is given in the heart of believers through the Holy Spirit, through whom *caritas* is shed in the hearts of believers.[9] But what was lying and was read in the letter by the people

---

1880), 507-08. Citing Jer 5:12, according to the Vulgate: '*They rejected me, and they said: it is not he*. Who is *he*? "The Messiah who comes is not he, but we await another." You see how openly the prophet has depicted your insanities. Likewise, he (says): "Behold the days are coming, says the Lord, and I will make for the house of Judah... a new covenant [*pactum*]." Whence is this one "new," if the old does not precede it? And therefore a new covenant, in order to abolish the old. And in order that you may know this covenant to have been arranged not as law but as Gospel, not only to Gentiles but also to Jews (who we are), listen: "Not according to the covenant which I made with their fathers, when I took their hand to lead them from the land of Egypt," that is a covenant of law [*pactum legis*]. You see the law has been abolished, and made as if rejected. And rightly the prophet announced this to occur after the time, because he foresaw that a testament of the Gospel [*testamentum Evangelii*] would be given, not in his own time but in the days to come.' But even here the contrast between the *pactum legis* and *Evangelii testamentum* shows the ambiguity—and in terminology that will remain a part of Christian discourse especially in the Reformed tradition.

7. See the role of Alcuin in the helpful study of Joanna Story, *Carolingian Connections: Anglo-Saxon England and Carolingian Francia, c.750-870* (Aldershot/ Burlington: Ashgate, 2003). A brief outline of his life is provided, pp.4f.

8. '[Jer 31:31-34] is said concerning the law: having been brought at Mt Sinai (which, it is agreed, was given on the fiftieth day [Pentecost]), their fathers did not continue in it, but they made a calf in Horeb and worshiped it. For it is not concerning that [covenant] which he proposed to their fathers—that is Abraham, Isaac, and Jacob. And all the sons of faith can be called sons of Abraham, just as it is written about the Lord himself in the Gospel: "For I say to you, that God is able from these stones to raise up sons for Abraham" (Matt 3:9). And this is the covenant [*testamentum*] which God will make, that is, he will accomplish for all the nations, in order that whoever might believe in Christ might truly be sons of Abraham, according to spiritual generation.' Alcuin of York, *Expositio in Epistolam Pauli Apostoli ad Hebraeos* (PL 100; Paris: 1863), 1070.

9. Cp. the Glossa: 'Not on tablets of stone, not by writing, but by the Spirit, by whom being present (who is the finger of God) charity is spread in the hearts, which is the fullness of the law.' *Glossa Ordinaria: Epistola ad Hebraeos* (PL 114; Paris: 1879), 657. This is the 'newness of the Spirit who heals the defect [*vitio*] of the old'—language

through the traditions of the teachers, this the coming Holy Spirit taught the apostles.... 'Paul, taking courage from the prophet, attacks more in that *testamentum*, revealing rightly that ours now flourishes, and the ancient things have almost perished.' But our youth will be renewed just as an eagle if we hurry to the fount of life, if we extend the wings and eyes to the sun of righteousness (*iustitia*).[10]

Though the broader context shows an interest in the *mutatio sacramentorum*, the central issue in citing Jeremiah is the contrast of the 'letter of the law' and 'grace given in the heart.' That the statement is made immediately after asserting the continuity of the 'sons of Abraham' implies a contrast between the Mosaic 'letter of the law' and the Abrahamic covenant 'according to the generation of the Spirit'. This might be the forerunner for the position of Oecolampadius outlined below, the contrast of Jeremiah's promise being a reversion to the purity of the Abrahamic promise, but too little is stated. More likely we simply find Augustine and John Chrysostom set side by side, with no explanation of the tension.

1. *Thomas and the* Mutatio Sacramentorum

Thomas Aquinas (c.1225-74) holds company with a very select few for influence in developments of Western theology—a place guaranteed to him by a series of papal approbations.[11] Thomas is normally thought of in terms of his philosophical, or at best theological, contributions. But many are now rightly voicing the imbalance of such portraits. So Nicholas Healy:

---

that may have been taken from Augustine.

10. York, *Hebraeos*, 1070. The citation in the middle is from Chrysostom, *Hebrews*, Hom. 14, §7. The same sentence is also quoted, with Alcuin's added exhortation, in the commentary on this text in the next generation by Rabanus Maurus (c.776-856), who entitles this section 'Ostendit Christum esse meliorem sacramentorum ministrum, ministris Veteris Testamenti': Rabanus Maurus, *Enarrationum in epistolas beati pauli* (PL 112; Paris: 1852), 768.

11. He was canonized in 1323 by Pope John XXII, and when named *doctores ecclesiae* in 1567 by Pope Pius V, only the four Latin fathers bore the title (Ambrose, Augustine, Jerome, and Gregory the Great; the four Eastern fathers were added at the same time: Athanasius, Basil, Gregory of Nazianzus, and John Chrysostom). More recently, and responsible in part for the immense boom in 'Thomist' philosophy and theology, is the 1879 *Providentissimus Deus* (Enchiridion Biblicum, no.81) by Pope Leo XIII, who referred to Thomas as 'the prince of theologians' and declared, 'The best preparation [for study of Scripture in the wake of Rationalism] will be a conscientious application to philosophy and theology under the guidance of St. Thomas of Aquin' (§16). See other papal praises in Thomas Aquinas, *Commentary on the Epistle to the Hebrews* (Tr. by Chrysostom Baer. South Bend: St. Augustine's Press, 2006), xi-xiii.

While almost all of Thomas' commentaries on Aristotle's philosophical works have been translated into English, only about half the biblical commentaries have, and of these, most are out of print.... It is therefore not surprising that some perceive Thomas to be the prime example of that form of traditional Catholic theological inquiry which emphasizes philosophical reasoning, in contradistinction to the Scripture-based tradition of the Reformers and their heirs. This perception is quite mistaken, however, and evidently so to anyone who has actually read Thomas' commentaries and is aware of their bearing upon his other work.[12]

The concern in this chapter will be Thomas as a reader of Scripture, and the theological use to which Scripture is put by Thomas.

By the time we arrive at the high medieval period the relationship between the *vetus* and *novum testamentum* had been given another chance to emerge in the center of discussions. This was largely through two opposing heresies: the Cathars and the lesser-known Passaginis. Malcolm Lambert's helpful work on medieval heresies gives a good flavor for the immense influence and diversity of the Cathars, as they weave in and out of his storyline.[13] But the significance for us is the fertile ground produced by this sect for the strong assertion of the Augustinian line. The Cathars stood as inheritors of the Manichaeans. Like the early heresy, the Cathars rejected the material world as the work of that evil deity represented in the Old Testament (which is hence rejected as well).[14] We aren't surprised, then, to find Augustine's work pressed into battle once

---

12. Nicholas Healy, "Introduction," in *Aquinas on Scripture* (Edinburgh: T&T Clark, 2005), 1. Or more basically, 'Thomas ist Philosoph nur in spezieller Funktion seines eingentlichen Auftrags und Selbstverständnisses als (biblisch-augustinisch orientierter) Lehrer der Theologie.' Ulrich Kühn, "Nova Lex. Die Eigenart der christlichen Ethik nach Thomas von Aquin," in *Lex et Libertas* (eds. L.J. Elders and K. Hedwig; Studi Tomisitici,. Vatican City: Libreria Editrice Vaticana, 1987), 244.

13. For general discussion, see Malcolm Lambert, *Medieval Heresy: Popular Movements from the Gregorian Reform to the Reformation* (3rd ed. Oxford: Blackwell, 2002).

14. Though Lambert (op. cit.) is less concerned with this latter aspect of Catharism (simply mentioning the rejection of the OT, e.g. p.66), it is clearly seen in his fuller study, Malcolm Lambert, *The Cathars* (Oxford: Blackwell, 1998). Thus, speaking of a group of heretics mentioned in a sermon, 'These heretics were unmistakably Cathar for their rejection of the Church's sacraments flowed from a profound rejection of creation, repudiating the Old Testament, believing that the law of Moses was given by the Devil, denying the resurrection of the body' (88); or, citing a manuscript of utterances reflecting 'ordinary believers' in this sect: 'The god of the Old Testament was malign: one should put faith only in the god who made a new heaven and a new earth' (161).

more with his rebuttal regarding a form of the unity of the people of God across redemptive-history.

The opposing heresy to the Cathars, and much more confined (perhaps only to Lombardy), was that of the Passaginis. Rather than denying the OT, this sect denied the divinity of Christ and placed a renewed value on the Mosaic laws such as circumcision, feasts, and food laws.[15] The heresy in this case was seen as a refusal to acknowledge the change of sacraments (*mutatio sacramentorum*). So we cannot be surprised to find the emphasis of this teaching as well. Each of these two disparate heresies, prevalent in the 12th century, set the theological field for discussions of the relationship of the testaments—whether the testaments/covenants be considered as books, eras, or states of affairs. One evidence of this is the late-12th c. treatise *Summa contra haereticos*, which moves back and forth summarizing and critiquing these two heresies. As the treatise demonstrates, the high medieval period had very real and present concerns demanding proper negotiation of the relation of the *vetus* and *novum testamentum*.[16]

The dominant trend in using Jer 31:31-34 would remain with reference to the change of sacraments as a contrast of the *vetus* and *nova lex*.[17] The remarks of the *Glossa ordinaria* at Jer 31:31-34 further affirm that this dominance was indebted in large part to Jerome. Edited in various places throughout the 12th c., the *Glossa* was a highly successful attempt to turn the mass of patristic (often via Carolingian) comments on the Bible into a tool useful in the schools and monasteries. Alexander Andrée comments:

> As a reference tool the practical use of which is impossible to underestimate, it was to be found in every library ready to be consulted by a Peter Lombard or a St Thomas Aquinas.[18]

---

15. See Walter L. Wakefield and Austin P. Evans, eds. *Heresies of the High Middle Ages: Translated with Notes* (New York: Columbia Univ. Press, 1991), 173-85. This includes excerpts from the Passagini summaries in the *Summa contra haereticos* (below).

16. *Summa Contra Haereticos: Ascribed to Praepositinus of Cremona* (Notre Dame: Univ. of Notre Dame Press, 1958), esp. §II ('Quod lex vetus a diabolo/Deus data est et nullus/plures ante Christum salvatus'), §VI ('Quod vetus testamentum observandum sit/non sit ad litteram'). The attribution to Prepositinus is disputed: it is affirmed hesitantly by Georges Lacombe, *La Vie et les Oeuvres de Prévostin* (Bibliothèque Thomiste 11; Le Saulchoir: 1927), 134-35. But the reasons are insufficient for the attribution to be certain. See the introduction to the above edition by Garvin and Corbett, pp.xiii-xv.

17. E.g. *Contra Haereticos*, §VI.B.10.

18. Alexander Andrée, *Gilbertus Universalis: Glossa Ordinaria in Lamentationes Ieremie Prophete. Prothemata et Liber I. A Critical Edition with an*

Given its importance, the fact that the editor(s) for Jeremiah leaned heavily—in many places solely—on Jerome's commentary explains something of the dominance of Jerome's reading of Jer 31:31-34. On this oracle the gloss gives nothing more than a summary of Jerome, making clear the issue of the change of sacraments in just the terms Jerome puts forward.[19] The gloss links the new covenant to the 'possession of all virtues' through the Spirit's work of instilling the knowledge of God. Also like Jerome, however, there is no notice of Augustine's concerns of what this might mean for the 'ancient fathers'.[20]

We shouldn't be surprised, then, that Thomas makes significant use of Jer 31:31-34 as a support for the *mutatio sacramentorum*. Thomas' first remarks on the text come from his commentary on Jeremiah—a cursory reading of the text likely produced while he was still a 'bachelor' under Albert the Great in Cologne (i.e. 1248-52).[21] Thomas finds in the text the promise of 'spiritual goods', opposed to the 'temporal goods' of 31:27-30. He organizes his comments under three parts: the promise itself (*res*), the course (*tenor*), and the use. (1) The promise itself is that of a new covenant, 'that is the Gospel,' in the 'days of grace'. Interestingly, the Vulgate rendering of בעלתי with *dominatus* leads Thomas to seeing a negative side to Yhwh's work with Israel in the earlier covenant ('*crudeliter, et potestative ulciscendo*') set over against this new covenant. Since this stands opposite to Jerome's reading it may be that Thomas did not

---

Introduction and a Translation (Stockholm: Almquist & Wiksell Intl, 2005), 30.

19. On v.31: 'By this testmiony Paul, etc., *until* both circumcision and the sabbath have been spiritually fulfilled.' On v.34: 'In order that they might not seek Jewish teachers and rulers of men, but be instructed by the Holy Spirit, if yet they will be the temple of God, and the Spirit of God will dwell in them—who breathes where he wills and has various graces: yet the knowledge of the one God is the possession of all virtues.' *Glossa Ordinaria: Prophetia Jeremiae* (PL 114; Paris: 1879), 46c. Cp. Jerome, *In Hieremiam*, VI.26.4-6: 'By this testimony the apostle Paul... in order that all things, sacrifices and circumcision and the sabbath might be spiritually fulfilled.... In order that they by no means might seek Jewish teachers and traditions and rules of men, but be instructed by the Holy Spirit, if yet they will merit to hear: you are the temple of God and the Spirit of God dwells in you. For the Spirit breathes where he wills, and has various graces, and the knowledge of the one God is the possession of all virtues.'

20. The comments from the *Glossa* on Hebrews, drawn largely from Chrysostom, likewise set this pattern of spiritual/carnal sacraments: 'There is a distance between the priesthood and priesthood. That was carnal, this spiritual. That was temporal, this eternal.' *Glossa ad Hebraeos*, 655. Or, 'This is the distance between the "old" and the "new, since that was in stone, this in the heart; the for a reward, hearth; here, the vision of God (p.657).'

21. Jean-Pierre Torrell, *Saint Thomas Aquinas: The Person and His Work* (Tr. by Robert Royal. Washington D.C.: Catholic Univ. of America, 2003), I.27.

have, or did not make use of access to Jerome at this point.[22] (2) The 'tenor' of the covenant is found in v.33a: written 'in the inner parts, not on tablets of stone.' (3) The 'usefulness' of the covenant or its end, is for obedience (33b), for wisdom (34a, 'in which the need for teaching is excluded'), and for forgiveness of sins (34b).

That Thomas conceives of the whole contrast as between two religio-historical eras is made obvious in his comment on 34a:

> And this is certainly fulfilled in the present time because we do not come into divine truth through prophetic methods or human planning, nor even through Jewish traditions; but in the future it will be completed entirely.[23]

The deferring of complete fulfillment to the future might show some hesitation to apply the 'new covenant' directly to the 'present time.' But of course, given Thomas' occupation as an instructor in divine truth, the admission may simply be prudence. The real contrast remains the time prior to and following Christ.

Thomas' commentary on Hebrews represents a developed view of the same line. The commentary was written around 1265-68, just three years before the second part of the *Summa Theologiae* (*STh*) in which an Augustinian reading emerges. In the comments on Hebrews the change from 'old' to 'new law' especially concerns a change of efficacy in the sacraments. So, commenting on 7:12 (Vg: 'for the priesthood being changed, it is necessary that a change also be made of the law') Thomas cites Jer 31:31-32 as 'concerning this change', combining it with Rom 8:2:

> For the law of the spirit of life, in Christ Jesus, hath delivered me from the law of sin and of death. For the old law is called the law of sin and death, by an accepted circumstance that it does not confer grace *ex opere operato* as do the sacraments of the new law.[24]

For Thomas the sacraments of the *vetus lex* required faith to be added to them in order to become effective instruments of grace. But in the *nova lex* this is no

---

22. Jerome comments: 'When Israel is taken from the land of Egypt, so great was that intimacy of God with the people, that he says he took them by the hand and gave the covenant.' Jerome, *In Hieremiam*, §VI.26.5-6.

23. Thomas Aquinas, *In Jeremiam prophetam expositio* (Sancti Thomae Aquinatis Doctoris angelici. Opera Omnia 14; Parma: 1863), cap. 31, l.10. For his point on 34a, see Alcuin above.

24. Aquinas, *Hebrews*, 152. Cf. Peter Lombard: 'The letter of the Gospel differs from the letter of the law, for different things are promised: earthly things in the latter, heavenly things in the former. The sacraments also differ, for the sacraments of the law only signified grace, those of the Gospel confer it.' *Sententiae in IV libris distinctae* (PL 192), S.III, d.40., c.3.

longer a necessary condition. Thus, in a question taken into the *STh*, Thomas comments on Heb 9:9 (the old sacrifices 'could not make the worshipper perfect'):

> But were not many perfect in the old law? ... I respond that although many were then holy and perfect, this was not because of works of the Law. Above 7:19: 'For the law brought nothing to perfection.' Rather, it was because of faith in Christ. Gen 15:6: 'Abram believed God, and it was reputed to him unto justice [*iustitia*].' Therefore, this was not in virtue of the ceremonies or the legal observances. Hence it is frequently said, as it is in Lev 5:10 and many other places, 'The priest shall pray for him, and for his sin, and it shall be forgiven him.' That this would cleanse was due to faith. But in the New Testament it is said in Mk 6:16: 'He that believeth and is baptized, shall be saved.' For there is no salvation without the sacraments of the new law. [cites Jn 3:5][25]

Thomas is not disputing the necessity of faith for salvation in the New Testament. The question is, in what way are the sacraments effective instruments of grace? In the *vetus lex*, due to the nature of the sacraments as 'purely corporeal,'[26] they could not be sufficient instruments for causing grace. The 'promised goods in the Old Testament were temporal goods.' But in the New Testament the promises are 'heavenly'.[27]

Thomas is consistent throughout his career in using Jer 31:31-34—or at least its instances in the New Testament—to speak of this change in the ceremonial laws. From sacraments whose efficacy is tied to faith, the *nova lex* institutes sacraments that are efficacious in themselves. His commentary on Galatians and Hebrews offer the most clear statements of the matter, but it also re-occurs in the discussion of the *Summa Theologiae*. He poses the question, 'Whether the ceremonies of the *vetus lex* ceased at the coming of Christ?' He will answer in the affirmative, but cites Heb 8:13 as his chief answer against the contradictions (the *sed contra*): 'In saying new, he has made the former old: and that which decays and grows old, is near its end.'[28] Thomas outlines three different 'states' (*stati*)

---

25. Ibid., 183-84. Or, 'if there were any in the old law who were just, they were not made just by the works of the Law [i.e. the 'ceremonial works' which 'neither confer grace nor contain grace in themselves'] but only by the faith of Christ "whom God hath proposed to be a propitiation through faith" (Rom 3:25)....' Ibid. This also represents the use of Jer 31:31-34 in his *Commentary on Saint Paul's Epistle to the Galatians* (Tr. by F.R. Larcher. Albany, NY: Magi Books, 1966), 139ff.

26. Aquinas, *Hebrews*, 184.

27. Ibid., 185.

28. Thomas Aquinas, *Summa Theologiae* (5 vols.; Ottawa: Studii Generalis, 1949), IaIIae, 103, a.3, s.c. I have used the translation of the English Dominicans (*Summa Theologica*, Benziger Bros., 1947) throughout, changed or updated as necessary.

for three different stages in which one joins external worship to internal worship: (1) faith and hope in heavenly goods as things yet to come, and their means as something yet to come (i.e. the era prior to Christ); (2) faith and hope in heavenly goods as things yet to come, and their means as having already come (i.e. the era after Christ); and (3) the possession of the heavenly goods and their means ('the state of the Blessed'). So, with the *nova lex* promised through Jer 31, the means of the heavenly goods have come—the *passio Christi* and the true sacraments. The clear religio-historical use of Jer 31:31-34 for the change of sacraments (*mutatio sacramentorum*) shows Thomas in this mainline of interpretation.

2. *Locating the Discussion in the* Summa

We must, however, say more about Thomas' reading of Jeremiah's new covenant in the *STh*, where the Augustinian reading emerges.[29] The *STh* was composed in its three parts later in Thomas' life, from c.1265-73 when he stopped abruptly on the topic of 'penance'. And many individual questions are taken more or less whole out of previous commentaries or other works. But Thomas puts forward the interrelation of the three parts explicitly by way of the prefaces, and now is generally acknowledged.[30] We find the treatment of Jer 31:31-34 in the midst of the treatise on Law in the *prima secundae*. And though one can find this treatise published on its own today, Thomas places it in direct relationship to the *prima pars*:

> [N]ow that we have treated of the exemplar, i.e. God, and of those things which came forth from the power of God in accordance with His will [i.e. part 1], it remains for us to treat of His image, i.e. man, inasmuch as he too is the principle of his actions, as having free-will and control of his actions.[31]

Within this goal Thomas gives a more particular goal for the discussion on Law, making use of the larger theme of the movement toward God, our 'happiness' and proper end:

> We have now to consider the extrinsic principles of acts. Now the extrinsic principle inclining to evil is the devil, of whose temptations we have

---

29. Contrary to the presentation of Leo J. Elders, "La relation entre l'ancienne et la nouvelle Alliance, selon saint Thomas d'Aquin," *RThom* 100 (2000). Elders interacts with the above texts, but inexplicably never with the important discussion in IaIIae q.106, which presents the crucial caveat.

30. See Leonard E. Boyle, "The Setting of the Summa Theologiae of St. Thomas—Revisited," in *The Ethics of Aquinas* (ed. Stephen J. Pope; Washington D.C.: Georgetown Univ. Press, 2002); Torrell, *Person and Work*, 145-47.

31. Aquinas, *STh*, Ia IIae, pro.

spoken.... But the extrinsic principle moving to good is God, who both instructs us by means of His Law, and assists us by His Grace: wherefore in the first place we must speak of law; in the second place, of grace.[32]

The *tertia pars* continues this logic, so that after teaching about the proper end of human life Thomas moves to the means by which we can obtain that end, namely Jesus Christ, the sacraments, and the resurrection. Thus we are concerned in the *secunda pars* with humanity, and in particular the actions of a person in relation to his or her proper end. What follows the treatise on Law is a discussion of grace (which fits well the natures of the old and new law), and then the *secunda secundae* which details the actions proper to the Christian life.

The contextual importance of the treatment of Law in relation to sin should be emphasized, in part because it is often overlooked despite the proximity of the questions (q.89 closes the treatment on sin, q.90 opens that on law) and the explicit link made by the prologue between them.[33] As Thomas Hibbs remarks: 'It is not accidental that the treatise on law in the Summa is comfortably ensconced between the treatises on sin and grace.'[34] The fundamental principle of the whole *secunda pars* is that the happiness and desire of all humankind – i.e. humankind's proper end – is the beatific vision of God.[35] That is where humankind ought to be headed. And yet the habits or dispositions which ought to lead us toward that end have been damaged by sin, and by original sin in particular.

Original sin corrupts 'the disposition of a complex nature, whereby that nature is well or ill disposed to something.'[36] It works like a disease that carries a person from health to sickness – an 'inordinate disposition of the body'. Further, following Anselm, original sin is the 'absence of original justice' (*carentia originalis iustitiae*). *Iustitia* has already been discussed as a cardinal virtue, tied

---

32. Ibid., Ia IIae, q.90, pro. The dual need of instruction (given by law) and assistance (the grace of the Spirit) is also seen in Hugh of St. Victor, *On the Sacraments of the Christian Faith (De Sacramentis)* (Tr. by Roy J. Deferrari. Cambridge, MA: Mediaeval Academy of America, 1951), I.viii.3.

33. Cf. the prologue above. Even Étiene, whose helpful article devotes some space to the place of the treatise on law within the whole fails to mention any connection here. Jacques Étiene, "Loi et grâce: Le concept de loi nouvelle dans la Somme théòlogique de S. Thomas d'Aquin," *RTL* 16 (1985).

34. Thomas S. Hibbs, "Divine Irony and the Natural Law: Speculation and Edification in Aquinas," *International Philosophical Quarterly* 30.4 (1990), 426.

35. 'The final and perfect blessing (*beatitudo*) cannot be anything except in the vision of the divine essence.' *STh*, Ia IIae, q.3, a.8, co.

36. Ia IIae, q.82, a.1, s.c. See the helpful treatment on this topic by Marie Leblanc, "Le péché originel dans la pensée de S. Thomas," *RThom* 93 (1993).

directly to one's nature and directing one's nature to the proper end.[37] Thus the absence of the cardinal virtue of *iustitia*, or the disposition of righteousness which is a part of our nature, rules us out of attaining either the natural or supernatural aspect of our proper end. In short, after original sin we are left with a significant problem: the lack of *iustitia* and the corrupted habits, so we are headed away from that end proper to our nature. The importance of that unresolved problem cannot be forgotten when Thomas turns to discussion of law.

3. *'Law' in Thomas: Natural, Human, and Divine*

Thomas begins his discussion of law here, immediately after establishing the place of sin leading us away from our proper end. And he ties law directly to the theme of our movement to 'happiness' or our proper end:

> Now the first principle in practical matters, which are the object of the practical reason, is the last end: and the last end of human life is bliss or happiness, as stated above. Consequently the law must regard principally the relationship to happiness.[38]

The idea is simple enough: all matters of practice are to be ordered towards our proper end. And laws have to do with matters of practice, so they must be set in the context of our proper end, the beatific vision. This is the foundation of the 'eternal law' (*lex aeterna*) undergirding all other laws. Already a popular concept at least as far back as Augustine, the eternal law in Thomas is the plan of divine wisdom (*ratio divinae sapientiae*) which 'moves all things to their

---

37. Ia IIae, qq.58-62. The (one) proper end of a person is twofold for Thomas, containing both a natural aspect – corresponding to one's nature and attainable by it – and a supernatural aspect which is impossible to attain except by the power of God. These two different aspects of the proper end correspond to two kinds of virtues, (a) the cardinal or principle virtues tied to our nature and (b) theological virtues which are infused in us by grace. For this see esp. Ia IIae, q.62, a.1, co.

38. Ia IIae, q. 90, a.2, co. Étiene rightly points towards the unity that this provides between 'law' and 'desire' in Thomas: 'Toute loi est ordonnée à une fin mais saint Thomas songe avant tout à la fin dernière, à la béatitude surnaturelle à laquelle Dieu invite ses enfants; il en résulte que, comprise dans taoute sa profondeur, la loi dont traite la Somme, loin d'évoquer une violence asservissante, apparaît, dans une perspective de sagesse, comme un chemin qui condui l'homme au bonheur parfait; loi et désir sont foncièrement réconciliés dans la vérité de l'homme telle que Dieu la révèle de sorte que chacun puisse s'y conformer par son agir.' Étiene, "Loi et grâce," 8. Or more simply, 'Gesetz und Evangelien sind kein Widerspruch.' Johannes Stöhr, "Bewahrt das Sittengesetz des alten Bundes seine Geltung im neuen Bund?," in *Lex et Libertas* (eds. L.J. Elders and K. Hedwig; Studi Tomisitici,. Vatican City: Libreria Editrice Vaticana, 1987), 220.

proper end'.³⁹ This is the governing category of law, in which the other kinds of law (natural, human and divine) find their place. It is a general 'way things ought to be' through the creative and sustaining providence of God in creation.⁴⁰

So 'law', grounded fundamentally in the eternal law, directs us toward our proper end. The three parts of this law—natural, human, and divine—are subsumed in different ways within this structure. Natural law, perhaps the most famous aspect of Thomas' thought, is the means by which rational creatures participate in the eternal law *in their nature*.⁴¹ That is, every rational creature is ordered by its created nature towards its proper end. Based on the Aristotelian conviction of the law of non-contradiction as a foundational principle, Thomas asserts as the foundational self-evident principle for the natural law, 'good is that which all things seek after' and its precept, 'good is to be done and pursued, and evil is to be avoided.'⁴² This is built into our nature as the bedrock of all 'natural' law (nature directed to happiness).

---

39. Ia IIae, q.93, a.1, co. Cf., e.g., Augustine, *De libero arbitrio* (CCL 29; Tournholt: Brepols, 1970), I.6.15.

40. See Ia IIae, q.93, a.5.

41. The discussion of Thomas on natural law is immense, though summarily we can mention three points. (1) There exists a traditional line of development which can be summarised in Jean Porter's words: 'Thomas' moral theology presupposes that the content of morality can be derived from independent, nontheological grounds.' Jean Porter, "Desire for God: Ground of the Moral Life in Aquinas," *TS* 47 (1986), 65. See her more lengthy discussion in *Natural & Divine Law: Reclaiming the Tradition for Christian Ethics* (Grand Rapids, MI: Eerdmans, 1999). (2) This reading is strongly (and rightly) disputed by other scholars: the 'curtailment or suspension of the theocentric intention of Aquinas's ethical considerations is bound to distort his account.' Fergus Kerr, "Aquinas and Analytic Philosophy: Natural Allies?," in *Aquinas in Dialogue: Thomas for the Twenty-First Century* (eds. Jim Fodor and F.C. Bauerschmidt; Oxford: Blackwell, 2004), 132 (summarizing another's views, with whom he sympathizes). Cf. Pamela M. Hall, *Narrative and the Natural Law: An Interpretation of Thomistic Ethics* (Notre Dame: Univ. of Notre Dame, 1994); Thomas S. Hibbs, "Interpretations of Aquinas's Ethics since Vatican II," in *The Ethics of Aquinas* (ed. Stephen J. Pope; Washington D.C.: Georgetown Univ. Press, 2002). (3) This discussion is inseparable from that of 'natural theology' in more general terms – a project to which Karl Barth strongly objects and associates with Thomas (akin to Porter's reading); but in light of (2), see Eugene F. Rogers, Jr., "Thomas and Barth in Convergence on Romans 1?," *Modern Theology* 12.1 (1996); Idem, "The Narrative of Natural Law in Aquinas's Commentary on Romans 1," *TS* 59.2 (1998).

42. Ia IIae, q.94, a.2, co.

The self-evidence of the principle aids to ensure that the natural law cannot be eliminated from the heart, even through sin.[43] Further, the general precepts of natural law are always necessarily available by virtue of the nature of man as a reasonable creature created within the eternal law.[44] But this does not mean that the act of deriving precepts from our nature is untouched by sin. Already we can begin to see the points that will be at issue in the giving of the divine law. By virtue of sin we are ruled out of the beatific vision, both by lack of *iustitia* and a disposition away from our proper end. Law is given to direct us to our proper end, and though still a part of our nature by virtue of the continuity of nature before and after sin, it cannot in itself take us to that proper end. Natural law can direct, but if one's dispositions are away from the good then simply being given the direction cannot be sufficient; something beyond law is necessary. Thomas will assert that this 'something beyond' is grace and the work of the Holy Spirit which he terms the 'new law'. The whole treatise heads towards this point.[45]

Thomas' discussion of human law can be treated briefly. Human laws are given to train or direct towards the common good. Thus Thomas states, 'man has a natural aptitude for virtue, but the perfection of virtue must be acquired by

---

43. Ia IIae, q.94, a.6.

44. The room for this is already established in Ia IIae, q.85, a.1. Sin does not change the nature of a created being. Thus his oft-cited dictum: 'gratia non destruit naturam, sed supponit et perficit eam.' This brings up the difficult principle of *synderesis*, which has been debated widely and would take us too far afield to attempt to resolve. In my mind Pamela Hall is right in following Daniel Mark Nelson, who does not downplay the importance of synderesis – that habit by which one is able to choose good – but instead emphasises the generality of the concept. In Hall's words, 'The first principle of practical reason does not then yield specific knowledge of genuine goods; it provides only the most general way to characterize the end of an action: as a good, as something to be desired.' Hall, *Narrative*, 31. This ties in well with the emphasis of Westberg who reminds us that the discussion of the laws is primarily addressed to the intellect, rather than the will, contrary to the later tradition in medieval thought (e.g. John Scotus and William Ockham). In other words, law addresses primarily what we desire as an end, and only derivatively what we ought and ought not to do. Daniel Westberg, *Right Practical Reason: Aristotle, Action and Prudence in Aquinas* (Oxford: Clarendon, 1994), 34-35.

45. Thus Pesch: 'Die allgemeine Lehre vom Gesetz, die als solche schon eine unverkennbare theozentrische Orientierung aufweist, wird nur als Prolegomenon der Lehre vom göttlichen Gesetz des Alten und Neuen Bundes vorangeschickt, auf der quantitativ und qualitativ das Schwergewicht des Gesetzestraktates liegt.' O.H. Pesch, *Die Theologie der Rechtfertigung bei Martin Luther und Thomas von Aquin: Versuch eines systematisch-theologischen Dialogs* (Mainz: Matthias-Grünewald-Verlag, 1985), 411.

man by means of some kind of training.'⁴⁶ Thus the institution of human laws, which have their origin in the natural law and are instituted by the proper authorities according to the particular determinations that seem best for the circumstances. Thomas distinguishes human law from natural law not only via the source of institution (by the creature rather than by the created order or nature), but because human law is malleable to the extent that it takes into account present circumstances and the current imperfection of the common good.⁴⁷ But as of yet we have no solution offered for the problems of sin and our attaining our proper end. Neither natural law nor human law can take us to that end, even if both continue to have an important place in human life.

Thomas introduces divine law by offering four reasons for its necessity above and beyond natural and human law:

> (1) The proper end of a person (beatific vision) is beyond his or her natural faculties to attain; therefore more than the natural law must be given.⁴⁸
>
> (2) Human discernment regarding the particulars of what ought and ought not to be done is uncertain.⁴⁹

---

46. One's 'natural aptitude for virtue' means that a person, by virtue of his or her nature as a rational creature, is prone towards the proper end (happiness) which entails the proper virtues. He does not here deny the earlier statements regarding the effect of sin upon one's habits: each question is handled in its appropriate place. He defends this statement in Ia IIae, q.63, a.1 and q.94, a.3; Ia IIae, q.95, a.1, co.

47. Ia IIae, q.97, a.1. The distinction here is easily stated: the command not to murder is a different kind of precept than the command to pay my taxes. The latter is only binding by virtue of the present institution, whereas the former is binding by virtue of the created order. The government has the authority to revoke the precept commanding taxes given whatever present circumstances; but the overturning of the command not to murder would entail an overturning of the created order and is thus impossible for man or even for God insofar as the natural law is simply that which leads to God. 'God cannot dispense a man so that it be lawful for him not to direct himself to God, or not to be subject to His justice, even in those matters in which men are directed to one another.' Ia IIae, q.100, a.8, ad.2.

48. More precisely: 'First, because it is by law that man is directed how to perform his proper acts in view of his last end. And indeed if man were ordained to no other end than that which is proportionate to his natural faculty, there would be no need for man to have any further direction of the part of his reason, besides the natural law and human law which is derived from it. But since man is ordained to an end of eternal happiness which is inproportionate to man's natural faculty, as stated above, therefore it was necessary that, besides the natural and the human law, man should be directed to his end by a law given by God.' Ia IIae, q.91, a.4, co.

49. The point will be continued through the Reformation: e.g. Philip Melanchthon, *On Christian Doctrine: Loci Communes 1555* (Tr. by Clyde L.

(3) The perfection of the proper end demands acting rightly in both external and internal actions. But human judgment, and therefore human law, is only competent for external acts.[50]

(4) Human law cannot punish or forbid all sin, for by so doing many good things would be forbidden and the common good would be hindered. Thus in order that all sin might be confronted, divine law was necessary.

While the latter two show the need for something beyond human law, the first reveals the shortcomings of the natural law itself. Thomas does not see natural law as capable of perfecting men and women, that is, of bringing us to our proper created end of friendship with God. The second reason adduced is a shortcoming in humanity and a foreshadowing of the discussion regarding the old law (*vetus lex*), where its necessity is placed on the reality of sin (though here it can be understood less strongly). In any case, Thomas does not hold the natural law to be sufficient for the proper ordering of humanity—either for humanity's supernatural end (1) or natural end (2). Thus our proper end stands in need of divine law.

Divine law has two parts: the *vetus* and *nova lex*, terminology that we have already seen is prevalent in Justin Martyr and that dominated medieval theology.[51] The characterisation of the *vetus lex* along three parts—moral, judicial and ceremonial—is by no means original to Thomas.[52] But the three parts enable him to tie the whole into the discussion of the eternal and especially the natural law in fruitful ways. As human law is tied to natural law (both grounded in the eternal law), so he claims that the moral precepts in the old law, summarized by the Decalogue, are a clarification of the natural law.[53]

Manschreck. Oxford: Oxford Univ. Press, 1965), 128-29.

50. A similar shortcoming is found regarding the *vetus lex* in Thomas Aquinas, *Scriptum super sententiis* (Sancti Thomae Aquinatis Doctoris angelici. Opera Omnia 6-7; Parma: 1858), lib.3, q.40, a.2, s.c.2: 'In Matt 5 the Lord goes beyond the precepts of the law, when what belongs to the exterior work, such murder, he makes an addition concerning the interior act of sin, just as with anger: which would not have been if the old law had restrained the spirit (*animus*). Therefore the old law does not restrain the spirit.'

51. E.g., Peter Lombard opens his influential Sentences with language of the 'veteris ac novae legis': *Sententiae*, S.I, d.1.

52. See Beryl Smalley, "William of Auvergne, John of La Rochelle and St. Thomas Aquinas on the Old Law," in *St. Thomas Aquinas: Commemorative Studies* (ed. Armand A. Maurer; Toronto: Pontifical Institute of Medieval Studies, 1974).

53. Cp. Peter Lombard, *Sententiae*, S.III., d.36, c.3: 'Indeed, even the ceremonial commands according to the spiritual understanding which they contain, and all the moral commands are attributed to charity. For all of them pertain to the ten commandments written in tablets, where a summary of all of them is offered, from which

It is therefore evident that since the moral precepts are about matters which concern good morals, and since good morals are those which are in accord with reason (*ratio*),[54] and since also every judgment of human reason must be derived in some way from natural reason, it follows of necessity, that all the moral precepts belong to the law of nature.[55]

A law, as we have seen, is in place in order to direct to one's proper end. This is no different for divine law in both its parts, 'old' and 'new'.[56] In fact to call the old law 'good' is simply to ascribe to it this quality of directing its subjects toward their proper end. One of the chief consequences of this is Thomas' strong view of the permanence of the moral part of the old law:

> Now the precepts of the Decalogue contain the very intention of the lawgiver, who is God. For the precepts of the first table, which direct us to God, contain the very order to the common and final good, which is God; while the precepts of the second table contain the order of justice to be observed among men, that nothing undue be done to anyone, and that each one be given his due; for it is in this sense that we are to take the precepts of the Decalogue. Consequently the precepts of the Decalogue admit of no dispensation whatever.[57]

The judicial and ceremonial precepts of the old law, however, were given in order to govern the relationships within Israel (judicial), and between Israel and

---

the other (commands) flow... And just as other (commands) are referred to the ten commands of the Decalogue , so aslo the ten pertain to the two commands of love (*charitas*). Therefore all pertain to the two commands of love, because they are fulfilled by love, and are to be referred to love as their end (*finis*).'

54. *Ratio* has already been identified as the central characteristic of those creatures who follow their proper end by choice, and as a faculty is tied directly to this proper end. Thus 'good morals are those which are in accord with *ratio*.' Reason is not here the 'brain in a vat' or separable from the end of the beatific vision.

55. Ia IIae, q.100, a.1, co. 'Nur die äußere schriftliche Form und seine spezielle Funktion, die durch den von ihm ausgeübten Zwang gekennzeichnet ist, unterscheidet den Dekalog vom Naturgesetz.' Ulrich Kühn, *Via Caritatis: Theologie des Gesetzes bei Thomas von Aquin* (Göttingen: Vandenhoeck & Ruprecht, 1965), 67.

56. 'As the Apostle says, "the end of the commandment is *caritas*"; since every law aims at establishing friendship, either between man and man, or between man and God. Wherefore the whole Law is comprised in this one commandment, "Thou shalt love thy neighbor as thyself," as expressing the end of all commandments: because love of one's neighbor includes love of God, when we love our neighbor for God's sake.' *STh*, Ia IIae, q.99, a.1, ad.2. The latter part of this statement is drawing on the Augustinian notion that all true (i.e. right) love of anything less than God must be a loving of it for God's sake. Only God is to be loved for his own sake. Augustine, *Christian Teaching*, Bk.1. It is common language by Thomas' time, as seen in Peter Lombard, *Sententiae*, S.I, d.1 c.2.

57. Ia IIae, q.100, a.8, co.

God (ceremonial). Thus, by virtue of being tied to God's institution and not intrinsic to nature, they are changeable (by God) and not necessarily binding for all people at all times.[58]

Yet however good the old law was, it was not 'perfect', since perfection implies an ending to movement: the old law would have to take us to our proper end in and of itself. Since it does not do so, it can only be called 'imperfectly good'.[59] This imperfection does not, however, mean that the law is not good and therefore not from God. A medicine, Thomas explains, does not have to restore to health in order to be a good medicine; it may simply need to stop the disease. It would be imperfect – not taking the subject to the complete state of wellness – but proper and good nonetheless. The central problem with the old law is its failure to confer grace (*vetus lex gratiam non conferebat*).[60] We still must face the problem of sin and our supernatural end, both of which have loomed over the whole discussion of 'law'.

4. *The 'New Law' in Thomas*

As many before him, Thomas makes use of Jer 31:31-34 in the contrast of the *vetus* and *nova lex*. But as the groundwork has begun to show, Thomas will use the text here as something other than a proof-text for the *mutatio sacramentorum*. Rather, Thomas explicitly agrees in the basic understanding of the contrast of old and new law with what was shown above in Augustine's contrast of *vetus* and *novum testamentum*. For Augustine the *vetus testamentum* was the law without grace or faith or the letter without the Spirit, which could not give life. Members of the *vetus testamentum* are thus identified by this standing before God and relationship to grace rather than by their location in a particular religio-historical era. Thomas, with certain nuances, takes the same basic position here. He posits the contrast of *vetus* and *nova lex* as between a law by itself

---

58. Ia IIae, q.104, a.1, co.

59. Ia IIae, q.98, a.1-2. Pamela Hall states the matter well: 'the Decalogue was directed toward constituting men and women who are good and thus capable, by divine similitude, of friendship with God; this friendship, as we know, is the end of the divine law. But in saying that the old law conduced and directed towards virtue and to likeness to God is not to say that it achieved this end.' Hall, *Narrative*, 59. Or Aubert, 'Dans les deux cas, en tant qui réalité humaine, la loi naturelle n'avait efficacité, que seule possède la grace de l'Esprit Saint donné par la Loi nouvelle, c'est à dire l'Evangile.... l'Evangile n'est pas synonyme d'absence de loi, d'opposition à la loi; mais il est l'accès rendu possible à l'homme de vivre une nouvelle vie dont la loi est l'amour.' Jean-Marie Aubert, "L'analogie entre Lex nova et la loi naturelle," in *Lex et Libertas* (eds. L.J. Elders and K. Hedwig; Studi Tomisitici,. Vatican City: Libreria Editrice Vaticana, 1987), 250-51.

60. As already seen in his Aquinas, *Sup. sent*, lib.3, q.40, a.2, s.c. 3.

without grace—which thus could never bring about man's eternal happiness—and the law of grace by which alone we can achieve that happiness. As such the divide between the old and new law cannot be reduced to a contrast between two eras in the divine economy.

We have already seen that Thomas does speak of the contrast of the old and new law as relative to divine economies in redemption.[61] This is evident here also in Thomas' discussion of why the old law was given in the time of Moses:

> [I]t was fitting that the Law should be given at such a time as would be appropriate for the overcoming of man's pride. For man was proud of two things, viz. of knowledge and of power. He was proud of his knowledge, as though his natural reason could suffice him for salvation: and accordingly, in order that his pride might be overcome in this matter, man was left to the guidance of his reason without the help of a written law: and man was able to learn from experience that his reason was deficient, since about the time of Abraham man had fallen headlong into idolatry and the most shameful vices. Wherefore, after those times, it was necessary for a written law to be given as a remedy for human ignorance.[62]

But the old law was not only given because of those who had fallen into idolatry. It was also rightly given at that time for the sake of the 'good':

> With regard to good men, the Law was given to them as a help; which was most needed by the people, at the time when the natural law began to be obscured on account of the exuberance of sin: for it was fitting that this help should be bestowed on men in an orderly manner, so that they might be led from imperfection to perfection; wherefore it was becoming that the old law should be given between the law of nature and the law of grace.[63]

---

61. This is the emphasis given in Romanus Cessario, *The Moral Virtues and Theological Ethics* (Notre Dame: Univ. of Notre Dame, 1991), 15, 20-21, et passim.

62. Ia IIae, q.98, a.6, co. Cp. Hugh of St. Victor: '[I]n the time of the natural law man was left entirely to himself, afterwards in the time of the written law counsel was given to him when he realized his ignorance, finally in the time of grace help was furnished him when he confessed his lack.' Victor, *On the Sacraments*, I.viii.3. As a side-note we can here (again) see Thomas' view that sin has clouded our ability to claim and recognize natural law without divine revelation. Or, as Hibbs: 'Revelation, then, is needed not only that man may grasp supernatural truths, but also that he may re-cognize those natural truths which the effects of sin have hidden from him.' Hibbs, "Divine Irony," 424.

63. Ia IIae, q.98, a.6, co. These two are brought together more succinctly, q.98, a.6, ad 1: 'It was not fitting for the old law to be given at once after the sin of the first man: both because man was so confident in his own reason, that he did not acknowledge his need of the old law; [and] because as yet the dictate of the natural law was not

Jeremiah's New Covenant 49

The economical aspect of these lines is rather clear and we can point to the last line in particular ('inter legem naturae et legem gratiae, oportuit legem veterem dari'). These three periods certainly cannot be considered entirely distinct – for the natural law is not constrained to one time only, nor as we will see is the law of grace. Perhaps Thomas is simply referring to the revealing of the various laws ('to give'—*dare*—is a vague term): they were revealed in a progressive manner in the history of God's bringing people to himself. In this case, as in Augustine, the revelation of a thing does not necessarily mean its institution.[64] That the new law is fully revealed only in Christ does not mean it did not exist prior to the Incarnation. Or if this is stretching the case, we are left with a tension in Thomas' work.

We see the major impetus behind Thomas' appeal to the new law at the close of the discussion of the moral part of the old law and the question whether or not the moral precepts of the old law justify.[65] In what becomes a complicated series of distinctions regarding the nature and use of *iustificatio*, Thomas emerges with the claim that the old law cannot in itself produce *iustificatio* as an infused virtue.[66] This is in keeping with the point made above that the old law is good but only as an imperfect good that directs us to our proper end but unable

---

darkened by habitual sinning.'

64. '[R]evelationes eorum considerantur in his nominibus, non institutiones': Augustine, *Contra epp. Pel*, §3.13.

65. The objection runs, 'It appears that the moral precepts of the law justify.' Ia IIae, q.100, a.12.

66. Summarily, a thing can be said to 'justify' either by (1) the causing of justice, or (2) as a sign or disposition toward justice. Within the latter the old law can be said to justify since it disposes one towards the justifying grace of Christ ('disponebant homines ad gratiam Christi iustificantem'), which the people of Israel typify (cf. Ia IIae, q.104, a.2, ad 2). Within the first category, something can cause *iustificatio* either (a) as a habit (*habitus*) or (b) as an act – the production of *iustitia*. If understood as the latter, then the old law justified man in various ways (the ceremonial in one way, the judicial in another, and the moral in another), through obedience to its precepts.

Considered as a habit or virtue, we have one last distinction. For virtues can be either acquired or infused (see Ia IIae, q.63). The latter are understood, by definition, to be those which 'God works in us, without us' (Ia IIae, q.63, a.4, s.c.). Further, it is this infused virtue which is *vera iustitia*, according to which it is said that one is *iustus apud Deum* as Abraham (Romans 4:2). The moral precepts, concerned as they are with human actions (and not divinely infused virtues), could never justify in this 'truest' sense. Incidentally one can already see the difficulties with this line of formulation for Luther and the magisterial Reformers, for whom *iustificatio* exists *extra nos* – not just as given from outside of us (*infusa*). For a diagram of Thomas' discussion, see Pesch, *Theologie der Rechtfertigung*, 429.

in itself to take us there, a teaching that is broadly indebted to Augustine and seen in Thomas' predecessors.[67] The new law is the provision of that which the old law is unable in itself to do: *lex nova est perfectior quam lex vetus*.[68]

All of this lays the ground for the nature of the new law. In summary form the *lex nova* for Thomas is the grace of God through the Holy Spirit.[69] Thomas identifies the *lex nova* with the Law of the *novum testamentum* ('lex nova est lex novi testamenti'), and defines the new law as the grace of the Holy Spirit:

> 'Each thing appears to be that which is foremost in it,' as the Philosopher states (Ethic., ix). That which is foremost in the Law of the *novum testamentum*, and in which all its power consists, is the grace of the Holy Spirit, which is given through faith in Christ. Consequently the *lex nova* is principally the grace itself of the Holy Spirit, which is given to those who believe in Christ.[70]

To establish his position he cites Jer 31:31,33 followed by two citations of Augustine from the De spiritu, the second of which reads: 'What else are the Divine laws written by God Himself on our hearts, but the very presence of his Holy Spirit?' So, from Augustine, Thomas learns to read the contrast in Jer

---

67. Cp. Peter Lombard, *Sententiae*, S.III, d.40, c.2; quoted below.

68. Aquinas, *Sup. sent*, lib.3, d.40, q.1, a.2, sc.1. 'Hierein liegt demnach der grundlegende Unterschied zwischen altem und neuem Gesetz: Das alte Gesetz ist unfähig, die eigentliche justificatio zu bewirken, das vermag nur das neue Gesetz, indem es in den Sakramenten über Mittel verfügt, die durch die dargereichte Gnade die erstrebte justitia als justitia infusa verwirklichen.' Kühn, *Via Caritatis*, 72. Or more succinctly, 'Das Alte Gestez ist dadurch charakterisiert, daß es nicht erreicht, was es fordert. Das Neue Gesetz ist dadurch gekennzeichnet, daß es auch erreicht, was es intendiert.' Pesch, *Theologie der Rechtfertigung*, 427.

69. Helpful discussions of the 'new law' include Pamela M. Hall, "The Old Law and the New Law," in *The Ethics of Aquinas* (ed. Stephen J. Pope; Washington D.C.: Georgetown Univ. Press, 2002); Philippe Delhaye, "La Loi nouvelle comme dynamisme de l'Esprit-Saint," in *Lex et Libertas* (eds. L.J. Elders and K. Hedwig; Studi Tomisitici. Vatican City: Libreria Editrice Vaticana, 1987); Étiene, "Loi et grâce." The most thorough discussion is Kühn, *Via Caritatis*.

70. Ia IIae, q.106, a.1, co. The secondary sense of the new law as written is of little importance for our discussion and is backgrounded sharply here by Thomas, though it grounds much of the teaching in IIa IIae. Since the new law contains some things that belong to the arranging or disposing of the grace of the Spirit and the use of that grace ('quaedam sicut dispositiva ad gratiam spiritus sancti, et ad usum huius gratiae pertinentia'), these things are written down for our instruction. Thus the written Gospels present the grace of the new law but are not properly called the *lex nova* itself. Ibid.

31:31f as between an old law that cannot justify, and the 'new' work of the Spirit in those who believe.

The consequences of this for Jeremiah's 'new covenant' are then spelled out by the objection confronted by Augustine: what of those prior to the *nova lex*? The objection reasons that, if the new law is the Spirit's work by which people are made friends of God, and if the ancient faithful had that Spirit's work, then you have the *novum testamentum* in the era of the *vetus*. Thus the new law cannot be defined this way:

> The Law of the Gospel is characteristic of those who are in the situation of the *novum testamentum*. But the Law that is inscribed [on the heart] is common both to those who are in the *novum testamentum* and those who are in the *vetus testamentum*. For it is said in Wisdom 7[:27]: 'Divine wisdom conveys herself through the nations into holy souls; she establishes the friends of God and the prophets.' Therefore the *lex nova* is not the Law inscribed.[71]

Thomas answers by appeal to an implicit distinction between membership in the *novum testamentum* and the 'situation [*status*] of the *novum testamentum*':

> No one ever possessed the grace of the Holy Spirit except through faith in Christ, explicit or implicit. Moreover, through faith in Christ a man belongs to the *novum testamentum*. Thus whoever had the Law of grace infused, accordingly belonged to the *novum testamentum*.[72]

At first glance it does not appear that Thomas answers the objection. He solves the dilemma by agreeing that there have always been those who had the Law of grace and belonged to the *novum testamentum*. The implicit point, however, is that 'belonging to the *novum testamentum*' is not the same as being in the *status novi testamenti* – otherwise the reply would not at all address the objection. Thomas thus drives a distinction between two realities: that of the situation of the Gospel or the *status novi testamenti*, and that of membership within the *novum testamentum*. And Jer 31:33-34 addresses the latter. Thus, in article 4 of the same question he asserts that the situation of the new law succeeds the situation of the old law ('*successit enim status novae legis statui veteris legis*'), a claim he finds consistent with the *novum testamentum* existing during the situation of the old law.

Matthew Levering summarizes the distinction being made this way: 'The state of the new law begins after the Incarnation, while the new law itself,

---

71. Ia IIae, q.106, a.1, ob.3.
72. Ia IIae, q.106, a.1, ad.3.

as the grace of the Holy Spirit, is found in all places and times.'[73] Or more fully is Colman O'Neill:

> [T]he new law exists as the mystery of salvation at work in the world from the time of the restoration of man to grace. Yet, though the new law thus transcends historical periods, the state of the new law does not. For the state of the new law is precisely that third state of revelation and faith which was initiated in the Incarnation and in the mysteries of Christ.[74]

That Thomas owes this position to Augustine is clear: Augustine is cited no fewer than 8 times in answer to this one question. And we can see the similarity to Augustine's distinctions. One can speak two different ways of the vetus and novum testamentum (or lex): either with reference to a 'state' or era, or with reference to the thing itself. If the former, then one can speak of the economical differences. But if the latter, then any view of temporal succession is impossible. And the point for our purposes is that Jeremiah is speaking of the latter. The *lex nova* spoken of in Jer 31:33-34 is available throughout all ages and without the possession of it, one's happiness (proper end) is unattainable – for that which is outside of a person cannot justify. The virtue of being just before God cannot be acquired unless given by God, and clearly those faithful of the ancient era were just before God. Thus 'in all times there have been some belonging to the *novum testamentum*', even if the *statu novi testamenti* awaited the coming of Christ.[75]

This point is made concrete in Thomas' treatment of David in Psalm 51 (Vg. 50) and Thomas' view of David as having the Holy Spirit (i.e. the *lex nova*):

> However, the reason for this manifestation [of guilt (*culpa*) being wiped clean] is divine mercy; for this manifestation is useful for the righteous so that they do not presume upon their righteousness. For if David sinned – after so many victories, after the gift of the Holy Spirit, after so much familiarity with God and the exercise of prophecy – then how much more ought we, who are fragile and sinful, to be wary?[76]

If Jeremiah's prophecy of the new covenant is a prophecy of the *lex nova*, which is contained fundamentally in the giving of the Holy Spirit, then David is here explicitly counted as a member of the new covenant. The exhortation even

---

73. Matthew Levering, *Christ's Fulfillment of Torah and Temple: Salvation according to Thomas Aquinas* (Notre Dame: Univ. of Notre Dame, 2002), 23.

74. Colman E. O'Neill, "St. Thomas on the Membership of the Church," *Thomist* 27 (1963), 99. I take this as also applicable to the somewhat obscure reply in Ia IIae, q.106, ad.2.

75. 'omni tempore fuerint aliqui ad novum testamentum pertinentes.' Ia IIae, q.106, a.3, ad.2.

76. *In psalmos Davidis expositio* (Opera Omnia 14; Parma: 1863), §50, n.1.

hinges upon an *a fortiori* privileging of the place of David: if even *David* can sin, how much more should *we* fear? There is only one way by which anyone is made right with God, and that is through the *novum testamentum* or the *lex nova*, which is the grace of the Holy Spirit given to those who believe. As he says elsewhere, immediately after citing Jer 31:31-34:

> The *vetus testamentum*, therefore, is written in a book, afterward sprinkled by blood, as is said in Hebrews... And so it is clear, that the *vetus lex* is a testament of the letter (*testamentum litteri*). But the *novum testamentum* is a testament of the Holy Spirit, by whom the love (*charitas*) of God is shed abroad in our hearts, as is said in Rom 5:5. And so, when the Holy Spirit produces love in us, which is the fulness of the law, it is the novum testamentum, not by the letter, that is, not written through letters, but by the Spirit, that is the Spirit who gives life.... Therefore the law without the Spirit impressing inwardly the law on the heart, is the occasion of death. And it was necessary to give the law of the Spirit, who gives life by producing love in the heart.[77]

This possessing of the Spirit who gives life, by which the *novum testamentum* is known, is for Augustine and Thomas known by the faithful regardless of era. And this right standing before God, brought by the Spirit's work, is the substance of Jeremiah's new covenant.

5. *Elsewhere in the High Medieval Tradition*

Thomas' strong view of unity between the two eras here—and the debt to Augustine—is not unique within high medieval theology (an unsurprising fact given the prominence of the Cathars). In a direct citation of Augustine on this issue, Prepositinus of Cremona (c.1145-c.1210)—a Lombardian theologian likely familiar with the Passagini and certainly with the Cathars (and known and read by Thomas)—makes use of this reading:

> We say, that those mandates [of the old law] did not justify nor were able to justify, in the way they had been delivered, and only external works were ordered by them. Yet there were some who spiritually believed in those mandates: Love the Lord your God, etc. For, as was stated above, love is twofold, exterior and interior: the exterior are signs of love, the interior consist in the devotion in the mind; and only those which were external were ordered for that coarse people. Yet there were some who spiritually understood and they were justified and did not belong to the *vetus testamentum*, but to the *novum*. As an authority says, 'there were some during that time who belonged to the *novum testamentum*, just as now

---

77. *Super II Epistolam B.Pauli ad Corinthios lectura* (Opera Omnia 13; Parma: 1863), cap.3, l.2.

> there are some who belong to the *vetus*, who nevertheless manage to serve for temporal things.'[78]

Landgraf, in his valuable essay on the subject, makes the same point citing a much broader formula found in Hugh of St. Victor's *Summa sententiarum*:

> Thus the *Summa sententiarum* puts forward a further interpretation of the axiom, which is nowhere represented as a shift of terminology: 'By this one distinguishes between the *vetus* and *novum testamentum*: there an act is prohibited, in the new the will and the act,' so that—and this is here the new—those who submitted to the commandment 'in the will and act' were no longer to be regarded as men of the old, but rather of the new testament.[79]

Landgraf asserts that this solution was already found in Gilbert of Porrée and he finds it in others as well. Each case preserves, some more and some less closely, the Augustinian view of the salvific contrast between the *vetus* and *novum testamentum*. The *vetus testamentum* is the possession of the law alone without grace (i.e. written only on tablets of stone) and as such, a ministry of death.[80] The *novum testamentum* is the possession of the Spirit, of grace, of faith, and so the possession of life.

Even in Peter Lombard's *Sentences*, in the midst of other statements throughout the work that seem at odds with the position, we read the following—quoting Augustine's *De baptismo* and then his "Letter 145":

> What is the Letter that Kills?—Augustine, *De baptismo*. If it is asked what is the letter the Apostle describes as that which kills, 'It is certainly the Decalogue. It is not called *the letter which kills* because the law is evil, but because by forbidding sin it increases lust (*concupiscentia*) and aggravates sin, unless grace sets us free,' which grace is not as abundant in the Law as in the Gospel. 'And so the law is good, but without grace it kills, since

---

78. Cited in the valuable essay, "Die Gnadenökonomie des alten Bundes," in A.M. Landgraf, *Dogmengeschichte der Frühscholastik* (Regensburg: Verlag Friedrich Pustet, 1954), III.i, 30. The manuscript Landgraf cites is Prepositinus' *Summa Theologica* (Cod. Erlangen. lat. 353): see discussion in Lacombe, *Prévostin*, 161.

79. Landgraf, *Dogmengeschichte*, III.i, @26-27. Hugh's full statement cites Augustine explicitly: By this one distinguishes between the *vetus* and *novum testamentum*: there an act is prohibited, in the new the will and the act. Augustine accepts *vetus testamentum* as the letter, not the Spirit, just as the Apostle everywhere does.' Hugh of St. Victor, *Summa sententiarum septem tractatibus* (PL 176; Paris: 1884), 4.6.

80. Thomas, *STh* Ia IIae, q.106, a.2, ad.3. 'Das Gesetz – Gott im Gesetz – tötet nicht effective, sondern nur occasionaliter, nämlich durch seine Unvollkommenheit. Das soll heißen: Tod und Sündenverstrickung sind keinesfalls direkte Intention des Gesetzes.' Pesch, *Theologie der Rechtfertigung*, 431.

it is "the power of sin" [1 Cor 15:56], which commands what cannot be fulfilled apart from grace.' Yet grace was lacking, and so the letter killed.[81]

The unity of the people of God, repeated through the 12th-13th c. in contradiction to the Cathars, is taken by Thomas and others and applied to the contrast in Jer 31:31-34 with the same force as put forward by Augustine. That Thomas does not solely read or use the text this way simply reveals the ambiguity long involved in Christian interpretations of the text.[82] That Thomas speaks of the natural, old, and new laws as on the one hand distinct eras and on the other as 'existential categories' (Pesch's term)[83] is likewise not unique. Hugh of St. Victor did the same two generations before. Hugh speaks unabashedly of the three eras in which God worked to restore his people (natural law, written law, and grace), and even corresponds these to the kinds of sacraments in each era.[84] But the primary reference for these three realities are as states before God in any era:

> [T]here are three kinds of men, that is, men of the natural law, men of the written law, men of grace. Those can be called men of the natural law who direct their lives by natural reason alone, or rather those men are called men of the natural law who walk according to the concupiscence in which they were born. Men of the written law are those who by exterior precepts are instructed unto right living. Men of grace are those who breathed upon by the inspiration of the Holy Ghost are illumined to recognize the good which must be done, and are inflamed as they love and strengthened to accomplish good... In the first kind are contained the pagans, in the second kind the Jews, in the third kind the Christians. These three kinds of men have never been wanting at any time from the beginning.[85]

---

81. *Sentences*, S.III. d.40. c2.

82. A possible avenue of further influence in this direction (without citing Jer 31:31-34), is his statement that 'for as faith is the way to love, so is the old law [the way] to the new,' clarified by asserting, 'because those things which in the old law were obersved from the law of love were perfect; thus they belonged to the new law, in which is the state [*status*] of perfection.' Aquinas, *Sup. sent*, lib.3, d.40, q.1, a.4, qc.2, co. and ad. 2.

83. Pesch, *Theologie der Rechtfertigung*, 451.

84. '[I]n the time of the natural law man was left entirely to himself, afterwards in the time of the written law counsel was given to him when he realized his ignorance, finally in the time of grace help was furnished him when he confessed his lack.' Victor, *On the Sacraments*, I.viii.3. 'Sacraments' for Hugh take a much broader meaning than comes to be the case. Fundamentally there are three 'sacraments' always necessarily simultaneous for efficacy: faith, the sacraments of faith, and good works. Ibid., I.ix.8.

85. Ibid., I.viii.11.

So the three 'states' properly refer to three ways of standing before God, seen in any era. Hugh emphasizes the unity of the people of God through the work of Christ.[86] Hugh's positing of the *limbus patrum* as a distinction between the eras certainly shows somewhat of a different conception of this unity to Augustine—or to the later Reformed. But even this is not a contrast between those who live now and those who lived then, but between those dead now and those who were dead then (for we do not reach perfection until after death either!).[87] For the whole Church there is 'the same Saviour, the same grace, the same faith—in the former in what was to come, in the latter in what was shown.'[88]

6. Conclusions

Overall, Thomas' varied uses of Jer 31:31-34 bear the same dual-aspect as Augustine, first a contrast between two successive eras and then a form of a 'salvific' contrast. But in Thomas the tension stands within the same work. For our purposes the most important aspect is the preservation of the Augustinian reading: for one to be a member of the *vetus lex* is to have the law without the

---

86. E.g., 'You should know, therefore, that at no time from the beginning of the world even to the end has there been or is there anyone truly good unless justified by grace and that no one could ever have obtained grace except through Christ, so that you should realize that all whether preceding or following were saved by the one remedy of sanctification. Behold, therefore, the cause of our King and the battle lines of His army resplendent with spiritual arms; behold by what a multitude of peoples preceding and following He is surrounded as He advances.' Ibid. Hugh disagrees (rather harshly), however, with Augustine's insistence on this 'faith' as entailing knowledge of Christ's death and resurrection: '[M]any before the Saviour's coming, holding to and loving omnipotent God, the gratuitous promise of their salvation, believing Him faithful in His promise, hoping for Him who most certainly pays, were saved in this faith and expectation, although when and how and in what order salvation was promised they did not know (I.x.6).'

87. 'The second difference [between the old and new sacraments] is that the ancient just who were imbued with these sacraments were not yet able to enter the gates of the kingdom of heaven until the Saviour by assuming flesh ascended heaven and opened the way to all who believed in Him and followed Him.' Ibid., I.xi.6. The first difference is the efficacy of the sacraments, seen in a more developed form in Thomas above. But even here faith is still always necessary to join to the sacraments (then as now)—I.ix.8. So the difference is not between us and them (or their benefits and ours), but in the objective substance of the sacraments themselves.

88. Ibid., I.xi.8. Cp. Thomas: 'The ancient fathers, serving the sacraments of the law (legalia sacramenta), were brought into Christ through the same faith and love by which we are also brought into him. On account of this the ancient fathers belonged to that same body of the church to which we belong.' *STh* III, q.8, a.3, ad.3.

Spirit in any period of the Church. Conversely, to be a member of the *nova lex* is to have the grace of the Spirit in any period. From an exegetical standpoint we can see clearly the tension or even contradiction between this reading of Jeremiah's new covenant and the same text as announcing the *mutatio sacramentorum*. One cannot hold that Jer 31:31-34 contrasts two successive economies or stages of the people of God, and not, at one and the same time.

But the tension in the language and thinking on these issues lies wider than simply Jeremiah's new covenant oracle—as seen in the language of Hugh of St. Victor. In the one case (properly speaking) the ancient fathers were not members of the 'written law', but of 'grace'. But in the other case (regarding the sacraments) they were necessarily members of the 'written law' and not of 'grace'. A formal contradiction (p and not-p, in the same way and at the same time) might be avoided by saying that we are speaking of a semantic divergence: they were members of the new covenant with respect to faith, but of the old covenant with respect to the sacraments. But even if this is possible to defend, the use of the same text in each case is puzzling, to say the least.[89] As was the case in late antiquity and will be the case for the early modern Reformed, the medieval tradition reveals the struggle in Christian theological uses of Jeremiah's new covenant.

---

89. The appeal to different ways of reading (e.g. literally vs. allegorically) may be possible, but unlikely. After all, which is which? Such might, however, explain the somewhat odd use in Thomas, *STh* I, q.106, a.1 ad.2, in which the 'knowledge of God' in Jer 31:34 is said to refer to the angelic 'immediate vident Dei essentiam'—which Thomas certainly does not see as now in force for the faithful. But he is here borrowing an older view (referring to the 'sabbati perenni gloria'): see Rupert of Deutz, *Liber de divinis officiis* (CCL 7; Tournholt: Brepols, 1967), 4.13.

4

The Early Modern Reformed Tradition

Thus far we have taken two 'soundings' in the Western history of interpretation of Jeremiah's new covenant: Augustine's view in late antiquity and then the high medieval period, focusing on Thomas Aquinas. In each case we have two exegetical alternatives. On the one hand, we find the common reading of the contrast in the old/new covenant as a contrast of two successive eras or economies—two successive ways in which God deals with his own people. And by and large this view is expressed in terms of a *mutatio sacramentorum*, a change of sacraments from one 'covenant' to the next. But Augustine offered another view that stands opposed to this first view. In this 'Augustinian' line of reading, the contrast of the old and new covenants is that absolute contrast of unbelief and faith. The 'old' implied in the 'new covenant' is unbelief, or a failure to join the possession of divine law to the grace of God and the work of the Spirit. The consequence was a loosening of the language of temporal succession: the faithful of any era—including Moses himself—are members of the 'new covenant'.

This 'Augustinian' line of interpretation survives in an attenuated form in the early modern Reformed theologians through the 16th-17th centuries. I will begin the chapter with Philip Melanchthon's 1521 *Loci communes*, which represents the continuity of the Augustinian reading into the Protestant mould in an immensely influential text. From there I will look at three models of early Reformed readings: the first two see Jer 31:31-34 as a contrast of accidents (Heinrich Bullinger), or a contrast of two kinds of eras, moving from complex to simple (Johannes Oecolampadius). These are simply variations on the basic reading as a contrast of religio-historical eras. But a third reading emerging in the work of John Calvin and Peter Martyr Vermigli incorporates—if unevenly—Augustine's central concerns. Overall this period provides a clear insight into the struggle for Christian interpretation of Jer 31:31-34, especially with the difficulties in asserting the contrast (in de Lubac's terms) as between 'two orders, established by God one after the other in order to regulate man's relationship with him.'[1]

1. *An Augustinian Start: Philip Melanchthon*

Philip Melanchthon's 1521 *Loci communes* stands as one of the most important texts of the early Reformation. Called (somewhat misleadingly) the 'first summa of the Reformation',[2] the *Loci* offered the first sustained presentation of the fundamentals of the Christian faith in its Protestant form. Melanchthon drew these fundamental topics (*loci*) largely from his reading of the chief points of Romans, for which he followed Luther, under whom Melanchthon earned his theological degree in 1519.[3] Given the early date and immense impact of the 1521 *Loci*, its partial preservation of Augustine's view of the contrast within Jer 31:31-34 makes it important for the development of Reformed and Lutheran thought. In one way there is little surprise to Melanchthon's presentation of the Augustinian view. Kenneth Hagen's study of Luther's thoughts on the relationship of the testaments argued explicitly a link to Augustine, summarizing his findings on Luther this way:

> The designation of old and new testament does not refer to two different testaments of God; rather during the time covered by the books of both the Old and New Testaments, the one testament of God is the *testamentum*

---

1. de Lubac, *Medieval Exegesis*, 1.227.

2. Salvatore Caponetto, *The Protestant Reformation in Sixteenth-Century Italy* (Tr. by Anne C. Tedeschi and John Tedeschi. Kirksville, MO: Thomas Jefferson Univ. Press, 1999), 22. Indeed, Melanchthon attempts to distance himself entirely from the 'summas' of the Schools: Philip Melanchthon, *Loci Communes Theologici (1521)*, 20-21; in *Melanchthon and Bucer* (ed. Wilhelm Pauck; London: SCM Press, 1969). For the Latin I have used Philip Melanchthon, *Loci communes von 1521* (Melanchthons Werke II.1; Gütersloh: Bertelsmann Verlag, 1952).

3. He calls Romans Paul's 'compendium of Christian doctrine': Melanchthon, *Loci (1521)*. On the structure of the *Loci*, Maurer states: "Damit [i.e. the *Theologica Institutio in Epistolam Pauli ad Romanos*, 1519] hat Melanchthon den Schlüssel gefunden zu einer exegetischen Methode, in der der Begriff der Loci eine entscheidende Rolle spielt. Er bietet – das können wir hier schon feststellen – nicht die Grundlage für eine Systematik, die die Summe der Erscheinungen einheitlich zusammenzufassen trachtet und dabei auch die religiösen Erfahrungen mit einbezieht; sondern die Loci sind Hilfsbegriffe, die, aus der Exegese gewonnen, das Verständnis biblischer Texte und damit der Heilsoffenbarung überhaupt erschließen sollen. Die exegetische Methode, in deren Dienste sie stehen, unterscheidet sich formal von der Auslegungsweise, die Luther etwa in seiner Römerbriefvorlesung verfolgt hatte.' Wilhelm Maurer, "Melanchthons Loci communes von 1521 als wissenschaftliche Programmschrift," *Luther-Jahrbuch* 27 (1960), 1-50.

> *Christi.* The testament of God becomes old when it is received by man as law; just as it becomes new when it is received by man as spirit... The difference between the testaments is the difference between receiving the *testamentum dei et Christi* as letter or spirit, as old or new.[4]

In similar language, Heinrich Bornkamm:

> The distinction between the testaments is the equivalent of that between law and gospel. It is primary, and precedes the differentiation between the books; Luther carried it right through the Old Testament writings.[5]

Though there is much to be said here about the differences with Augustine (perhaps too easily glided over by Hagen) the main outline as put by these two scholars appears similar to the absolute or 'salvific' contrast of Jer 31:31-34 that emerged in Augustine's later work. More interestingly, Luther's lectures on Hebrews on which Hagen's study is based were finished the same year (1518) that Melanchthon came to Wittenberg. So when examining Melanchthon's views on the difference between the testaments—one of the *loci* drawn from Romans—one is hardly surprised to find a similar line in the (24 year-old) student as in the teacher.

As with much of the text, Melanchthon adopts an elenctic approach to determine the difference between the testaments:

> The Schools fail just as miserably in this area as in their distinction between law and gospel; they call the Old Testament a kind of law which demands external works only, and the New Testament a law which demands the heart in addition to external works.[6]

Melanchthon will essentially challenge only the second part of this formula. So his definitions of the two testaments are summarily put:

> I consider the Old Testament a promise of material things linked up with the demands of the law. For God demands righteousness through the law and also promises its reward, the Land of Canaan, wealth, etc... By contrast, the New Testament is nothing else than the promise of all good things without regard to the law and with no respect to our own righteousness. In the Old Testament good things were promised, but at the same time it was demanded of the people that they keep the law. In the New

---

4. Hagen, *Theology of Testament*, 69

5. Heinrich Bornkamm, *Luther and the Old Testament* (Tr. by Gritsch, Eric W. and Ruth C. Philadelphia: Fortress Press, 1969), 82.

6. Melanchthon, *Loci (1521),* 120. See the statement of Hugh of St. Victor already cited above: 'By this one distinguishes between the *vetus* and *novum testamentum*: there an act is prohibited, in the new the will and the act.' Victor, *Summa sententiarum septem tractatibus*, 4.6.

Testament good things are promised unconditionally, since nothing is demanded of us in turn.[7]

So while Melanchthon is willing to grant the view of the *vetus testamentum* as the external and temporal requirements given under law, he radically departs from the presentation of the *novum testamentum* as he sees it in the Schools. At issue is the clouding of the *novum testamentum* with 'law' rather than 'gospel', which is its actual property:

> Here [with the *novum testamentum*] you see briefly what the glory of the gospel is; it bestows salvation gratuitously without regard for our righteousness or our works.[8]

Immediately on the heels of these definitions Melanchthon tells us that, 'Jer, ch.31, indicates this difference between the Old and New Testaments.'[9] More precisely, Jer 31:31-34 promises the abrogation of the Decalogue or moral law—*not* the abrogation of the ceremonies.[10] But Melanchthon acts quickly to silence thoughts of antinomianism (a point that would soon gain focus in Melanchthon's dispute with John of Agricola, beginning the year the *Loci* were published).[11] The abrogation concerns not the freedom to disobey the Decalogue,

---

7. Melanchthon, *Loci (1521)*, 120. Or earlier: '[S]ome [promises] are of material things, as are all those of the *vetus testamentum*. Others are spiritual, which properly pertain to the *novum testamentum*. One can move from the material to the spiritual (if one has the Spirit), but to do so is to move to the *novum testamentum* (properly). Ibid., 96. Cp. Luther: 'For the Old Testament, which he gave through Moses, was a promise – not of remission of sins or of eternal things, but of temporal things, namely, of the land of Canaan; no man was thereby renewed in his spirit to lay hold of the heavenly inheritance.' Martin Luther, *The Babylonian Captivity of the Church* (Luther's Works 36; Tr. by A.T.W. Steinhäuser, F.C. Ahrens, A.R. Wentz. Philadelphia: Fortress Press, 1959), 40. This is not entirely divorced from the Scholastic tradition: e.g. 'The letter of the Gospel differs from the letter of the law, for different things are promised: earthly things in the latter, heavenly things in the former.' Peter Lombard, *Sentences*, S.III. d.40. c.2. Cf. Augustine, *Enarrationes in Psalmos*, on Psalm 73:1.

8. Melanchthon, *Loci (1521)*, 121.

9. Ibid.

10. 'That part of the law called the Decalogue or the moral commandments has been abrogated by the New Testament. The proof of this is first of all, the passage of Jeremiah quoted in Hebrews where the prophet contends that the law has been divinely abrogated because the people made it invalid... Israel sinned not merely against the ceremonies, but rather against the Decalogue, the highest part of the law, as Christ calls it'. Ibid.

11. See the helpful treatment of the dispute in Timothy J. Wengert, *Law and Gospel: Philip Melanchthon's Debate with John Agricola of Eisleben over Poenitentia* (Grand Rapids, MI: Baker, 1997).

but the Decalogue's power to judge and condemn: 'our freedom consists in this, that every right of accusing and condemning us has been taken away from the law.'[12] The new covenant is 'the gospel', i.e. 'nothing else than the promulgation of this freedom.'[13]

To this point Melanchthon sounds rather far from Augustine in many respects, and particularly in the view of the law. But with this identification of the 'new covenant' and the 'gospel' we begin to merge into a new form of Augustine's reading of the text. Melanchthon had in fact made this connection earlier in his *locus* on grace:

> To sum it all up, grace is nothing but the forgiveness or remission of sins. The Holy Spirit is the gift [of grace] that regenerates and sanctifies hearts... The gospel promises grace as well as the gift of grace. The Scriptures are plain on this, and therefore it seems enough to cite one passage, Jer 31:33...[14]

So Jer 31:31-34 promises nothing other than the gospel: forgiveness of sins and the Holy Spirit. Melanchthon then makes the link to Augustine explicit as he argues that the abrogation of the Decalogue by the new covenant is not so that we do not obey but rather, since we are given the Spirit, in order that we might be able to obey:

> The law is the will of God; the Holy Spirit is nothing else than the living will of God and its being in action (*agitatio*). Therefore, when we have been regenerated by the Spirit of God, who is the living will of God, we now will spontaneously that very thing which the law used to demand.[15]

---

12. Melanchthon, *Loci (1521),* 121. My emphasis. Or in language more directly related to Augustine: 'Therefore, the law has been abrogated, not that it not be kept, but in order that, even though not kept, it not condemn, and then too in order that it can be kept (125).' This is the movement from Augustine's famous statement: 'Lex ergo data est, ut gratia quaereretur, gratia data est, ut lex impleretur.' Augustine, *De spiritu*, §34. As in Augustine, this is possible by the 'gift of grace' identified as the Spirit (below).

13. Melanchthon, *Loci (1521),* 122-23.

14. Ibid., 88.

15. Ibid., 123. Cp. Martin Luther, *Lectures on Deuteronomy* (Luther's Works 9; Tr. by R.R. Caemmerer. St. Louis, MO: Concordia, 1960), 179: 'The commands of the New Testament are directed to those who are justified and are new men in the Spirit. Nothing is taught or commanded there except what pertains solely to believers, who do everything spontaneously, not from necessity or contrary to their own will.' Or, elsewhere applied directly to Jer 31: 'His [i.e. the Christian's] law is faith, that is, a living spiritual flame, by which hearts are set afire, born anew and converted through the Holy Spirit, so that they desire, will, do, and are exactly what the law of Moses expressly commands and requires. Jer 32 [31:33!] says of it: "I will put my law within their souls

Melanchthon assures his readers that Augustine has already discussed all of this in the *De spiritu*, to which assurance he appends the contrast of Jer 31:31-34:

> Augustine discusses Christian freedom at length in this manner in his book *The Spirit and the Letter*. Jer 31:31-34 says... [full citation]. In this passage the prophet mentions a twofold covenant, the old and the new; the old, justification by the law, he says, has been made void. For who could keep the law? Therefore, he says that since the demand has been taken away, the law must now be inscribed in men's hearts so that it can be kept. Therefore, freedom does not consist in this, that we do not observe the law, but that we will and desire spontaneously and from the heart what the law demands.[16]

The contrast is clearly 'salvific' in terms of being under the law and under grace, or justification by the law vs. the gift of the Spirit. To be a member of the old covenant is to stand under the condemnation of the law.

That the new covenant cannot be denied to the 'fathers' is then explicitly stated, again following the Augustinian line:

> In this way the fathers who had the Spirit of Christ were also free [from the law] even before his incarnation... [cit. of Acts 15:10]. [T]hey were justified by faith. That is, although the fathers could not fulfill the law, they knew that they also were free through Christ, and they were justified by faith in Christ, not by the merits of their own works of righteousness.[17]

Or more firmly:

> You will say, however, that if those who have the Spirit of Christ are free, were both David and Moses free? Absolutely! For this is what Peter says in Acts 15:10... [T]hey believed and they were saved by trusting in the mercy of God; when they had received God's Spirit, they realized they

---

and I will write it upon their hearts, etc.'" Martin Luther, *The Misuse of the Mass* (Luther's Works 36; Tr. by F.C. Ahrens. Philadelphia: Fortress, 1959), 200. Except for the statement of spontaneity, the basic point is not entirely dissimilar to Thomas' view, citing Gregory: 'love (*caritas*) is not idle; for if it exists it works great things. But if it does not work, there is no love there. Thus the manifest sign of love is promptness of fulfilling the divine precepts; for so we see that a lover works great and difficult things on account of his beloved.' Thomas Aquinas, "De decem praeceptis," in *Recherches Thomasiennes* (ed. Jean-Pierre Torrell; Paris: Librairie Philosophique J.Vrin, 2000), II.37-40. 'Caritas', of course, is the work of the Spirit shed in our hearts.

16. Melanchthon, *Loci (1521)*, 123. His next line, 'This no one could ever do before', must be read as 'before the Spirit' or 'before becoming a member of the new covenant', not 'before Christ'—see below.

17. Ibid., 124.

were free from the curse of the law, and also from every burden or demand of the law.[18]

The discussion is rounded out by an explanation of the abrogation of the ceremonies. But Melanchthon offers the same treatment as the abrogation of the Decalogue, and again in elenctic fashion:

> Generally speaking, men hold that the ceremonies have been abrogated because they were simply shadows of the gospel, and that now there is no need of them since the body, namely the gospel itself, has come. I have no idea whether Paul has anywhere pursued this argument... This goes for Hebrews too; in the whole letter the author teaches that not only ceremonies are abrogated *because they cannot justify*, but also the whole law, or, as we said above, it is abrogated because it cannot be fulfilled.[19]

The fathers, then, were also freed from the ceremonial law in this way (though they generally continued in them since 'that freedom had not yet been revealed').[20] This leads directly into the next locus: the contrast of the 'old man and the new', which is once more a salvific contrast centred on the abrogation of the law's condemning function and the gift of the Spirit.

So Melanchthon's reading of Jer 31:31-34 in 1521 is explicitly taken from Augustine's *De spiritu* and reflects—now in an unmistakeably Lutheran or Protestant formulation—the basic salvific contrast Augustine saw there. By the final (German) edition of 1555 there are some changes to this view—most notably the inclusion of Jer 31:31-34 as a part of the *mutatio sacramentorum* (though even here, possibly, the same 'salvific' idea is present).[21] Melanchthon

---

18. He uses Acts 15:10 elsewhere also to show the inclusion of the 'fathers' into the same justifying grace: after citing the text, 'Peter therefore means that all the works of the fathers, of David, Isaiah, and Jeremiah, were sin, but that they were justified by trust alone, trust in the mercy of God promised in Christ'. Ibid., 95-96.

19. Ibid., 127. My emphasis. This is owing, no doubt, to Luther's lectures on Hebrews—cf. Hagen, *Theology of Testament*.

20. Ibid., 130.

21. '[W]e must know that in the New Testament worship is not just external forms and showy works, but is a divine light, faith, fear, comfort, and joy in God in the heart; and the beginning of eternal life and suitable works follow the divine light and life in the heart, as the prophet says, "I will put my law within them...". Therefore, the ceremonies and sacrifices of the law of Moses are abolished, for the New Testament demands spiritual sacrifices of the heart.' Melanchthon, *Loci (1555)*, 225-26. Similarly in the locus on the kingdom of Christ the text is cited as proof that 'the kingdom of Christ is spiritual' (275).

also by this time adopts the language used by the Swiss Protestants to express the unity of the people of God:

> The promise of grace is the eternal covenant, the eternal testament, for through it eternal salvation is given, for the promise is sure and firm for all times and for all men who accept it with faith.[22]

Further, while he still identifies the *vetus testamentum* as temporal or the externals of the 'laws and ceremonies' of Israel, he now places more emphasis its institution to prepare a 'lodging place for the divine promises of the Savior Christ.' And now this temporal state of affairs ordained by God has become 'the Old Covenant, properly speaking.'[23]

But even here we can identify the same salvific contrast and the inclusion of the 'fathers' within the *novum testamentum*. Thus, he defines the *novum testamentum* with the key-word of the 'promise' of Christ and the work of the Spirit:

> the New Testament is the promise in which God said that he would send his only begotten Son, and through him, on account of his obedience, without any merit on our part, would give to believers forgiveness of sins, grace, the Holy Spirit, eternal righteousness, and blessedness.[24]

None of these are denied to the 'fathers', and in fact we find each aspect directly attributed to them:

> It is certainly true men have in all times been turned to God and saved; Adam, Eve, Seth, Enoch, Noah, Abraham, Moses, Samuel, David, Elijah, and Daniel received forgiveness of sins, and were justified; that is, they were pleasing to God, received the Holy Spirit, and were made heirs of eternal blessedness for the sake of the promised Savior, through faith in the promised Savior... The Son of God produced life in them through the promise, and gave them his Holy Spirit.[25]

So while Melanchthon's views develop and shift, his 1521 *Loci* offers a bridge from the medieval discussions into the Protestant concerns with respect

---

22. Ibid., 148.

23. 'For the word "testament" the Hebrew language uses this word, "covenant," or "promise," or "obligation"; and the Old Testament, or the Old Covenant, properly speaking, is the promise in accordance with which God gave a certain country to the stem of Israel. He established a worldly government, bound it with his own laws and ceremonies, and promised the people help and protection, all so that this country and government might be a lodging place for the divine promises of the Savior Christ.' Ibid., 192.

24. Ibid., 193.

25. Ibid. Italics removed.

to the contrast of Jer 31:31-34. Though he explicitly distances himself from 'the Schools', 'the Sophists' and 'the Parisians', the similarities in the contrast of 'old' and 'new' to Thomas above are evident—both acknowledging their debt to Augustine. The discourse has shifted, but we still find Augustine's contrast of old and new covenants as between the law in itself (or by itself) as insufficient, and the gift of grace and the Spirit.

The impact of Philip Melanchthon on the Reformed tradition has long been known, and has received significant recent attention. John Schofield recently showed at length the influence of Melanchthon on the English Reformation, revealing how widely Melanchthon was read in England.[26] Further, while the notion of a close friendship between Melanchthon and John Calvin has been questioned,[27] it still stands that Melanchthon's *Loci* received a warm preface by Calvin in its French translation and had at the very least a methodological influence on Calvin's structuring of the *Institutes* (below). Naturally, Melanchthon was able to wield a much more direct impact on what developed as the German Reformed tradition, having directly taught a number of prominent 'Calvinist' thinkers—above all the Heidelberg theologian Zacharius Ursinus, with whom Melanchthon corresponded until his death in 1560.[28] The remainder of this

---

26. John Schofield, *Philip Melanchthon and the English Reformation* (St. Andrews Studies in Reformation History; Ashgate: Aldershot, 2006). Clyde Manschrek asserts in his "Preface" that 'Melanchthon's *Loci* was required reading at Cambridge, and Queen Elizabeth I memorized large portions of it in order to converse learnedly about theology.' Melanchthon, *Loci (1555)*, xx.

27. Timothy J. Wengert, "We will Feast Together in Heaven Forever: The Epistolary Friendship of John Calvin and Philip Melanchthon," in *Melanchthon in Europe: His Work and Influence beyond Wittenberg* (ed. Karin Maag; Grand Rapids, MI: Baker, 1997); Riemer Faber, "The Humanism of Melanchthon and of Calvin," in *Melanchthon und der Calvinismus* (eds. Günter Frank and Herman J. Selderhuis; Stuttgart: Friedrich Frommann Verlag, 2005).

28. Lyle D. Bierma, "What Hath Wittenberg to do with Heidelberg? Philip Melanchthon and the Heidelberg Catechism," in *Melanchthon in Europe: His Work and Influence beyond Wittenberg* (ed. Karin Maag; Grand Rapids, MI: Baker, 1999), 106-07; Herman J. Selderhuis, "Ille Phoenix: Melanchton und der Heidelberger Calvinismus 1583-1622," in *Melanchthon und der Calvinismus* (eds. Günter Frank and Herman J. Selderhuis; Stuttgart: Friedrich Frommann Verlag, 2005). Selderhuis calls Ursinus 'der bedeutendste Vermittler zwischen melanchthonischem Denken und reformierter Theologie (p.50).' The disputes on this influence can be found in Derk Visser, *Zachary Ursinus: The Reluctant Reformer, His Life and Times* (New York: UCC Press, 1983). For deeper influence in the tradition, see also Andreas J. Beck, "Zur Rezeption Melancthons bei Gisbertus Voetius (1589-1676), namentlich in seiner Gotteslehre," in *Melanchthon und der Calvinismus* (eds. Günter Frank and Herman J. Selderhuis; Stuttgart: Friedrich

chapter will turn to the early modern Reformed, located especially in the Swiss confederacy. But the influence of Melanchthon, his ties (and distance) to the medieval tradition, and his carrying through of the Augustinian position make him an important figure for any remnants of Augustine's reading of Jeremiah's new covenant among the Reformed.

2. A Contrast of Accidents: Heinrich Bullinger

The centre of the Reformation in the Swiss Confederacy (and arguably beyond) was the city of Zurich and the work of Huldrych Zwingli.[29] But in recent years historians have begun to express the enormous influence of his successor Heinrich Bullinger (1504-75) in his 43 years as head of the influential Zurich church.[30] The pattern of Augustinian readings of Jer 31:31-34 thus far has been shaped in the atmosphere of perceived denials of some kind to the Old Testament era: the denial of the Holy Spirit to the Old Testament by Julian of Aeclanum or (in general influence) the Catharism in the high medieval era. In line with this, looming over all of the Swiss Reformed discussions of Jer 31:31-34 we find the dispute with the Anabaptists.[31] Zwingli responded early to the Anabaptists by asserting a unity of the covenant through the eras prior to and after Christ.[32] And by the early 1530's the question of the place of the Old Testament for theological thought was perhaps the central point of the disputes. In a letter from Bullinger to Berchtold Haller in Bern, as preparation for the 1532 disputation with the Anabaptists, Bullinger advises the following for the first debated proposition:

Frommann Verlag, 2005).

29. 'Huldrych Zwingli was the dominant force in the Swiss Reformation: without his vision, his preaching, his theological profundity and dexterity, and his political acumen, there would have been no Reformation in the Swiss Confederation. It would be impossible to sustain that Zwingli himself was the author of the Reformations in Berne, Basle, or Schaffhausen... but he was responsible for what happened in Zurich, and without Zurich there would have been no other Reformations.' Bruce Gordon, *The Swiss Reformation* (Manchester: Manchester Univ. Press, 2002), 142-43.

30. See now above all, Peter Opitz, *Heinrich Bullinger als Theologe: Eine Studie zu den "Dekaden"* (Zurich: Theologischer Verlag, 2004); Bruce Gordon, "Introduction: Architect of Reformation," in *Architect of Reformation: An Introduction to Heinrich Bullinger, 1504-1575* (eds. Bruce Gordon and Emidio Campi; Grand Rapids, MI: Baker, 2004).

31. Cf. Gordon, *Swiss Reformation*, 191-227.

32. A developed form is seen in his 1527 "Refutation of the tricks of the Baptists," in *Ulrich Zwingli (1484-1531): Selected Works* (Philadelphia: Univ. of Pennsylvania Press, 1972).

When tensions and conflicts arise between Christians concerning matters of faith, they should be decided and clarified with Holy Scripture of Old and New Testament.[33]

The point at issue, naturally, is the inclusion here of the Old Testament. Bullinger warns Haller to maintain this proposition ('Don't give in an inch; press them and hold them bound to the spot') and to be wary of an equivocation on the term 'Law' and its use to refer to the whole of the Old Testament being done away with: all with a reference to Heb 8 and the conclusion drawn there from Jer 31:31-34.[34] The role of the Old Testament in Christian theology, and the place of Jer 31 in that dispute, was clearly of importance. And one central issue, as for Augustine, lies in the definition of terms ('law' or 'old testament').

Bullinger's reading of Jer 31:31-34 remains consisted and is illustrated well by his influential treatise *De testamento seu foedere Dei unico & aeterno*, published in 1534 and ultimately going through 15 editions. The treatise has given rise to Bullinger being named the 'first bona fide federal theologian'—though such a claim will hinge entirely on one's definition of the terms.[35] The use of the covenant to structure a system of theology, if that is what is meant, does not occur in Bullinger's work. But doubtless the grounds for such a system is present:

> [I]t is evident that nothing else was handed down to the saints of all ages, throughout the entire Scripture, other than what is included in these main

---

33. Heinold Fast and John H. Yoder, "How to Deal with Anabaptists: An Unpublished Letter of Heinrich Bullinger," *The Mennonite Quarterly Review* 33 (1959): , 84. This had been an emphasis of Bullinger's since at least 1523, as noted by Opitz, *Heinrich Bullinger*, 321. One sees in this letter the seed of the Reformed scholastic insistence on a 'prolegomena' that consists primarily of a doctrine of Scripture: 'What counts is to define at the very beginning with what weapons the battle is to be waged [i.e. the Scriptures].'

34. 'Be forewarned against the word "Law." Most of the argument on this subject [of the authority of the Old Testament] will turn around it, and they will shamelessly misuse the double meaning of the word. For they will set up the following argument: "The Law is done away with (Heb. 8:13). Therefore the authority of the Old Testament for purposes of debate is nil."' Bullinger's conclusion, as will be consistently seen below, is that the reference there is only to the 'ceremonial law'. Fast and Yoder, "Deal with Anabaptists," 86.

35. Stephen Strehle, *Calvinism, Federalism, and Scholasticism: A Study of the Reformed Doctrine of Covenant* (Bern: Peter Lang, 1988), 134. The best recent discussion of Bullinger on the covenant is Opitz, *Heinrich Bullinger*, 317-52. The older study by Baker is still very useful, though perhaps flawed by its underlying premise: J. Wayne Baker, *Heinrich Bullinger and the Covenant* (Athens: Ohio Univ. Press, 1980). See further below.

points of the covenant, although each point is set forth more profusely and more clearly in the succession of times.³⁶

Bullinger's central solution to the Anabaptist arguments, as for Zwingli, rests in a particular view of the continuity and sufficiency of the covenant. In the treatise Bullinger aims to establish that there is one single covenant of God that has always been in operation: the same essence, with the same basic requirements (faith and love), even if it comes with varying accompaniments.³⁷ The payoff is the continuity of the way in which God deals with the children of believers – at least as far as baptism.³⁸ This view in one way or another becomes

---

36. Heinrich Bullinger, *De testamento seu foedere Dei unico & aeterno* (Zürich: 1534). The English translations generally follow Heinrich Bullinger, "A Brief Exposition of the One and Eternal Testament or Covenant of God," in *Fountainhead of Federalism* (eds. Charles S. McCoy and J. Wayne Baker; Louisville, KY: Westminster John Knox, 1991), 112. Likewise, in 1527 he had claimed: 'This is certain: all the books of Holy Scripture we see having a common scope, which is: the God of heaven, the omnipotent God made with the human race an everlasting *testamentum, pactum,* or *foedus*.' Heinrich Bullinger, *Studiorum Ratio: Text und Übersetzung* (Zürich: Theologischer Verlag, 1987), §20. This is picked up in later Reformed thought: e.g., 'all the word of God appertains to some covenant; for God speaks nothing to man without a covenant.' Robert Rollock, *A Treatise of God's Effectual Calling* (Tr. by Henry Holland. London: 1603), 33.

37. As in the *Decades*: 'Verily, there is no difference of the people, of the testament, of the church, or of the manner of salvation betwixt them, among whom there is found to be one and the same doctrine, the same faith, the same Spirit, the same hope, the same inheritance, the same expectation, the same invocation, and the same sacraments.... In respect of the substance there neither was, nor is, any more than one testament; that the old fathers are one and the same people that we are, living in the same church and communion, and saved not in any other but in Christ alone, the Son of God, in whom also we look for salvation.' *The Decades* (5 vols.; Tr. by Thomas Harding. Cambridge: Cambridge Univ. Press, 1849), III.283. See also his discussion of this topic in *Der alt gloub* (1537), given an early English translation by Miles Coverdale in 1541 (*The olde Fayth*, no publisher listed), which was later republished with a more provocative title: *Looke from Adam, And behold the Protestant's Faith and Religion* (Tr. by Miles Coverdale. London: 1624). A full discussion of this unity, in coordination with the doctrine of *sola fide* can be found in Aurelio A. Garcia Archilla, *The Theology of History and Apologetic Historiography in Heinrich Bullinger* (San Fransisco: Mellen Research Univ. Press, 1992), 37-69. Such is necessary given the misguided critique of, e.g., Strehle, *Calvinism*, 136-37.

38. 'Now is it probable that the most merciful God acted less favourably and more harshly toward our children after he sent the Savior than he had acted toward those children whom he had chosen as his possession before Christ had been sent? No!' Bullinger, "Brief Exposition," 108.

determinative for the Reformed tradition. Bullinger stresses the unity of the covenant from the start, but states it later with a quotation from Augustine:

> 'The same church that gave birth to Abel, Enoch, Noah, and Abraham also at a later time gave birth to Moses and the prophets before the coming of the Lord; and that very same church gave birth to everyone who appeared, born at different times but joined together in the fellowship of one people'... From all of this I think it is truly evident that there is only one church and one covenant, the same for the patriarchs and for us.[39]

This unity is immediately qualified, however, by those texts in scripture that give clear testimony to 'two' testaments or covenants. And, though only given brief mention in the treatise, Bullinger's view of Jer 31:31f. comes as part of the qualification of the unity. Having just cited Jer 31:31, among other texts, Bullinger says:

> [T]he nomenclature of the old and new covenant, spirit, and people did not arise from the very essence (*substantia*) of the covenant but from certain foreign and unessential things (*accidentibus*) because the diversity of the times recommended that now this, now that be added according to the difference of the Jewish people. These additions (*accessere*) did not exist as perpetual and particularly necessary things for salvation, but they arose as changeable things according to the time, the persons, and the circumstances. The covenant itself could easily continue without them.[40]

Here we find Bullinger's great solution: the unity of the substance, but the diversity of the accidents. The old Aristotelian distinction was common and scholastic (Bullinger was a scholastic here): *substantia* is that which makes a thing what it is, or the concrete essence or *forma*. But the *accidentalia* are the nine predicates of the thing, all of which can change over time without affecting the thing itself: quantity, quality, relation, action, passivity, place, time circumstance, and state (habit). So Bullinger cites the ceremonies of the ancient era as the content of the 'accidents.'[41] By maintaining that the 'old covenant' faithful

---

39. Ibid, 120. The Augustine citation is from *De baptismo contra Donatistas*. Thus Schrenk's comment, 'Die Gläubigen des Alten Bundes stehen mit uns in Glaubensgemeinschaft.' Gottlieb Schrenk, *Gottesreich und Bund im älteren Protestantismus vornhemlich bei Johannes Coccejus* (Giessen: Brunnen Verlag, 1985), 43.

40. Bullinger, "Brief Exposition," 120. For 'difference' in the fourth line, McCoy and Baker use 'contrariety', which carries a more negative meaning that *diuersitate* ought here: *De testamento*, 29a.

41. 'Indeed, the ceremonies are of this sort, as well as the Aaronic priesthood itself, the law prescribing the manner of sacrificing, purifying, and slaying...' "Brief Exposition," 120.

possessed saving knowledge of God, forgiveness of sins,[42] the work of the same Spirit[43] (law on the heart) – i.e. all those things called a part of the 'new covenant' in Jer 31:33-34 and that would make up the *substantia* of the covenant – Bullinger is left with only the *mutatio sacramentorum* never in fact a part of Jeremiah's oracle.

Bullinger's commentary on Jeremiah, written around 1560 (when Calvin begins his work on the book), bears out this same reading in more detail. He claims that the text undoubtedly addresses the contrast of law and gospel, and endeavours to show in what way the new is superior to the old, and in what way the law is abrogated.[44] Bullinger assumes throughout that the new applies 'to the time of Christ' (*applicauit Christi temporibus*). He again appeals to the distinction between the *substantia* and the *accidentalia* in the covenant, by this time common for the Reformed. The Decalogue is part of the former, while the cere-

---

42. 'The diversity [regarding the covenant and the people of God with reference to the Decalogue] has arisen from the minds of men and from the additions foreign to the covenant, so that the covenant, which is one among all faithful people, began to be called "old" and "new", "carnal" and "spiritual," on account of certain alien elements and rather superstitious people. Indeed, it is called the "old" because the "new" follows it (as the rule of relations demands); *it even promises the remission of sins, which it offers through Christ*; and it also teaches faith and love. But it cannot be called "new" entirely on account of these facts, since it teaches nothing new.... [C]onsequently it is called "new" from the fact that all the ceremonies were fulfilled by Christ, whom alone it proclaims.' Ibid., 122-23. My emphasis. Or elsewhere, after citing Jer 31:31-34, 'This full and perfect forgiveness is not therefore called the new Testament, as though there had been no remission of sins among the old Fathers, but because the promise made long before unto the Fathers, is now confirmed and renewed: and the old figures that represented the same are abrogate.' Bullinger, *Looke from Adam*, 84.

43. '[T]he names "old" and "new," both of the people and of the Covenant, cannot tear asunder the very covenant and the very church of the ancient people and of our people[.] Even the Spirit is the same in both Testaments.' Ibid., 124. Or from the Bullinger, *Decades*, III.286-87: 'And since it is evident that our forefathers were justified by the grace of God, it is manifest that that justification was not wrought without the Spirit of God; through which Spirit even our justification at this day is wrought and finished. Therefore the fathers were governed by the very same Spirit that we of this age are directed by.'

44. 'Moreover, in the words here recited he prophesies concerning the grace of Christ. He opposes [*confert*] the Law and Gospel, and recommends and celebrates the superiority of the latter. He explains also regarding the abrogation of the law; and both sides by the old and the new testament....' Heinrich Bullinger, *Ieremias fidelissimus et laboriosissimus Dei propheta, expositus per Heinrychum Bullingerum* (Zürich: 1575), 187b.

monies are part of the latter. And the latter are at stake in the contrast of the 'new covenant' in Jer 31:

> And it is to be observed, in the covenant there are certain things that are essential (*substanialia*), as they call it, and certain things that are accessories (*accessoria*) or accidental (*accidentalia*). The essential things are comprehended by the two tables through the ten commandments; the accidental things are the tabernacle with all of its instruments, the priests with their sacrifices, prohibitions, festivals, and the remaining kinds of such ceremonies... Above all, we understand the ceremonies to be spoken of by the old covenant, of which Jeremian speaks at present.[45]

So the old covenant concerns the accidental things, and in particular the cultic activities: 'Therefore the *vetus testamentum* is the law itself with the whole of the Levitical cult.'[46] The substance of the covenant continues, of course, but the accidents—the cultic accompaniments—change. In short, the old and new covenants contrast the change of sacraments (*mutatio sacramentorum*) rooted in the fulfillment of the cultic activity.

Even when the question emerges of the possession of the Holy Spirit by the ancient believers—the central question for Augustine and Thomas—Bullinger remains fimly settled in the realm of temporal contrast:

> The ancient covenant of God was written in tablets of stone; now the new covenant is written in the hearts. And only God through his Spirit writes it in human hearts. God gives his faithful the Holy Spirit in their hearts, who regenerates, incites faith, through whom they are justified, who finally inspires love (*caritas*), and the spontaneous study of the law of God, so now what before displeased us might begin to please. *Certainly the Spirit is given also to the ancient fathers in the old covenant: but everything in the new covenant is brighter, greater, and more common.*[47]

His assertion of the contrast between tablets of stone and the heart—and the association of the Spirit with the new covenant on the heart—all sounds strikingly similar to Augustine or Melanchthon (or Thomas, for that matter). But Bullinger does not allow such matters to mitigate the temporal contrast he insists upon, falling back to an appeal regarding the quality (an accident), which Bullinger applies throughout: the ancient fathers were the people of God, but in the new testament these people are *illustriora multo*, the knowledge of God is now both *illustrissima* and spread throughout the world. And, as before, Bullinger applies the same logic to the forgiveness of sins:

---

45. Ibid., 188a.
46. Ibid.
47. Ibid., 188b.

Indeed, not through any other than through the Messiah is the remission of sins enjoyed under the ancient covenant; yet in the new all things are now completed and perfected which were about to be accomplished by the Messiah they believed was to come. Therefore everything in the new covenant is superior.[48]

As in the *De testamento*, Bullinger posits unambiguously a temporal contrast, with the centrality of the *mutatio sacramentorum* and the general qualitative principle of superiority.

While Bullinger may have possessed a diminishing of interest in using the 'covenant' as a lens for all of Scripture's teaching (though this can be debated), his view on reading Jer 31:31-34 remains the same throughout his long career. It is already present in a letter of 1526 that substantially presents in outline the argument of the later treatise *De testamento*.[49] This letter, not coincidentally, was penned the same time as Bullinger wrote on the epistle to the Hebrews, where he offers the same reading of the new covenant as the dismissal of the ceremonial law.[50] Indeed, this view of the contrast is already found in Bullinger's 1525 letter 'Von dem Touff', though he does not cite Jeremiah in the discussion: the language of 'new' arises from speaking before and after the Messiah, and with respect to the 'carnal ceremonies.'[51] And Bullinger remains with

---

48. Ibid., 188b-9a.

49. 'Zum ersten ist obgemelt, was das testament sye. Hie wöllend wir nun anzöugen, das es einig und ewig sye, und also wir und die alten vor Christus purt ein volck, ein kilchen, under einem gott, testament und glouben syend.... Worumb gebrucht dann Hieremias deß wörtlins? Antwurt: Sidmal durch die zůkunfft Christi Jesu all figuren uff Christum, den waren lichnam bedütende, verblichen sind und das testament vervolckomnet, nempt die geschrifft das einig testament nüw, angesehen, daß ein nüw liecht kummen und die alten schatten veraltet sind'. "Antwort an Burchard," in *Heinrich Bullinger Werke* (eds. Hans-Georg vom Berg and Bernhard Schneider; vol. III.2; Zurich: Theologischer Verlag, 1991), 151-52. For the dating of the text, see J. Wayne Baker, "Das Datum von Bullingers 'Antwort an Johannes Burchard'," *Zwingliana* 14 (1976).

50. "Vorlesung über den Hebräerbrief," in *Heinrich Bullinger Werke* (eds. Hans-Georg vom Berg and Susanna Hausammann; vol. III.1; Zurich: Theologischer Verlag, 1983), 191-94.

51. The question of unity in the face of being called 'new' and 'old' is handled the same way: 'So es nu ein testament ist, das wir bishar habend für zwey gehalten, worumb nemmend wirs dann das alt und nüw?—Antwort: Es isst nitt me dann ein einigs gmecht, dardurch alle fommghkeit imm glouben znn Messiam entspringt. Dorumb aber heissend dise zyten nüwe testament, daß uns Christus gleistet ist. Wann der da nempt das nüw, der vertillget das altö und daß der pundt ouch gemachet ist mitt einem nüwen volck, mitt den heiden, nitt alein mitt den Juden wie vor, besich Ephe. 2.ca. (14)!' "Von dem Touff," in *Heinrich Bullingers Werke* (ed. Hans-Georg vom Berg; vol. III.2; Zurich:

this view even in his mature works such as the *Decades*—the most influential of Bullinger's writings.[52] After citing the alleged differences of the covenants based on Hebrews, he states:

> Yet for all this let no man think that the fathers obtained no remission of their sins. For as they by faith had free forgiveness of their sins, so did God both write his law and pour his Spirit into their hearts. For which of us at this day can say, that we excel in knowledge and in faith either Abraham, Moses, Samuel, David, Isaiah, Daniel, or Zacharias? So then the difference is not, in that the fathers of the old testament were without the remission of sins and the illumination of the Holy Ghost, and that we alone, which are the people of the new testament, have obtained them: *but the difference doth consist in the greatness, ampleness, largeness, and plentifulness of the gifts*, to wit, because they are more liberally bestowed and more plentifully poured out upon more now than they were of old.[53]

Bullinger's reading, and the positing of a unity of substance and contrast of accidents, shows what will emerge as the boundary markers of Reformed thought on the subject. Such language is not unique to Bullinger and will become common for the Reformed and will influence the whole of the tradition through the period of orthodoxy and into contemporary Reformed theology.[54] Bullinger stands firmly in line with Jerome's temporal contrast, but rather than posit a change of people—from Israel to the Church (as Jerome)—Bullinger posits a change with respect to the 'accidents' of the one covenant. By doing this Bullinger is able to take the main point of Augustine's emphasis on the unity of the people of God, and combine it with a religio-historical contrast in Jer 31:31-34. Where the necessity of the Holy Spirit in the ancient era drove Augustine to positing a distinction in uses of *vetus testamentum*, Bullinger presents another option: the quality of the Spirit's work as a part of the *accidentalia* of the covenant. The difficulty of limiting the contrast in the oracle to 'accidents', however, will be felt by a number of the Reformed and, as I will argue, is entirely mistaken.

Theologischer Verlag, 1991), 78-79.

52. See Peter Opitz, "Bullinger's *Decades*: Instruction in Faith and Conduct," in *Architect of Reformation: An Introduction to Heinrich Bullinger, 1504-1575* (eds. Bruce Gordon and Emidio Campi; Grand Rapids, MI: Baker, 2004), 101-02.

53. Bullinger, *Decades*, III.297-98. My emphasis.

54. Already in 1527 Martin Bucer is using similar language: Martin Bucer, *In sacra quatuor Euangelia, enarrationes perpetuae, secundum & postremum recognitae* (Geneva: 1553), 46a.

3. *From Complexity to Simplicity: Oecolampadius*

Though we find certain 'boundaries' of Reformed thinking evidenced in Bullinger's work, this by no means entailed unanimity regarding Jer 31:31-34. Johannes Oecolampadius (1482-1531), though less-known today than Bullinger or Calvin, has been called the 'greatest scholar of the early Swiss Reformation' and was the leading Reformer in the important city of Basel for many years.[55] Oecolampadius put forward a variation on the contrast of 'accidents' in the move from the old to the new covenants. While Bullinger saw the contrast of quality as moving from less to more clear/plentiful/illustrious, Oecolampadius saw the contrast of Jer 31:31-34 as a move from complexity to simplicity in the era prior to and following Christ. This is contrary to some interpretations that have understood Oecolampadius as in some ways closer to the Augustinian line. So J. Wayne Baker states:

> All the elect, all people of faith from the beginning of the world participated in the new covenant. It was the new spiritual law written in the heart by God.[56]

But as we will see, while there is truth in the summary—and truth that makes Oecolampadius important for our study—such a view must be significantly qualified.

Oecolampadius first remarks on Jer 31:31-34 in his commentary on Isaiah, published in 1525. The brevity of his remarks on the subject generally may be because the debates with the Anabaptists had not yet consumed the discussions. Oecolampadius simply speaks of the fulfillment of Jer 31:33-34 at Pentecost, and to the 'new law, given not on Mt. Sinai but Zion'. This *nova lex* is the *lex Spiritus*: the Gospel standing over against the Pharisaical view of the Law as sufficient for justification and sent out with the Spirit for the inclusion of the nations.[57] So while the commentary is unmistakeably Lutheran (Protestant),

---

55. Gordon, *Swiss Reformation*, 204. For introductions to Oecolampadius, see Karl Hammer, "Der Reformater Oekolampad (1482-1531)," *Zwingliana* 19.1 (1992); Mark W. Elliott, "Oecolampadius," in *The Dictionary of Historical Theology* (ed. Trevor A. Hart; Grand Rapids, MI: Wm. B. Eerdmans, 2000); Thomas A. Fudge, "Icarus of Basel? Oecolampadius and the Early Swiss Reformation," *JRH* 21.3 (1997).

56. Baker, *Bullinger*, 187.

57. Johannes Oecolampadius, *In Jesaiam Prophetam Hypomnematon* (Basel: 1525): e.g. on Isa 51:4 (p.256a): 'For the Pharisees were not true people of God. but this consoles the church of the faithful, and shows the way of salvation, which is not through waging war in the future, but through the giving of a new law [*nova lex*], not on Mt. Sinai, but Zion, by the gathered apostles on the day of Pentecost. That is truly the law of the Spirit [*lex spiritus*], concerning which (speaks) Jer 31 and Heb 10. And this is the

Oecolampadius takes his terminology straight from the medieval discussions, but with rather little by way of full explanation of the 'new covenant' in Jer 31.

The most significant discussion of the text from Oecolampadius comes from his 1527 lectures on Jeremiah, edited and posthumously published by Wolfgang Capito in 1533. Staehelin has argued against viewing this commentary as a true representation of Oecolampadius' thought because of Capito's admission to editing and filling in what Oecolampadius said.[58] Deciding to what extent the comments on Jer 31:31-34 belong to Captio or Oecolampadius is difficult: a marked shift has occurred since the comments in 1525 and so we can imagine this a prime illustration of Capito's hijacking of Oecolampadius' reputation. But Oecolampadius would certainly have known of Bullinger's remarks and might easily have agreed given the concern of the Anabaptists. So a shift in his statements and thoughts would not be surprising. In any case, the commentary had its future influence (*Wirkungsgeschichte*) as the work of Oecolampadius, and will be so treated here. The comments begin by clarifying what is meant by a *foedus* which has 'laws on both sides,' as opposed to a *testamentum* that is unilateral and requires blood to be shed or the death of the one instituting it.[59] The distinction was minimized by Bullinger, but played a significant part in much of the debates of the 16th and into the 17th century with Reformed theologians using the distinction to hold to a single *testamentum*, made principally with Christ, and multiple *foedera* made with the people of God.[60]

---

covenant [*testamentum*] which I will make with the house of Israel, says the Lord, giving my law in their midst and in their hearts I will inscribe it. This law will go out from God which before was given through the Mosaic law, which had led nothing to perfection. Now giving himself, he will bring about to fulfill the law, and through this law will the nations be enlightened, and the number of the faithful be increased.'

Or on 51:7 (p.257a), commenting on the line 'Listen to me all you who know righteousness [*iustitia*],' he says: 'Now he consoles his own, taking away from them human fear, and these same are exhorted to hear, commending to them his law, which is the law of the Spirit [*lex spiritus*] written in the heart, as is (said), Jer 31.' Cf. also Isa 35:3-4 (193b); 59:21 (285).

58. Ernst Staehelin, *Das theologische Lebenswerk Johannes Oekolampads* (Quellen und Forschungen zur Reformationsgeschichte 21; Leipzig: M. Heinsius, 1939), 407-08. Capito's admission—as well Matthias Aparius' comments from his preface to Oecolampadius' lectures on Hebrews—are in Idem, *Briefe und Akten zum Leben Oekolampads* (2 vols.; Leipzig: 1934), n.970, n.976 (esp. p.757).

59. Johannes Oecolampadius, *In Hieremiam prophetam commentariorum libri tres Ioannis Oecolampadii* (Argentinae: 1533), II.161a.

60. See the helpful recent work by Brian J. Lee, *Johannes Cocceius and the Exegetical Roots of Federal Theology: Reformation Developments in the Interpretation*

Oecolampadius states that in the covenant (*foedus*) God makes, he undertakes to 'act as a defender, and supplies every good thing. God undertakes this is his law, in order that he might be what he truly is, namely the God of those whom he elected into friendship (*amicitia*).' On the other side, the people are 'to listen to his word and trust him to be for their good.'[61] This is, in fact, not far from his earlier comments regarding the covenant that was broken in Jer 11:

> For the covenant is friendship (*amicitia*) between God and the people, so that the people obey, God protects. The words of the covenant were precepts and blessings, with curses, and words of promise from the people. Moreover, the signs (were) circumcision, the sprinkling of blood, and that sort, and these are sometimes called the covenant. So Christ concerning the wine, 'This is the new testament in my blood.'... He subjoins the words of the testament, that he might hear his voice, that is, for your part, it requires to be obedient, and on the part of God, he will be a defense and blessing. And if for your part comes disobedience, it will bring from God a curse.[62]

Both covenants have the end of *amicitia dei*, and God acts the same in both.[63] But there are key differences hinted at above but made explicit in discussion of 31:31-34:

> But we find a two-fold covenant: old and new, carnal and spiritual, external and internal, perfect and imperfect. The former is that which God formerly entered with the people because they were[64] carnal, imperfect, and old. And, leading them by the hand by shadows but not leading them to perfection, the covenant was therefore to be abolished. And such a covenant was carnal—as were the people and the promises.[65]

---

of Hebrews 7-10 (Göttingen: Vandenhoeck & Ruprecht, 2009), 23-72.

61. Ibid, II.161a.
62. Ibid., I.66b-7a.
63. The notion of the 'amicitia dei' as the heart of the covenant, which becomes standard in Reformed thought, is seen also in Zwingli's comments published 1531: Ulrich Zwingli, *Jeremia-Erklärungen: Complanationis Ieremiae prophetae foetura prima* (Huldrych Zwingli Sämtliche Werke 14; Zurich: Verlag Berichthaus, 1959), 612. But again this is a scholastic idea—we have already seen Thomas speak of this as the goal of divine law: *STh* Ia IIae, q.99, a.1, ad.2. More interestingly elsewhere, 'Therefore, as is well known that friendship (*amicitia*) is most perfect between those who relate it to love, including all the preceding things; hence love (*caritas*) is to be placed in the class of this rule, which is a certain love of man to God, through which man esteems (*diligit*) God, and God (esteems) man.' Aquinas, *Sup. sent*, lib.3, d.27, q.2, a.1, co.
64. Or 'it was.'
65. Oecolampadius, *In Hieremiam*, II.161b.

At first blush this appears quite distinct from Bullinger's line of thought, so much so that some have accused Bullinger of misusing Oecolampadius.[66] But such a conclusion appears somewhat hasty. The most important point for understanding Oecolampadius on Jer 31:31-34 is his three-fold distinction of the covenant as made with Abraham, Moses, and Christ. The 'one gracious covenant' was given first to Abraham, and repeated to Isaac and Jacob, exemplifying the kindness of God and 'pure grace' while requiring 'the simple obedience of faith.' But with Moses God adds 'further laws' as a part of the conditions of the covenant—thus, 'if you continue in all that I have commanded, and impress them on your offspring after you.'[67] Importantly, Oecolampadius sees these conditions added by Moses as entirely external, the 'outer word' commanding what ought not be done, in order to drive one to reliance upon God and the pure grace of the covenant with Abraham:

> This ministry, characteristic of Moses, is only external—although [God] arranged for chiefly internal things to be advanced among his own. Thus he promises the circumcision of the heart to be done by the Lord.... They are ultimately going to seek the One Lord with the whole heart. He [i.e. Moses] promises perfect redemption in the fullness of days, and he prays more than once that the Lord might give to the people a heart that understands. He wept desperately, having endeavoured after so many years, with the Lord not yet having given to them a heart that understood.[68]

The idea is the second use of the law (as it would come to be called), Oecolampadius even pointing to Paul's speaking of Christ as 'the end of the law.' The law requires of the people what was possible to do only by the Spirit working in them:

> For Moses demands from his people those things that no one fulfills without the Spirit of Christ: to value God above all things, to be beyond all concupiscence, to value their neighbours as themselves: who, I ask, having

---

66. Charles S. McCoy and J. Wayne Baker, *Fountainhead of Federalism: Heinrich Bullinger and the Covenantal Tradition* (Louisville, KY: Westminster John Knox Press, 1991), 128, n.23.

67. *In Hieremiam*, II.162a. The same theme is seen in his comments on Ezek 40:28-37, and the three courts of the temple in the vision there representing three covenants with the same substance of the forgiveness of sins through the goodness of God: Johannes Oecolampadius, *In Ezechielem: Prophetam Commentarii Ioannis Oecolampadii* (Geneva: 1583), 201.

68. *In Hieremiam*, II.162a. For the externality of the *vetus testamentum*, cf. Augustine, *De spiritu*, §41 (above).

struggled by human strength, will attain these? Therefore the law is spiritual, since to fulfill it, it has need of the Spirit.[69]

But rather than condemning the entirety of the era as devoid of God's Spirit, Oecolampadius claims that the faithful 'generally understood this plan (*ratio*)', which Moses and the prophets used to drive to Christ. Thus:

> There were members of Christ under Moses, just as under Paul. Here is the light of midday and a proper summer, on account of the plan of the time and the revelation of God; then only the cloud shone, which shielded the heat of divine wrath from the people, which diffused its splendour from rays of light, although it was very slight on account of the plan for the time. For clearly this is not to detract from the merit of Christ's suffering, for the lamb was slain before God from the beginning of the world, his power lay hidden in the dispensation of shadows.[70]

The appeal to Rev. 13:8 and a (Platonic) conclusion on that ground for the eternal efficacy of the atonement sets another common theme for Reformed thought. And in this light Oecolampadius can elsewhere characterize the covenant given at Sinai as 'a friendship between God and the people'—the same characterization he gives for the one covenant of grace.[71] The contrast thus returns to something very similar to Bullinger: the increased clarity and understanding marking the difference between the eras of the the one covenant. In language even closer to Bullinger:

> Before God there is one covenant that is eternal, which is dispensed variously on account of the diversity of times. And in the interiority of man also it was always one and will constantly remain so—not only as it exists in eternal predestination. But if you join to it the ministry of those men with whom it was contracted at the time, it is necessary that you acknowledge the covenants to be divided also with respect to substance. For when you include the administration of the covenant in the substance, the conditions which are in the covenants (*pacta*) are likewise included. In this way the covenant of Abraham, the covenant of Moses, and the covenant of Christ are by nature very diverse among themselves, and they are affirmed to be different through Scripture.[72]

The diversity of the covenants comes from their diverse administration and so a substantial difference is true only if the administration is part of the substance. But the three-fold difference between Abraham, Moses and Christ shows how Jer 31:31-34 is to be read: the contrast lies in the 'conditions', the

---

69. *In Hieremiam*, II.162a.
70. Ibid., II.162b.
71. 'Foedus autem, est amicitia inter Deum & populum'. Ibid., I.66b-7a.
72. Ibid., II.162b.

'plans' utilized for the one eternal covenant. And this variety is a movement from a simple (Abraham) to a complex (Moses), and back to a simple (Christ) state of affairs:

> Now hear the kind of difference of the covenants: the Lord covenanted with Abraham by words; nothing other than obedience was stipulated by him. Under Moses many wonders and dreadful things were added, not known to only one leader, but clear to the whole multitude. Further, it was surrounded by so many legal circumstances which all were referred to those ten words of the covenantal table. But in Christ is truth and life, extending over the ministry of the church of Abraham.[73]

Such a movement may bear some resemblance to the view of Alcuin briefly mentioned earlier where the covenant through Christ comes as a return to the simplicity of the covenant with Abraham. And Wolfgang Musculus will offer a similar notion, though more Lutheran in the discussion of 'law', in his influential *Loci communes* of 1560.[74] But Oecolampadius offers more precision by raising an objection to this reading of Jer 31:31-34—an objection entirely missing in Musculus' discussion:

> For you see, I ask myself whether Abel, Noah, Abraham and other spiritual persons were not in the *novum testamentum*. For everything that they say here is appropriate to them, for God had given them the law in their hearts and they had been taught by the Lord, and their sins had been forgiven.... For would God be so unfair (*personarum receptor*) that he would disdain the old with this grace, or deny the greatest gifts to his closest friends? You must admit that the fathers shared in the same Spirit of faith, and that they ate the same food who stood out as spiritual people in that age.[75]

---

73. Ibid., II.163a. This is cited by Bullinger, *De testamento,* 38-39. The general view has some Reformed supporters today: E.g., 'The new covenant is anticipated as a renewed Abrahamaic (rather than Mosaic) covenant, for instance, in Jeremiah 31.' Michael S. Horton, *Covenant and Eschatology: The Divine Drama* (Louisville: Westminster John Knox, 2002), 134. Similarly, Wayne Grudem, *Systematic Theology: An Introduction to Biblical Doctrine* (Grand Rapids, MI: Zondervan, 1994), 521.

74. Wolfgang Musculus, *Loci communes theologicae sacrae* (Ultima ed. Basel: 1599), 140-47. His views here fit well with his description as 'an independent thinker whose theological formulations fell somewhere between Zurich and Wittenberg.' Gordon, *Swiss Reformation*, 177.

75. Oecolampadius, *In Hieremiam*, II.163a. That only pre-Mosaic figures are named seems to me accidental to Oecolampadius and his argument. If he had intended Moses to be the temporal dividing line, the argument surely would have moved in that way. But it doesn't, and as will be seen none of the following arguments are applicable

If each part of Jer 31:33-34 can be attributed (indeed, must be attributed) to the 'spiritual persons' of the ancient era, then how can one say that they are not members of the new covenant? Oecolampadius gives two answers: first, 'as long as the *testamentum* was not consecrated by the blood of Christ, it is not said to have been instituted.'[76] This does not mean that the plan (*ratio*) of God was entirely foreign to those before Christ (he cites again Rev 13:8); only God's plan was 'confirmed' by Christ's blood being shed, and is now made manifest by the Spirit.[77] This appears to be a sleight of hand, changing the terminology from *foedus* to *testamentum*. As stated at the outset of his discussion, a *testamentum* is only valid by the shedding of blood and instead of having requirements on both sides, is unilateral: only revealing the will of the one making it.[78] So while Oecolampadius has overlooked the difference in terminology in the intervening discussion, he returns to it here so the 'fathers' might have all the things promised in Jer 31:33-34 but still not be members of the *novum testamentum*, the latter only validated by death. They were thus members of the one (bilateral) covenant, but not members of the *novum testamentum*.

His second answer, tied as an explication of the first, brings us back to the movement from complexity to simplicity, in which the *foedus* (!) is 'made new, because it is made with respect to its fulness.' This fulness has to do with the increased fruitfulness of the Spirit and the fulfillment of the ceremonies—clearly a temporal matter. But, he remarks, it is also due to the new covenant being on the heart, and therefore not being broken.[79] But in this latter case, 'you see the new and eternal to be the same', for God's words and Spirit are always active in the hearts of the elect.[80] Thus he can hold that 'the first covenant was also eternal, insofar as it pertained to God.'[81] And in this sense Baker's statement at the outset of this section can be true: all the members of the elect are members of the first, eternal covenant, which is the new covenant. But Oecolampadius repeats his caveats: being eternal, the covenant existed in the ancient era but was not truly the 'new' covenant because it was written on tablets of stone and concerned 'external things'. But 'this new, eternal, bare (covenant) is simply of the inner person, and therefore has its beginning, middle and end by

---

solely to those before Moses.
    76.   Ibid.
    77.   Ibid., II.163a-3b.
    78.   Ibid., II.161a.
    79.   Ibid., II.163b. He includes here a similarity to Melanchthon and Luther in the 'sponteneity' that comes ('faciatque populum spontaneum').
    80.   Ibid.
    81.   Or, 'when one held fast to God': Ibid., II.161b.

the Spirit.' Such is opposite the covenant with Moses, and the external necessities only 'obliquely' leading to the Spirit.[82] The contrast is, once more, with the (merely) external additions to the eternal covenant, and a 'new' era marked by pure internality.

So with Oecolampadius a variation on a standard contrast of administration emerges: the movement from the eternal covenant with its external accessories (the 'old covenant') to its 'bare' state in Christ. The theological payoff is that Oecolampadius can speak of the 'fathers' as having every part of the new covenant in Jer 31:33-34, because these are a part of the eternal covenant promised and known by Abraham and all 'spiritual persons' of every age. But it is truly called 'new' only when stripped of its external accompaniments. Rather than the covenant surrounded by Mosaic externalities, the Church has the simplicity of the Gospel and worship.[83] The boundaries seen in Bullinger are maintained in Oecolampadius' discussion, and the same payoff against the Anabaptist position, but the point of contrast is not simply a mutatio sacramentorum or an increase of qualitas. The movement is from a complex to a simple era, centred on the sacraments.

4. *Augustinian Remnants (a): John Calvin*

Among the early modern Reformed, we find the most obvious wrestling with both an Augustinian and religio-historical reading of Jer 31:31-34 from the French reformer John Calvin (1509-64). Calvin's relationship to the Swiss theologians, somewhat like Geneva to the Swiss confederacy, was a mixture of dependency, protection, and distance.[84] But the theological difference between Geneva and Zurich can be overstated. Some recent scholarship has done just this on the issue of 'covenant'—clearly a discussion of some interest for the present topic. J. Wayne Baker, for instance, sees in Bullinger and Calvin a difference between a two-sided responsibility in the covenant (Bullinger) over against a unilateral soteriology in the latter (Calvin).[85] Though learned and provocative,

---

82. Ibid., II.163b.

83. Here one naturally thinks of the iconoclastic side of the Swiss Reformation.

84. 'Huldrych Zwingli was one of Calvin's least favourite topics'. Bruce Gordon, "Calvin and the Swiss Reformed Churches," in *Calvinism in Europe, 1540-1620* (eds. Andrew Pettegree et al.; Cambridge: Cambridge Univ. Press, 1994), 65. Calvin's relationship with Bullinger was more fruitful: cf. F. Büßer, "Calvin und Bullinger," in *Calvinus Servus Christi* (ed. Wilhelm H. Neuser; Budapest: 1988); Hans Scholl, "Calvin und die Schweiz—Die Schweiz und Calvin," in *Calvin im Kontext der Schweizer Reformation* (ed. Peter Opitz; Zurich: Theologische Verlag, 2003).

85. Baker, *Bullinger*; J. Wayne Baker, "Heinrich Bullinger, the Covenant, and the Reformed Tradition in Retrospect," *The Sixteenth Century Journal* 29 (1988).

such a reading has been shown reductive in both its parts.[86] For our purposes it is sufficient to state that, as we will see, Calvin reads Jer 31:31-34 from within the same theological boundaries on the unity of the covenant that we find in his Swiss neighbours.

Calvin mentions the contrast of old and new covenants in his first theological publication: his 1534 preface to Pierre Robert Olivétan's French New Testament.[87] And he posits the contrast as a simple one of two eras. After Adam's fall from his created state into ruin, and God's 'abhorrence' of humanity on that account, God nonetheless gave humanity 'time and opportunity to return to him'.[88] God extended his hand both through nature and through speaking to Israel in particular:

> And as though he were nothing to the other nations, he willed expressly to be called the God of Israel, and to have Israel called his people, on condition that they would recognize no other Lord and receive none else as their God. And this covenant (*alliance*) was confirmed and handed down by authentic instruments of testament and testimony given by himself.[89]

But Israel failed, leaving both Jews and Gentiles unfaithful before God. Thus the young Calvin claims:

> Wherefore, if God were to approach his people, whether Jew or Gentile, a new covenant was needed: one which would be certain, sure, and inviolable. And to establish and confirm it, it was necessary to have a Mediator...[90]

---

86. E.g. Lyle D. Bierma, "Federal Theology in the Sixteenth Century: Two Traditions?," *WTJ* 45 (1983); Idem, "The Role of Covenant Theology in Early Reformed Orthodoxy," *The Sixteenth Century Journal* 21, no.3 (1990); Cornelis P. Venema, *Heinrich Bullinger and the Doctrine of Predestination: Author of "the other Reformed Tradition"?* (Grand Rapids, MI: Baker, 2002); Peter A. Lillback, *The Binding of God: Calvin's Role in the Development of Covenant Theology* (Grand Rapids, MI: Baker, 2001); Idem, "Ursinus' Development of the Covenant of Creation: A Debt to Melanchthon or Calvin?," *WTJ* 43 (1981); M. Eugene Osterhaven, "Calvin on the Covenant," in *Readings in Calvin's Theology* (ed. Donald K. McKim; Grand Rapids, MI: Baker, 1984). Cf. the remarks of Richard A. Muller, *The Unaccomodated Calvin: Studies in the Foundation of a Theological Tradition* (Oxford Univ. Press, 2000), 155.

87. For discussion of Calvin's relationship to Olivétan, see Bruce Gordon, *Calvin* (New Haven: Yale Univ. Press, 2009), 18-19.

88. John Calvin, "Preface to Olivétan's New Testament," in *Calvin: Commentaries* (ed. Joseph Haroutunian; Philadelphia: Westminster Press, 1958), 58-59.

89. Ibid., 59.

90. Ibid., 61. The line of argument here is functionally the same in his *Argumentum* of Romans: John Calvin, *Iohannes Calvini Commentarius in Epistolam*

Calvin then moves to pointing to the various prophecies that testified to the coming Messiah (including Gen. 3:15, on which he would later change his mind). What we have in the New Testament is the making of this new covenant through the coming of that Messiah:

> And this book is called the New Testament in relation to the Old, which, in so far as it had to be succeeded by and related to the New, and was shaky and imperfect in itself, was abolished and abrogated. It is the new and the eternal, which will never grow old and fail, because Jesus Christ is its Mediator.[91]

Ganoczy is right to find little explicit evidence of interaction with fully Protestant views in the preface, though he overstates the matter.[92] And we find no hint that Calvin has read the literature on the topic of the two testaments from the Swiss.[93] Calvin lacks any discussion of the 'substance' of the covenant.[94]

Pauli ad Romanos (Leiden: E.J. Brill, 1981), VI.50f. The commentary is based on lectures begun in Geneva in 1536.

91. Calvin, "Preface to NT," 64.

92. 'One has the impression that Calvin used no other source than the Bible itself and—let us willingly add—the responses that his readings of the Scriptures inspired in his own heart. The preface exhibits Lutheran thought in only a few statements.... But the text as a whole primarily praises Christ in elegant terms as the only mediator of the New Testament and as the end and fulfillment of the entire ancient law.' Alexandre Ganoczy, *The Young Calvin* (Tr. by David Foxgrover and Wade Provo. Edinburgh: T&T Clark, 1987), 96. Even the 'few statements' of Lutheran thought would by no means be heterodox to many within Roman Catholic positions at the time, though Calvin's Latin forward (only appearing in the 1535 ed.) to the Bible reveals already his distaste for the Sorbonne theologians: John Calvin, *Ioannes Calvinus caesaribus, regibus, principibus, gentibusque omnibus Christ imperio subditis salutem* (Ioannes Calvini Opera 9; Brunswick: 1870).

93. Against the (hesitant) suggestion of Irena Backus and Claire Chimelli, eds. *La Vraie Piété: Divers traités de Jean Calvin et Confession de foi de Guillaume Farel* (Geneva: 1986), 20-21. The closest parallel would be to Heinrich Bullinger, "De scripturae negotio," in *Heinrich Bullingers Werke* (ed. Hans-Georg vom Berg; III.2; Zurich: Theologischer Verlag, 1991). Orig. publ., 1523.

94. Though Beza's Latin translation addresses this by changing a sentence around to read, 'And so that the full and lasting faith in the goodness of God might be revealed, the Lord Jesus himself, who is the sponsor of that covenant and is himself the substance of it, appointed the apostles to himself...' (Atque ut huius Dei beneplaciti plena fides et perpetua exstaret, Dominus Iesus ipse, qui foederis istius sponsor est atque ipsamet illius substantia, apostolos sibi designavit...). The French reads, 'Pour laquelle [i.e. reconciliation] chose declairer, le Seigneur Iesus, qui en estoit le fondement et la substance, a ordonné ses Apostres....' John Calvin, *A tous amateurs de Iesus Christ, et de*

And the unity under discussion regards the unified witness to the promise, not a unity of the 'covenant' itself.[95] The contrast concerns the move from the one era to the next, abolishing and abrogating the 'old' and beginning the 'new and the eternal' with the coming of Christ.

Five years later, however, Calvin shows clear familiarity with the Swiss discussion on the covenants in the 1539 edition of his *Institutes*.[96] Calvin here first began to use Melanchthon's *Loci* to overlay the catechetical structure of the earlier editions, and thus first included a *locus* on the two testaments.[97] That Calvin made use of the covenant motif in many of his works, from every period of his life, is evident.[98] But since our goal is not an exhaustive presentation of Calvin's views or their development, I will focus on the last edition of the *Institutes* (1559) and the commentary on Jeremiah—published in 1563 from lectures given in 1560-62[99]—as revealing the mature Calvin's struggle to understand Jer 31:31-34.

As was the case for Bullinger and Oecolampadius, Calvin's interpretation of Jer 31:31f was an important part of his disputes with the Anabaptists.[100] But a further external influence for Calvin comes from the treatment of the topic

---

son S. Evangile, salut (Ioannes Calvini Opera 9; Brunsfield: 1870).

95. Calvin, "Preface to NT," 65.

96. See Büßer, "Calvin und Bullinger," 119-20.

97. See Richard A. Muller, "Ordo Docendi: Melanchthon and the Organization of Calvin's Institutes," in *Melanchthon in Europe: His Work and Influence beyond Wittenberg* (ed. Karin Maag; Grand Rapids, MI: Baker, 1999); Idem, *Unaccommodated Calvin*, 125-39. Parker speaks of this as a move to a more 'systematic' approach over the catechetical: T.H.L. Parker, *Calvin's New Testament Commentaries* (Louisville, KY: Westminster John Knox Press, 1993), 89f.

98. See Lillback, *Binding of God*, 126-41; Anthony A. Hoekema, "The Covenant of Grace in Calvin's Teaching," *Calvin Theological Journal* 2 (1967): , esp. 141f. Strehle's claim (*Calvinism, Federalism*, 149-50) that Calvin's use of 'covenant' is 'intercalated rather sparingly' in the *Institutes* is only superficially true. Better (if still imprecise) is Vos: Calvin 'is the forerunner of such Reformed theologians who allocate to it [i.e. the covenant] a subordinate place as a separate locus.' Geerhardus Vos, "The Doctrine of the Covenant in Reformed Theology," in *Redemptive History and Biblical Interpretation: the Shorter Writings of Geerhardus Vos* (ed. Richard B. Gaffin; Phlipsburg, NJ: P&R, 1980), 236.

99. Pete Wilcox, "Calvin as Commentator on the Prophets," in *Calvin and the Bible* (ed. Donald K. McKim; Grand Rapids, MI: Baker, 1997), 107-30.

100. For full discussion see Willem Balke, *Calvin and the Anabaptist Radicals* (Tr. by William J. Heynen. Grand Rapids, MI: Wm. B. Eerdmans, 1981).

by Michael Servetus, with whom Calvin was familiar at least as early as 1534.[101] Though Servetus was not unknown to the Zurich and Basel reformers—even spending nearly a year in Basel in 1530, just prior to Oecolampadius' death—the deliberate response to Servetus' views on the testaments fell to Calvin.

Servetus treats the subject in an appendix to his 1532 *Diologorum de trinitate*, where the old and new covenant are seen as the contrast between law and gospel, combined with a temporal contrast so that the era of law is set absolutely against the era of the gospel.[102] Thus he excludes 'the Jews' from membership in the kingdom of God and adoption,[103] from the true forgiveness of sins,[104] and from true justification.[105] He concludes:

---

101. Ganoczy, *Young Calvin*, 86.

102. Thus his claim that 'the Lutherans...do not enough distinguish the law from the Gospel.' In "On the Righteousness of Christ's Kingdom", Michael Servetus, *The Two Treatises of Servetus on the Trinity* (HTS 16; Tr. by Earl Morse Wilbur. Cambridge, MA: Harvard Univ. Press, 1932), §3.11. Calvin's grouping of Servetus with the Swiss Brethren at this point might be justified: see the summary of the latter's position in John D. Roth, "Harmonizing the Scriptures: Swiss Brethren understandings of the relationship between the Old and New Testament during the last half of the sixteenth century," in *Radical Reformation Studies: Essays presented to James M. Stayer* (eds. Werner O. Packull and Geoffrey L. Dipple; St. Andrews Studies in Reformation History,. Aldershot: Ashgate, 1999), 48.

103. 'Under the law there was never any one in the kingdom of heaven, for the kingdom of God had not yet come, which came to us when Christ came.... None of them was ever elect, or predestined by that election which God presdestined concerning us, namely, that we should receive the adoption of sons, and be brethren of Christ.' Servetus, *Two Treatises*, §3.1.

104. 'Indeed, in the law no other forgiveness of sins was known than a carnal and earthly one.... For this carnal expiation, sacrifices were appointed in Leviticus, and the shedding of blood for sin and for transgression, in which there was no true forgiveness of sins, as the Apostle teaches. The Lord never gave them rest of conscience, but under this shadow they always had their hearts veiled.' Ibid., §3.2.

105. '[I]n the law it was a righteousness of the flesh; while we have a righteousness of the Spirit. All, even the most holy, who were under the law, were carnal. Although the Holy Spirit spoke prophecies through them, although they foresaw the future, yet in their deeds they savored of nothing but the carnal.' Ibid., §3.3. 'Although Abraham saw the day of Christ in the birth of a son that had been promised, namely, Isaac, yet notwithstanding this he was carnal, and asked God for carnal things, and his righteousness was carnal, prefiguring one that was spiritual.' Ibid. Summarily, 'From what has been said above it appears, in the first place, that there was in the law no justification of the spirit, nor was there any true justification, just as there was also no true forgiveness of sins, although for a time it was given them for salvation, that they

> They therefore fall into no mean error who confuse the Testaments... they lessen the grace of the coming of Christ by making the Jews equal to us. They have not the spirit of Paul so as to know how great are those things which have been given us by Christ. Indeed, if they pay attention, they are treating the Spirit of grace with despite. They have their hearts veiled lest the light and glory of the Gospel shine upon them, so that they wish still to live under the shadow of the law.[106]

Such statements throw Calvin's discussion into sharp relief. Calvin is best known in this regard for his insistence on the unity of the covenant throughout redemptive history:

> all men adopted by God into the company of his people since the beginning of the world were covenanted to him by the same law and by the bond of the same doctrine as obtains among us.[107]

Or, even more strongly from the commentary on Jeremiah:

> He then who once made a covenant with his chosen people, had not changed his purpose, as though he had forgotten his faithfulness. It then follows, that the first covenant was inviolable; besides, he had already made his covenant with Abraham, and the Law was a confirmation of that covenant. As then the Law depended on that covenant which God made with his servant Abraham, it follows that God could never have made a new, that is, a contrary or a different covenant.[108]

Calvin summarizes the unity and diversity of the testaments in line with Bucer, Bullinger, and others, delineating a unity in 'substance' and a diversity in 'administration' or 'dispensation':

---

might live under the shadow.' Ibid., §3.10.

106. Ibid., §3.3. Worth noting is that Servetus appeals to Jer 31:31-34 as a part of this strong contrast (§1.4, 3.2).

107. John Calvin, *Institutes of the Christian Religion* (Tr. by Ford Lewis Battles. Philadelphia: Westminster Press, 1960), II.x.1. Schrenk states, 'Ja, so stark hat Calvin die innere Einheit der Testamente hervorgehoben, daß er wie Zwingli nachher den Schein abwehren muß, als ob er keine Unterschiede statuiere.' Schrenk, *Gottesreich und Bund*, 47. Strehle refers to it as 'the excessive amalgamation of the two testaments', though such language clearly begs the question. Strehle, *Calvinism*, 150.

108. *Commentaries on the Book of the Prophet Jeremiah and the Lamentations* (5 vols.; Tr. by John Owen. Grand Rapids, MI: Baker, 1979), IV.126. Or, 'God has never made any other covenant that that which he made formerly with Abraham, and at length confirmed by the hand of Moses (4.127).'

> The covenant made with all the patriarchs is so much like ours in substance and reality that the two are actually one and the same. Yet they differ in the mode of dispensation [*administratio tamen variat*].[109]

Calvin then spends the next sections of the *Institutes* establishing both parts of the thesis—unity of substance, diversity of administration—though his special concern lies with the unity, even calling the addition of the chapter on diversity (new to 1559) an 'appendix'.[110]

We see the emergence of a 'salvific' contrast in Jer 31:31-34—and our first remnant of Augustine's reading—in Calvin's five-fold difference between the testaments. The third point begins with a citation of Jer 31:31-34, adding this summary of 2 Cor 3:6-11:

> From these words [of Jeremiah] the apostle took occasion to make a comparison between the law and the gospel, calling the former literal, the latter spiritual doctrine; the former he speaks of as carved on tablets of stone, the latter as written upon men's hearts; the former is the preaching of death, the latter of life; the former of condemnation, the latter of righteousness; the former to be made void, the latter to abide.[111]

Calvin, after pointing to a difference between Jeremiah and Paul raised by the *ad hominem* nature of Paul's argument, defines for us the point of contrast at stake in each:

---

109. *Institutes*, II.x.2. The same two-fold concern is seen often, e.g. his comments on Isa 2:3: 'Two things, therefore, must be observed: first, that the doctrine of God is the same, and always agrees with itself; that no one may charge God with changeableness, as if he were inconsistent; and though the law of the Lord be now the same that it ever was, yet it came out of Zion with a new garment; secondly, when ceremonies and shadows had been abolished, Christ was revealed, in whom the reality of them is perceived.' *Commentary on the Book of the Prophet Isaiah* (Tr. by William Pringle. Grand Rapids, MI: Baker, 1979), ad loc. He equates the covenant made with Abraham and the 'eternal covenant' at, e.g., *The Sermons of M. Iohn Calvin upon the Fifth Booke of Moses called Deuteronomie* (Tr. by Arthur Golding. London: 1583), 4a. For discussion, see Hans Heinrich Wolf, *Die Einheit des Bundes: Das Verhältnis von Altem und Neuem Testament bei Calvin* (Neukirchen: Verlag der Buchhandlung des Erziehungsvereins Neukirchen Kreis Moers, 1958), 19-24, et passim; Osterhaven, "Calvin on Covenant," 98f.

110. Calvin, *Institutes*, II.x.1. So Parker: 'Calvin's whole intention has been to establish the similarity or unity of the Old and New Covenants. The chapter on the differences should on no account be taken as a balance to that on the similarity. There could be no such balance, but either only a confirmation or a demolition of the case.' T.H.L. Parker, *Calvin's Old Testament Commentaries* (Edinburgh: T&T Clark, 1986), 50.

111. *Institutes*, II.xi.7.

Jeremiah's New Covenant

> [B]oth Jeremiah and Paul, because they are contrasting the Old and New Testaments, consider *nothing in the law except what properly belongs to it*. For example: the law contains here and there promises of mercy, but because they have been borrowed from elsewhere, they are not counted part of the law, when only the nature of the law is under discussion. *They ascribe to it only this function: to enjoin what is right, to forbid what is wicked*; to promise a reward to the keepers of righteousness, and threaten transgressors with punishment; but at the same time not to change or correct the depravity of heart that by nature inheres in all men.[112]

In other words, for Calvin the point of contrast in Jeremiah as described here is not concerning eras as such, but the proper definition of the law in itself – the *nuda lex* – apart from the life-giving Spirit of the Gospel.[113] So he immediately states:

> The Old Testament is of the letter, for it was published without the working of the Spirit. The New is spiritual because the Lord has engraved it spiritually upon men's hearts. The second antithesis is by way of clarification of the first. The Old brings death, for it can but envelop the whole human race in a curse. The New is the instrument of life, for it frees men from the curse and restores them to God's favor...[114]

---

112. Ibid, II.xi.7. My emphasis. Or elsewhere, 'But as evangelic promises are only found scattered in the writings of Moses, and these also somewhat obscure, and as the precepts and rewards, allotted to the observers of the law, frequently occur, it rightly appertained to Moses as his own and peculiar office, to teach what is the real righteousness of works, and then to show what remuneration awaits the observance of it, and what punishment awaits those who come short of it. For this reason Moses is by John compared with Christ, when it is said, "That the law was given by Moses, but that grace and truth came by Christ." (John 1:17) And whenever the word law is thus strictly taken, Moses is by implication opposed to Christ: and then we must consider what the law contains, as separate from the gospel. Hence what is said here of the righteousness of the law, must be applied, not to the whole office of Moses, but to that part which was in a manner peculiarly committed to him.' *Commentaries on the Epistle of Paul the Apostle to the Romans* (Tr. by John Owen. Grand Rapids, MI: Baker, 1979), at 10:5-10.

113. 'If [Moses] is considered without Christ in his narrow office of lawgiver, his message was only letter that produced death. But if Moses is considered in his whole teaching, he is a preacher of the gospel which is found in the New Covenant.' Lillback, *Binding of God*, 154. For discussion, see Wolf, *Einheit des Bundes*, 38-54. This distinction is somehow missed by Mark W. Karlberg, "Reformed Interpretation of the Mosaic Covenant," *WTJ* 43.1 (1980), 12-16.

114. *Institutes*, II.xi.8. Elsewhere, in confrontation with semi-Pelagianism: 'that statement of Jeremiah cannot be refuted by any cavils: that the covenant of God made with the ancient people was invalid because it was only of the letter; moreover, that it is not otherwise established than when the Spirit enters into it to dispose their hearts to

The point of contrast for Jeremiah (and Paul) is the letter of the law apart from the working of the Spirit—i.e. the gospel.[115] Calvin at this moment stands squarely in the tradition of Augustine: Jeremiah presents a 'salvific' contrast between faith (the Spirit's work) and unbelief (law without the Spirit).

Further, we can see why the contrast cannot be viewed as temporal succession. Calvin explicitly claims for the ancient Fathers both faith in Christ and possession of the Spirit, which are only available as divine acts of mercy.[116] Calvin even claims that, though in comparison with the present age there were few in ancient Israel 'who embraced the Lord's covenant with their whole hearts and minds. Yet, reckoned by themselves without comparison, there were many.'[117]

Calvin's debt to Augustine in this way of reading is then explicitly stated. Calvin has just given his first four comparisons between the two testaments—(1) heavenly benefits known through temporal promises vs. known directly (cf. Melanchthon's *Loci*), (2) figures vs. shadows, (3) letter vs. spirit, and (4) bondage of fear vs. joy of freedom. He then comments:

> The three latter comparisons to which we have referred are of the law and the gospel. In them the law is signified by the name "Old Testament," the gospel by "New Testament." The first [comparison] extends more widely, for it includes within itself also the promises published before the law. *Augustine, however, said that these should not be reckoned under the name "Old Testament." This was very sensible. He meant the same thing as we*

---

obedience.' Ibid., II.v.9.

115. Thus his comment on Deut 30:11: 'But if God cures the depravity of the heart by the Spirit of regeneration, and he mollifies its hardness, this is not of the law but is properly of the Gospel.' Cited in Wolf, *Einheit des Bundes*, 44. Cp. the statement of Bucer: 'Thus he enacts nothing by the new law, but he gives his Spirit, who places the Law in our inmost place, and in our heart writes it: thus we both know and love him, and by him we live according to his will.' Bucer, *In quatuor Euangelia*, 46b.

116. See *Institutes*, II.x. Cf. II.v.4 (where Augustine's *De spiritu* looms large). Calvin states here that it is the testimony of Moses and the prophets themselves that 'men become wise only when an understanding heart is given them'. And elsewhere: 'almost no one can be found in the Christian church who in excellence of faith is to be compared with Abraham' (II.xi.6). Since 'faith is the principal work of the Spirit' (III.i.4), this claim would establish Abraham's possession of the Spirit.

117. Ibid., II.xi.8. So, commenting on Ps 119:13, he states: 'In this verse he declares that the law of God was not only deeply engraven on his own heart, but that it was his earnest and strenuous endeavor to gain over many of his fellow-disciples into subjection to God.' (cf. at 119:54.) *Commentary on the Book of the Psalms* (Tr. by James Anderson. Grand Rapids, MI: Baker, 1979), ad loc.

are teaching: for he was referring to those statements of Jeremiah and Paul wherein the Old Testament is distinguished from the word of grace and mercy. In the same passage he very aptly adds the following: the children of the promise, reborn of God, who have obeyed the commands by faith working through love, have belonged to the New Covenant since the world began. This they did, not in hope of carnal, earthly, and temporal things, but in hope of spiritual, heavenly, and eternal benefits. For they believed especially in the Mediator; and they did not doubt that through him the Spirit was given to them that they might do good, and that they were pardoned whenever they sinned. It is that very point which I intended to affirm: all the saints whom Scripture mentions as being peculiarly chosen of God from the beginning of the world have shared with us the same blessing unto eternal salvation. *This, then, is the difference between our analysis and his: ours distinguishes between the clarity of the gospel and the obscurer dispensation of the Word that had preceded it... Augustine's division simply separates the weakness of the law from the firmness of the gospel.*[118]

Calvin agrees explicitly with Augustine that the contrast in Jeremiah is a salvific one, and further that all the 'children of promise... have belonged to the new covenant since the world began.' Yet in the next breath Calvin also affirms that the contrast is concerned with the *claritas* of the two covenants, clearly a temporal contrast.[119] The only way in which he is able to do this without blatant contradiction is through the broadening of the term 'Old Testament' in the first of the comparisons, as he admits to doing ('The first extends more widely...'). This notion is given summary form in an earlier statement: 'where the *whole law* is concerned, the gospel differs from it only in clarity of manifestation.'[120] The 'whole law' is clearly the period of the law, or the books

---

118. *Institutes*, II.xi.10. My emphasis.

119. Cp. his comment on Matt 5:17 in *Commentary on a Harmony of the Evangelists, Matthew, Mark and Luke* (Tr. by William Pringle. Grand Rapids, MI: Baker, 1979): 'God had, indeed, promised a new covenant at the coming of Christ: but had, at the same time, showed that it would not be different from the first, but that, on the contrary, its design was, to give a perpetual sanction to the covenant, which he had made, from the beginning, with his own people. "I will write my law (says he) in their hearts, and I will remember their iniquities no more" (Jer 31:33-34). By these words he is so far from departing from the former covenant, that, on the contrary, he declares, that it will be confirmed and ratified, when it shall be succeeded by the new.' The unity is the central point here, but it is a unity in temporal succession.

120. *Institutes*, II.ix.4. My emphasis. This general use of 'law' is explicitly in mind in the later discussion of the use of the 'law': 'I understand by the word "law" not only the Ten Commandments, which set forth a godly and righteous rule of living [what was called 'proper' earlier], but the form of religion handed down by God through

of the Old Testament, rather than the law properly defined as the *nuda lex*. Thus it appears that properly speaking the contrast in Jeremiah is salvific; while improperly, the contrast is one of clarity.[121]

Calvin offers another instance of adding a qualitative contrast to the salvific in his discussion of the two eras as 'bondage' vs. 'freedom':

> But suppose that our opponents object that, among the Israelites, the holy patriarchs were an exception: since they were obviously endowed with the same Spirit of faith as we, it follows that they shared the same freedom of joy. To this we reply: neither of these arose from the law. But when through the law the patriarchs felt themselves both oppressed by their enslaved condition, and wearied by anxiety of conscience, they fled for refuge to the gospel. It was therefore a particular fruit of the New Testament that, apart from the common law of the Old Testament, they were exempted from those evils. Further, we shall deny that they were so endowed with the spirit of freedom and assurance as not in some degree to experience the fear and bondage arising from the law.[122]

Calvin depends upon the proper definition of 'law' for the first answer establishing the continuity of experience: they had the Spirit as fruit of the 'new testament'. But he adds a contrast of quality for the sake of preserving the discontinuity of experience. The conclusion is then explicitly temporal.[123]

Moses. And Moses was not made a lawgiver to wipe out the blessing promised to the race of Abraham. Rather, we see him repeatedly reminding the Jews of that freely given covenant made with their fathers of which they were the heirs. It was as if he were sent to renew it. This fact was very clearly revealed in the ceremonies (II.vii.1).' (Note the contrast here to Oecolampadius!) Though even here it appears that the following discussion wavers back and forth.

121. So, more broadly, Wolf: 'Wenn es bei der Einheit des Bundes bleiben soll, dann kann diese Unterscheidung von Gesetz und Evangelium nur eine uneigentliche sein, die das Verhältnis von A.T. und N.T. in keiner Weise letztgültig bestimmen kann.' *Einheit des Bundes*, 44.

122. *Institutes*, II.xi.9. For the last point, cp. Bullinger, *Decades*, III.296: 'The liberty of the fathers was by the weight and heap of ceremonies so oppressed and covered, that although they were free in spirit before the Lord, yet notwithstanding they did in outward shew differ little or nothing from very bond-slaves, by reason of the burden of the law that lay upon their shoulders. For insomuch as the law was not as yet abrogated, they were compelled precisely to observe it.'

123. 'Hence, they are rightly said, *in contrast to us*, to have been under the testament of bondage and fear, when we consider that common dispensation by which the Lord at that time dealt with the Israelites.' Ibid. My emphasis.

Calvin, like Melanchthon, distances his reading of Jeremiah from the matter of the *mutatio sacramentorum*, while affirming this change in the language of old and new testaments:

> [The law which is abrogated] is to be referred to the ceremonial law. For because the Old bore the image of things absent, it had to die and vanish with time. The gospel, because it reveals the very substance, stands fast forever. Indeed, Jeremiah calls even the moral law a weak and fragile covenant. But that is for another reason: by the sudden defection of an ungrateful people it was soon broken off. However, because the people were to blame for such a violation, it cannot properly be charged against the covenant. Now the ceremonies, because by their own weakness they were abrogated at Christ's advent, had the cause of their weakness within themselves.[124]

Calvin distinguishes between the weakness of the 'old' in Jeremiah, which referred to the moral law and thus a weakness in the people, and the weakness of the ceremonies, which was inherent in their being *figurae*. In any case, in the *Institutes* we are left with an unresolved tension. On the one hand is the (necessarily) temporal distinction between the old and the new as less and then more 'clear'. On the other is the contrast between old and new as salvific, the contrast of unbelief and faith without reference to temporal eras.[125]

---

124. Ibid., II.xi.8. Calvin thus appears to agree with Melanchthon that Jeremiah's point of contrast is the moral law (above), though avoiding the consequence of its abrogation by his appeal to the narrow definition of law.

125. Worth comparison is the commentary on Hebrews (from 1549), in which a similar tension exists but the contrast is more clearly qualitative: 'Yes, it is evident that they worshipped God with a sincere heart and a pure conscience, and that they walked in his commandments, and this could not have been the case except that they had been inwardly taught by the Spirit; and it is also evident, that whenever they thought of their sins, they were raised up by the assurance of a gratuitous pardon. And yet the Apostle, by referring the prophecy of Jeremiah to the coming of Christ, seems to rob them of these blessings. To this I reply, that he does not expressly deny that God formerly wrote his Law on their hearts and pardoned their sins, but he makes a comparison between the less and the greater.' But what of the example of Abraham, for 'hardly any such an example can at this day be found in the whole world'? Calvin retorts that the point of contrast is not the individuals, but the general 'economic condition'. These 'spiritual gifts' were 'accidental as it were to their age.' Thus he resorts again to the narrow use of Law: 'Hence it was not without reason that the Apostle, in comparing the Gospel with the Law, took away from the latter what is peculiar to the former. *There is yet no reason why God should not have extended the grace of the new covenant to the fathers.* This is the true solution of the question.' *Commentaries on the Epistle of Paul the Apostle to the Hebrews* (Tr. by John Owen. Grand Rapids, MI: Baker, 1998), 190-91. My emphasis.

This same tension is evident in the commentary on Jeremiah. The 'newness' does not lie in the 'substance', but the 'form' of the covenant, defined as 'first Christ, then the grace of the Holy Spirit, and the whole external way of teaching.'[126] Calvin's difficulty comes in the second as a part of the temporal contrast. So he states:

> But the coming of Christ would not have been sufficient, had not regeneration by the Holy Spirit been added. It was, then, in some respects, a new thing, that God regenerated the faithful by his Spirit, so that it became not only a doctrine as to the letter, but also efficacious, which not only strikes the ear, but penetrates into the heart, and really forms us for the service of God.[127]

Tying the law on the heart to the regenerating work of the Spirit is not unique here.[128] But as Graafland points out, how can the regenerating work of the Holy Spirit be considered in any respect temporally 'new' within Calvin's thought, or be regarded only as part of the 'form' or accidental shape of the covenant?[129]

---

126. *Jeremiah*, IV.127.

127. Ibid.

128. Esp. in his sermons on Deuteronomy: e.g., on Deut 9:15-21: 'we have as it were a figure or image, that God's once writing of his Law is not enough for us: but that we have need of a second writing of it, to the intent it may avail us, and the doctrine thereof benefit us by showing itself to be lively and of effectual force and power. And that is the thing which the Prophets mean in saying, that God will make a new covenant with his faithful ones, not as he did with their fathers in Egypt, but by writing his Law in their hearts.... And so, as oft as we come to any sermon, or read the holy Scripture: let us pray God to touch us inwardly, and to make the doctrine available which we shall have heard, so as it may not be spoken to the stones, but to such as have been foretaught by his holy spirit.' *Sermons on Deuteronomy*, 404a-b. Cf., 421b-22a (on 10:1-8); 132a-b (4:10-14); 912a (26:16-19). In all of these instances it can be argued that Calvin reads Jer 31:31f as a non-temporal contrast: it is the law without the Spirit vs. the efficacious work of the Holy Spirit (at 132a it is even the contrast of the Gospel and the Law in this sense of efficacy by the Spirit); and Calvin could not in his soteriology – and more importantly does not – deny the work of the Spirit in the lives of the Old Testament believers (as explicitly below). But in one or two of these texts there is ambiguity, which is only complicated by the non-ambiguity of the sermon on 32:44-47 (p.1175a-b). There the contrast is obviously temporal, centred on the 'full opening' of the eternal covenant.

129. 'Man fragt sich, ob dieser Unterschied zu der Form des Bundes gerechnet werden könne. Wohl ist deutlich, daß Calvin in diesem Fall am engsten an Jer 31 anknüpfen kann, weil auch im Text explizit über den Geist gesprochen wird, der im neuen Bund das Gesetz ins Herz schreiben wird. Calvin war also vom Text hier gezwungen, diesen Unterschied zu nennen.... Ist das aber wirklich gut möglich? In bezug auf Jer 31 ist das jedenfalls fragwürdig, aber auch im Rahmen von Calvins Theologie ist es nicht sofort akzeptabel. Denn aus Calvins Theologie wird deutlich, daß das Werk des

Calvin must face the same question raised by Melanchthon and Oecolampadius, and he answers it in Augustinian language:

> A question may however be here moved, Was the grace of regeneration wanting to the Fathers under the law? But this is quite preposterous... [T]he Fathers, who were formerly regenerated, obtained this favour through Christ, so that we may say, that it was as it were transferred to them from another source. The power then to penetrate into the heart was not inherent in the Law, but it was a benefit transferred to the Law from the Gospel... But still the main thing is, to consider what the Law of itself is, and what is peculiar to the Gospel... [The Law] only sets before the eyes of men what is right, and sounds it also in their ears... But the Gospel—what is it? It is spirit, that is, God not only addresses his word to the ears of men and sets it before their eyes, but he also inwardly teaches their hearts and minds. This is then the solution of the question: the Prophet speaks of the Law in itself, as apart from the Gospel, for the Law then is dead and destitute of the Spirit of regeneration.[130]

Further on he remarks that

> to write the Law in the heart imports nothing less than so to form it, that the Law should rule there, and that there should be no feeling of the heart, not conformable and not consenting to its doctrine. It is hence then sufficiently clear, that no one can be turned as to obey the Law, until he be regenerated by the Spirit of God... in a word, that the doctrine of the letter is always dead, until God vivifies it by his Spirit.[131]

The borrowing from Augustine is no less strong in these passages than is admitted in the *Institutes*, and is invoked to resolve the question of the attributes of the member of the new covenant which are clearly evidenced in the ancients. If the new covenant member is identified by the law on the heart, which is regeneration, then those who were regenerate before Christ were members of the new covenant. But Calvin has simply side-stepped the difficulty raised in identifying the law on the heart (regeneration) with the 'form' of the covenant.

Geistes zu der Substanz des Heils gehört.... Denn diese Gnade ist nichts anderes als der Bund zwischen Gott und seinem Volk selbst als eine wechselseitige Beziehung.' Cornelis Graafland, "Alter und neuer Bund: Calvins Auslegung von Jeremia 31,31-34 und Hebräer 8,8-13," *Zwingliana* 19.2 (1993), 131. He is drawing on Calvin's reference to the covenant formula (31:33) as 'the nature of the covenant with God'.

130. *Jeremiah*, IV.130-31.

131. Ibid., IV.133. Here he is close to Melanchthon's and Luther's notion of the Holy Spirit as immediately compelling obedience to the decalogue, but does not assert the necessary causality that is important for the Lutheran approach. Instead he draws the conclusion of the need for the Holy Spirit for a life lived according to the Law, showing he is here drawing on Augustine rather than Melanchthon or Luther.

Further, as in the *Institutes*, Calvin adds a temporal contrast based on clarity, reverting to the 'improper' use of 'Law' and 'Gospel' as successive realities in redemptive history. This is immediately evident:

> Here is mentioned another difference between the old and the new covenant, even that God, who had obscurely manifested himself under the Law, would send forth a fuller light...[132]

The Law here must be seen as the era of the Old Testament with its (dim) promises. The conclusion to the text reveals the tension of both the salvific and the temporal readings pressing unresolved on Calvin:

> I answer... that the Law was not destitute of those benefits which we at this day receive under the Gospel, but that these benefits were then, as it were, adventitious, and that they do not properly belong to the Law... If Moses be regarded, not as opposed to Christ, he was the herald and witness of God's paternal kindness towards his people; his doctrine also contained promises of a free salvation, and opened to the faithful the door of access to God. But if Moses be set in opposition to Christ, he becomes the minister of death, and his doctrine leads to destruction; for the letter, as Paul in 2 Cor. iii.6, calls it, killeth... It then follows that nothing remains in Moses when considered in himself. But God promised salvation to his ancient people, and also regenerated his chosen, and illuminated them by his Spirit.

Such a statement is in line with Augustine's suggestion of the point of contrast: the Law by itself without grace as the 'old covenant'. But the next sentence reverts once more to the contrast with law 'broadly' understood:

> This he did not do so freely and extensively as now. As then God's grace is at this day more abundant, it is justly extolled in high terms by all the Prophets; and then, as I have already said, whatever God at that time conferred, was, as it were, adventitious, for all these benefits were dependant on Christ and the promulgation of the Gospel.[133]

It appears that Calvin, having moved far from his early and easy assertions of 1532, continues to wrestle with the question of unity and diversity with respect to the 'new covenant'. On the one hand we see a clear exposition of Augustine's reading of Jer 31:31-34, but on the other hand we find that exposition

---

132. Ibid., IV.134. Or, '[The prophet] shows to us the superior brightness of the gospel light, as God, under the Law, did not so perfectly teach his people as he does us at this day (IV.135).' 'Though, then, many are now ignorant among the children of God, and among those who are really of the number of the faithful, yet if we consider how great was the obscurity of the Law, those who are at this day the least among the disciples, are not otherwise than prophets and teachers (IV.137).' Cp. Bullinger, above.

133. Ibid., IV.141.

placed directly alongside a contrast of the two religio-historical eras of 'Old Testament' and 'New'. A number of commentators have noted this tension in Calvin's work.[134] It is as though Calvin sits with (at least metaphorically) Augustine open on one side of the desk and Bullinger on the other. The necessary equivocations, however, show the incompatibility of such an approach for the exegesis of Jer 31:31-34.

5. Augustinian Remnants (b): Peter Martyr Vermigli

An unapologetic endorsement of the Augustinian 'salvific' contrast of Jer 31:31-34 comes from the Italian Reformer Peter Martyr Vermigli (1499-1562). Vermigli left his native Italy under threat of persecution for his reforming convictions in 1542, and spent the rest of his life as a teacher, variously at Strassburg, Oxford, and finally as professor of Old Testament at Zurich.[135] Vermigli had been living in the Augustinian Order prior to fleeing Italy, and was fluent in scholastic theology. Interestingly for our purposes, he claims for himself a great debt to Thomas Aquinas.[136] Recent scholarship has further shown Vermigli's debt to the reception of Augustine.[137] The two debts form a tempting

---

134. E.g. Graafland, "Alter und neuer Bund", 32 'Calvins Antwort ist mindestens merkwürdig zu nennen.' Also Lyle D. Bierma, *German Calvinism in the Confessional Age: The Covenant Theology of Caspar Olevianus* (Grand Rapids, MI: Baker, 1996), 45-47; Wolf, *Einheit des Bundes*, 47-48. It is missed, however, by David L. Puckett, *John Calvin's Exegesis of the Old Testament* (Louisville, KY: Westminster John Knox Press, 1995), 41ff. Puckett rightly states that for Calvin some in the ancient era 'were reborn of God obeyed out of faith working through love and thus belonged to the New Covenant (43)', but gives no recognition of the exegetical tension this might create with the temporality of the contrast. Lillback's resolution of the tension is interesting and perhaps useful, but cannot count for either proper exegesis of Jer 31 or of Calvin: Lillback, *Binding of God*, 158f.

135. The early biography by Josiah Simler (of 1563) is given in Peter Martyr Vermigli, *The Life, Early Letters & Eucharistic Writings of Peter Martyr* (Oxford: Sutton Courtenay Press, 1989), 22-94. More recently, see Philip McNair, *Peter Martyr in Italy: An Anatomy of Apostasy* (Oxford: Clarendon, 1967).

136. Thus Donnelly's pronouncement that Vermigli shows that 'a Protestant theology could rest on a Thomistic base.' John Patrick Donnelly, *Calvinism and Scholasticism in Vermigli's Doctrine of Man and Grace* (Leiden: E.J. Brill, 1976), 27. Donnelly's claims are nuanced helpfully by Frank James, cited below.

137. For Vermigli's debt to the *schola Augustiniana moderna*, and especially Gregory of Rimini on predestination, see Frank A. III James, *Peter Martyr Vermigli and Predestination: The Augustinian Inheritance of an Italian Reformer* (Oxford: Oxford Univ. Press, 1998). More broadly, Alfred Schindler, "Vermigli und die Kirchenväter," in *Peter Martyr Vermigli: Humanism, Republicanism, Reformation* (ed. Emidio Campi; Geneva: Librairie Droz, 2002).

invitation to see whether the influence of reading Augustine and Thomas might have trickled into his reading of Jer 31:31-34—an invitation that does not disappoint.

Vermigli's published theological work was almost entirely in the form of commentaries, following Martin Bucer's style of including the *loci* of theology at what the appropriate places throughout one's exegesis. Such an approach made it possible shortly after his death to put together a *Loci communes* by abstracting the *loci* from the commentaries. The use of such a derivative compendium is, naturally, filled with pitfalls—as one scholar states, it puts us 'twice removed from their original oral form'.[138] But the work is nonetheless a useful tool for our purposes so long as we keep this in mind, not least because of the tremendous influence of the *Loci* on the developing Reformed tradition—particularly in England. Diarmaid MacCulloch goes so far as to claim for Vermigli's *Loci communes*, with Bullinger's *Decades*: 'Between them, one might consider these two works to have been more central to the Elizabethan Church of England than all the writings of John Calvin.'[139] Christoph Strohm even puts the *Loci communes* above the *Decades* as (along with Calvin's *Institutes*) 'the most influential overview of Christian teaching in early Reformed Protestantism.'[140]

Peter Lillback rightly emphasizes Vermigli's agreement in the generalities of understanding the covenant with the Swiss Reformed, including Calvin.[141] Vermigli holds to one covenant in two parts, old and new, and 'in either covenant, the thing itself and the substance is entirely one and the same—only certain qualities vary.'[142] The variation is found chiefly in the difference

---

138. Marvin Walter Anderson, *Peter Martyr, A Reformer in Exile (1542-1562): A Chronology of Biblical Writings in England & Europe* (Nieuwkoop: B. de Graaf, 1975), 29. Of course, the second step of editing the lectures into published form was (at least generally), taken by Vermigli himself.

139. Diarmaid MacCulloch, "Peter Martyr and Thomas Cranmer," in *Peter Martyr Vermigli: Humanism, Republicanism, Reformation* (ed. Emidio Campi; Geneva: Libraririe Droz, 2002), 200.

140. Christoph Strohm, "Bullingers *Dekaden* und Calvins *Institutio*. Gemeinsamkeiten und Eigenarten," in *Calvin im Kontext der Schweizer Reformation* (ed. Peter Opitz; Zurich: Theologischer Verlag, 2003), 215.

141. Peter A. Lillback, "The Early Reformed Covenant Paradigm: Vermigli in the Context of Bullinger, Luther and Calvin," in *Peter Martyr Vermigli and the European Reformations: Semper Reformanda* (ed. Frank A. III James; Leiden: Brill, 2004).

142. Peter Martyr Vermigli, *Loci Communes D. Petri Martyris Vermilii. ex varis ipsius authoris scriptis in unum librum collecti & in quatuor Classes distributi* (London: 1583), §2.16.2. The discussion appears to be drawn in the main from (in English) *The Most fruitfull & learned Commentaries of Doctor Peter Martir Vermil [on Judges]* (Tr.

between: the Messiah as promised and the Messiah as having come; the extension of the covenant to the Gentiles; and the external aspects of the sacraments.[143] In sum, 'all things are contained more openly, plainly, and manifestly in the *novum testamentum* than in the *vetus*.'[144] Such makes possible the following statement, in line with Bullinger:

> So then they [the 'fathers'] had the fruits of those things which God promised to give in the new covenant. The only difference was touching the largeness and perspicuity.[145]

But the discussion becomes complicated as the various passages on the contrast of old and new covenant emerge. So, regarding Gal and 2 Cor 3, Vermigli asserts,

> But in these sorts of places Paul speaks of the *vetus testamentum* as it was thrust upon them by the false apostles—apart from Christ and faith. Then it is just as if you take away its soul and leave nothing but death and the punishment of the flesh.[146]

Vermigli appeals to an *ad hominem* view of the *vetus testamentum* in Paul's discussions. The similarity to Augustine's view in the *De spiritu et littera*—a text known by Vermigli—is clear.[147] And Vermigli applies the same line of thinking to Jer 31:31f (and Heb 8) while answering the objection that forgiveness of sin is reserved to the 'new covenant':

> But if you look upon the sacraments or ceremonies with respect to the work (*quoad opus*), they did not remit sins—and nor do our sacraments do

---

by John Day. London: 1564), 2:23. Perhaps importantly, these lectures—given first in Strasbourg in 1554-56—were revised by Vermigli while in Zurich, according to Anderson, *Peter Martyr*, 291, 383. Cf. also Vermigli, *In Epistolam S. Pauli Apostoli ad Romanos* (3rd ed. Basel: 1568), 11:26-27; Idem, *In Mosis Genesim. Commentarii* (Basel: 1554), ch.17.

143. Though he holds *quoad res,* there is no difference between the sacraments: Vermigli, *Loci communes*, §2.16.3. Cf. his "Treatise on the sacrament of the Eucharist," from Oxford, 1549: 'Our opponents... would have our sacraments completely distinguished from the mysteries of the ancients in many ways. We grant this too, both as to the different symbols and different times, as well as other properties. But concerning the reality (*res*) of the sacraments, which was received by the holy patriarchs, we hold it to have been the very same meat and drink as forms the substance of our sacraments.' in Vermigli, *Life*, 183.

144. *Loci communes*, §2.16.2.

145. Ibid., §2.16.5.

146. Ibid., §2.16.8.

147. He cites the *De spiritu* at, e.g., Ibid., §2.15.22.

> so. When Paul says to the Hebrews, that 'the blood of goats, bulls, and calves, could not take away sins', we do not deny it. But neither does Paul deny that the faith of the ancients, by which they saw Christ and embraced him in the sign of those sacrifices, justified and obtained the casting off of their sins. The blood of those sacrificial victims certainly did not wash away the sins of the world, but only the blood of Christ, as he himself says: This cup is the *novum testamentum* in my blood which will be shed for the remission of sins, for you and for many.[148]

Vermigli perhaps has the medieval scholastic discussions in mind here and denies the sacramental views of Thomas as well as Biel. But more relevant to our concern is that Vermigli is reading Hebrews as contrasting the sacraments *apart from Christ* and the sacraments with Christ—the latter of which is the 'new covenant' and was effective for the 'ancients'. Applied directly to Jer 31:31 he says:

> There the covenant is taken for Law as distinguished from Gospel, which is clear from his saying that he will write his laws in their hearts, and carve them in their inward parts, which does not agree with the Law at all—which only reveals sin, condemns and accuses. Nor does it give strength, but rather in a certain way it commands infinite things, and imposes a burden on us that we cannot bear. Therefore it is said there by the prophet that 'they did not remain in his *testamentum*'. So this word *foedus*, or *testamentum* is not taken there in the way now taken by us [in the preceding discussion]. As we discuss it here, it includes both Law and Gospel together. And in this respect there is no difference between the *vetus* and *novum testamentum* except what we have already said.[149]

Thus the contrast in Jeremiah is different from the contrast of accidents that he has discussed above, differentiated along the lines similar to Augustine. One can speak of the old covenant as 'both Law and Gospel,' and so designate the *era* of the Old Testament. And Vermigli takes the term this way in his earlier discussion. But this is explicitly not the way in which he reads Jer 31:31f, which contrasts the *nuda lex* and the Gospel. In other words, Jeremiah's 'new covenant' clearly has to do with a 'salvific' contrast. So the faithful of the ancient era had the law written on the hearts by the Spirit—indeed, this was necessary for faith; and they had the knowledge of God and forgiveness of sins.[150] The only

---

148. Ibid., §2.16.10.
149. Ibid., §2.16.11.
150. Ibid., §2.16.5. He also unapologetically claims full possession of the spirit of Christ for the faithful in the ancient era (even if it was mitigated for some by their own weakness): Ibid., §2.16.25.

potential difference between the eras is the accidental qualities of these things; and Vermigli claims that this difference is not at stake in Jer 31:31f.

Vermigli is in Zurich, however. So perhaps with some political acumen, he states that if one reads Jeremiah as a contrast of eras—holding both law and Gospel in each part—then the general structure of the earlier discussion is applicable:

> But if you prefer to understand the prophet there using this word *testamentum* as we ouselves now speak of it, we will concede that some things are abrogated through the coming of Christ—when those accidents, conditions, and qualities which we pointed out to have existed in the *vetus testamentum* have been abrogated. Then it is said by the figure of a synecdoche, by which something is said simply to be antiquated or abolished, when it is only removed to some extent.[151]

But this appears to be a covering comment, his own view of the passage being given above. For Vermigli the contrast in Jer 31:31-34 is the salvific one between the law apart from Christ, and the Gospel. Whatever differences in *accidentalia* exist between the two eras, they are not addressed by Jeremiah's promise of a new covenant. In this he is very clearly in the line of Augustine, who never denied differences between the eras or the use of *vetus* and *novum testamentum* to talk about those eras. But this is something other than what is being said in Jer 31:31-34.

6. Conclusions

The boundaries of the Reformed tradition, forged in controversy with the Anabaptists, formed around a unity to the people of God in terms of God's one single redemptive act in Christ, applicable to all the faithful of any era. But the contrast of covenants in Jer 31:31-34 then becomes a point of tension: if nothing in the new covenant can rightly be denied to the 'fathers', then what is contrasted? Bullinger appealed to the *accidentalia* of the covenant, and the change of sacraments or ceremonies in particular. What continues is the essence, so what is contrasted in Jer 31 can be nothing other than the accidents. Such an approach becomes common, but with variations. Oecolampadius, for instance, stated the contrast in terms of a movement from a complex era, in which existed both the (eternal) covenant of grace and the Mosaic (external) covenant, to a simple era of the covenant of grace promulgated alone.

A reading more faithful to Augustine's 'salvific' contrast can be found in Philip Melanchthon, and in particular his 1521 edition of the *Loci communes*. For Melanchthon the contrast of Jer 31:31-34 was a part of the contrast between

---

151. Ibid., §2.16.11. Such a line of argument was already presented in §2.16.5.

the *nuda lex*, which cannot save, and the Gospel. And so all who by the gift of the Spirit are made partakers of the Gospel are then moving from the 'law' to 'grace,' and so from the old to the new covenant. Melanchthon combines this with various other designations of the temporal nature of the promises (akin to Oecolampadius in certain regards), but puts forward a statement generally consistent with (and explicitly related to) Augustine's reading. We see the same in the *Loci communes* of Peter Martyr Vermigli, who was able to circumvent the contrast by appeal to the Augustinian view of an absolute or salvific contrast. The view was entertained by Calvin as well: Jer 31:31-34 as a contrast of the *nuda lex* and the work of the Spirit. But Calvin is a prime example of the ambivalence in the Reformed tradition on this matter. In certain points—namely, those concerning the place of Old Testament believers—he appeals to the Augustinian contrast for Jeremiah's new covenant. But in other points he is happy to read Jer 31 as a contrast of *qualitas* between two eras.

At the least, we can draw the conclusion that there is no single 'Reformed' reading of Jer 31:31-34 even if there are set boundaries within which those readings take place. Whether one can sustain a reading of simple 'accidents' being contrasted will be an important question for the inheritors of the Reformed tradition, but generally what we see is a continuation of the struggle typified in Calvin between a 'salvific' Augustinian contrast in Jer 31:31-34, and a contrast of two successive eras of God's dealings with his people.

5

17th Century Reformed: The Continued Struggle

The legacy of the early modern Reformers in reading Jeremiah's 'new covenant' was an uneasy situation between Augustine's absolute ('salvific') contrast and Jerome's contrast of two successive religio-historical eras. The boundaries of Reformed thought—above all the unity of the covenant of grace—provides a unique challenge to a religio-historical contrast in Jer 31:31-34. These challenges led to the three main models discussed above: Bullinger's contrast of accidentals, centred on the mutatio sacramentorum, Oecolampadius' movement from a complex to a simple era, and Vermigli's assertion of a salvific contrast (abandoning the religio-historical contrast for reading Jer 31:31-34). Calvin provides the best explanation of Augustine's own position, but reveals the equivocating necessary if one is to live with both a salvific and religio-historical contrast within Reformed thought.

In this chapter I will push further into the Reformed tradition to look at the fate of the Augustinian reading in the later development of Reformed orthodoxy.[1] This is a period of theological history that has witnessed a large amount of interest regarding its relation to the earlier Reformers. We have a number of important developments that occur—the most significant for our purposes will be the (almost) ubiquitous language of the 'covenant of grace' as the chief theological construction for explaining the doctrine of salvation. This language is found in Calvin, Bullinger, and Oecolampadius and as the so-called 'Muller thesis' holds, the difference of form does not appear a difference of substance.[2]

---

1. Following Muller, I use the term 'Reformed orthodox' to indicate 'an individual or a theology that stands within the confessional framework of the Reformed churches and which is understood as conveying the "right teaching" of those churches, whether scholastic, catechetical, exegetical, or homiletical, as determined by the standards of the era. "Orthodoxy," in other words, functions as a historical denominator—and reference to the era of orthodoxy indicates the time of the institutionalization of the Reformation according to its confessional norms'. Richard A. Muller, *Post-Reformation Reformed Dogmatics* (4 vols.; Grand Rapids, MI: Baker, 2003), 1.30.

2. Martin I. Klauber, "Continuity and Discontinuity in Post-Reformation Reformed Theology: An Evaluation of the Muller Thesis," *JETS* 33.4 (1990).

But the move towards rigidity in codifying the tradition is not without its points of interest: matters of ambiguity or ambivalence can often become more pronounced. And such is the case here. The tradition continues to represent the struggle and tensions of the earlier Reformed writers. But we find the tensions even more pronounced and sometimes more inexplicable in their contradictions.

I have chosen only three representative heads from this period, each a significant figure in Reformed orthodoxy and each a showcase for the continued wrestling with an Augustinian approach. The purpose of the chapter is to establish that the interpretation of Jeremiah's 'new covenant' remained a prominent theological topic and to show some of the issues that will continue (in altered form) even through the 20th century. So though I will supplement the three representative figures with certain coordinating views and offer some comments on the wider sense of this struggle, a full examination of the developments and interpretations within Reformed orthodoxy in its historical context is beyond the scope of the present work. For the present work, the general contours of these various sides of the tradition are sufficient.

The three figures of this chapter cut across the three main centres of Reformed thought as it develops: the German Reformed centred in Heidelberg (Caspar Olevianus), the British Reformed centred in the theology of the Westminster Assembly documents (John Ball), and the Dutch Reformed of the mid- to late-17th century (Herman Witsius). In each case and stretching across the continental Reformed tradition, we find the struggle for (and difficulty of) a theologically and exegetically appropriate reading of Jeremiah's new covenant.

1. *Caspar Olevianus*

One of the strongest statements of an Augustinian theology leading to a contrast of 'accidents' in Jeremiah's new covenant lies in the work of the German Reformed theologian Caspar Olevianus (1537-87). As far as is known, Olevianus came into the Protestant tradition while studying law at Orleans in 1552.[3] He was quickly brought into the centre of the Reformed discussions in 1558 when, after a brief visit to Zurich where he met with Bullinger and Vermigli (with whom he would continue to correspond), he began theological studies at the newly-formed Genevan Academy. Olevianus arrived in Heidelberg in 1561 after a tumultuous time in his hometown of Trier. He would remain in Heidelberg with his colleague Zacharius Ursinus (where they produced one of

---

3. See R. Scott Clark, *Caspar Olevianus and the Substance of the Covenant: The Double Benefit of Christ* (Rutherford Studies in Historical Theology; Edinburgh: Rutherford House, 2005), 9-38.

the classics of Reformed orthodoxy in the Heidelberg Catechism)[4] until the banishment of the 'Calvinists' in 1576. He spent his remaining years—the most productive for publishing—in the Wetterau counties just to the North, chiefly in Herborn. Olevianus' theological world was, thus, deeply informed by just those figures so far discussed: Melanchthon, Bullinger, Calvin, and Vermigli.

The most noticeable aspect of Olevianus' theology, in contradistinction to his mentors, is the more explicitly covenantal shape of the whole of his thought. Olevianus casts his Christology, and even more blatantly his soteriology (both justification and sanctification), in terms of 'covenant'.[5] This is done in his 1585 *De substantia foederis gratuiti* by opening with a citation of Jer 31:31-34.[6] After which, as Strehle remarks, 'much of the ensuing discussion becomes either an exegesis or paraphrase of this one central pericope.'[7] Olevianus follows what was the already-common distinction of the covenant into its substance and accidents and explicitly links Jer 31:31-34 (the new covenant) with the substance, and so with the elect:

> This covenant [of 31:33-34] is such that truly promises to us knowledge of God, which also includes the gracious forgiveness of sins in Christ, as well as the renewal of man to the image of God.... Yet we accept the covenant as two-fold: first with respect to the substance of the covenant or with respect to the thing itself by God's promises; or with respect to its administration in the visible church. It is taken in the former meaning by the place already cited from Jeremiah. And it is peculiar to the elect.[8]

The text of Jeremiah encapsulates the central parts of the substance of the covenant: God as the author, the elect for whom the covenant is promised,[9] the kind

---

4. Though Olevianus' role has been challenged, see the cogent discussion in Lyle D. Bierma, "Olevianus and the Authorship of the Heidelberg Catechism: Another Look," *The Sixteenth Century Journal* 13.4 (1982).

5. See the excellent work of R. Scott Clark, *Olevianus*, 104-209.

6. Caspar Olevianus, *De substantia foederis gratuiti inter deum et electos, itemque De mediis, quibus ea ipsa substantia nobis communicatur* (Geneva: 1585), §I.1.i. Mark Karlberg refers to this treatise as 'Perhaps the most important and influential treatise on the covenant to appear in the sixteenth century' (though he offers neither explanation nor defence of the statement). Karlberg, "Reformed Interpretation," 19.

7. Strehle, *Calvinism*, 170.

8. Olevianus, *De subst. foed*, §I.1.i-ii.

9. 'These are all whom God decreed of grace to adopt from among the multitude of the condemned.' Ibid., §I.1.ix.

of covenant,[10] the end to which it is promised,[11] and 'both of the essential parts of the covenant promised by God.'[12] Olevianus summarizes his own point—still with reference to Jer 31:33-34:

> The whole of the gracious substance of the covenant is: [1] with respect to God, he properly strikes the covenant with us when he seals the promise of gracious reconciliation offered in the gospel in our hearts by the Holy Spirit, and begins the renewal unto eternal life... [2] With respect to us who were dead in sin the covenant is received while by grace the Holy Spirit is given to us, by whom one is aroused from death into life, that we might not only desire and be able to believe the gracious promise of reconciliation through Christ and the renewal of ourselves so that we might approach the inheritance of the kingdom of heaven, but also that we might believe or grasp faith itself.[13]

In short, Jer 31:33-34 outlines the whole of the substance of the covenant.[14] This is the same approach already taken in his 1576 exposition of the Apostle's Creed, which was already given an English translation by 1581 (showing some of the significance of this theologian). The 'new covenant' in Jeremiah is that covenant which 'the Lord has made with us through faith in Christ.'[15] Indeed, every part of the new covenant promise is listed in this context:

> ...God says that this whole covenant is free and undeserved, and that it consists in the knowledge of him, or rather by faith: and through which

---

10. 'he promises a covenant of the kind whose whole essence (*uniuersa essentia*) depends upon him, and is established by him in Christ.' Ibid., §I.1.x.

11. 'The end... is twofold: one, in order that all glory of our salvation might return to him alone... The other end is the firm and eternal peace of our consciences.' Ibid., §I.1.xii.

12. Ibid., §I.1.iii.

13. Ibid., §I.1.xiii.

14. And so it is used throughout, e.g.: 'The promised knowledge of God (Jer 31) is of this kind, by which also I might be certain of the gracious remission of sins, and by which the image of God might be renewed in us.' Ibid., §I.1.xiv. '[This] faith is promised in the new covenant, when it says, I will give knowledge of me into their midst, Jer 31.' Ibid., §I.9.i. 'I believe in the divine mind all sins, even of the entire catholic church, have been remitted according to the promise of the covenant: their sins I will remember no more, Jer 31.' Ibid., §I.1.x.

15. Caspar Olevianus, *An Exposition of the Symbole of the Apostles, or rather of the Articles of Faith. In which the chiefe points of the everlasting and free covenant betweene God and the faithfull is briefly and plainly handled* (Tr. by John Fielde. London: 1581), 53. He also cites Isa 53:54 and Hos 2.

after he has abolished the remembrance of our sins, he will renew our hearts—which he called 'writing his laws in our hearts'.[16]

Such a line of interpretation leaves the door wide open for an Augustinian view of the contrast—indeed, it is hard to see what else one can do with it.

Olevianus furnishes even further reason for seeing an Augustinian view. The graces of this covenant (whose substance is in Jer 31:33-34) cannot be reserved for only that era after Christ: 'the same favour of justification in Christ is common to all under the old and new testament.'[17] As he makes clear regarding forgiveness of sins and over against the doctrine of the *limbus patrum*:

> Now the beginning of the error concerning Limbus, is that many thought and yet do think, that sins were not forgiven before Christ suffered. But the passion of Christ had its effect and power from everlasting. For Christ yesterday and today, is for ever and the same world without end. Hebr. 13.18. And Paul to the Romans, ch.4, defines justification by David: Blessed are they whose iniquities are forgiven. Therefore in the time of David, before Christ had suffered, sins were forgiven by confidence and trust in that sacrifice of Christ to come. And in the same Chapter he says, that we obtain happiness and remission of sins by no other means, than whereby Abraham obtained it who is the father of all believers.[18]

Jeremiah's oracle teaches the two-fold benefit of the work of Christ: ingrafting into Christ by the Spirit (justification), and the testimony of that ingrafting by the Spirit's working of a 'new obedience'—neither of which are denied to the ancient era.[19]

---

16. Ibid., 55. Translations are slightly updated.
17. Ibid., 240.
18. Ibid., 169.
19. Ibid., 244-45. Olevianus does not deny this work of the Holy Spirit to the believers in the ancient era: e.g., Caspar Olevianus, *A Firm Foundation: An Aid to Interpreting the Heidelberg Catechism* (Tr. by Lyle D. Bierma. Grand Rapids, MI: Baker, 1995), q.129 (original publ., 1567): 'Is it absolutely necessary, then, that we have the Holy Spirit? A: Yes, unless we should want to do without all the fruits mentioned above. For there is no other means whereby we can share in Christ and all his benefits than the Holy Spirit, who incorporates us into Christ. As it says in Romans 8[:9], "Whoever does not have the Spirit of Christ, he is not his."... Thus we can understand how necessary it is for each person to have the Holy Spirit.' With q.135, A: 'just as there is only one Head of the Church, Christ, so also all believers from Adam to the end of the world are His members and one body through the Holy Spirit.' Thus Schrenk: 'Aber Olevianus sagt diese Gliedschaft nicht nur von den Gläubigen des Neuen Testaments aus. Weil Christus von Anfang an der einzige Weg des Heiles war, schon im Alten Bunde, sind auch alle,

Yet further, Olevianus characterises the 'old' covenant of 31:31 as a 'legal pact' entirely unlike the one God makes with his adopted children. Those living under that old covenant were twice condemned: by the order of creation and by this old *pactum*, which demanded perfect obedience from their own strength. But God makes with his true children the free and gracious covenant as found in Jer 31:33-34.[20]

In all of these ways Olevianus seems akin to an Augustinian reading: the new covenant as simply the experience or membership in a faithful state before God. But then, and somewhat startlingly, Olevianus turns to explain the contrast of the text as a change of accidents, citing Jer 31:31-34 and declaring:

> Yet the position of participation (*communionis*) is not a change in anything whatsoever in the substance of the covenant, but makes a distinction in the *qualitas* or *claritas* of revelation on the part of God and in turn of the knowledge in us... and further in the *quantitas* or fullness of the Spirit.[21]

This latter is then applied directly to the sacraments under the new testament (*sub nouo testamento*) as the means by which the Spirit increasingly confirms our ingrafting into Christ, our regeneration, adoption, and our fellowship with Christ.[22] The implication is that these sacraments do this work of confirming more effectually. So while Jeremiah's new covenant is explicitly about 'substance' in one place, it becomes explicitly about 'accidents' in another.

Bierma attempts to mitigate the difficulty of Olevianus' discussion on the subject by maintaining that the old era had both the covenant of grace and this legal covenant: but '[a]fter Christ, the covenant of grace and its covenanters move forward unfettered by the covenant of law.'[23] Such would place Olevianus

---

welche je seit Adam geglaubt haben, Glieder Christi durch den Heiligen Geist.' Schrenk, *Gottesreich und Bund*, 62.

20. *De subst. foed*, §I.1.ix.

21. Ibid., §I.9.xvi. Cp. Ursinus: '[Unity of the testaments is found] In the promise of grace concerning the remission of sins, and eternal life granted freely to such as believe by and for the sake of Christ, which promise was common to those who lived under the old covenant, as well as to us; although it is now delivered more clearly... [The two testaments differ] In the gifts which they confer: In the old, the effusion of the Holy Spirit was small and limited; in the new it is large and full. "I will make a new covenant."' Zacharius Ursinus, *Commentary of Dr. Zacharius Ursinus on the Heidelberg Catechism* (Tr. by G.W. Williard. Cincinnati, OH: 1852), 99-100.

22. *De subst. foed*, §I.9.xvii; §II.41.

23. Bierma, *German Calvinism*, 136. Bierma is drawing mainly on the commentaries.

close to Oecolampadius and the movement from a complex era (legal covenant and covenant of grace) to a simple era. The faithful in the ancient era were saved only in the covenant of grace, while the other existed to drive them to the first: the law was given to drive to the promise.[24] The attraction of this solution for theologians may be clear enough. But unless we limit the 'old covenant' to the ceremonial and cultic laws—which Olevianus does not seem to allow—I am unsure exactly what distinction exists between the eras here, for the use of the law as driving to Christ still exists for Olevianus in the new era.[25] Such a limiting would also face rather significant exegetical challenges, at the least. Or from the other side and similar to Melanchthon's question: are we going to say that the ancient believers were somehow *not* freed from the covenant of law? But this would be difficult to state given the exclusive natures of the two covenants. If Bierma is right, then Olevianus leaves us with at best a rather tenuous reading of Jer 31:31-34.

Olevianus is important for showing how the positive elements of the new covenant of Jer 31:33-34 cannot be called *accidentalia* of the covenant. He explains at length how the promises of Jer 31:33-34 form the 'substance' and 'essence' of the covenant of grace. But then we are in an odd position of the new covenant describing the *substantia*, but the contrast regarding the *dispensatio*. What is 'new' is not what is described as the new covenant, but the way in which such is given (e.g. quality, clarity, and quantity)—appealing to something *not said* (like Oecolampadius or Bullinger) to discover the 'newness'. The logic of this solution in all of its various forms is clear: (1) the point of contrast is with the state of affairs instituted at Sinai; (2) that state of affairs had, for the faithful, all the benefits described as the 'new covenant'; (3) therefore the contrast can only be accidental.[26] But standing on what is not said for the point of 'new-

---

24. This is closer to the view developed by the Scottish Reformed theologian Robert Rollock: 'The name of the *vetus testamentum* extends widely to the law or covenant of works together with the covenant of grace when joined to the law. The apostle to the Hebrews shows the name of *vetus testamentum* so accepted, Heb 8:8-9.' Robert Rollock, *Quaestiones et responsiones aliquot de foedere Dei* (Edinburgh: 1596), B5b-6a. Or, '*Q: Whether the covenant of grace was also struck with the church and people of old?* R: It was: though its mention was obscure in the teaching of the covenant of works and law.' Ibid., A6a. Or elsewhere, 'The name of the old covenant, not the legal covenant alone, whose condition contains legal works, nor grace alone, which was shown darkly with the legal covenant; in truth, by the name of the old covenant I understand both legal and gracious; legal of which express mention is made, gracious of which is not except for obscurely heeded in the old Scriptures.' Robert Rollock, *Analysis Logica in Epistolam ad Hebraeos* (Edinburgh: 1605), 105. See below on the 17th c. Reformed.

25. Olevianus, *De subst. foed*, §II.6-7.

26. Already seen in this shape in Bucer's 1535 dialogue between Synnprecht

ness'—a recurring problem we will face through the modern period—is by its nature unconvincing.

2. *John Ball*

So from Heidelberg and the tension given direct shape by Olevianus, we step to Westminster and the British Reformed, one generation further on. And here we have another opportunity to see Jeremiah's new covenant at the heart of yet another theological dispute, this time in the early-mid 17th century dispute over the nature of the Mosaic covenant. That the 'covenant' was a (though not *the*) central uniting theme for the British Reformed has been affirmed by a number of studies and is clear in even a cursory look at the texts.[27] The general shape of this covenant theology followed the two-fold division already seen in this discussion: the *foedus operum* and *foedus gratiae*. The roots of this system have been the source of much inquiry, though only rarely is the close connection of these terms to the (far) older discussion of Law/Gospel or

---

and Friedlieb (the latter, clearly being the 'correct' view): 'Synnprecht: Der Herr verhaißt als ain besondere aigenschaft des newen Testaments, das er wölle yetz sein gesatz in die hertzen schreiben. Fridlieb: Diß hatt er im newen Testament etwas reichlicher thün woolen dann bei den alten. Er hatt aber solche gnaden allen erwöleten im alten Testament auch gethon. Dann schlecht die allweg Got ain grewel gewesen seind, die Gottes wort nicht in der warhait geglaubet und in von hertzen gliebet haben. Das volck Gotes seind ye und ye allain die gläubigen gewesen. "On den glauben mag Gott nyeman gefallen" [Heb. 11,6]. Den glauben aber hatt der Herr nach der erhöhung Christi ettwas reicher und dann auch allen völckeren gegeben und derhalb hat er auch seine gläubigen nit mehr mit so vilen eüsserun gebreüchen üben und treiben wöllen.' Martin Bucer, *Dialogi oder Gespreech von der gemainsame und den Kirchenübungen der Christen und was yeder Oberkait von ampts wegen auß Göttlichen befelch an denselbigen züversehen und zü besserteb gebüre* (Martin Bucers Deutsche Schriften 6.2; Gütersloh: Verlagshaus Gerd Mohn, 1984).

27. 'There is good reason to view the development of English theology – from Lambeth and the Irish Articles through the thought of Ussher, Downham, Ball, Leigh and their contemporaries, to the Westminster Standards – as a cohesive movement in Reformed theology. The central issues confronting the Reformed in this movement – divine sovereignty and human responsibility and the doctrinal *loci* of Scripture, predestination, covenant and the Person of the Mediator – were drawn together into a confessionally defined orthodoxy.' Richard A. Muller, "Reformed Confessions and Catechisms," in *Dictionary of Historical Theology* (ed. Trevor A. Hart; Grand Rapids, MI: Wm. B. Eerdmans, 2000), 482b. Or David Mullan's comments on Scottish theology: 'In evaluating the [Scottish] religious thought of the period 1600-40 the most obvious feature, along with the Augustinian-Calvinist view of grace, is the notion of the religio-political covenant.' David George Mullan, *Scottish Puritanism 1590-1638* (Oxford: Oxford Univ. Press, 2000), 171.

vetus/nova lex considered.[28] So while the construct of the two covenants may be new, and may develop with new formulations and in various directions, at least some part of the discussion ties the roots to language of the role of Law/Gospel (whether in a Lutheran or Reformed sense).[29]

The two-covenant construct begins to impact readings of Jer 31:31-34 by virtue of the near universal assumption (which I will suggest is mistaken) that the 'new covenant' in Jer 31 stands in contrast to the 'Mosaic covenant.' Yet no unanimity existed in English Reformed thought for how the Mosaic covenant was to be understood. Anthony Burgess, a representative at the Westminster Assembly, reported four main options:

> In expressing this [Mosaic] Covenant there is difference among the Learned: some make the Law a Covenant of works, and upon that ground that it is abrogated: others call it a subservient covenant to the covenant of grace, and make it only occasionally, as it were, introduced, to put more luster and splendour upon grace: Others call it a mixed covenant of works and grace; but that is hardly to be understood as possible, much less as true. I therefore think that opinion true... that the Law given by Moses was a Covenant of grace.[30]

---

28. Most conspicuous in this regard is David A. Weir, *The Origins of the Federal Theology in Sixteenth-Century Reformation Thought* (Oxford: Clarendon Press, 1990). Better (though still with only passing prominence) are Robert Letham, "The Foedus Operum: Some Factors Accounting for Its Development," *Sixteenth Century Journal* 14.4 (1983); Michael McGiffert, "Grace and Works: The Rise and Division of Covenant Divinity in Elizabethan Puritanism," *HTR* 75.4 (1982); Idem, "From Moses to Adam: The Making of the Covenant of Works," *Sixteenth Century Journal* 19.2 (1988).

29. See, e.g., William Pemble: 'By the Covenant of Grace we understand in one word, the Gospel.... By the Covenant of Works, we understand that we call in one word the Law.' *Vindiciae Fidei, or A Treatise of Justification by Faith* (Oxford: 1625), 136. This connection is already present in Dudley Fenner: 'The covenant made with the Jews is a covenant of works, which God stipulates to the Jews to maintain themselves as a possession [*peculium*: Ex 19:5] among all the people, if they continue in all the things which are written in the book of the law.' *Sacra Theologia, sive Veritas quae est secundum Pietatem* (n.a.: 1585), VIII.282. Also William Perkins (latin publ. 1590): 'the Decalogue, or Ten Commandments, is an abridgment of the whole law and the covenant of works.' *A Golden Chaine* (Cambridge: 1591), §19. Cp. the language of *pactum legis* and *Evangelii testamentum* in Paul Alvarez (above, p.31).

30. Anthony Burgess, *Vindiciae Legis: or, A Vindication of the Morall Law and the Covenants* (London: 1646), 213. Cf. Samuel Bolton, *The True Bounds of Christian Freedom* (Carlisle, PA: Banner of Truth, 1964), 93-94. Orig. publ., 1645. The discussion of Calamy seems to desire a further option, in which the Mosaic covenant is *neither* the covenant of works or of grace, but rather a confirmation given for those who

The 'mixed covenant' is seen in the work of Robert Rollock, hinted at above in Bierma's discussion of Olevianus. This was a view in the line of Oecolampadius. And a notion of a 'subservient covenant' refers to the work of John Cameron—the influential Scottish theologian at Saumur, who first delivered and published his main theses on the covenant in Heidelberg while Olevianus was still present.[31] The option of the Mosaic covenant as solely a covenant of works is often thought to be represented by the 'Antinomians' such as John Saltmarsh or Topias Crisp, though John Preston would be a more orthodox (if less consistent) illustration, and one more potentially convergent with the Augustinian line.[32]

---

are already in the covenant of grace. Edmund Calamy, *Two Solemne Covenants Made between God and Man* (London: 1646). Discussions of this topic are less than outstanding. The best work with sympathies towards the majority Reformed position is Ernest F. Kevan, *The Grace of Law: A Study of Puritan Theology* (Grand Rapids, MI: Baker, 1976). For more sympathy toward the 'Antinomian' party, see J. Wayne Baker, "Sola Fide, Sola Gratia: The Battle for Luther in Seventeenth-Century England," *The Sixteenth Century Journal* 16.1 (1985); Tim Cooper, "The Antinomians Redeemed: Removing Some of the "Radical" from Mid-Seventeenth-Century English Religion," *JRH* 24.3 (2000); M. W. Karlberg, "The Mosaic Covenant and the Concept of Works in Reformed Hermeneutics: A Historical-Critical Analysis with Particular Attention to Early Covenant Eschatology" (Ph.D, Westminster Theological Seminary, 1980). The last is, unfortunately, significantly flawed in its largely unargued insistence to delimit the 'true' or 'pure' Reformed line around a particular view of the 'Mosaic covenant' (defined by the author).

31. See Rollock, *De foedere*; John Cameron, "De triplici Dei cum homine foedere theses," in *Ioannis Cameronis Scoto-Britanni Theologi Examii TA ΣΩZOMENA siue Opera Partim ab auctore ipse edita* (Geneva: 1642). Thus Cameron: 'Therefore we say the covenant is partly of nature, partly of grace, partly subservient to the covenant of grace (which in Scripture is called the 'old covenant') (§7).' More fully: 'The old covenant, or subservient covenant, we call that which God entered with the Israelite people on Mt. Sinai, to their preparing unto faith, and to the inflaming of their longing for the promise, and the evangelical covenant (which otherwise languished in their souls); and at the same time as if having applied a harness for repressing wickedness, right until that time they would be released by the Spirit of adoption in their hearts, and until they would be governed by the law of liberty (§42).'

32. Preston's discussion makes much of the absolute contrast of the old/new covenant as law/gospel in his posthumously published sermons: John Preston, *The New Covenant, or The Saints Portion* (London: 1629), II.71ff. Thus his exhortation to his hearers to move from one covenant to the other—e.g., his *The Law Out-Lawed or, The Charter of the Gospel shewing the priviledge and prerogative of the Saints by vertue of the Covenant* (Edinburgh: 1631), 2f. But he also treats Jer 31:31-34 as a qualitative difference of the same covenant: *New Covenant*, 82-83. Again, how these can both be true is unclear.

But the dominant line, which Burgess endorses, saw the Mosaic covenant as a covenant of grace. A number of treatises along these lines emerged in this period—most prominently by Burgess, Samuel Rutherford, William Strong, Thomas Blake, John Ball and George Gillespie.[33] Of these authors, only Ball (d.1640) and Blake were not members of the Westminster Assembly, which began its meetings in 1643. And by this time the ethos of Reformed thought in its British context had shifted from the almost fully dominant Calvinist structures to a Puritan movement of outsiders (non-conformity becoming a mark of the 'truly' Reformed) fighting a strong Arminian rise associated with the rise of Archbishop Laud.[34] With the return of Charles II to the throne, this outsider status would become even more acute. These treatises should not, then, be considered simply abstract theological works but a part of the theological crisis that was felt by the increasingly marginal Reformed orthodox in Britain.

By far the most influential treatise in this group was Ball's *Treatise of the Covenant of Grace*, published posthumously in 1645. Ball's reputation had already been established through his earlier (pre-1617) treatise on the structure of theology – a structure that is carried over in large part to the Westminster Standards.[35] Ball's prominence is stated well by Muller:

> [Ball was] one of the theologians most influential in the development of English Reformed theology in the transition from the early orthodox position of Perkins… to the full development of Puritan and Presbyterian theology in the Westminster Standards.[36]

---

33. Burgess, *Vindiciae Legis*; Samuel Rutherford, *The Covenant of Life Opened: or, a Treatise of the Covenant of Grace* (Edinburgh: 1654); William Strong, *A Discourse of the Two Covenants: wherein the Nature, Differences, and Effects of the Covenant of Works and of Grace are distinctly, rationally, spiritually and practically discussed; together with a considerable quantity of Practical Cases dependent thereon* (London: 1678); Thomas Blake, *Vindiciae Foederis: or, A Treatise of the Covenant of God entered with Man-Kinde, in the several Kindes and Degrees of it* (2nd ed. London: 1658); John Ball, *A Treatise of the Covenant of Grace wherein The graduall breakings out of Gospel grace from Adam to Christ are clearly discovered* (London: 1645). And the two-part work by George Gillespie, *The Ark of the Testament Opened* (London: 1661); *The Ark of the Covenant Opened* (London: 1677).

34. See Nicholas Tyacke, *Aspects of English Protestantism c.1530-1700* (Manchester: Manchester Univ. Press, 2001), 132-75.

35. John Ball, *A Short Treatise: Containing all the principall grounds of Christian Religion* (London: 1617). This edition is the 'second impression'; I have been unable to find the first. Richard Muller ("Reformed Confessions," 483a) mistakenly cites for the treatise the date of 1629, by which time it had gone through seven editions.

36. Ibid., 482b-3a. Ball has also been called 'perhaps the most important

Ball received his B.A. from Oxford in 1604 – incidentally the same year that William Laud took his B.A. from the same university. It was the start of much ferment at the institution between the Calvinist majority and the movement away from that majority coming from the increasing patronage of non-Reformed figures like Laud.[37]

Ball's treatise traces the history of the covenant of grace through its development as presented in Scripture—a similar approach to the later work of the Dutch theologian Johannes Cocceius. But Ball's conclusions are emphatically not those of Cocceius (below). Ball maintains the view of the Mosaic covenant as a covenant of grace—and hence the contrast of Jer 31:31-34 to be one of accidents—but he is clearly puzzled by the discussions surrounding this point. His summary is worth citing in full as a perfect statement of the struggle and confusion on the subject:

> Most Divines hold the old and new Covenant to be one in substance and kind, to differ only in degrees: but in setting down the differences they speak so obscurely, that it is hard to find how they consent with themselves. For most commonly they distinguish them thus: The old Testament promises life to them that obey the Law, and condemns all not perfectly conformable: the new doth freely pardon sins, and give Salvation to them that believe in Christ. The old was written by the finger of God in tablets of stone: the new by the Spirit of God in the fleshy tables of the heart. The old was the ministry of death, a killing letter: the new the ministry of the quickening Spirit. The old did lay upon the necks of the Fathers an intolerable yoke of rites and commandments: the new doth impose the easy yoke of the Spirit, enduing us with the Spirit of Adoption and liberty of the Sons of God. The old doth involve the Doctrine of the Grace of the Messiah under the shadows of types and rites: the new doth contain the fulfilling of the types and figures. Moses is the typical mediator of the Old Testament: Christ is the true Mediator of the New... The old was imperfect, intolerable, weak, and therefore to be abolished: the new perfect, easy, and to continue forever, etc.[38]

---

ecclesiological scholar of his generation', but that would take us to another aspect of his work. Tom Webster, *Godly Clergy in Early Stuart England: the Caroline Puritan Movement c.1620-1643* (Cambridge: Cambridge Univ. Press, 1997), 25. Cf. p.301ff for discussion of Ball and the ecclesiological disputes.

    37. C.M. Dent, *Protestant Reformers in Elizabethan Oxford* (Oxford Univ. Press, 1983), 221-37. The main source for details of Ball's life is Samuel Clarke, "The Lives of Thirty-two English divines," in *A General Martyrologie, containing a collection of all the greatest persecutions which have befallen the Church of Christ* (London: 1677), 147-54.

    38. Ball, *Covenant of Grace*, 95-96.

Jeremiah's New Covenant

Ball points precisely to the central difficulty in these common (Reformed orthodox) statements: 'many things herein are spoken truly, but how all these differences should stand, if they be not Covenants opposite in kind, it is not easy to understand.'[39] How can one be the ministry of life and the other of death, yet still be the same covenant? Ball's solution to this question is the distinction between the second and third uses of the law:

> [The law] was so delivered as it might serve to discover sin, drive the Jews to deny themselves and fly to the mercy of God revealed in Jesus: but it was given to be a rule of life to a people in Covenant, directing them how to walk before God in holiness and righteousness, that they might inherit the promises of grace and mercy.[40]

So the continuity of the law is established, provided its proper setting or provided a distinction between *ratio* and *telos*: it was given in such a way that 'it might serve' in its familiar second use (*ratio* or method). But its purpose (*telos*) in being given was for ordering one's life in the covenant.[41] In an important step in the discussion of the question, Ball looks at the 'broken covenant' of Jer 11, taken (rightly, I will argue) as the point of contrast to the new covenant, and asks what kind of covenant it is. He concludes unambiguously that it is one 'of grace and mercy':

> What Covenant, but of grace and mercy? even that wherein God promises to be their God, and take them to be his people, if they obey his commandments. For since the fall of Adam, the Covenant which the Lord hath entered into with all his people, was ever free and gracious: For when all men are sinners by nature, dead in trespasses, and enemies to God, how can a Covenant betwixt God and man be stricken without forgiveness of former transgressions?[42]

---

39. Ibid., 96.

40. Ibid., 102. The distinction between the law as a rule of life and as a covenant is made early: Ibid., 15. This becomes a standard way of phrasing the issue: e.g. Bolton, *True Bounds*, 28.

41. Cf. Strong, *Discourse of the Two Covenants*, 88, 90f, 109.

42. Ball, *Covenant of Grace*, 103. 'It was such a Covenant whereby the spiritual seed was made a Kingdom of Priests, a holy nation, and a peculiar treasure unto the Lord. The word *Segulla* signifies one's own proper good, which he loves, and keeps in store for himself, for his special use: a rare and exquisite treasure; a thing desired, dear and singular or proper to a man himself.' Ibid. Calamy, in spite of his disagreements with the idea of Israel entering into a covenant at Sinai (a rather eccentric idea), appears to agree nonetheless on the basic point: 'the Law at Mount Sinai was... only given to those that were in covenant as a rule of obedience... that is by the covenant of grace made with Jesus Christ and confirmed to Abraham.' Calamy, *Two Covenants*, 8.

The covenant had to be one of grace, and so the law had to be given simply as a rule of life within the covenant. Further, in language that brings us back towards Jer 31:31-34:

> the Law given by Moses is engraven in the heart of the spiritual seed, or people effectually in Covenant, as they are called a people in whose heart is the Law. No man will deny the Covenant which God keepeth with them that love him and keep his Commandments, to be the Covenant of Grace. But the Covenant which Israel entered into, is that which the Lord keeps with them that love him, and keep his Commandments.[43]

The law on the heart is the property of those 'effectually in covenant' with God, and as such was known in Israel by the faithful.

This fits Ball's earlier claim that the 'covenant of promise' (the promised covenant of grace) – of which the Old Testament believers were a part – was written on the heart, had forgiveness of sins, and the Spirit of adoption.[44] In fact, all of the benefits of reconciliation and access to the Father were known and communicated to the believers of the ancient era.[45] In short:

---

43. Ball, *Covenant of Grace*, 108. Or, 'As Adam in the state of Innocency was made able to fulfil the Covenant made with him: so is the Covenant of Grace written in the hearts of them that be heirs of the Promise in Christ.' Ibid., 24-25.

44. 'Internally the Spirit doth seal up the truth of this Covenant in the hearts of the faithful. For when the adoption and the inheritance pertained to the Fathers under the Covenant of promise, the Spirit of adoption and earnest of the inheritance pertained unto them likewise.' Ibid., 29. Cp. Rutherford: 'Abraham, David... and the Jews by faith, have remission of sins and salvation, as also the Gentiles have.' They have 'the condition [of the covenant] and perseverance therein, and a new heart, righteousness, pardon, and life.' Rutherford, *Covenant of Life*, 62.

45. '...the fruit of them [i.e. reconciliation and access to the Father, which demanded Christ's coming in the flesh] was communicated to the Fathers under the Old Testament, by force of the divine Promise, and certainty in the things to come.' Ball, *Covenant of Grace*, 28. He continues, in a way anticipating some of the debate on the Continent later in the century, but likely with an eye on the doctrine of *limbus patrum*: 'If it be objected, that the cause is before the effect, and therefore the incarnation and death of Christ must go before the communication of the fruit and benefit thereof unto the Fathers... The answer is, That in natural causes the proposition holds true, but in moral causes the effect may be before the case: and so the fruit and virtue of Christ's death was communicated to the Fathers before his Incarnation... yet the manner and reason of that Mediation was proposed more obscurely, the force and efficacy of it was less, and did redound to fewer.' Ibid.

> [T]he faithful before Christ were saved by the free mercy of God in Christ, did know God and Christ, had the spiritual promise of life eternal, and were equal to us Christians in all substantial graces of the Covenant.[46]

The content of the 'new covenant' in Jer 31:33-34, then, was known to the faithful before Christ. Rutherford is similar in speaking of Jer 31:33 to mean 'gifted with a new heart, and such as shall never be cast off, but shall persevere to the end', contrasted with the 'stiff-hearted Jews' who were God's people 'by external calling only.'[47] The contrast quite clearly appears as 'salvific'. The matter is put even more strongly by Thomas Blake:

> There is not a promise in the New covenant, whether it be for privileges, conferred upon us, or graces wrought in us, but by the help of that light, we may find in the Old covenant, the same held out.[48]

That this is fitting to the 'Augustinian' line is even more clear in Ball's explaining the the contrasts of Law and Gospel, though more likely taken from Calvin than Augustine:

> Paul proves the Law... *separated from faith*, to be the cause, not of life, but of death: as that which did not only want Christ, who is the soul of the Law, but is opposite to him. And therefore Paul doth this, because the Jews, (faith being let pass) did seek righteousness in the dead works of the Law, and did oppose the Law to the Gospel and Christ, who was the end and scope of the Law.[49]

Or similarly, here is Rutherford:

> [Paul] speaks of the Law absolutely, as contradistinguished from the Gospel... so it is a Covenant of Works begetting children to bondage.[50]

Paul is confronting a view of the law without faith, in which sense it is opposed to the Gospel since it does not lead to Christ by faith, 'the end and soul of the Law'.[51]

But if this is the case, and if the faithful of the Old Testament era had the Spirit of faith and grace as well as the Law written on the heart, then Paul's contrast does not address them. In fact, we can speak of the faithful of the an-

---

46. Ibid., 30.
47. Rutherford, *Covenant of Life*, 347. My emphasis. Cp. his *The Trial and Triumph of Faith* (Edinburgh: Banner of Truth, 2001), 86, 88.
48. Blake, *Vindiciae Foederis*, 208.
49. Ball, *Covenant of Grace*, 115. My emphasis.
50. Rutherford, *Covenant of Life*, 63. Cf. Strong, *Discourse*, 88f.
51. Ball, *Covenant of Grace*, 105.

cient era as simply being members of the *one* covenant – even the 'new' covenant:

> Unto such as used the old Testament as they ought, only as an Introduction to the new, there was indeed but one Testament: For as the Schools speak, *Ubi unum propter aliud, ibi unum tantum.* But such as rested in the Law, and used it not as a pedagogy to Christ, but sought justification by the observation of the Law Moral or Ceremonial, and opposed Christ the soul of the Law, such were held under damnable bondage, and cut from Christ.[52]

Following Calvin, Ball points out that there is no new 'law' offered in Jer 31:33.[53] The text in fact says nothing more than what was already promised in the Law at Deut 30 and the circumcision of the heart—a point that will resurface with an altered significance in the 20th century. What is promised in Jeremiah is nothing other than the work of the Holy Spirit through faith on the heart. Again, Ball is worth citing in full:

> Therefore the words of the Prophet as touching the writing of God's Law in our hearts, can import nothing but this, that the Laws which were before by the ministry of Moses delivered only in ink and paper, should by the power of the holy Ghost, through the faith of Christ be wrought and written in the affections of the heart: that God in Christ would not only administer outwardly the letter of the Law, whether in writing or preaching, but would by the regeneration of the Spirit, give grace inwardly to the obedience thereof... The Law is not opposed to the Law: but the writing to writing. Writing in tables of stone pertained to Moses or to the Old Testament: writing in the heart to Christ, or the new Covenant. The Law is the same, but otherwise administered in the hand of Christ, then in times past in the hand of Moses. Moses gave the Law in tables of stone, but could not give power or ability to do what the Law required: but Christ writeth the Law in the heart, and enableth the faithful in some measure to do what he commandeth.[54]

True to the Augustinian reading of the old/new covenant, Ball maintains that this work of Christ through the Spirit cannot be restricted to a future era—a point made above. The contrast of law and gospel, and of the testaments, is for Ball the contrast of the law without the Spirit over against the work of the Spirit in grace and faith. So the author of Hebrews disputes as 'old' a covenant

---

52. Ibid., 117.

53. Ibid., 118.

54. Ibid. Cp. another polemicist against the antinomians: 'The Spirit of God doth write this [moral] law in the heart of all God's children; according to the promise, "I will put my Law in their inward parts, and write it in their hearts."' John Sedgwick, *Antinomianism Atomized* (London: 1643), 17.

which in and of itself could 'not be rested in', since it was only the shadows rather than the substance ('as if we could be justified by the works of the law').[55] Likewise, Paul's polemic in Gal 4 and 2 Cor 3 stems from those who 'perverted the right use and end of the law'.[56] Further, as Blake remarks, as one can 'in a rigid interpretation' make Old Testament texts to hold out a covenant of works, one can do the same to texts in the New Testament. But this does not make it *in se* a covenant of works.[57]

But Ball, in a startling turn akin to Olevianus, fails to apply this reading once he turns to the second part of his treatise, 'Of the New Testament or Covenant'. In fact the discussions here bear almost no resemblance to the examinations of the same passages earlier in the treatise. Thus:

> the Covenant of Grace is fitly called the new Covenant or Testament, Jer 31:31, Heb 8:8, 2 Cor 3:6, for it is diverse from that which God made with the Fathers before Christ, most necessary and excellent, never to wax old, or to decay. By it a new light of the doctrine of the Gospel shined to the world, it had new worship, new adoration, a new form of the Church, new witnesses, new tables, new Sacraments and Ordinances.[58]

The newness lies in the change of worship, the 'form of the church', and its lasting nature – but none of these are the contrasts of Jer 31, Heb 8, or 2 Cor 3 which he has already provided. Ball returns to acknowledging the status of the 'faithful before Christ' in defining the nature of the 'new covenant' and does so in terms almost entirely given over to the *mutatio sacramentorum* and the clarity that comes from the covenant now 'plainly and openly propounded'.[59] I

---

55. Ball, *Covenant of Grace*, 118-19. My emphasis. This is already seen, in fact, at the very opening of the treatise (p.15): Hebrews 8:7 is cited as a contrast between the covenant of grace and that covenant which 'could not give life', i.e. the covenant of works made with Adam.

56. Ibid., 122.

57. Blake, *Vindiciae Foederis*, 215-16.

58. Ball, *Covenant of Grace*, 195. Cp. Rutherford: 'The Author to the Hebrews, ch.8, applieth the saying of Jeremiah to Christ and his dispensation under the Gospel, and the former covenant to the law and dispensation of the old testament...' Samuel Rutherford, *A Survey of the Spirituall Antichrist* (London: 1648), I.308. Or, The contrast is 'comparatively spoken... because forgiveness of sins is promised darkly in the first covenant, but plainly in the other, because Grace is promised sparingly in the former, but here abundantly, the Law being written on the heart.' Rutherford, *Covenant of Life*, 63.

59. Ball, *Covenant of Grace*, 196-97. This is in some form anticipated in the earlier remarks: 'The Covenant of Grace is either promised or promulgated and established. Promised to the Fathers, first to *Adam*, and afterwards to the Patriarchs, and lastly to the people of Israel, and that before their coming into the Land of Canaan, and

am tempted to blame the posthumous nature of the treatise for such a glaring inconsistency, but it is just what we saw in Olevianus and what we then find in Thomas Blake. Here is Blake's full statement, part of which was cited above, revealing the thrust:

> There is not a promise in the New covenant... [but] we may find in the Old covenant, the same held out.... The betterness is, in the greater ease being freed from that bondage of the ceremonial yoke, and in their more distinct clearness.[60]

The logic remains the same: the contrast cannot be in the substance given the nature of the 'new'. Therefore the contrast must be in the *accidentalia*—the *mutatio sacramentorum* and the *claritas*. Again, and not for the last time, we find a commentator appealing to things not mentioned to explain the true 'newness' of the new covenant.

The same exercise could be done with the treatise of William Strong, one of the delegates at the Westminster Assembly. Strong takes the common view that the 'covenant for the substance of it is the same both unto Jews and Gentiles.'[61] He even asserts that the Law as given upon Sinai by Moses was a

---

after their return from the Babylonish captivity. Promulgated, after the fullness of time came. And hence the Covenant of Grace is distributed into the Covenant of Promise, or the New Covenant, so called by way of excellency. For the Foundation and Mediator of the Covenant of Grace is our Lord Jesus Christ, but either to be incarnate, crucified, and raised from the dead, or as already incarnate, crucified, and truly raised from the dead, and ascended into Heaven (p.27).'

60. Blake, *Vindiciae Foederis*, 208. He appeals to the Geneva Bible here (published first in 1560), to show that some things spoken absolutely are really meant only comparatively. The 'almost incalculably influential' Geneva Bible (Daniell) offers a standard contrast of accidents: 'Though the covenant of redemption made to the fathers, and this which was given after, seem diverse, yet they are all one, and grounded on Jesus Christ, save that this is called new because of the manifestation of Christ, and the abundant graces of the holy Ghost given to his Church under the Gospel.' *The Bible: That is, the Holy Scriptures, contained in the Olde and Newe Testament. with most profitable Annotations upon all the hard places, and other things of great importance* (London: 1595), ad loc. See David Daniell, "Review of *Translating the Bible. From the 7th to the 17th century*. By Lynne Long," *JEH* 54.4 (2003), 765. The Bible was the standard translation for the English Reformed until the Authorized Version of 1611, and according to Bebbington was the preferred text in Scotland until the 18th century. See D.G. Danner, "The Contribution of the Geneva Bible of 1560 to the English Protestant Tradition," *The Sixteenth Century Journal* 12.3 (1981), 5-7; David Bebbington, "Evangelicals and Eschatology in Britain" (unpublished paper presented at the University of St. Andrews, 2007).

61. Strong, *Discourse*, 238; cf. p.65, et passim.

covenant of grace, as most of the divines.[62] So Israel quite clearly knew and enjoyed the covenant of grace, wherein alone salvation was found. Then Strong makes a number of distinctions, among which is the following:

> The Covenant has two parts; (1) One inward and spiritual, which is by Faith and Conversion, and the benefits of it are Justification, Adoption, and Sanctification,[63] which is the Covenant spoken of, Jer 31.33 [quotation]. (2) Another external, which entitles a man to outward priviledges only, and this is the Covenant in regard of the outward administrations owning them for a visible Church of God; thus God is said to break with the Jews; for the Covenant of Grace in the spiritual part of it is everlasting, and cannot be broken.[64]

So even contrasting with the 'administration' of the covenant of grace, Strong sees Jeremiah's new covenant as the 'spiritual' or 'inward'—i.e. salvific—aspect of the covenant, which is everlasting. The administration can change, be broken, and this will include for Strong the change of sacraments.[65] But that is not the proper location for discussion of Jeremiah's 'new covenant': the new

---

62. Similar to Calvin's distinction above, he states: 'Law is taken in Scripture two ways, as it was given by God upon Mount Sinai for a double end: (1) It is taken largely, for the whole Doctrine delivered by God upon Mount Sinai, with the precepts and the Promises thereof; and so Grace is the Law written in the heart, it is the Epistle of Christ ministered by us. (2) It is taken strictly setting down an exact rule of righteousness, and promising life upon condition of personal and perfect obedience.... Now if we take the Moral Law as given upon Mount Sinai, in the first sense, so it is a Covenant of Grace; but if we take it in the latter sense, so it is a Covenant of Works.' Ibid., 88. Or, 'By all this you see that the Covenant, of which Circumcision was a signa dn a seal, was not the Covenant of Works, but was the same that was made with Abraham, because the Covenant was the same... nor was the Covenant that God made with Moses a Covenant of Words, for Moses was (Heb 11:23) a Believer.... It was to the carnal Jews plainly a Covenant of Works, not in God's intention, but by their own corruption...' Ibid.

63. Cf. *Westminster Larger Catechism*, q.69: 'What is the communion in grace which the members of the invisible church have with Christ? A: The communion in grace which the members of the invisible church have with Christ, is their partaking of the virtue of his mediation, in their justification, adoption, sanctification, and whatever else, in this life, manifests their union with him.' (Cp. *Westminster Shorter Catechism*, q.32.)

64. Ibid., 239. See also the common language of 'new covenant' for the simple covenant of grace, e.g. 260f.

65. 'unto the spiritual part of the Covenant there is added the *Seal of the Spirit*, which is secret between God and the Soul; and unto the external part of the Covenant there are added visible Seals before men, and these visible Seals are different amongst the Jews and the Christians; the Ordinance and Seal of Admission amongst the Jews was Circumcision, but it's Baptism amongst Christians; therefore the administration is varied, though the Covenant remain the same.' Ibid.

covenant is the covenant of grace considered from its 'spiritual' and saving aspects.

Likewise, speaking of the contrast of the covenant of works (first covenant) and the covenant of grace (second), he states:

> The great difference between the first and second Covenant lay in this: the promises of the first Covenant were all of them conditional, being given unto grace received, and did suppose grace in the person to whom they were made; but there were no absolute promises to give grace: that Covenant did suppose grace, but it did not give grace... and herein lies the great glory of the promises of the new Covenant, and the grace of them, it gives grace, and then it crowns grace; and therefore they are said to be better promises.[66]

Or, in listing the promises of the covenant of grace, he lists first Ezek 36:26 ('I will take away your heart of stone, and give a heart of flesh') and second Jer 31:33 and then says: 'these two are promises of conversion and of the power of God in Christ put forth upon the Elect of God.'[67]

Yet, Strong elsewhere is happy to cite Jeremiah's new covenant (at least as it stands in Hebrews) to refer to an era *within* the covenant of grace. So he says:

> There is indeed a *Triplex Era*, a *three-fold account*, or three several periods in Scripture of the Covenant of Grace. [1] As it was made with Adam after his fall... called the Covenant of Promise. [2] As it was more fully revealed after Christ's coming in the flesh, Heb 8.6,7., so the Covenant as to the Fathers being in the Promise, is called the first Covenant, and as performed, and Christ exhibited, the second.... [3] As shall be more gloriously revealed at the calling of the Jews, when the Lord shall make this Covenant with them, that is take them into this Covenant again... [Rom 11].[68]

So the 'first covenant' is the promise before Christ's coming and the 'second' is after he is exhibited. The language comes straight from the earlier and common discussions regarding Jeremiah's 'new covenant' in Reformed writers, and the language of two 'administrations' is prominent throughout.[69] But the tension nonetheless stands: the new covenant describes the (one, eternal) covenant of

---

66. Ibid., 245.
67. Ibid., 251; cf. p.119, 245.
68. Ibid., 66. Or elsewhere: 'it is therefore commonly called a *New Covenant*, because, though it be the same, yet it's under new outward administrations (239).' This is the *mutatio sacramentorum* once more, but here supported with a rather questionable interpretation of Dan 9:27.
69. Ibid., 240-41.

grace over against the covenant of works, and yet is also a distinction within the covenant of grace by a change of administration.

Calamy, somewhat unique in his discussion of the matter, nonetheless faces the same issues. On the one hand, he states:

> [I]t is true, when Christ was sacrificed he put an end to all sacrifices and ceremonies that tipified him, crucified for sins, all those types and shadowes are done away, it is called the first covenant, and the manifesting of Christ crucified, by the History of the foure Evangelists is called the new covenant, see Heb. 8:7, 8, 9.[70]

Yet he immediately faces the objection concerning the 'writing on the hearts' as tied to the new covenant. (It's worth remembering this is still the same objection from Augustine's time.) He says—similar to Augustine—that 'it is not said that this shall only be done in the times after the Incarnation of Christ, although grace shall more abound then before his death.'[71] His solution appears to be that, by abstracting the covenant of grace entirely into the eternal covenant between the Father and Son, then its various outworkings are mere manifestations of that eternal covenant. So Jeremiah's 'new covenant' is not really itself a covenant, but merely a further manifestation of the covenant of grace. But then once we turn to the material within that 'new covenant,' he falls into the difficulty of admitting it was known before Christ. But to keep some form of distinction relies again on the 'accidents' (*more* abound).

In Ball—as with Blake and Rutherford—we come closest among the 17th century British to an Augustinian reading of an absolute contrast regarding Jeremiah's new covenant: unbelief vs. faith and the work of the Spirit. But after the opening exegetical discussions he reverts once again to the contrast of two religio-historical eras marked out by the 'accidents', undercutting his earlier comments and leaving at least this reader more than a bit puzzled. Like Calvin before him (no Calvin vs. the Calvinists here!), the inconsistency stands in the text and the question of how one ought to read Jer 31:31-34 receives two mutually exclusive answers, one necessarily of temporal succession and one necessarily without temporal succession. The same tension can be found in a number of the English Reformed around Ball's time in the early and mid-17th century—a tension marked by the desire to use Jeremiah's new covenant to explain the central components of the covenant of grace, the inability to say any part of Jer 31:33-34 was foreign to the faithful in the ancient era, and yet the felt need to make the distinction one of two successive eras nonetheless. The solutions

---

70. Calamy, *Two Covenants*, 16-17.
71. Ibid., 17.

offered may stand as logical within a system of doctrine, but do nothing to help the exegetical difficulties attending them.

3. *Herman Witsius*

The struggle in Reformed readings of Jer 31:31-34 is further exemplified by Dutch Reformed orthodoxy in the 17th century. The Dutch provinces in this century became the most important location for Reformed thought, with only the possible exception of Britain.[72] But the 'Golden Age' of the Dutch Republic was by no means a calm period for theological development. One of the most divisive periods in the Dutch Reformed tradition was the 'theologico-political *Kulturkampf*' between the 'Voetians' and 'Cocceians' in the 17th century.[73] Gispertus Voetius (1588/89-1676) was a popular preacher and academic in Utrecht, and a leader of the *Nadere Reformatie* in Holland—a movement often paralleled with their 'Puritan' contemporaries in England.[74] Like its counterpart in Britain, the movement made much of the public enforcement of the norms of behaviour found in their reading of Scripture. The fault-line between the two parties was opened by the arguments against the continuity of the Sabbath regulations in the 'New Testament' era by the Hebraist scholar at Utrecht, Johannes Cocceius (1603-69). The fallout on this issue began to tear apart the Dutch churches and would ultimately cause both the North and South synods to split, the universities to draw lines within their faculties, and the political leaders to enforce a silence on the issues in a (failed) effort to quiet the matter. So again

---

72. On the rise of Reformed thought in the Dutch provinces, see Alastair Duke, *Reformation and Revolt in the Low Countries* (London: Hambledon Press, 1990). Andrew Pettegree, "Coming to terms with victory: the upbuilding of a Calvinist church in Holland, 1572-1590," in *Calvinism in Europe, 1540-1620* (eds. Andrew Pettegree et al.; Cambridge: Cambridge Univ. Press, 1994). For the Dutch provinces generally through the 17th century, see Jonathan Israel, *The Dutch Republic: Its Rise, Greatness, and Fall 1477-1806* (Oxford History of Early Modern Europe; Oxford: Clarendon Press, 1995).

73. The phrase is from Ibid., 664.

74. See the summaries of the *Nadere Reformatie* in Joel R. Beeke, "The Dutch Second Reformation (Nadere Reformatie)," in *Christian's Reasonable Service* (Grand Rapids, MI: Reformation Heritage Books, 1992); M.E. Osterhaven, "The Experiential Theology of Early Dutch Calvinism," *Reformed Review* 27.3 (1974); J.N. Geisler, *The Thousand Generation Covenant: Dutch Reformed Covenant Theology and Group Identity in Colonial South Africa, 1652-1814* (Studies in the History of Christian Thought; Leiden: E.J. Brill, 1991), 68-79. Cf. Keith L. Sprunger, *Dutch Puritanism: A History of English and Scottish Churches of the Netherlands in the Sixteenth and Seventeenth Centuries* (Studies in the History of Christian Thought; Leiden: E.J. Brill, 1982).

we find Jeremiah's new covenant brought into battle on two sides of a theological (and political) dispute.

The Voetian-Cocceian dispute is complex and ranges over other topics of the day, moving from Sabbath-enforcement to views of contingency within divine action—which latter raised fears of the still-ongoing Remonstrant (Arminian) disputes so divisive a generation before. The debate also came to enfold the ultimately more important disagreements between the Cartesians and anti-Cartesians in the Dutch Universities. The followers of Cocceius often (though not always) found agreement with the 'new philosophy', to Voetius' chagrin.[75] But one aspect of the dispute, which seems to have most impressed Voetius and Cocceius themselves, was the theological divide on the relationship between the eras before and after Christ with respect to the covenant. Willem van Asselt has recently summarized the point of the dispute precisely along such lines:

> The main issue was a different interpretation of the continuity and discontinuity of redemptive history in the Old and New Testaments. Whereas the Voetians stressed the substantial unity of salvation for believers in the Old and New Testament dispensations, Cocceius underlined the progression of salvation in history and, therefore, the different status of the Old and New Testament believers.[76]

Instead of examining the dispute in its main protagonists and the views of Jer 31:31-34 in each case, I will look at one of the figures standing in the wake of the divide. Herman Witsius (1636-1708) was a student at Utrecht under Voetius, and more importantly, has been said—along with Wilhelmus à Brakel (seen briefly below)—to 'represent the normative form of Reformed federalism

---

75. The dispute over Cartesian thought, with Voetius as a central figure against it, is well-addressed in English scholarship with the works of J.A. van Ruler, *The Crisis of Causality: Voetius and Descartes on God, Nature and Change* (Brill's Studies in Intellectual History; Leiden: E.J. Brill, 1995); Aza Goudriaan, *Reformed Orthodoxy and Philosophy, 1625-1750: Gisbertus Voetius, Petrus van Mastricht, and Anthonius Driessen* (Leiden: E.J. Brill, 2006). Some of the particulars of the immediate dispute between Voetius and Descartes in the events of 1643 (perfectly contemporary to the Westminster Assembly) are presented in the editorial appendix to René Descartes, *The Correspondence of René Descartes: 1643* (Utrecht: Utrecht University, 2004), 183-92.

76. Willem J. van Asselt, "*Amicitia Dei* as Ultimate Reality: An Outline of the Covenant Theology of Johannes Cocceius (1603-1669)," *Ultimate Reality and Meaning. Interdisciplinary Studies in the Philosophy of Understanding* 21.1 (1998), 37. Van Asselt's recent treatment of Cocceius is very valuable: Willem J. van Asselt, *The Federal Theology of Johannes Cocceius (1603-1669)* (Studies in the History of Christian Thought; Tr. by Raymond A. Blacketer. Leiden: Brill, 2001).

fashioned in the wake of debate over Coccceius' doctrine.'⁷⁷ With Witsius we see another form of that structure seen in Oecolampadius, the contrast being a movement from a complex to a simple era. Witsius posits a third (a 'national') covenant that covers much the same ground as Oecolampadius' discussion of the Mosaic 'additions' to the covenant of grace—now in dialogue with Coccceius rather than the Anabaptists. What is held out in Jer 31:33-34 is an abrogation of this national covenant and a full pronouncement of the bare covenant of grace.

Witsius has sometimes been considered a mediator of the Voetian-Coccceian dispute who betrays significant influence from Coccceius.[78] The title and structure of Witsius' chief theological work on the covenant, *The Economy of the Covenants between God and Man*, does show a willingness to depart somewhat from Voetius' approach. But from the outset Witsius explicitly distances himself from the 5-fold gradual abrogation of the covenant of works that forms the heart of Coccceius' system.[79] Thus, after listing the things supposedly abrogated he states:

---

77. Richard A. Muller, "The Covenant of Works and the Stability of Divine Law in Seventeenth-Century Reformed Orthodoxy: A Study in the Theology of Herman Witsius and Wilhelmus à Brakel," *Calvin Theological Journal* 29 (1994): , 80, n.12. See the essay, including biographical sketch, by Arie de Reuver, *Sweet Communion: Trajectories of Spirituality from the Middle Ages through the Further Reformation* (Tr. by James A. De Jong. Grand Rapids, MI: Baker, 2007), 261-80.

78. Thus, e.g., Herman Bavinck, *Reformed Dogmatics* (4 vols.; Tr. by John Vriend. Grand Rapids, MI: Baker, 2003), III.210, n.33. More helpful is the chart of Coccceius' influence given by van Asselt, *Federal Theology*, 340. Witsius appears directly between Voetius and Coccceius, with à Brakel more directly under Voetius.

79. Here is Coccceius' own summary: 'For the abolition of the law or the covenant of works proceeds by these steps: It is made ancient, (1) with respect to the possibility of giving life, through sin; (2) with respect to damnation, in the promise being displayed through Christ, and apprehended by faith; (3) with respect to fear, or the efficient power of dread of death and of servitude, through the promulgation of the new covenant (*foederis novi*), the expiation of sin being made. Which, being made, they who are redeemed are under the law of the Redeemer. This was in order that the same law abolished by the Redeemer as the law of sin might become the law of the Saviour and might account righteousness to them who are his.... (4) With respect to the struggle with sin, through the death of the body; (5) with respect to all effects, through the Resurrection of the dead.' Johannes Coccceius, *Summa doctrinae de foedere et testamento Dei* (Opera 6; Amsterdam: 1673), §58. For the difficulties of interpreting Coccceius on this abrogation, see Willem J. van Asselt, "The Doctrine of the Abrogations in the Federal Theology of Johannes Coccceius (1603-1669)," *Calvin Theological Journal* 29 (1994); Idem, *Federal Theology*, 271-87; for the fullest summary and explanation see Lee, *Johannes Coccceius*, 113-71.

> [I]t will be more proper to treat of these things when we speak of the fruits and effects of the covenant of grace, than when considering the abolition of the covenant of works: which is on no account abolished, but insofar as it is become impossible for man to attain to life by his own personal works.[80]

So Witsius proves an interesting perspective on Dutch Reformed views of the old and new covenants: drawing on Cocceius and Voetius, while identifying directly with neither. And, true to the form of Olevianus and Ball, offers yet one more instance of the struggle and tension in reading Jeremiah's new covenant within the bounds of Reformed orthodoxy.

We find the tension already appearing in Witsius' discussion of the covenant of grace, which was made with the elect as the outworking of the eternal *pactum* between Father and Son. Two aspects of this are of interest: first, this covenant is made with the elect and so embracing all believers in any time:

> ...as we restrict this covenant to the Elect, it is evident that we are speaking of the internal, mystical, and spiritual communion of the covenant. For salvation itself, and everything belonging to it, or inseparably connected with it, are promised in this covenant, all which, none but the Elect can attain to.[81]

Second, the promises of this covenant, namely of 'grace and glory', are summarized in Jer 31:33:

> We may likewise not improperly say, that in the covenant of grace are promised both salvation itself, and all the means leading to it, which the Lord hath briefly comprised, Jer 31:33... [full citation].[82]

This is precisely the move seen above in Olevianus. And since the text of Jer 31:33 is the summary of the covenant of grace itself, the new covenant cannot be denied to any of the elect without denying salvation itself and/or its means. Thus the ancient believers, who were among the elect, would need to be a part of the new covenant.

But also like Olevianus, Witsius moves from this point into the use of Jer 31 as a contrast between the two eras of the one covenant of grace. Witsius

---

80. Herman Witsius, *The Economy of the Covenants between God and Man* (Tr. by William Crookshank. London: 1822), §I.9.xxiii. Emphasis are removed throughout, except when stated.

81. Ibid., §III.1.v.

82. Ibid., §III.1.vi. Or, 'when God proposes the form of the covenant of grace, his words, to this purpose, are mere promises, as we have lately seen, Jer 31 and 32.' Ibid., §III.1.xii. Likewise, his use of Cloppenburg who refers to the *new* covenant, in explaining the nature of the covenant of grace: Ibid., §III.1.xv.

begins his more thorough discussion of the matter by insisting that the contrast of old and new covenant is not that regarding the 'legal covenant', but of the two parts of the covenant of grace: 'that dispensation, which subsisted before the coming of Christ in the flesh, and was proposed formerly to the fathers' and 'that dispensation, which succeeded the former, after being consecrated and established by the blood of Christ.'[83] Thus Witsius reverts (momentarily) to the standard religio-historical contrast within the covenant of grace.

The central point of dispute between Witsius and Cocceius is the latter's (inconsistent) denial of what Witsius calls the 'permanent benefits' of the covenant of grace to the believers of the ancient era. These benefits are the *sine qua non* for membership in the covenant of grace. The tendency to the contrast of degree in the question over against Cocceius is made explicit:

> It is one thing to say that Israel had not some degree or measure of true and permanent benefits; another, that they had not the blessings themselves. He who would assert the former, which is true, should not use words that signify the latter, which is absolutely false.[84]

But the discussion becomes more involved than merely a contrast of quality once particular issues arise, such as the law on the heart in the ancient era. Witsius opens with the assertion that, 'The excellence of the Old Testament is too much lessened by asserting, that the circumcision of the heart, mentioned, Deut 30:6 was a blessing peculiar to the New Testament.'[85] Witsius cites Cocceius' definition of circumcision of the heart as 'regeneration by the spirit of adoption', or 'sanctification by the spirit of faith and the love of God and consolation in hope of eternal life', and then Cocceius' positing that circumcision of the heart was reserved for the 'New Testament' era.[86] This appears to entail that the Old Testament era had no regeneration or sanctification, but, as Witsius notes, Cocceius does not grant the point of 'the fathers' being without circumcision of

---

83. Ibid., §III.3.i. This is tied directly to Jer 31:32 at §III.3.xxvii.

84. Ibid., §IV.12.xii. Or, '[I]t is wrong to infer…that under a mutable economy which was, in due time, to be changed, there were no permanent blessings either bestowed or made known.' Ibid., §IV.12.xiv.

85. Ibid., §IV.12.xvi.

86. Cocceius, on Deut 30:6: 'Above all it signifies Regeneration or sanctification through the spirit of faith and love of God… Second, it means Consolation in hope of eternal life, through the expiation of Christ.' Johannes Cocceius, *De ultimis Mosis considerationes* (Opera 1; Amsterdam: 1673), §337-38. Put together with Johannes Cocceius, *Summa Theologiae ex Scripturis Repetita* (Opera 6; Amsterdam: 1673), §53.7; Cocceius, *Sum. doctr*, §352.

the heart.[87] Instead Cocceius appeals to a sense of 'fullness',[88] and then to a third aspect of the circumcision of the heart – i.e., *ablationem veli*, the removal of the veil of the ceremonies so that we serve without such a 'yoke':

> Third, it makes the removal of the veil from the eyes and the yoke from the conscience for the serving of God without fear of death, in liberty and delight. For in circumcision, the removal of the substance of flesh doubtless also signifies partly the casting-out of 'trust in the flesh' (Phil 3:3, 'and confidence is not in the flesh'), that is, in his strength and the external work of the law of flesh; and partly liberation from the yoke of such a law.[89]

Witsius uses strong language to assert the experience of circumcision of the heart as a necessary part of the covenant of grace,[90] and essentially doubts only the third aspect of Cocceius' understanding—both because the text of Deut 30:6 cannot be taken to be referring to the abrogation of the ceremonies, and because 'carnal' can only be applied insofar as the external rite is performed without 'the spirit or mind, but [merely] in the members of the body.'[91]

Witsius then immediately turns to the similar promise of Jer 31:33 and the law on the heart, again using a *reductio ad absurdum*:

> In the same base manner, they make the writing the law on the heart, a blessing peculiar to the New Testament: because Heb 8:10 it is said from Jer 31:34 [he means v.33, cited in full]...; that is, says our author [Cocceius]... 'I will cause them to receive my law, delight therein, and not forget

---

87. 'And they had each of these as well as the fathers. For they were not without the Spirit of God... and the creation of a pure heart... and circumcision of the heart, they were able to call Christ 'Lord': thus David (Psa 110:1). And they had the hope and joy of salvation.' Cocceius, *De ult. Mos*, §339.

88. 'And it will so seem that here spiritual grace is signified to an extent common with men of both the old testament and the new, in its fullness it is properly attributed to the latter: and here, properly attributed to the new testament, it is so promised to be superadded to the things received.' Ibid., §335.

89. Ibid., §340.

90. 'And as circumcision of the heart, is this very regeneration and sanctification, without which none can see God, we must of necessity say, that it is the privilege of all those that were saved at any time. A greater or less degree of sanctification alters not the species. Nor do I imagine any believer at this time will, even as to the degrees of sanctification, claim to himself a superiority above David, or Moses, or Abraham.' Witsius, *Economy*, §IV.12.xix. This last line is reminiscent of Bullinger, *Decades*, III.298: 'For which of us at this day can say, that we excel in knowledge and in faith either Abraham, Moses, Samuel, David, Isaiah, Daniel, or Zacharias?'

91. Witsius, *Economy*, §IV.12.xx-xxi.

> it.' If these words be taken as they lie, it follows, that the ancient believers, who lived before the times of the New Testament, did not receive the law of God, nor delight in it but forgot it. But that these things are most eminently false, appears from the example of David alone…[92]

Witsius attaches this to Coccieus' statement that the ancient fathers could not fulfill the commandment to 'love the Lord thy God' because they had fear (and, 'where there is fear there is no perfect love', 1 Jn 4:18). But the difficulty Witsius has is the witness of the Old Testament itself:

> But I do not meet with these things in the sacred writings; for they declare that even the ancient believers loved God, Ps 18:1 and 116:1. And that as their Father, Isa 63:16… and without any fear that did become the children of God, Ps 46:2 and 33:3, nay, that they had a joyful sense of the love of God shed abroad in their hearts, Ps 4:7.[93]

So we still have to ask, what *is* the contrast in Hebrews and Jeremiah? Witsius gives an answer that takes us back towards Oecolampadius, though now in the terminology of a 'national covenant':

> I answer: the apostle does not here oppose the covenant of grace, as it is dispensed after the coming of Christ, to the same covenant of grace, as it was dispensed before: but opposes the covenant of grace, as in its full efficacy under the New Testament, to the national covenant made with the Israelites at mount Sinai; and as a spiritual covenant to a typical…. Here a better covenant is opposed to that Israelitish covenant, which is not formally the covenant of grace, but is only considered with respect to typical or shadowy pomp, the effect of which is the writing the law on the heart, and communion with God as the fountain of salvation.[94]

This runs directly against what Witsius has already said on the matter of contrast of dispensations above. Nonetheless, in this 'national covenant' God 'did not promise to give them a heart to obey… And therefore, in consequence of *this* covenant, the law was not written on the heart of the people of Israel.'[95] This third covenant is, more or less, the commands of the theocratic state, with the ceremonies, divorced from any spiritual promises—the externals of the Mosaic era, akin to the Mosaic 'additions' in Oecolampadius. The ancient believers were members of *both* the covenant of grace via Abraham and the 'national covenant' of types and shadows which in itself was weak and unprofitable for spir-

---

92. Ibid., §IV.12.xxiii.
93. Ibid., §IV.12.xxv. Emphasis original.
94. Ibid., §IV.12.xxvi.
95. Ibid. My emphasis.

itual benefit.⁹⁶ So the temporal contrast is a movement from complex to simple: a time of the covenant of grace bound up with the national covenant, to the covenant of grace alone.

But Witsius is not yet finished. In the most thorough discussion of Jer 31:31-34, Witsius is explicit that the point of contrast for the new covenant is the state of affairs 'which Moses has fully set forth, Exod 24:3ff.' More specifically, the '*manner* of ratifying this covenant [of Moses], consisting in ceremonies and sacrifices, is, in this place, called the old covenant.'⁹⁷ This being so, the nature of the new covenant is the *ablationem veli*, brought back into the discussion:

> To that old covenant is contradistinguished the new, which can be no other, but God's agreement with Israel, without the veil of ceremonies; in which there can be nothing typical or shadowy, but all things real and substantial.⁹⁸

The old covenant 'had not...the promise of sanctifying grace', even though the believers had such grace, as above. The old covenant was 'external' but the new 'spiritual'—even though the old believers also had the spiritual. In fact, the only points of temporal novelty come in the claim that the new will have 'true expiation' rather than 'typical', and that the new holds out an 'irrevocable grace...without the veil of ceremonies.'⁹⁹ The latter is the standard *mutatio sacramentorum*. The former is grounded in Witsius' agreement with Cocceius that those before Christ did not have 'true expiation', though he maintains that they themselves had their sins fully forgiven and had pure consciences.¹⁰⁰ By this he means that the sins still existed 'in the account of the surety, who was to answer them'.¹⁰¹ But such a move transfers the temporal distinction to the abstract 'ac-

---

96. 'However, the elect among Israel, even in the ancient times, besides their engagements by the Sinaitic covenant, were joined to God by the covenant of grace which he had solemnly renewed with Abraham. And from that covenant they had everything that the writing the law on the heart comprises, and God himself for their God, that is, the fountain of salvation.' Ibid.

97. Ibid., §IV.14.xviii. My emphasis.

98. Ibid., §IV.14.xix.

99. Ibid., §IV.14.xxi.

100. For the latter points, see Ibid., §IV.12.xxix-xliii and §IV.12.l-lv. See the discussion in Herman Witsius, *Sacred Dissertations, on what is commonly called the Apostles' Creed* (2 vols.; Tr. by Donald Fraser. Edinburgh: 1823), §XXV.8-14.

101. Witsius, *Economy*, §IV.13.iv. And, 'This then was the first defect of the Old Testament, that it had not the cause of salvation completed, and consequently not a true expiation of sins.' This was a central point of contention among the orthodox (cf. Olevianus on *limbus patrum* above). For the opposite view, see (e.g.) Francis Turretin:

count' of the *sponsio*, Christ—the experience of the benefits by the elect remains unaffected between the eras. In any case, for Witsius the contrast here is patently between a covenant of grace without the ceremonies ('new covenant'), and a 'national covenant' of external commands ('old covenant'). Thus Witsius' most important contribution places the contrast in the same essential realm as seen in Oecolampadius: a covenant of temporal and national concerns contrasted to the one eternal covenant of grace.

Witsius has found a following in at least one recent study of the topic.[102] But as an exegetical solution this clearly has a long way to go. First, if the nature of the 'old covenant' is the cultic activities and theocratic laws, then we are given no indication whatsoever of this in the book of Jeremiah. Indeed, as we will see, the exact opposite is the case: the broken covenant is explicitly distanced from proper cultic activities and is everywhere concerned with the broader concern of fidelity in relationship to Yhwh. And second, the difficulty is again with the description of the 'new covenant' being completely divorced from the supposed 'old covenant' to which it is contrasted. What is 'new' is what is *not said*, since all that is called 'new' was known and experienced in the ancient era as part of the substance of the covenant of grace. Like Ball or Olevianus, Witsius expresses the difficulty of denying any aspect of the 'new covenant' to the faithful in the presentation of the Old Testament. But his conclusion of what this must mean for reading Jer 31:31f leaves much to be desired.

4. *Widening the Struggle*

The struggle of Reformed orthodoxy to read Jer 31:31-34 is widely attested, especially among the Dutch Reformed. The influential Leiden Synopsis

---

'Yea, since the works of God are known to him from eternity (Acts 15:18) by the light of omniscience that sponsion was observed by God not only as future, but even as present, yea, as actually performed; and its efficacy gave the same benefits to the fathers which we enjoy'. Francis Turretin, *Institutes of Elenctic Theology* (4 vols.; Tr. by George Musgrave Giger. Phillipsburg, NJ: P&R Publishing, 1994), Loc.12.q.IX.viii Or Witsius' younger contemporary, Wilhelmus à Brakel: 'The apostle shows that the death of Christ had to occur but once, and that this one sacrifice was efficacious from the foundation of the world. He thus forcefully confirms that this one death of Christ was already efficacious then [in the ancient era], this being such as if He both at that time and since that time had actually suffered.' Wilhelmus à Brakel, *The Christian's Reasonable Service* (4 vols.; Tr. by Bartel Elshout. Grand Rapids, MI: Reformation Heritage Books, 1992), 1.453-54.

102. Henri Blocher, "Old Covenant, New Covenant," in *Always Reforming: Explorations in Systematic Theology* (ed. A.T.B. McGowan; Leicester, England: Apollos, 2006).

of 1625—fashioned as a handbook for dogmatic disputations in the wake of the Synod of Dort by four Leiden professors—reveals a similar dual-presentation as expressed by Ball. The University of Leiden in the 17th century has been called 'the most renowned university of the Republic in its most flourishing period.'[103] And the value of the *Synopsis* ought to be seen in this light. The disputation *De veteri et novo testamenti* fell to the French theologian Andre Rivet and again opens with the issue of definition:

> Properly, the name of *vetus testamentum* means the Law, which was given through Moses to the Jewish people, promising life under condition of curse against transgressors, together with the intolerable burden of legal rituals and the yoke of very strenuous policies, which is therefore called the letter that kills, the ministry of death and condemnation, begetting servitude, the image of Hagar... This is opposed in its proper meaning by the *novum testamentum*, the teaching, of course, of spiritual grace and salvation.[104]

Thus, defined properly, the terms are mutually exclusive, contrasting *essentialiter*, with all salvation and grace being found in the *novum testamentum*.[105] The old kills, the new is the life giving Spirit—all in words that could have been drawn straight from Augustine and applied to 2 Cor 3 and Heb 10:1.[106]

A further connection with Augustine is in the definition of vetus and novum testamentum. Figuratively the terms are applied to the books of the Old and New Testaments, but 'strictly speaking' the two are direct opposites that cannot be reconciled.[107] Such language is by no means unique to the *Synopsis*

---

103. Peter T. van Rooden, *Theology, Biblical Scholarship and Rabbinical Studies in the Seventeenth Century: Constantijn L'Empereur (1591-1648) Professor of Hebrew and Theology at Leiden* (Leiden: E.J. Brill, 1989), 13.

104. Johannes Polyander et al., *Synopsis Purioris Theologiae* (Leiden: D. Donner, 1881), §23.v.

105. 'In this meaning the *vetus* and *novum testament* differ not only in certain circumstances and accidents, but essentially (*essentialiter*).' Ibid., §23.vi.

106. 'Therefore in this sense, the vetus testamentum is said to be a ministry of death, a letter that kills (2 Cor 3:6), an intolerable yoke pressing worshippers with servitude (Acts 15:10); only a shadow of future goods (Heb 10:1), imperfect, to be abolished, etc. It is opposite the *novum testamentum*, those things which we said by signification, is the ministry of the life-giving Spirit, the easy yoke of Christ, giving to us the spirit of adoption, and the freedom of the sons of God... having the true image of things, perfect and eternal.' Ibid., §23.vii.

107. 'For each is taken strictly, in that meaning that we said is its proper attribute, and by which they are directly opposed, so that they cannot be brought together; and hence it is not necessary that we establish extensive agreement between them.' XXIII.xii. Or, 'Thus also the *novum testamentum* is taken broadly, for the teaching first

given the interests in definitions in the Reformed scholastics. But here they are near copies of Augustine's formulation of the distinction.[108]

Yet this does not rule out the use of *vetus testamentum* for the era of the lesser state of the covenant of grace:

> But nothing hinders the lesser covenant of grace, or the promise made, dressed in the circumstances of its pedagogy, coming by the name of the *vetus testamentum*, since something in it was to be renewed and left unchanged—just as Paul in Heb 8:13 and 9:1... takes the first *testamentum* for the whole cult of the religion of the old tabernacle, in which promise was surely contained and confirmed. Though as we said, strictly speaking, it [i.e. *vetus testamentum*] properly designates the covenant of works and by the name of the 'new' is understood nothing other than the covenant of grace.[109]

The use of Heb 8 makes it likely that Rivet envisioned Jeremiah's new covenant to be read according to this use, rather than the 'proper' use of the terms. The discussion then turns to a comparison of the covenant of grace in the ancient era with the fullness of the covenant in Christ, almost entirely consisting in contrasts of degrees (with the '*mutatio Sacerdotii*') and using some of the same texts that before were used for the strict (absolute) contrast: Heb 8 and 10, Rom 8, Acts 15, and Gal 4.[110] The same dual-exegesis as Ball—with the same puzzling result—is anticipated.

Likewise, the Polish theologian Johannes Maccovius (1588-1644), long-time professor in the Netherlands and sometime colleague of Coccejus at Franeker, appeals to Jer 31:31f as a part of both the *principalia* and the *accessoria* of the covenant of grace. The promises of the new covenant are explicitly those of the *principalia*: 'the goods of heavenly and eternal life' and the means of obtaining them—the latter of which he ties explicitly to Jer

---

of grace of faith, then repentance (*resipiscentia*) and gratitude, or new obedience." Ibid., §23.xi.

108. Elsewhere see, e.g., Voetius who (in a series of definitions of 'law' and 'gospel'), defines 'gospel' as 'The good news and teaching that contains the *foedus novum*, or the promises of the *foedus novum*, the same as was preached whether before the coming of Christ or after; as also until now is distinguished from the teaching of the law.' Or, 'For the *foedus novum* is one plan (*ratio*), through which (and) under which salvation is conferred and acquired, our union with God, blessedness. Gispertus Voetius, *Selectarum Disputationum Theologicarum* (5 vols.; Utrecht: 1648), 4.17, 24.

109. Polyander et al., *Synopsis*, §23.xiii.

110. Jer 31:31 only emerges as showing that the cause of our salvation lies not in regeneration or the conditions of the Gospel ('faith and new obedience': i.e. the work of the Spirit), but in God's promise: Ibid., §23.xxix.

31:33-34.[111] Maccovius makes emphatic that we do not find here a contrast of 'substance' with the covenant but a contrast of 'efficacy': the old covenant was broken and the new is not.[112] Once more we see the dilemma. Maccovius cannot deny any of the principle parts of the covenant of grace to the ancient members of it. But since one cannot deny any of the *principalia* to the ancient members of the covenant of grace, Jeremiah calls it 'new' on account of its increased clarity—Bullinger's answer stated once more.[113]

But the text for Macccovius is also concerned with the *accessoria* of the covenant of grace:

> Jeremiah calls it new (ch.31) by reason of what was already alleged a little earlier; although it is also called new not with respect to time, as if it did not exist before the Messiah, but by reason of its nature and in comparison to that legal covenant, whose knowledge certainly had been born with us and had been previously known to us by nature. The covenant of the Gospel is, in fact, entirely new and is brought forward from the bosom of the father from eternity, and was unknown to all the world. Although this covenant can be called new by that name under the New Testament in the time of Christ, because it was promulgated by abolishing the old ceremonies with the signs of the new sacraments.[114]

---

111. 'The principal things are: first, goods of heavenly and eternal life; second, the means which lead to it—these are, justification, regeneration, faith, and perseverence in them. And indeed, this latter is also promised in the covenant of grace, most clearly evident in Jer 31. For the Lord here promises to maintain [it], so that the covenant he would enter into with his own people would not be like the covenant which he entered with his people Israel; which, he says, they violated. And so God enters into a covenant with the people of the N.T., which the people of the N.T. will not violate.' Johannes Maccovius, *Loci communes theologici* (Amsterdam: 1658), 501a. The reference to 'perseverance' may be borrowed from Zanchius: see John L. Farthing, "*Foedus Evangelicum*: Jerome Zanchi on the Covenant," *Calvin Theological Journal* 29 (1994).

112. 'For it is not concerned about the substance of the covenant, but about its efficacy, in that place in which it must be closely observed. Of course the prophet in the name of the Lord does not say thus: "I will not make with you a covenant, which I will enforce in order that you might do it and live," but he says, "I will not make a covenant with you, because you might violate it," of which he joins this rule [ratio], because "I will write" my law in your hearts.' Maccovius, *Loci communes*, 501a.

113. 'And I might avoid that these are said in a future time, not because they did not already exist then, but because they were not as clear (*illustris*), on account of which God promised to them in this place the forgiveness of sins, not as if it did not exist then, but because it was not so clear (*illustris*).' Ibid.

114. Ibid., 501b-2a.

So the covenant of the Gospel is 'new' from eternity, contrasted to the legal covenant. He appears to be drawing on a particular form of the Augustinian contrast for this, but is unwilling to say either that Jeremiah refers to this contrast, or that 'new' means something more than the *mutatio sacramentorum*—presumably the content of what he means by an increased clarity. So on the one hand the contrast is not regarding *substantia*, but on the other it is regarding *natura*? It is not with the *foedus operum*, but with the *foedus legale* known to us by nature and creation (both distinctions without difference)? The contrast is that of temporal efficacy, yet not with respect to time? Like in Olevianus, Jer 31:33-34 becomes a perfect illustration of the promise of the essential aspects (*principalia*) of the covenant of grace in any era. But then 'new' can only mean 'new degree', which is conjoined to the change of sacraments.

One final illustration of the struggle among the Dutch Reformed is the influential pietistic theologian Wilhelmus á Brakel.[115] Á Brakel offers the most blunt presentation of the logic leading to the contrast of old/new covenant as one of 'quality' or 'accidents'. So, writing against Cocceius and his followers, á Brakel states unambiguously that everything in the 'new covenant' of Jer 31:33-34 must already have been known by the faithful in the ancient era. So, he concludes, the contrast must be in the 'administration' and 'degree':

> [W]hatever is promised to the New Testament church in this text, already existed in the Old Testament church. The contrast does not pertain to the matter itself, but to the manner of administration and the degree of application.[116]

This is more fully explained in the standard form of the *qualitas* response, worth citing in full as the purest and simplest expression of the argument:

> *Answer*: It is a fact that there is a distinction here between the Old and New Testaments. It is equally certain that the New Testament did not exist during the days of the Old Testament, but came after the Old Testament; that is, it replaced and set aside the Old Testament. Furthermore, it is true that the New Testament is the covenant of grace, comprehending the spiritual benefits in Christ – and to remain with the text: the writing of the law

---

115. There is a helpful introduction to his life by W. Fieret, "Wilhelmus à Brakel," in *Christian's Reasonable Service* (Grand Rapids, MI: Reformation Heritage Books, 1992). This pietistic dogmatics was immensely popular, going through twenty Dutch editions in the 18th century and has been called the 'crowning achievement of the *Nadere Reformatie*.' (John Bolt, in the 'Editor's Introduction' to Bavinck, *Reformed Dogmatics*, I.12, n.6). See also de Reuver, *Sweet Communion*, 231-58, who reminds us that this work 'does not belong to the genre of systematic theology' but 'a popular statement of doctrine with pastoral applications' (234).

116. à Brakel, *Christian's Service*, 4.475.

in their hearts, to have God as their God (v. 33), to have enlightened eyes of the understanding, and to have the forgiveness of sins (v. 34). Moreover, it is equally certain that the Old Testament comprehended all these benefits of the covenant of grace and the covenant of grace itself...

At this point Augustine might have been used to illustrate the difference of definition: the 'new testament' did not exist during the days of the 'old testament'? That, Augustine said, depends upon the definition. But á Brakel continues the argument without regard or notice of Augustine's position. So he moves directly to the minor premise:

> It is also agreed that the covenant of grace has been since Adam and will remain the same in essence until the end of the world... Consequently it follows with equal certainty that the contrast between the Old and New Testaments cannot be one of essence. Since the New Testament is the covenant of grace – the New Testament having been nonexistent during the Old Testament, existing subsequent to, instead of, and the setting aside of the Old Testament being implied – then all who lived prior to the time of the New Testament would not have had a covenant of grace. There would then have been no fear of God, no knowledge of the mystery of salvation, and no forgiveness of sins; whereas people were indeed saved and did possess all the benefits of the covenant of grace.
>
> Therefore, the contrast pertains to the circumstances, the manner of administration, and the measure of light, faith, hope, and love. Old Testament believers had the law written in their hearts, had God as their God, had the knowledge of the mystery of salvation, and had the forgiveness of sins. They did not have this, however, with the same clarity as New Testament believers.[117]

What we have seen in a variety of forms from Bullinger onward is simply made transparent by á Brakel. Jer 31:33-34 offers nothing that can in fairness be denied to those prior to the era of the 'New Testament', and so one must appeal solely to a contrast of degree. The argument is coherent and (perhaps) theologically satisfying—at the least, the logic is valid. But the difficulty comes in such a view put forward as an exegetical statement of Jer 31:31-34. One must point to things *not said* to describe the 'newness': the 'new' is not the knowledge of God but the *clearer* knowledge of God. But such a move lacks any exegetical warrant and clearly emerges from a line of reasoning little concerned with immediate exegetical reflection.

---

117. Ibid., 4.409-10.

5. *Conclusions*

The struggles in Reformed readings of Jeremiah's new covenant that are clearly a part of 16th century discussions can be traced just as clearly (or more so) in the period of Reformed orthodoxy. The three main lines found from the 16th century Reformed readings still exist: (1) the movement from complexity to simplicity that Oecolampadius champions is seen in varied forms in John Cameron, Samuel Bolton, Robert Rollock, or Herman Witsius. (2) The movement towards a simple appeal of accidental contrast, seen in Bullinger, continues to show itself in the work of Maccovius or Wilhelmus á Brakel. (3) And the confusion or ambivalence of Calvin is given even sharper form in Caspar Olevianus and John Ball. In both Olevianus and Ball we find two-part works, the first of which makes use of Jer 31:33-34 to state the substance of the covenant of grace—the covenant in which all (and only) the faithful are saved regardless of era. What is true of the 'new covenant' in Jer 31:33-34 is true for all the faithful in any era. But then in the second part of their works both Olevianus and Ball return to a contrast of 'accidents' at stake in Jeremiah's 'new covenant', undercutting their own exegesis earlier offered and presenting no reasons or apology for the two conflicting readings. But nonetheless, we find in these influential theologians (as well as others) the preservation of the Augustinian 'salvific' contrast, however mixed or confused it might be.

This struggle within Reformed confessional orthodoxy does not cease after the fall of institutional orthodoxy. And in the mid-19th century the Augustinian option reappears in an unambiguous form in the work of the American Presbyterian theologian Robert Dabney (1820-98). So Dabney states:

> There is unquestionably, a difference asserted here [in Jer 31:31f]; and it is the difference between law and grace. But it is the Covenant of Sinai viewed in one of its limited aspects only, which is here set in antithesis to the Covenant of Grace.... The prophet points out to [the people] that the fate of the nation, under that theocratic bond, had been disaster and ruin; and this, because the people had ever been too perverse to comply with its legal terms, especially, inasmuch as God had left them to their own strength. But the spiritual covenant was to differ (*as it always had*), in this vital respect: that God, while covenanting with His people for their obedience, would make it His part to write His law in their hearts.[118]

Or more recently, and more directly similar to Augustine, is the 20th century American Presbyterian J. Oliver Buswell, Jr.:

---

118. Robert L. Dabney, *Lectures in Systematic Theology* (Grand Rapids, MI: Zondervan, 1972), 440-63, esp. 456-60. My emphasis.

Jeremiah's New Covenant

> A careful examination of these Scriptures [Jer 31:31-34; 2 Cor 3:6-16; Hebrews 7-8] will show that the Scripture writers themselves used the term 'old testament' to refer, not to the thirty-nine books which preceded the earthly life of Christ, nor to the revealed system of worship which the thirty-nine books contained, but to refer to a legalistic, self-righteous attitude in the contemplation of those books and their provisions. Similarly the words 'new testament' in Scripture refer not to the twenty-seven books given since the time of Christ on earth, but to that renewed relationship into which God's elect, in every age since the fall of man, have entered by faith.[119]

But by this time the entire discourse of biblical studies has shifted. And since the aim of this book is a reading of the 'new covenant' in Jer 31:31-34 that is both theologically interested *and* exegetically responsible, the focus will now take a final leap to follow the shift. We move now from the Reformed orthodox to 20th century exegetical discussions. Here we can leave off the idea of a 'sounding' within the theological tradition and step into more familiar territory for Old Testament studies. Nonetheless the territory cannot and does not escape the struggles and difficulties found throughout Christian interpretive history. And many modern readings, unaware of the deeper tradition, falter on similar grounds.

---

119. J. Oliver Buswell, Jr., *A Systematic Theology of the Christian Religion* (2 vols.; Grand Rapids, MI: Zondervan, 1962), I.307-08.

6

The New Covenant in Modern Discourse

We have throughout this study been content to take soundings of the Christian tradition, paying particular attention either to those readings which express an Augustinian reading of the contrast, or those marked by a tension due to shared concerns with the Augustinian reading (most of the Reformed). At each point we have stepped into a new context, explored the uses and readings of Jeremiah's new covenant, only to leap ahead to yet another place for exploration. Our next leap brings us into the modern period and the interpretations of Jeremiah that are the main concern of contemporary readers of the oracle. The movement into 'modern' readings of the Old Testament is one that has been told at various times and in various ways.[1] And even a cursory reading of the treatments of Jeremiah's new covenant in the modern period in comparison with earlier readings provides ample demonstration that significant shifts have occurred. But our interest is not the tracing of those shifts in approaches to reading the Old Testament, or of their philosophical or socio-political causes except insofar as is necessary to see the ways in which Jeremiah's oracle has been read up to the present.

Reading 20th century interpretations is something like watching Odysseus hold down Proteus: interpretations like new faces emerging constantly, some unique and some flatly contradictory. And the keypoint in each case is the search for a context—a constructed story or 'world'—in which the oracle is given its role to play. Putting the matter simplistically, the context for pre-modern Christian interpreters had as a necessary ingredient the oracle's ontology as divine communication. Thus Jeremiah's 'new covenant' played its role in the larger concern of the ways in which God revealed himself, his will, or truth more broadly to his people: it played a role within the coherent world of discourse given shape by who God is and what he has done. This is true for either Jerome or Augustine, or in a broad sense of any of the figures so far discussed. Such insistence on the oracle's divine origins was not in every case a dismissal of his-

---

1. See e.g., Henning Graf Reventlow, *The Authority of the Bible and the Rise of the Modern World* (Tr. by John Bowden. London: SCM Press, 1984).

tory—a bald and unfortunate caricature.² But the historical situating of the oracle was theologically secondary for its 'meaning', and even questions of history were answered within the context of other dogmatic or theological claims. This was emphatically not the case in the turn to modern readings of the prophets where the meaning of the oracle was to be tied to a publicly accessible historical context, and because publicly accessible, was forcibly divorced from dogmatics (the *Einleitung* of 19th-20th century biblical studies). As stated programmatically by Abraham Kuenen:

> It is an *historical* investigation for which we are preparing. That involves in it that all dogmatic pre-suppositions are set aside—that we continually consult the documents, and allow ourselves to be guided exclusively by their well-guaranteed testimonies.³

Thus the central concern in biblical studies became a 'historical' (and non-theological) context in which the oracle was seen to play its role—whether that is within the psychological experience of the 'great life' of Jeremiah,⁴ the wishes of an over-zealous scribe, the propaganda of the Deuteronomist reform or the response of later anti-Deuteronomists—or any number of other options.⁵ One significant result of this shift in allowable 'contexts' is the ignoring or displacing of those issues that most concerned pre-modernist readers such as Augustine or Vermigli. The theological claim of the unity of Scripture is displaced by the anthropological claim of historical development (*Entwicklung*). Thus, questions regarding whether Jer 31:31-34 can be harmonized with theological claims (as Augustine), or even with the witness of other biblical texts, are easily

---

2.   E.g. Gunkel's dismissal of the entire tradition: 'Orthodoxy... [saw] in the prophets the mere mechanical instruments of a simply supernatural revelation.' Hermann Gunkel, "The Secret Experiences of the Prophets," *Expositor* 9.1, 9.2 (1924): , 356.

3.   A. Kuenen, *The Prophets and Prophecy in Israel* (Tr. by Adam Milroy. London: Longmans, Green, & Co, 1877), 22. His emphasis. Cp. Vatke, 'Als historische Wissenschaft ist die biblische Theologie unabhängig von der Kirchenlehre und von den dogmatischen Systemen, und entlehnt ihren Stoff bloß aus der Schrift'. Cited in Lothar Perlitt, *Vatke und Wellhausen: Geschichtsphilosophische Voraussetzungen und historiographische Motive für die Darstellung der Religion und Geschichte Israels durch Wilhelm Vatke und Julius Wellhausen* (Berlin: Verlag Alfred Töpelmann, 1965), 94-95. For the philosophical statement of this shift, see Immanuel Kant, "An Answer to the Question: What is Enlightenment?," in *Practical Philosophy* (ed. Mary J. Giger; Cambridge: Cambridge Univ. Press, 1996).

4.   The phrase is from George Adam Smith, *Jeremiah* (London: Hodder & Stoughton, 1923), 7.

5.   For the purposes of this work I have focused on Old Testament scholarship as it has developed around the book of Jeremiah. Jer 31:31-34 continues to play a role, as can be expected, in dogmatic studies (e.g. Karl Barth or Hans Urs von Balthasar).

sidestepped or dismissed as inappropriate to what Skinner called the 'historical view of religion.'[6]

So as we leap into this new era, one more familiar to most readers of Jeremiah, I will tell the story as a search for a context in which the new covenant oracle can be made to play its 'original' role. As the faces seen in the oracle change we find one thread of unity: 'interiority' (though often in a vague or vacuous sense). But this turns us immediately back to Augustine, for his governing concern was one form of the denial of 'interiority' to the saints of the ancient era. In the end I will suggest that modern readers have largely been asking the wrong question regarding the point of contrast, assuming a particular narrative arc (or a variety of similar and dissimilar arcs) which remain in the theological and exegetical difficulties that have always plagued the non-Augustinian line of interpretation. At the end of the chapter, then, we will be ready to re-instate an Augustinian reading within the modern context of reading Jeremiah's new covenant.

1. *Bernard Duhm*

Bernard Duhm's seminal commentary of 1901 set the tone for modern exegetical studies of Jer 31:31-34, and represents well the continuity of the struggle and the discontinuity of the governing narrative over against pre-modern and early modern readings. Duhm's discussion is dominated by the conviction of the opposition between deuteronomistic and prophetic views of religion, developing Graf's and Ewald's distinction between the law and the prophets and indebted in no small part to Hegelian *Entwicklung*.[7] As early as 1875 Duhm had put forward a view of the prophets in the model of preachers of 'ethical mono-

---

6. John Skinner, *Prophecy and Religion: Studies in the Life of Jeremiah* (Cambridge: Cambridge Univ. Press, 1961), 331.

7. See, e.g., Bernhard Duhm, *Über Ziel und Methode der theologischen Wissenschaft* (Basel: Benno Schwabe, 1889). Duhm was likewise considerably influenced by German Romanticism, centering true religious thought in 'prophetic' (direct) communion with God. Thus the task of the theologian: 'Der Theologe hat, wenn er einem Jeremia, oder Paulus, oder Muhammed, oder Buddha gegenübersteht, erst noch zu prüfen, was an diesen Gestalten prophetisch ist und was nicht; diese Autoritäten grosser Religionsgesellschaften sind für ihn komplizierte Grössen und noch mehr sind es ihre Nachwirkungen (7).' For mention of Duhm's mysticism ('a strong divinatory strain')—which fits well with a Romantic view of the organic nature of the world into which one is drawn (*das Absolut*), and within which the 'prophetic' task is engaged—see Rudolf Smend, *From Astruc to Zimmerli: Old Testament Scholarship in Three Centuries* (Tr. by Margaret Kohl. Tübingen: Mohr Siebeck, 2007), 106-07. Smend also notes that Duhm's first theological book was Ewald's *Propheten* (p.104).

theism' standing outside and against the cultic and increasingly 'externalist' religion that would become Judaism.[8] Thus his narrative construct: the struggle between two views of religion in Israel's religious development as it progresses into the 'consummate religion' (to borrow Hegel's term) of Christianity. And within this construct we find the significance—or insignificance—of Jer 31:31-34:

> I have long struggled to understand this as those for whom it is undoubtedly a document from Jeremiah's hand.... Already this text, if due to Jeremiah, would be very important for other reasons, because in it the contrast between the prophetic and deuteronomistic views of religion would have to reveal itself. But such is not the case here. Admittedly, it promises a 'new covenant', but no new law—rather only an inner healing of the people with the law, and it lays the accent on the good consequences of this for the people, but it has no need for a higher kind of religion.[9]

So long as one is not 'dazzled' by some of the language ('new covenant' or 'written on the heart'), Duhm informs us, then we will simply see in the oracle a fulfilment of what was already envisioned as desirable and promised in Deuteronomy (citing 6:6-8 and 30:11). The text does not fit Duhm's view of the prophetic view of religion and thus cannot be attributed to Jeremiah:

> It is impossible for me to hold any longer to the jeremianic origin of this text. I find in it only the outburst of a scribe, who has for his highest ideal that everyone among the Jewish people know the law by heart and understand that all Jews are scribes.[10]

Duhm emphasizes the continuity of the Torah in each case, which he clearly finds distasteful. Hence he dismisses the oracls as a mere 'pious wish' that all would follow the same Torah as was always desired by the 'scribes':

> Had the author meant another law to be written on the heart, built on substantially different contents and character and better suited than the old, then he would have had to speak of it and in detail, for such would have been more important than everything of which he speaks—it would have been the truly reformed thought that one seeks in this text.... He is a fervent follower of the Torah and wishes nothing more ardently than that all Jews would be the same way, but throughout he offers us nothing more than this wish dressed up as a promise, without being able to say to us

---

8. Bernhard Duhm, *Die Theologie der Propheten als Grundlage für die innere Entwicklungsgeschichte der israelitischen Religion* (Bonn: Verlag von Adolph Marcus, 1875), esp. 73-91.

9. Bernhard Duhm, *Jeremia* (Tubingen: J.C.B. Mohr (Paul Siebeck), 1901), 254.

10. Ibid., 255.

from where he takes the right to promise what until now could only have been a pious wish (*ein frommer Wunsch*).[11]

The text lacks the 'creative spirit' expected of a prophet. Indeed:

> When he calls it a new covenant, it is yet in truth only a renewed covenant and the only difference is that in the future Yhwh will better ensure that the Israelites remain true to him.[12]

Duhm points out that even the final thought of the forgiveness of sins already existed and, far from ushering in a period governed by this principle of forgiveness, future sins would yet be punished in this pictured order if necessary (31:30). So there can be nothing 'new' here, other than the fulfillment of a 'pious wish' grounded in an inadequate view of religion.

Duhm was not the first to question the authenticity of the oracle to Jeremiah.[13] But he clearly meant to be provocative in doing so. The two main parts of his argument show a significant step in the movement from pre-modern to modern assumptions for reading the 'new covenant'. First, he claims that nothing here is foreign to the hopes and promises elsewhere found in the Old Testament, and especially in Deuteronomy and the Torah Psalms (1, 19 and 119). We find the same law and the same hope of faithfulness to it. Yet we have

---

11. Ibid., 256. The same basic arguments recur, with more focus on the continuation of the cultic laws, in Duhm, *Israels Propheten* (2nd ed. Tubingen: J.C.B. Mohr (Paul Siebeck), 1922), 456-58.

12. *Jeremia*, 256-57.

13. In the judgment of one earlier scholar, 'It was Smend... who first clearly set forth the internal evidence against the Jeremianic authorship of both chaps.' Nathaniel Schmidt, "Jeremiah (Book)," in *Encyclopaedia Biblica* (eds. T.K. Cheyne and J. Sutherland Black; London: Adam & Charles Black, 1901), 2384b. Schmidt follows the late dating here and in Nathaniel Schmidt, "Covenant," in *Encyclopaedia Biblical* (eds. T.K. Cheyne and J. Sutherland Black; London: Adam & Charles Black, 1899), 934b (it is set in 'the time of the Graeco-Persian war, when the writer confidently looked for extraordinary proofs of Yahwe's pardoning grace'). For Smend the oracle concerned a post-exilic 'Realisierung des prophetischen Ideals'. Rudolf Smend, *Lehrbuch der alttestamentlichen Religionsgeschichte* (Leipzig: J.C.B. Mohr (Paul Siebeck), 1893), 239-41, n.1. But Schmidt was apparently unaware that the authenticity is already questioned by Rowland Williams in 1871, who speaks of chs. 30-31 (including 31:31-34) as 'a song of encouragement by some Baruch or later Isaiah, far on in the exile, who yet may have used relics of the older prophet (perhaps his master?) as key-notes, from which to start his strain.' Rowland Williams, *The Hebrew Prophets* (2; London: Williams and Norgate, 1871), 277. And he is following the suggestion of F.C. Movers, *De utriusque recensionis vaticiniorum Ieremiae, Graecae Alexandrinae et Hebraicae marorethicae, indole et origine commentatio critica* (Hamburg: 1837), 37f.

already seen this put forward by (e.g.) John Ball, even pointing us to the same texts. In itself Duhm's claim is nothing unique. But the second and decisive step for Duhm lies in his narrative of the inner-development of Israelite religion. Thus, while for Ball this similarity of the oracle to Deuteronomy entailed a unity in the covenant (via a doctrine of the unity of God and Scripture), for Duhm the same similarity effects a dismissal of the oracle as a misguided religious approach. So Duhm happily limits the contrast to one factor, a healing of the old way of things:

> [T]he old and new covenants... do not stand as two substantially different views of religion, as the Christian likes to think, but only as two opposite historical periods: the first of which ended badly, but the second should run better. The new covenant is only new, therefore, because God will once more heal instead of simply abolishing the fragile covenant.

Whatever else one can say here about the Christian liking to think of two 'substantially different views of religion,' the traditional issues are still present, only transposed into a new realm of discourse. The only moment of truly theological inquiry comes when Duhm asks, 'why did Yhwh not do this same thing the first time?'[14] In essence this is similar to the question we saw in Oecolampadius: 'would God be so unfair that he would disdain the old with this grace?' But what Oecolampadius asks to render a more precise reading, Duhm asks to render the 'scribe' a fool. By asking the question Duhm considers his role complete.

There were many early responses to Duhm, but his general narrative of the inner-development of religious thought in Israel remained more or less unquestioned. The concern became to rescue the oracle as worthy of a prophet standing against the deuteronomic view of religion. The oracle was spoken of in prominence unseen in older commentaries. For instance, Samuel Driver offers his view with the full flourish of late Victorian rhetoric:

> This prophecy of the New Covenant is one of those great passages in the prophets, perhaps the greatest of all, which stand out from the rest and impress us by the wonderful spirituality of their tone, and by their evangelical character. Though this particular passage is not among those recorded to have been quoted by our Lord, it breathes emphatically His spirit, and is a striking declaration of the great principles of spontaneous personal service [!] on which in His ministry He so frequently insists.[15]

---

14. 'Aber zunächst hat man doch zu fragen: warum hat Jahwe das nicht gleich das erste Mal gethan?' Duhm, *Jeremia*, 256.

15. S.R. Driver, *The Ideals of the Prophets* (Edinburgh: T&T Clark, 1915), 44. This is from a posthumously published sermon.

Whatever else one might say about the claims, Jer 31:31-34 never had so many acclaimed admirers as we find in the Victorian era, Duhm's dismissal notwithstanding.

Among the first responses to Duhm is that of C.H. Cornill. Cornill acknowledges the two views of religion—though exempting the Decalogue as playing a part in this ('Is not the foundation of religion and morality for all time written into the Decalogue?').[16] Citing Jer 7:22-23 he claims that the new covenant Torah cannot be contrasted with 'cultic-religious' laws as Duhm implies, but must contrast with the 'practical-ethical regulations' as summarized in the Decalogue.[17] Yet the Decalogue could not be removed—'even Jesus did not waive it'. Citing Vatke, and with clear Hegelian overtones, Cornill remarks:

> Thus the content of the new covenant is not new in principle, and does not need to be... The newness is much more concerning 'the aspect of its reality', it is a 'covenant of conviction or the spiritual reality (*geistigen Realität*) of the earlier covenant'.[18]

What was external in the old is made internal in the new—made a 'spiritual reality'. This is, in one sense, not entirely different from earlier readings. But clearly the context and the function of the claim have shifted drastically. Cornill finds the 'novelty' in the classic internal vs. external distinction, set in contrast to the state of affairs presented in Exodus and now given form in Kantian moral categories:

> If we think think of the obvious relationship of our words to Ex. 31:18, their full content becomes clear: that the eternal moral law, whose observance Yhwh demands of humanity, and which he once wrote on cold stone at Sinai so that humanity faced it as something objective—as a rigid norm of a heteronomous morality—in the future, in the new gracious covenant with Israel, he will write on the warm heart of the one converted, that it would become for humanity as one's own internal voice, as a living impulse of an autonomous morality.[19]

---

16. C.H. Cornill, *Das Buch Jeremia* (Leipzig: Chr. Herm. Tauchnitz, 1905), 350. His view of the development of Israelite religion (again, a dialectical development) is more thoroughly seen in *The Prophets of Israel* (Tr. by Sutton F. Corkran. 4th ed. Chicago: The Open Court, 1899). There the 'sublime figure of Jeremiah' stands over against 'the disastrous consequences of the priestly reforms' of Deuteronomy, and presents the 'ideality and universality of religion' (91, 98).

17. Cornill, *Jeremia*, 349. Cf. W.J. Moulton, "The New Covenant in Jeremiah," *The Expositor, 7th Series* 1 (1906), 374.

18. Cornill, *Jeremia*, 350.

19. Ibid., 351. In Kantian moral philosophy the heteronomous moral principle

Thus, with the great movement of interiority and its moral imperative springing from a new heart and acting in justice and righteousness (which he takes from 22:16 as the 'formal definition' of 'know Yhwh') we have 'the quintessence of [Jeremiah's] whole theology and one of the greatest triumphs of faith'.[20]

W.J. Moulton takes a similar line of response to Duhm, though less overtly theological. Moulton asserts that the terminology used (כרת ברית) is not used by P. Thus for Moulton, 'we find ourselves driven back in our search for the old Covenant to the two descriptions of the transactions at Sinai contained in Exod 20-23 and in the early chapters of Deuteronomy.'[21] That the contrast might be within the book of Jeremiah does not even come into consideration. But moving back to Deuteronomy, 'we are at once arrested' by the language of Deut 4:13:

> Deut 4:13 And he declared to you his covenant, which he commanded you to perform—even the ten commandments. And he wrote them on two tablets of stone.

The point of contrast is found, from this, in the Decalogue itself understood as a 'covenant' and written on tablets of stone. The language does not sit far in this one respect from some of Reformed orthodoxy (e.g. Samuel Bolton) and a movement from the Law as a covenant to an interior reality. But of course we are transposed into far different settings. Moulton concludes rather confidently:

> As the result then of this discussion, arrived at without presuppositions, but from a study of linguistic use, we claim that we have shown that by the old Covenant the author of Jer 31:31ff. means the Decalogue and nothing else.[22]

This, Moulton suggests, render Duhm's skepticism about the import of the oracle rather benign. The true teaching is that the 'same Divine Hand' writes the Decalogue 'no longer on cold and lifeless stone, but on the warm and fleshly tables of the heart', pointing to Paul in 2 Cor 3.[23] Hence, for Moulton the prophet is exonerated from the charge of being linked to deuteronomic theology. That

---

stands outside and commands, the autonomous is within and spurs one on. Since the heteronomous can be followed out of impure motives, the autonomous is seen as a higher ethical principle. See Immanuel Kant, *Groundwork for the Metaphysics of Morals*, in *Practical Philosophy* (ed. Mary J. Giger; Cambridge: Cambrige Univ. Press, 1996), 83ff.

20. Cornill, *Jeremia*, 352.
21. Moulton, "New Covenant," 374.
22. Ibid., 376.
23. Ibid., 377.

earlier generations would have considered the contrast he cites as 'salvific' and force us to further questions does not appear in any form. It need not: the context for meaning has been exhausted by a description of historical development of religious thought within Israel.

2. *The New Covenant in the Life Experience of the Prophet*

Already in these early responses, the theme of the 'interiority' of the new as an improvement on the old is evident. This, we will see, remains a constant thread tying together the varied strands of interpretation in the modern period. But worth noting is that this is not new in interpretation. Beyond the immediate predecessors of Duhm,[24] we have seen the notion of 'internal' vs. 'external' at every point we have examined in the history of interpretation. But in the place of theological nuancing and reasoning for describing the significance of the internal/external contrast, we find instead a constructed narrative of Israelite religious history in which the contrast is made to play its role—and in particular, a view of the struggle between two 'views of religion' in that narrative.

This narrative takes further shape in the early 20th century when combined with a portrait of Jeremiah as a preacher of 'individualism', especially within the romanticized psychological approaches to the prophetic literature—an approach seen in lesser form in Duhm or Cornill, though inherent to the whole image of the prophet as given by Ewald.[25] Jeremiah's oracle is now to be under-

---

24. E.g. Graf, again in Hegelian garb: 'Das am Sinai bekannt gemachte Gesetz wird nicht etwa aufgehoben und durch ein anderes ersetzt, es treten keine neuen Rechte und Verpflichtungen ein, aber die Beziehung Israels zu dem unveränderlichen göttlichen Gesetze wird eine andere; das Gesetz steht ihm nicht mehr als etwas äusserlich Gegebenes und Auferlegtes gegenüber, von dem es sich mit Leichtsinn oder Widerwillen abwendet oder dem es als einer Last und Fessel widerspenstig und feindselig entgegentritt, sondern dasselbe wird ihm ein innerliches, geht in seine eigene Gesinnung über, der Wille jedes Einzelnen im Volke fühlt sich mit dem göttlichen Willen Eins, und die Forderung, die von Anfang an an das Volk gestellt (vgl. 7,23. 11,4. Lev 26,12. Deut. 26,17f.), aber bis jetzt unerfüllt geblieben war, geht jetzt in Erfüllung.' Karl Heinrich Graf, *Der Prophet Jeremia* (Leipzig: T.O. Weigel, 1862), 396.

25. 'If, then, a phenomenon, which refers also or chiefly to others, creates in an individual's mind so vivid and divine a conception that he recognizes it not as his own but as God's conception, its irresistible, intense power will urge him to declare it as such publicly to others; and with the same immediateness and strength with which it lives in him he will communicate it in that quarter where it was occasioned and where it appears necessary for the welfare of men.... It is precisely this that brings us to what we call *prophecy*.' Heinrich Ewald, *Commentary on the Prophets of the Old Testament* (5 vols.; Tr. by John Frederick Smith. London: Williams and Norgate, 1875), I.6-7. And see the

stood as a part of the life-experience of the prophet: the scholar is to 'penetrate... into the psychological and ethical and religious experience of his inner life'.[26] So the context shifts from a general description of Israelite religious development and placed within the psychological development and experience of the prophet. And in this context the prophet again proclaims with the 'new covenant' a new form of interiorization (an immediacy of relationship with God) and a new individualism. Jeremiah becomes 'the pioneer of a new individualism'[27] or 'the prophet of personal religion.'[28] We see all of these aspects in H.W. Robinson's 1925 remarks:

> This [Jer 31:31-34] is a description of *personal religion in its individualized experience*, and it implies fundamentally three things: (1) the moral inwardness of true religion; (2) its dependence on supernatural agencies; (3) its realization of a direct personal fellowship with God.... This recognition of the inwardness of sin is one of the definite contributions of Jeremiah to the truth about man.[29]

---

discussion of Jeremiah ('the prophet of such a tender heart, of such purity and innocence of mind, who was only too sincere, too affectionate, and too sympathetic towards his age'), who stands at the turning of prophecy, the 'evening star of the declining day of prophecy', allowing the 'feelings of the heart' to intrude upon the otherwise purely ('manful') prophetic discourse: Ibid., III.69f.

26. H. Wheeler Robinson, *The Cross of Jeremiah* (London: SCM Press, 1925), 4.

27. Idem, "Hebrew Psychology," in *The People and the Book* (ed. A.S. Peake; Oxford: Clarendon Press, 1925), 373. Cp. Volz: 'Und so wird endlich auh Jeremias Religion eine ganz persönliche, Gesinnung, Heryenssache, jedes Menschen Beruf, innerlichste Gemeinschaft zwischen Gott und der Seele.... Bei Jeremia quillt alles aus dem persönlichsten Erfahren heraus: von Mutterleib an persönlich ausersehen und geführt, keine größere Lust kennend als die Zweisprache mit Gott, von allen anderen Quellen der Freude und des Trostes abgeschnitten, in den verzweifelsten Kampf hineingestellt, ist er der eigentliche Gründer der persönlichen Religion geworden.' D. Paul Volz, *Der Prophet Jeremia* (2nd ed. Leipzig: A. Deichertsche Verlagsbuchhandlung D. Werner Scholl, 1928), xxvii.

28. A.R. Gordon, "A Study of Jeremiah," *The Biblical World* 22.2 (1903), 100. This movement stands against the earlier (and better) estimation of Smend: 'ist auch hier von einer eigentlichen Individualisierung der Religion nicht die Rede': Smend, *Religionsgeschichte*, 239.

29. Ibid., 67-68, 76. My emphasis. Or, 'Because the root of all the trouble is in the evil will of individual men, and habit has made it impossible for them of themselves to repent, the prophet dares to conceive some new realization of the eternal covenant-relation... Yahweh will not again give an external law, which men will disobey as before; He will work from within and by a spiritual change inspire a new and effectual knowledge of Himself in the hearts of men. The new relation will be upheld like that

But throughout such readings the basic narrative movement is the same (developing and competing views of religion) and more importantly, the basic principle is the same: the oracle's significance is found by carving out a role for it to play in the narrative. So John Skinner, representing the same dichotomy as Duhm but finding the opposite teaching in the oracle:

> If anything is vital in Jeremiah, it is his experience of religion as immediate fellowship with God, and his conviction that the reality of it consists in a right inward disposition, in the instinctive response of the heart to the revelation of God. The [Deuteronomic] Covenant, on the contrary, only establishes an external relation... It represents a view of religion which was natural and beneficial in the early history of Israel, but could only produce a false sense of security in the age of Deuteronomy.[30]

And again, Skinner is not far from a number of more traditional positions, the contrast seen as between the external commands of Deuteronomy and a future internal reality. But by reducing the task to a construction of religious development, one can no longer ask Augustine's question: did not the ancient fathers have such 'fellowship with God' and a 'right inward disposition'? Such a question cannot be answered by the 'historian'. The historian's concern ends with a description of Jeremiah's life-experience and showing the oracle's role as an expression of that life-experience. And for Skinner this means proclaiming the oracle as hailing 'a new religious relationship' centred on individualism and inwardness.[31]

---

between the prophet and his God in the intimacies of personal religion, which has got beyond the stage at which a human teacher is needed.... Jeremiah, psychologist as he is, is content to emphasize the inner conditions of such divine activity, the individual relation, the inner change, the touch of God'. Ibid., 85.

30. Skinner, *Prophecy*, 325. Or George Adam Smith: 'Jeremiah was called to prophesy about the time that the religion of Israel was re-codified in Deuteronomy—the finest system of national religion which the world has seen, but only and exclusively national—and he was still comparatively young when that system collapsed for the time and the religion itself seemed about to perish with it.' Smith, *Jeremiah*, 5.

31. 'The central truth, therefore, on which the emphasis of the prophecy lies, is the inwardness of true religion—the spiritual illumination of the individual mind and conscience, and the doing of the will of God from a spontaneous impulse of the renewed heart.' Skinner, *Prophecy*, 329-30. Note the similarity in language of 'spontaneous impulse' to the earlier Lutheran views. Further, in language that would have been clearly 'salvific' in a previous generation: 'If this is not to create a new heart in the Christian sense, it is only because the figure employed is inadequate to express the fulness of the idea which the writer has in his mind (331).'

These readings take a number of various shapes. George Adam Smith gives the narrative its fullest pathos in his 1922 Baird lectures:

> But when the rotten surface of the national life thus broke under the Prophet he fell upon the deeper levels of the individual heart, and not only found the native sinfulness of this to be the explanation of the public and social corruption but discovered also soil for the seed-bed of new truths and new hopes. Among these there is none more potent than that of the immediate relation of the individual to God.[32]

Paul Volz gives the same narrative a different shape by setting up a contrast between Jeremiah's perception of human character over against the 'deuteronomistic-Josianic reforms'. The latter failed to see that the Mosaic covenant itself was insufficient: what is needed is that 'Yhwh create new humans'.[33] Volz's discussion is not entirely absent from the emphasis on individuality (the communion of 'God and the soul'), though he puts this a step away from the oracle.[34] Jeremiah's proclamation of the new covenant offers the 'seed (*Keim*) of the future development' regarding 'the independence of the religious individual'.[35] With this oracle we take one step closer to the full realization of true 'religion' in its fully individualized state. Whether the overtones of Hegel are significant or not, we still remain with the task of locating the oracle within the psychological development of the 'great life' of Jeremiah, which itself occurs within a constructed narrative of Israel's religious history.

---

32. Smith, *Jeremiah*, 368.

33. 'Es machte auf die nachdenklichen Geister tiefsten Eindruck, daß die deuteronomisch-josianische Reform den Charakter des Volkes nicht geändert hatte, ja an ihm zerbrochen war.... Nicht etwa bloß Josias Beritschluß, nein die MoseßBerit muß aufgehoben werden; damit ist überhaupt die gegenwärtige Weltzeit zu Ende, Jahwe schafft neue Menschen, Menschen des Wohlgefallens.' Volz, *Jeremia*, 298.

34. 'Die Hoffnung bleibt zunächst noch im Rahmen Israels; an die Stelle der idealen Mosegemeinde, die sich im geschichtlichen Verlauf nicht hatte halten können, tritt das neue Israel der dauernden Zukunft. Wie überall im A.T. sind auch hier Gott und das Volk verbunden, noch nicht Gott und die Seele, und in gewissem Sinn behält dies ja auch für alle Zeiten seine Geltung. Aber Jeremias Weissagung leitet doch über von der nationalgefaßten Religion Israels, in der Jahwe das Volk geführt und sich in der Geschichte geoffenbart hatte, zu der neuen, unbeschränkten Religion, in der die Stimme Gottes an die Seele ergeht. Und so verschwindet bei dieser Berit alles Nationale, aller Erwählungsglaube in dem rein Menschlichen und Innerlichen: wer Gott erkennt, gehört zum Volke Gottes.' Ibid., 297.

35. Ibid., 298.

3. *The New Covenant in the Prophetic Traditions*

These readings of the prophets as great 'inspired' individuals begin to fade by the mid-century. One can still find the perspective represented but with the increasing recognition that the prophets could not be seen as Ewald's visionary individuals standing outside of the cult and tradition. Clements suggests that this shift developed out of Gunkel's and Mowinkel's proposals of prophetic forms of discourse that stemmed from cultic activities.[36] But even more important in the larger scheme has been the fall from grace of romantic hermeneutics that make such readings appear to us as rather naïve. So perhaps the inevitable result occurred, and the prophets by mid-century were seen as a part of Israel's traditions, and the books which bear their names were given shape by and in those (often opposing) traditions. So by the middle of the century one still finds references to the phenomenon of 'prophetic religion', but this is itself put forward as essentially a particular 'tradition' in which the prophet stood.[37]

Gerhard von Rad, a prince among Old Testament interpreters in the 20th century, led much of the charge in locating the prophets within the developing traditions of Israel:

> If the prophets' teaching can no longer be derived simply from their religious experience, the question of its origin has to be put in a different

---

36. The former—perhaps accidental to the shift at best—is emphasised by R.E. Clements, *A Century of Old Testament Study* (London: Lutterworth Press, 1976), 70. Helpful surveys of modern prophetic scholarship can be found in Clements (ibid); and Robert P. Gordon, "A Story of Two Paradigm Shifts," in *"The Place Is Too Small for Us": The Israelite Prophets in Recent Scholarship* (ed. Robert P. Gordon; Winona Lake: Eisenbrauns, 1995). German-language studies from mid-19th c. to the 1960's are well covered by Peter H.A. Neumann, "Prophetenforschung seit Heinrich Ewald," in *Das Prophetenverständnis in der deutschsprachigen Forschung seit Heinrich Ewald* (ed. Peter H.A. Neumann; Darmstadt: Wissenschaftliche Buchgesellschaft, 1979).

37. So, e.g., J.P. Hyatt, *Prophetic Religion* (NY: Abingdon Cokesbury, 1947). This is not to say the influence of the earlier line disappeared—see, e.g., Artur Weiser's comments: 'Jeremia redet hier aus eigener Erfahrung. Diese Gedanken... sind gewonnen auf dem Weg, den der Prophet in der Unmittelbarkeit seines persönlichen Vewrhältnisses zu Gott und seinem Auftrag geführt wurde...; daher auch die eigenartig individuelle Zuspitzung des Bundesverhältnisses und die persönliche Vertiefung der Erkenntnis Gottes, die dem Bundesgedanken jene neue Note gibt, welche den neuen Bund vom alten abhebt.' Artur Weiser, *Der Prophet Jeremia 25,14-52,34* (Göttingen: Vandenhoeck & Ruprecht, 1955), 295. The emphasis on a distinct 'prophetic tradition' has received significant recent support, and most relevantly for our project in H. Lalleman-de Winkel, *Jeremiah in Prophetic Tradition: An Examination of the Book of Jeremiah in the Light of Israel's Prophetic Traditions* (Leuven: Peeters, 1997).

way—in what theological milieu was their unique independence and religious authority active?[38]

Von Rad presents a reconstructed history of Israel's traditions as Israel continued reflecting and re-reflecting on her existence as the people of God, one eye firmly set upon her traditions and the other upon current developing situations. So we re-set the new covenant oracle again, this time into these developing traditions and reflections. Von Rad begins by claiming that Jer 30-31, oracles originally given to the North, might lead one to think that 'the time of salvation of which Jeremiah speaks is in all essentials a restoration of previous conditions. The truth', however, 'is quite opposite.'[39] Von Rad sets Jeremiah over against the previous 'basis of salvation' on which Israel relied and paints the contrast in the starkest terms:

> The adjective 'new' in Jer 31:31 implies the complete negation of the saving events on which Israel had hitherto depended [the election traditions, etc.]. Such a judgment was infinitely harsher than any previous one for it was an out and out challenge to the validity of the basis of salvation on which Israel relied. It is as though these prophets had changed the outlook of faith by 180 degrees. The saving power of the old ordinances is abolished, and Israel can only find salvation in new, future saving appointments on Jahweh's part.[40]

The point of novelty that drives this great wedge between the past and the future 'saving events' is found in 'one essential feature': the law on the heart.

> [H]ere is the point where the new factor comes into operation—there is to be a change in the way in which the divine will is to be conveyed to men. At Sinai, Jahweh had spoken from the mountain top, and the Elohist—thus early—reports that Israel could not endure this address... If we understand Jeremiah correctly, the new thing is to be that the whole process of God's speaking and man's listening is to be dropped. This road of listening to the divine will had not led Israel to obedience. Jahweh is, as it were, to bypass the process of speaking and listening, and to put his will straight into Israel's heart.[41]

Von Rad admits that this ideal was present on 'every page of Deuteronomy': but it is the *mechanism* that von Rad sees as new. The hope in Deuteronomy was that the law would be placed on the heart through its being heard,

---

38. Gerhard von Rad, *Old Testament Theology* (2 vols.; Tr. by D.G.M. Stalker. Edinburgh: Oliver and Boyd, 1962), II.5.
39. Ibid., II.212.
40. Ibid., II.271.
41. Ibid., II.213.

154 Modern Discourse

studied, and memorized. Now that whole way of demanding obedience from the outside is eliminated and God will put his will into the heart directly, creating 'a man who is able to obey perfectly because of a miraculous change of his nature.'[42]

With von Rad we have moved out of earlier ideas of 'individualism,' rightly dismissed as entirely foreign to the oracle.[43] But in a way structurally similar to Oecolampadius, the novelty of the 'new covenant' in the future era comes from what is *not* said: i.e. no further mediating of the law. Yhwh himself will place the Torah on the heart, thus eliminating the need for teaching/hearing. Von Rad is by no means the only modern interpreter to take this approach.[44] Yet the argument is difficult to sustain. The oracle's statement that Yhwh will put the law on the heart says nothing about the way in which this is to be done.[45] Indeed, there are plenty of instances in Jeremiah of divine action as mediated, yet still spoken of as the direct work of Yhwh: Judah's judgment is everywhere re-

---

42. Ibid., II.213-14.
43. Ibid., II.216.
44. So Moshe Weinfeld: the Torah 'would not be enforced from without through learning and indoctrination which could be forgotten and put out of mind.' Moshe Weinfeld, "Jeremiah and the Spiritual Metamorphosis of Israel," *ZAW* 88.1 (1976), 28. Or more bluntly, Unterman: 'This [transmission of the Torah to the heart] will be accomplished without any intermediary—a direct transmission without the use of an agent, neither human (a prophet or a priestly instructor) nor material (tablets or book). Furthermore, the re-giving of the torah will not be accompanied by a revelation which affects the senses of sight and hearing.' Jeremiah Unterman, *From Repentance to Redemption: Jeremiah's Thought in Transition* (JSOTSup 54; Sheffield: Sheffield Academic Press, 1987), 98. Or, 'A new law is not properly envisaged at all, but only a new way of Israel's knowing and keeping the existing law of the covenant made on Sinai (Horeb).' R.E. Clements, *Jeremiah* (Atlanta: John Knox Press, 1988), 191. See also Jože Krašovec, *Reward, Punishment, and Forgiveness: The Thinking and Beliefs of Ancient Israel in the Light of Greek and Modern Views* (VTSup 78; Leiden: Brill, 1999), 455; Beate Ego, "'In meinem Herzen berge ich dein Wort': Zur Rezeption von Jer 31,33 in der Torafrömmigkeit der Psalmen," *Jahrbuch für Biblische Theologie* 12 (1997), 280-81; Lalleman-de Winkel, *Jeremiah*, 201; Gräbe, *New Covenant*, 54-55. Or, Potter: 'God will give direct, intuitive knowledge of his law... This then is what is new about the covenant: it will no longer be mediated by scribes and the élite, but will be universally apprehended by one and all, from the greatest to the least.' H.D. Potter, "The New Covenant in Jeremiah XXXI 31-34," *VT* 33.3 (1983), 353.
45. So, in a fashion, Coppens, 'Le texte de Jérémie...entrevoit la présence future de la loi dans la sein des croyants comme un don de Deiu. Il reste que ce don n'exclut pas nécessairement la grâce simultanée d'une promulgation externe des volontés divines.' J. Coppens, "La nouvelle alliance en Jer 31,31-34," *CBQ* 25.1 (1963), 17.

ferred to in just this way (e.g. 30:14, '*I* have dealt you the blow of an enemy'). If the judgment can be mediated yet the direct act of God, why not the restoration? This is not to say that the text requires mediation, but that it does not address the issue: it is Yhwh's work, however it may come about. Von Rad is dependent upon the text not mentioning mediation for Yhwh's work, but this cannot be said to be a conclusive 'novelty' by its absence.[46]

In John Bright's work we find a further development, returning somewhat to a deliberate reflection on the career of Jeremiah but avoiding a divorce between the prophets and tradition. The structure of Bright's commentary—rearranging the various oracles into their reconstructed chronological order—is itself a sign of the power of the contextual narrative for determining the significance and meaning of the disparate oracles. Reconstructed history displaces the canonical shape. The oracle, Bright claims, 'is complete in itself and without original connection with the sayings that precede it and follow it.'[47] This, I take to be a crucial first step that is only somewhat more explicit than others before him: freed from the role the oracle plays in the book Bright can place it where he wills. So he places it in Jeremiah's preaching to Judah after 587, though allowing some re-working by later editors.[48] In order to 'grasp its force,' however, we

---

46. This, not to mention the theological issues that would return us to Augustine: if they had the law on the heart apart from divine action, we are back with Julian of Aeclanum. Such comes into focus especially in the discussions of Thiel and Coppens. Thiel says, 'Was im Dtn als Forderung genannt wird, steht hier als Gabe Jahwes in Aussicht... Der vom Propheten überwiegend als Desiderat in der Anklage oder in der Jahweklage verwendete Begriff wird von D als Gabe Jahwes in die Zukunft projiziert.' Winfried Thiel, *Die deuteronomistische Redaktion von Jeremia 26-45* (Neukirchen-Vluyn: Neukirchener Verlag, 1981), 25-26. Or Coppens: 'Une différence subsiste toutefois notable entre ces textes et Jer 31,31-34. Le Deutéronome considère la présence de la loi dans le coeur des fidèles comme l'aboutissement d'actes que les enfants d'Israël auront à accomplir généreusement pour s'assimiler les commandements divins.' Coppens, "Nouvelle alliance," 16. Against this way of division, Dumbrell is more sure guide: 'Of course, the Old Testament calls upon the individual to ensure that the law is in the heart. This does not mean, however, that the individual puts it there... Whatever tensions may exist between calls to lodge the law in the heart and the implication that only God may put it there, they are not peculiar, as we well know, to the salvation experience of the Old Testament.' W.J. Dumbrell, *Covenant and Creation: A Theology of the Old Testament Covenants* (Exeter: Paternoster, 1984), 180.

47. John Bright, "An Exercise in Hermeneutics: Jeremiah 31:31-34," *Int* 20.2 (1966), 192.

48. The text 'is an accurate representation of the mind, if not necessarily the precise phraseology, of the Prophet himself.' Ibid., 193. Or, 'Although the passage may not preserve the prophet's *ipsissima verba*, it represents what might well be considered the high point of his theology.' John Bright, *Jeremiah* (The Anchor Bible 21; New York:

must first see the situation in which Jeremiah is standing. Jeremiah 'was plainly convinced' that Israel had broken the covenant and had become 'incorrigible' in their sins; the reforms of Josiah had only disillusioned Jeremiah, who became increasingly pessimistic so that he soon saw judgment as the only possible solution. But Jeremiah was convinced that this could not be 'the end of God's dealings with Israel' and so pronounces this 'renewed covenant' that will overcome Israel's inability to live in the covenant.[49] The career and experience of Jeremiah provide the narrative in which the oracle plays its role of announcing a new interiority, stemming from Jeremiah's personal disappointments with external forces of change.

Though clearly seeing the main teaching of the text as a contrast between the era of the Old Testament and that of a future era (brought in by Christ), in the sermon attached to his treatment of the text Bright takes a sudden turn to the subjectivity of the contrast that Jeremiah pronounces: what Bright calls the 'B.C.' aspect of every person and every era.[50] The hope that Jeremiah offers refers also to this subjective aspect of standing before God and our covenantal failures, he remarks. These statements are not far from the way of thinking for Augustine's reading: the absoluteness of the contrast before God, regardless of era. But with Bright this point is entirely displaced. The central difference between Bright and any Augustinian reading is Bright's dismissal of deuteronomic thought as essentially Pelagian. For Augustine the contrast of *vetus* and *novum testamentum* as 'salvific' meant that one could not speak of that previous era as simply the *vetus testamentum* (in Jeremiah's sense). With Bright we find no such conclusions.

Instead, Bright has moved the entire issue into the life-story of Jeremiah which becomes paradigmatic for ourselves. So until we become disillusioned with any human efforts to bring about true reform in ourselves and our society (as attempted by Josiah, Ezra and Nehemiah), we stand needing to hear the promise of the 'new covenant'—that is, the hope of the Gospel.[51] Bright has

---

Doubleday, 1965), 287.

49. The full pathos of the narrative construal is seen in John Bright, *Covenant and Promise* (London: SCM Press, 1977), 140-98; Bright, "Exercise in Hermeneutics," 196-98.

50. '[T]heologically speaking, B.C. is not an epoch that ended with the birth of Christ; it is a condition of living. Whoever is not subject to the lordship of Christ is B.C.: for him, Christ has not yet come. So our world is still largely a B.C. world.... Moreover, B.C. continues in the church and in each one of us.' Ibid., 200.

51. The link to earlier readings is clear, if somewhat less overt (cp. Volz above). Another earlier interpreter is less subtle: '[J]ust as Paul and Luther were led through the errors of Pharisaism and Romanism to their matchless insight into the gospel

turned his constructed narrative of Jeremiah's life (despair in human reforms becoming hope in divine action) into the paradigm Christian narrative moving from belief in ourselves to trust in God (the new covenant). Or to put it another way, with the oracle of the new covenant the Pelagian deuteronomists are overcome by the Augustinian Jeremiah.[52]

Such a reading of the life of Jeremiah, moving from despair in outward reforms to hope in a divine working on the heart—with its strong ties to the earlier readings of Cornill, Skinner and others—has been a popular modern option.[53] And, like von Rad or Bright, this hope in a new interior working is typically set over against the hopes of the deuteronomistic reforms.[54] Thus the sum-

---

of salvation by faith, so Jeremiah was led through practical experience of the impotence of the "renewed covenant" [of Josiah and Deuteronomy] to his almost Christian [sic!] conception of the "new covenant"—the covenant, not of the letter and of law, but of the Spirit and of grace.' Gordon, "A Study of Jeremiah," 106.

52. Or, as Carroll critiques such readings: 'Jeremiah emerges as a Luther opposing the Catholic Church's devotion to rituals, images and superstitions and preaching an alternative religion of the heart.' Robert P. Carroll, *From Chaos to Covenant* (London: SCM Press, 1981), 97.

53. 'The passage may be the fruit of reflection on the failure of the Deuteronomic reform of 621: Jeremiah has realized that you cannot save human beings by telling them to behave. He will thus anticipate teaching on grace.' Bernard P. Robinson, "Jeremiah's New Covenant: Jer 31,31-34," *Scandinavian Journal of the Old Testament* 15.2 (2001), 197. Similarly, Werner E. Lemke, "Jeremiah 31:31-34," *Int* 37.2 (1983); R.E. Clements, *Prophecy and Covenant* (London: SCM Press, 1965), 113. (Though Clements later distances the oracle somewhat from Jeremiah: Clements, *Jeremiah*, 189-90.)

54. Again Robinson: 'I take the passage to be Jeremianic in substance. The individual heart, it implies, is so corrupt that it cannot of itself make the necessary response, so a bilateral covenant as made between YHWH and his spouse Israel on Sinai/Horeb will not serve... Through experience of the Deuteronomic reform, and reflection on the Hosea tradition, Jeremiah came to see the need for unilateral action on YHWH's part on the heart of the individual'. Robinson, "New Covenant," 204. Somewhat uniquely, but still in this same line is Koch: the oracle holds out an 'eschatological future' in which 'God and man will come close to one another in spirit and discernment—so close that the divine will that creates community and fellowship will be freely accepted by the mind of every individual and will be followed understandingly.' Given that this rules out apostasy, he claims the oracle stands 'in diametrical opposition to Deuteronomy, where election to the covenant counts as irrepealable'. Klaus Koch, *The Prophets* (2: The Babylonian and Persian Periods; London: SCM Press, 1983), II.68, 67. Setting aside the reading of Deuteronomy, the Jeremianic side of this statement is only possible by ignoring 31:35-37 entirely (among others).

mary of Artur Weiser, where we find Jeremiah speaking 'from his own experience':

> [The new covenant is 'new' only] to the extent that the people's relationship to God experiences a reorganization (*Neugestaltung*) in the new covenant, as the demand of God becomes the gift of God in which God gives his law to the people in the heart and thus provides the voluntariness and power of a joyful obedience.[55]

The oracle shows Jeremiah's own movement from a covenant of 'demand' to one of 'gift'—from law to grace. Again, the overtones of earlier theological issues and concerns lie immediately under the text and in particular with respect to Lutheran theology. But divorced from the large-scale discussion and set within the reconstructed history of religious development in Israel, we have a complete lack of the theological concerns raised by pre-modern interpreters. Happy to dismiss the 'deuteronomists' as Pelagian, the authors never notice Augustine's concerns against reading the oracle as contrasting two religio-historical eras.

Two final illustrations of this line of modern thought are worth noting. William Holladay, like Bright and others, also offers a large-scale reconstruction of the life of Jeremiah as the context in which the oracles are given a role to play. Holladay reads Jeremiah 30-31 as initially preached to the north by the prophet, and then reworked in the context of the fall of Jerusalem. But Holladay closes this redacted scroll at 31:28, leaving 31:31-34 as an even later supplement (though still jeremianic). The oracle, Holladay suggests, arose in Jeremiah's 'counter-proclamation to the recitation of Deuteronomy in Jerusalem at the festival of booths in September/October 587.'[56] The reader can feel the tension of Holladay's narrative: standing in the newly-destroyed temple with a straggling remnant of people reciting Deuteronomy, Jeremiah rises and delivers this oracle deliberately using deuteronomic diction and themes. In uttering the 'shocking' words, he 'implies that Yahweh will draw up a fresh contract without the defects of the old, implying in turn that he could improve on the old one, that he had learned something from the failure of the old'.[57] Offering a reading similar to Cornill, Holladay points to two contrasts for the new covenant—sin engraved on the heart (17:1) and the law engraved on stone (Deut 5:22)—then concludes:

---

55. Weiser, *Jeremia 25-52*, 295.

56. William L. Holladay, *Jeremiah* (2 vols.; Minneapolis: Fortress, 1986), 165. This setting is reiterated in Idem, "Elusive Deuteronomists, Jeremiah, and Proto-Deuteronomy," *CBQ* 66.1 (2004), 70-73.

57. Holladay, *Jeremiah*, 197.

The difficulty with the old covenant, then, is that it was written exteriorly and allowed for insincere obedience... or for outright rebellion on the part of the people. Yahweh's new action will bring about a new situation wherein the people will obey freely and gladly, and rebellion will be a thing of the past.[58]

Holladay's narrative is interesting, not only for the unique location of the oracle in Jeremiah's career, but also for the shift from a changing view of religion in the prophet or community (anthropological perspective) to Jeremiah's asserted changeability in God—Yhwh himself 'had learned something' from the failure of the deuteronomic reforms. In another movement within Yhwh we find the forgiveness of sins in v.34: 'What Yahweh yearned to do before, he will now be able to do.'[59] Duhm's question ('Why did God not do this before?') seems to be answered: because either he couldn't or he didn't know better.

A final illustration of this line of thought is developed, without the large-scale reconstructions, by Bernard Renaud. Renaud asserts that the 'theological originality of the oracle favors its jeremianic authenticity'.[60] Again, Jeremiah's 'anthropological pessimism' is emphasized as the (psychological?) cause of the turn to the 'pure grace' of 31:31-34.[61] Renaud sees the oracle as a strong contrast to the deuteronomistic ideals and a rejection of them in favor of a future (eschatological) act of divine grace that would transform all 'Israel and Judah' so that the law is accomplished 'spontaneously' from the 'depths of one's being'.[62] Thus, as opposed to the 'externalities' of the earlier covenant, Jeremiah announces the 'radical novelty of the covenant to come, a novelty characterised by the interiorisation of the law in the heart and the intimate and direct knowledge of God that results from it.'[63] But this leaves a problem for Israel as they wait for this future divine act: what is to ensure that they will survive as a people with Yhwh until he brings about this act of 'pure grace'? Instead of appealing to Jer 31:35-37, which he brackets out of the discussion, he appeals to a history of

---

58. Ibid., 198.
59. Ibid., 199.
60. Bernard Renaud, *Nouvelle ou Éternelle Alliance? Le message des prophètes* (Paris: Les Éditions du Cerf, 2002), 73.
61. Ibid., 71, 70, cf. 55f. et passim.
62. 'la nouvelle alliance offre une telle immédiateté au cœur, c'est-à-dire à la conscience de l'homme, que de l'être profond (*beqirbam*) jaillira l'élan spontané vers son accomplissement.' Ibid., 56.
63. Ibid., 75. Elsewhere he adds to these two, 'une personnalisation des relations au cœur même de la communauté d'alliance (55).' For the interior/exterior contrast, see his remark on 31:33, 'Il y aurait donc contraste entre un passé marqué par le don d'une loi extérieure et un future caractérisé par l'inériorisation de cette loi (34).'

reception of the oracle by Jeremiah's and Ezekiel's disciples and the terminology of the ברית עולם ('eternal covenant'). This latter concept emerges to fill the gap to guarantee Israel as a people before Yhwh until the fulfillment of the ברית חדשה.[64]

In all of these lines of thought—relatively consistent from the responses to Duhm by Moulton and Cornill through the psychological readings and into von Rad, Holladay and Renaud—we find a consistent line of thought: Jeremiah was confronting the externality of the deuteronomists (or some such religious perspective) with a new interiority. The reading of the oracle becomes intertwined with some re-constructed narrative of the life and work of Jeremiah—the oracle given its role to play within such a re-constructed narrative.

4. *The New Covenant and the Deuteronomists*

Thus far we have seen the oracle—with the exception of Duhm—treated as a part of the life or traditions of Jeremiah. But since Mowinkel's influential work in 1914 scholars have often found (or asserted) another source lurking behind Jeremiah's composition: the deuteronomist.[65] And as with nearly

---

64. See also his earlier article on this development, Bernard Renaud, "L'alliance éternelle d'Ez 16,59-63 et l'alliance nouvelle de Jr 31,31-34," in *Ezekiel and his Book* (ed. J. Lust; Leuven: Univ. of Leuven, 1986). He is disputed in this by Vermeylen, for whom 'comme en Ez 16, la seule différence entre les deux alliances réside dans le fait que la fidélité d'Israël et désormais assurée par Dieu lui-même, et que la trahison n'est donc plus possible.' J. Vermeylen, "L'alliance renouvellée (Jr 31,31-34). L'histoire littéraire d'un text célèbre," in *Lectures et relectures de la Bible* (eds. J.-M. Auwers and A. Wénin; Leuven: Leuven Univ. Press, 1999), 78. For full discussion of ברית עולם in the Pentateuch (and offering no support to Renaud's thesis), see Steven D. Mason, *"Eternal Covenant" in the Pentateuch: The Contours of an Elusive Phrase* (Library of Hebrew Bible/Old Testament Studies; Edinburgh: T&T Clark, 2008).

65. Sigmund Mowinckel, *Zur Komposition des Buches Jeremia* (Dybwad: Kristiania, 1914). Such discussions have become more tentative in recent years: see the essays by Norbert Lohfink, "Was There a Deuteronomistic Movement?"; Richard Coggins, "What Does "Deuteronomistic" Mean?"; Robert R. Wilson, "Who Was the Deuteronomist? (Who Was Not the Deuteronomist?): Reflections on Pan-Deuteronomism;" all in the volume, *Those Elusive Deuteronomists* (eds. Linda S. Schearing and Steven L. McKenzie; Sheffield: Sheffield Press, 1999). So now Christl Maier, for instance, speaks of standing 'zwischen Pandeuteronomismus" und "Nulldeuteronomismus"'. *Jeremia als Lehrer der Tora: Soziale Gebote des Deuteronomiums in Fortschreibungen des Jeremiabuches* (Gottingen: Vandenhoeck & Ruprecht, 2002), 34f.

every oracle, 31:31-34 has from time to time been asserted to be a fruit of this deuteronomic redactor (or school of redactors).

In one strand of this position three scholars—Kutsch, Perlitt and Nicholson—follow the lead of Julius Wellhausen by mounting the argument upon a development of 'covenant' as a theological term. In such a scheme the earlier traditions were largely concerned with ברית as 'obligation' (*Verpflichtung*), and only in later developments did this become a theological expression of a relationship between Yhwh and the people.[66] Since Kutsch places the oracle prior to this 'theological' understanding of covenant, Jer 31:31-34 contrasts two sets of obligations: the deuteronomistic obligation to put the law on one's own heart (old covenant), and a divine 'self-obligation' that will make the Torah interior and so followed 'automatically' (new covenant).[67] The same line is taken in Nicholson, who places the oracle late in the deuteronomic tradition, holding out a 'paradoxical theory according to which God himself promises to make possible the very response which he inexorably demands.'[68] The goal and pattern of the two covenants (old and new) are the same, Nicholson maintains, with this single difference of divine enablement.[69]

---

66. Kutsch puts off the development of ברית as initiating relationship between two parties until the translations of the Old Testament (Targumim, LXX). Perlitt and Nicholson find the development in the Old Testament traditions themselves. Ernst Kutsch, *Verheissung und Gesetz* (Berlin: Walter de Gruyter, 1973); Lothar Perlitt, *Bundestheologie im Alten Testament* (Neukirchen-Vluyn: Neukirchener Verlag, 1969); Ernest W. Nicholson, *God and His People: Covenant and Theology in the Old Testament* (Oxford: Clarendon Press, 1986).

67. 'Der Sinn von v.31-33 ist somit folgender: Jahwe hat bei der Herausführung aus Ägypten den Israeliten eine *berît* = Verpflichtung festgesetzt. Diese Verpflichtung haben die Israeliten nicht eingehalten, sie haben sie zunichte gemacht, gebrochen.... Nun will Jahwe—"nach diesen Tagen" (v.33aα)—noch einmal einen Neuanfang setzen mit Israel. Er wird eine "neue *berît*" festsetzen, eine neue Verepflichtung. Im Unterschied zu der früheren werden die Israeliten diesmal die Verpflichtung nicht brechen, sondern einhalten; denn: die Verpflichtung wird derart sein (כי זאת הברית), daß Jahwe sine Tora den Israeliten "in ihr Inneres gibt und auf ihr Herz schreibt", so daß sie dann ohne gegenseitge Belehrung "Jahwe kennen" (v.34a.bα), ihm gehorchen, seine Tora befolgen werden.' The movement is from the 'Verpflichtung der Israeliten' to a 'Selbstverpflichtung'. Kutsch, *Verheissung*, 145-46.

68. Nicholson, *God and His People*, 216. Cp. his earlier view 'that the "new covenant" passage...is entirely the work of the Deuteronomists'. Ernest W. Nicholson, *Preaching to the Exiles: A Study of the Prose Tradition in the Book of Jeremiah* (Oxford: Blackwell, 1970), 138, n.1. This 'paradoxical theory', of course, has been a part of Christian theology for quite some time.

69. 'What is different is that in a new act of grace Yahweh is so to transform

That Augustine would see this as damning the whole of the ancient era, leaving the ancient fathers to themselves apart from divine enablement, does not come into the discussion: again, the oracle's significance is not understood with respect to divine realities and actions (as for Augustine) but with respect to publicly accessible historical developments in ancient Israelite religion. So, as in the above readings, here we find the same type of assertion of a 'new interiority' over against the elusive 'deuteronomist', now simply transplanted into a new narrative apart from Jeremiah the prophet.

This new post-Jeremianic construction of the oracle is taken in a different direction by H.-J. Kraus and Robert Carroll. For Kraus the oracle—far from a challenge to deuteronomic theology—is a fulfillment of deuteronomistic hopes. And so he finds it best to view the oracle as a late stage in the theological development of this position. 'Deuteronomistic preaching and teaching pursued only one goal: that the Torah penetrate into the heart of people.'[70] Jeremiah looked and saw that the failure of the people was just this problem with the heart (17:9), and so gave rise to later thoughts of the new covenant oracle. But with the promise of the law on the heart, the Torah finally reaches its goal and is fulfilled through this future 'new relationship with God.'[71] Kraus garners some support for this in examining the reception of this ideal in post-exilic Judaism, beginning with the Torah Psalms (1, 19b, 119). These Psalms 'stand in an unmistakable relationship with the deuteronomic and deuteronomistic tradition.'[72] Further, their standing in the line of Jeremiah is buttressed by the individualism (once again) implied in Deuteronomy's and Jeremiah's emphasis on

---

the will of Israel that it will henceforth spontaneously live as his people.' Nicholson, *God and His People*, 212. Or, 'the new covenant like the old involves a response from Israel in terms of observance of the Law, with this major difference, however, that Israel's past failure to obey it is now to be replaced by both the will and the ability to obey which Yahweh will graciously place in her heart'. Nicholson, *Preaching*, 83. Likewise Perlitt, who explicitly uses von Rad: Perlitt, *Bundestheologie*, 180.

70. Hans-Joachim Kraus, *Biblisch-theologisches Aufsätze* (Neukirchen-Vluyn: Neukirchener Verlag, 1972), 182.

71. 'Jahwes tora soll unter allen Umständen zum Ziel gelangen sie soll aufgenommen, befolgt und erfüllt werden. Mehr noch: Jahwes tora wird—das ist der Inhalt der Verheißung—tatsächlich erfüllbar sein in einem neuen Bund, in einem neuen Gottesverhältnis der Zukunft.' Ibid., 183.

72. Ibid., 185. This thesis is challenged by Ego, "Zur Rezeption." But this challenge is only sound if Ego is reading Jer 31:31-34 correctly—which I dispute. Kraus's view of the Psalms as part of the reception-history of Jer 31:31-34 is not entirely novel: cf. the remarks on Ps 40:8 ('I delight to do your will, my God/ Your law is in my heart') by W.F. Cobb, *The Book of Psalms* (London: Methuen, 1905).

'heart.'[73] Thus emerges Kraus's narrative context for the oracle's meaning: the line of idealism about the Torah comes to a new point with Jeremiah's view of interiority, which is then continued and evidenced in the later promise of a new covenant, and reflected in the Torah Psalms.

Kraus continues this emphasis on continuity with deuteronomistic hopes in a more recent essay. In contradistinction to Bultmann, he states:

> It must be very strongly stressed that no one can deem what is said in v.32 about the election, liberation and leading—about this love of Yhwh for the fathers—to be 'the old', 'the surpassed', 'the previous', which had to be removed and replaced by something 'entirely new'.[74]

He points to Calvin's (and Barth's) view of the contrast as between 'economies' rather than 'substance.' The previous covenant of 'love' becomes 'new' by the inscribing of it on the heart—a 'more intensive way' of God's taking his people by the hand.[75] Thus the truly 'new' thing is the overcoming of the need for external teaching: 'With the inscribing of the law on the hearts of Israel the oral Torah-instruction and the whole institution of priestly and prophetic teachers is abolished.'[76] The oracle, placed in the story of deuteronomistic thinking, is a climax in the hopes of this 'school' by promising this new interiority.

So where Kutsch and Nicholson find the oracle post-jeremianic and anti-deuteronomic, Kraus finds the oracle to be post-jeremianic and pro-deuteronomic. But Kraus's argument fails in the same way as von Rad: if the interiority is simply a non-mediated obedience to the law, then why is nothing said about non-mediated obedience? Again, to say that Yhwh will do something does not (in the book of Jeremiah) mean that Yhwh will do it apart from any mediate causes. Kraus points us to the continuity of the 'hopes' of deuteronomic theo-

---

73. 'Aber es wird zu beachten sein, daß namentlich das Deuteronomium, und dann auch die Prophetie Jeremias, durch das Du der Gemeinschaft hindurch das Du des einzelnen gesucht, angesprochen und aufgerufen haben. Das Herz des Menschen—darum ging es.' Kraus, *Biblisch-theoligisches*, 185.

74. Hans-Joachim Kraus, "Der Erste und der Neue Bund," in *Eine Bibel—zwei Testamente* (eds. Christoph Dohmen and Thomas Söding; Paderborn: Ferdinand Schöningh, 1995), 65.

75. 'Wie könnte auch der liebende, rettende Gott, der die "Väter bei der Hand nahm", diese Hand zurückziehen und die Erretteten sogar von sich stoßen?! Müßte nicht der "neue Bund" darin bestehen und sich erweisen, daß dieses "Bei-der-Hand-Nehmen" jetzt auf eine neue, noch festere und innigere Weise vollzogen und bewährt wird?! So ist die ins "Innere" und ins "Herz" eingeschriebene Tora eine neue, intensivere Weise des "Bei-der-Hand-Nehmens", des Erbarmens Gottes mit seinem Volk.' Ibid.

76. Ibid., 68.

logy, and the importance of the Torah Psalms for expressing a view of the law on the heart, but he fails to adequately describe why this covenant is called new in the context of the book of Jeremiah or why we should think that it entails the abolishment of priestly and prophetic teachers.

Robert Carroll offers a more radical approach on similar lines, and in fact carries us back to where we began this discussion with Bernhard Duhm. Carroll's distancing of 31:31-34 from the prophet is in line with two of his critical assumptions. First, Carroll takes it as axiomatic that 'a major poet... does not use banal prose for the majority of his most important statements'—especially not prose as 'banal' as that of the deuteronomists.[77] And since the oracle is in prose and uses 'deuteronomistic phrasings', Carroll deduces it must be non-jeremianic.[78] The second assumption is that the same person could not stand behind both the oracles of judgment and restoration:

> If the figure detected behind the poetic tradition of the judgment oracles is at all a reliable one (a very large if), then it is very difficult to see how a man who proclaimed judgment against all false sense and objects of security could subsequently with equanimity reinstate those objects within a permanent restoration of the community to its land. The climate of the salvation oracles would suffocate a Jeremiah, or send him into paroxysms of rage against such smug belief in the perfectibility of human society.[79]

Carroll offers a strained link to the prophet Jeremiah's early preaching to the North founded in hopes that Assyria would be 'crushed soon by Yahweh', which hopes were taken up in the tradition and expanded to give us these oracles in chs. 30-31.[80] But this is a far cry from Bright (and even further from Skinner). For Carroll the teaching of 31:31-34 is deuteronomistic, and in language sounding much like Duhm he asserts, 'What is envisaged by the text remains essen-

---

77. Carroll, *Chaos*, 9. He clarifies the (obviously untenable) first statement: 'It is not simply a question of whether he only wrote poetry or whether he wrote prose as well! It is a matter of whether he spoke or wrote this kind of prose, i.e., deuteronomist material. If the prose elements were distinctive or unique in the biblical traditions, then a case might be made out for accepting them as the prophet's. That they are not and, furthermore, that they are traceable to specific sources (i.e., deuteronomistic) warrant their rejection as part of the prophet's original work (10).' So the assumption is that a great poet does not use prose in a style that other people use (it must be 'distinctive or unique'): quite where this conviction springs (or why to believe it) is unclear.

78. Ibid., 217.
79. Ibid., 199-200.
80. Ibid., 200.

tially the core of the deuteronomistic view of community religion, except that it will be realized more effectively in the future.'[81] Or, more negatively:

> If ever an institution was created which was a complete failure from the beginning it must be the deuteronomist covenant! Yet here in Jer 31.31-34 the redactors are proposing yet another covenant, a new one. What a triumph of hope over experience![82]

Carroll goes even further and sets the prophet over against the oracle: 'For Jeremiah, the only grounds for national deliverance is the return of the people to Yahweh; for the deuteronomists the answer lies in a *new* covenant.'[83] But, as I will argue, Carroll has misconstrued the oracle by presenting a false dilemma: restoration must be either a return of the people to Yhwh or the offering of a new covenant. But I will argue that the new covenant just *is* the return of the people to Yhwh.

Like Duhm, Carroll admits a novelty in the internalization of the Torah, thus abolishing the need for teachers.[84] Carroll, however, takes clear delight in pointing out that this has not been the case in either Judaism or Christianity—each of whom have produced their great teachers and continue to need them. In the end Carroll's comparison to Duhm is apt: both find the oracle a simple heightening of a deuteronomistic (covenantal) view of religion they find unsatisfactory; both find it a part of that line of thought that flowered in Pharisaism;[85]

---

81. Ibid., 221. In his 1986 commentary this is somewhat shifted: 'I would regard the relation between 31.31-34 and the Deuteronomistic strand in the tradition to be one of critical dialogue'. This is not yet 'anti-deuteronomist' however: 'It is a post-Deuteronomistic hope but one which has learned its theology from Deuteronomism and made the leap of hope into the utopian future.' Robert P. Carroll, *Jeremiah* (OTL; London: SCM Press, 1986), 613-14. A similar view, again akin to Duhm, is the 'curious hypothesis' (Renaud, *Nouvelle ou Éternelle?*, 48) of the oracle as simply one further step in the devotion to the Torah in the Jewish community—perhaps even responsible for the beginning of wearing phylacteries—put forward by J. Swetnam, "Why was Jeremiah's New Covenant New?," in *Studies on Prophecy* (ed. J.A. Emerton; VTSup, 26; Leiden: Brill, 1974).

82. Carroll, *Chaos*, 217.

83. Ibid. His emphasis.

84. 'The only difference between the old and new forms of the covenant would appear to be the internalization principle employed in the new covenant.' Ibid., 218.

85. 'If fulfilment of the new covenant expectation must be sought, let it be found in the achievements of the Pharisees, who helped to create the spiritual way of life of a very practical but deeply internalized rabbinical religion.' Ibid., 225. Carroll gives this a veneer of praise, under which lies his already stated views on the 'defects' of the whole line of thought.

and what Duhm calls a 'pious wish', Carroll dismisses as a 'pious hope'—a 'utopianism... [that] represents a fundamental weakness of biblical prophecy.'[86]

Yet again the pendulum (or face of Proteus) shifts again in the relationship of the 'new covenant' and the deuteronomists. We have seen nearly every variation of that relationship, but two further significant contributions in this line are worth a closer look. If Kraus, for instance, finds the 'interiority' to be the fulfillment of the assumed deuteronomic program, Walter Groß and Adrian Schenker have found the interiority to stand against those (rather flexible?) deuteronomists.

Schenker, in a 1980 article, posited a difference between the deuteronomistic hope of Deut 4:25-31 and 30:1-14 over against Jer 31:31-34. The former holds out the possibility of a never-to-be-withdrawn Torah, waiting for Israel to seize it. The latter, however, has as its necessary pre-condition the inability of Israel ever to be able to do so.[87] A stark opposition stands between the Torah as 'external', yet to be ultimately grasped by Israel through an act of eschatological grace (Deut 30), and the 'jeremianic theology' of a 'new creation.'[88] In its essentials, such a reading can be grouped with that of Bright: the overcoming of the Pelagian deuteronomists by an Augustinian Jeremiah (or disciple of Jeremiah), though Schenker now locates the matter at a later stage of Israel's religious development.

Walter Groß offers a much more forceful argument in this direction, over against the readings of Lohfink and Zenger (below). Groß claims that Yhwh is pictured as working 'neither with regard to the *berit* that Israel broke, nor another older *berit*, rather he makes a new one' that 'replaces the *berit* that

---

86. Carroll, *Jeremiah*, 612.

87. 'In Jer 31,33f. bleibt die Tora auch, denn es ist dieselbe Tora... Aber im gegenwärtigen Zustand bleibt die Tora außerhalb des Menschen; sie kann nicht bei ihm ankommen; Tora und Mensch kommen nicht zusammen. So ist die Lösung von Dt 4,25-31; 30,1-14 für Jer 31,33f. ein Ding der Unmöglichkeit: Die Tora ist zwar angeboten, aber sie kann nicht ergriffen werden! Jer 31,33f. hat ein krankes, gelähmtes Israel vor Augen, das seine Hand nicht mehr der Tora entgegenstrecken kann; Dt 4,25-31; 30,1-14 erinnert ein gesundess, aber störrisches Israel an das Angebot der Tora, das nie zurückgezogen wurde, und das Israel ergreifen kann, sobald es will.' Adrian Schenker, "Unwiderrufliche Umkehr und neuer Bund: Vergleich zwischen der Wiederherstellung Israels in Dt 4,25-31; 30,1-14 und dem neuen Bund in Jer 31,31-34," *Freiburger Zeitschrift für Philosophie und Theologie* 27 (1980), 102.

88. 'Bei den Deuteronomisten ist die eschatologische Gnade bekehrend, heilend und festigend im Guten, bei Jeremia ist sie Neuschöpfung und Vereinigung mit Gottes Denken und Wollen.' Ibid., 106.

the people broke with a *berit* that will no longer be broken.'[89] The contrast for the oracle, according to Groß, is the Deuteronomic 'theology of teachers and learners.' So rather than the 'dtr-dtn principle of the written Torah', the text puts forward a view of the Torah written on the heart.[90] Since von Rad and before such a position has been asserted. But where most appear happy to assert (or repeat) the position as self-justifying, Groß offers a textual argument for this contrast. Jer 31:33 presents a chiasm, whose central facet is the location of the Torah:

(a) I will place my law (b) *in their inner parts*,

(b') And *on their hearts* (a') I will write it.[91]

Since the center of the chiasm concerns the location of the Torah, Groß concludes the chiasm carries the implicit question, 'on the heart *rather than where*?' And the answer, which he finds obvious, is the scroll of the deuteronomists.[92] But this is unlikely as a grammatical point for chiasms, which simply cannot hold such a load. Take another standard chiasm (Prov 7:1):

My son (a) keep (b) *my sayings*

and (b') *my commandments* (a') treasure up within you.

The chiastic structure is clear and the centre is 'my sayings/commandments'. But to claim as a grammatical point that this carries the implicit contrast 'rather than keeping whose sayings?' (we might even suggest that it is rather than the sayings of the 'deuteronomists'), would be more than a little suspect. Chiasms do not have to present such implicit questions. The focused attention of the law on the heart/inner parts in 31:33 is easily enough explained: because this is where the law is most needed. As will be emphasized below, the demand was always for a faithful heart, but the present state of affairs consisted in anything but the law on the heart. If there is emphasis to be drawn from the centre of a

---

89. Walter Groß, *Zukunft für Israel: Alttestamentliche Bundeskonzepte und die aktuelle Debatte um den neuen Bund* (Stuttgart: Verlag Katholisches Bibelwerk GmbH, 1998), 144.

90. Ibid., 145-46. Cp., e.g., Ego: the oracle signifies 'das Ende allen Lernens und Lehrens'. Ego, "Zur Rezeption," 288.

91. See the final chapter for a full discussion of the verse.

92. Groß, *Zukunft*, 145. Also Schmid: 'in Jer 31 liegt der Ton nicht auf der Aufhebung der Sünde bzw. der Pervertierung der Tora, sondern auf dem Schreiben על לבם, wie die Pendenskonstruktion in V.33aγ andererseits zeigt.... Nicht auf eine Buchrolle oder auf die Türpfosten, sondern "auf ihr Herz" wird Jhwh seine Tora schreiben.' Konrad Schmid, *Buchgestalten des Jeremiabuches: Untersuchungen zur Redaktions- und Rezeptionsgeschichte von Jer 30-33 im Kontext des Buches* (WMANT 72; Neukirchen-Vluyn: Neukirchener Verlag, 1996), 68.

chiasm (a point not obvious in itself), then the emphasis is clear: the heart—the centre of the person—will be changed. But the question must still be answered, why this is called 'new'?

In Schenker and Groß the same themes seen throughout this chapter emerge again: Jer 31:31-34 standing over against the 'deuteronomists' and their view of religion. The oracle is 'anti-deuteronomic',[93] standing against those who would hold that the law must be put on the heart by human means. Where pre-modern discussions were concerned to identify the nature of the 'old covenant' (*nuda lex*? *accidentalia*? whole of the era?), we now have a different but related answer: (Pelagian) deuteronomic theology. Throughout the modern period, the context of the contrast is no longer the theological question of God's dealings with his people, but the anthropological question of the developing views of religion in ancient Israel.

5. *A Renewed Covenant? Levin, Lohfink, and Zenger*

On Nov. 17, 1980 Pope John Paul II sparked a new interest and somewhat new (or renewed) direction for reading Jeremiah's new covenant. Speaking to the Central Council of Jews in Mainz, Germany he said:

> The first dimension of this dialogue, namely the meeting between the people of God of the old covenant, never revoked by God, and the people of God of the new covenant is likewise a dialogue within our Church, as it were between the first and second parts of her Bible.[94]

---

93. Ibid., 299.

94. 'Die erste Dimension dieses Dialoges, nämlich die Begegnung zwischen dem Gottesvolk des von Gott nie gekündigten Alten Bundes und dem des Neuen Bundes, ist zugleich ein Dialog innerhalb unserer Kirche, gleichsam zwischen dem ersten und zweiten Teil ihrer Bibel.' The forerunner for such a statement is in the declaration Nostra Aetate from the Vatican Council in 1965: 'the Jews should not be presented as rejected or accursed by God, as if this followed from the Holy Scriptures (§4).' Just as intriguing is the statement from the Protestant Rhineland Synod, also from 1980: 'Wir glauben die bleibende Erwählung des jüdischen Volkes als Gottes Volk und erkennen, daß die Kirche durch Jesus Christus in den Bund Gottes mit seinem Volk hineingenommen ist... Durch Jahrhunderte wurde das Wort "neu" in der Bibelauslegung gegen das jüdische Volk gerichtet: Der neue Bund wurde als Gegensatz zum alten Bund, das neue Gottesvolk als Ersetzung des alten Gottesvolkes verstanden. Diese Nichtachtung der bleibenden Erwählung Israels und seine Verurteilung zur Nichtexistenz haben immer wieder christliche Theologie, kirchliche Predigt und kirchliches Handeln bis heute gekennzeichnet. Dadurch haben wir uns auch an der physischen Auslöschung des jüdischen Volkes schuldig gemacht.' Both Pope John Paul II's statement and that of the Protestant synod are found in Rolf Rendtorff and H.H. Henrix, eds. *Die Kirchen und das*

The statement itself would be interesting for our examination given certain of its assumptions, but the more pressing issue is the impetus that this language of an 'unrevoked old covenant' gave towards a re-reading of Jer 31:31-34, especially in German scholarship. Only five years after the above declaration a sustained argument for reading the 'new covenant' as a 'renewed' covenant in some form came from Christoph Levin. Levin, taking apart the various pieces of the oracle, weaves them into a story of the development of Israelite covenantal traditions, producing a complex text in an even more complex narrative.[95] In his discussion of the emergence of the phraseology ברית חדשה Levin argues that the term חדשה ought to be taken as 'renewed', whose opposite is an 'earlier' covenant.[96] The emphasis is not on 'new' as a developmental way of thinking, but rather as bringing something out yet again—akin to the 'new day', 'new moon': 'fresh' as opposed to 'progression'. Levin thus reads this original addition to the oracle as a statement of a renewed relationship: *'restitutio ad integrum'*—a restoration to a state of integrity set over against the brokenness of the relationship in the covenant.[97]

Such a reading, which is similar in some respects to what will be proposed below, clearly can converge with the Augustinian understanding of the contrast as one of unbelief over against faithfulness. But in Levin this is only one moment of the text's development. Levin asserts that the later addition of v.33a (the law on the heart) assumes—distortingly—a 'qualitatively new rela-

---

Judentum. Dokumente von 1945-1985 (2nd ed. Munich: Paderborn, 1989), 75, 594-95.

95. Levin begins with 31:27a, 20aβγb-30a and 31:31a, 34abα as the core to which is later added 31:31b-32, 33b, and 34bα2βγ, and then much later comes 33a. Christoph Levin, *Die Verheißung des neuen Bundes: in ihrem theologiegeschichtlichen Zusammenhang ausgelegt* (Göttingen: Vandenhoeck & Ruprecht, 1985). As Christl Maier tersely comments, 'Die Forschung ist der literar-kritischen These Levins zu Recht nicht gefolgt.' Maier, *Jeremia*, 339. Another bluntly speaks of it as 'rather wild literary criticism'. Frank Crüsemann, *The Torah: Theology and Social History of Old Testament Law* (Tr. by Allan W. Mahnke. Edinburgh: T&T Clark, 1996), 41, n.81. Multiple recensions of the text are also supported (without success) by Vermeylen, "L'alliance renouvellée."

96. Levin, *Verheißung*, 138-41. His discussion provides plenty of illustrations of the possibility. He has been followed at this point by, among others, Erich Zenger, *Das Erste Testament: Die jüdischen Bibeln und die Christen* (2nd ppb. ed. Düsseldorf: Patmos, 2004), 115; Bob Becking, *Between Fear and Freedom: Essays on the Interpretation of Jeremiah 30-31* (Leiden: Brill, 2004), 260.

97. Levin, *Verheißung*, 140.

tionship with God,' drawing on Jer 7:23f.[98] Its addition stems from the apparent discrepancy of the earlier parts:

> The reason for this second addition of the promise of the new covenant is undoubtedly the discrepancy that a 'new covenant' (v.31) was initially promised that would be different than the one made with the remnant from the land of Egypt, but then this covenant was in fact nothing other than a re-validation of the long-known covenant formula (v.33b).[99]

But Levin is not yet finished. With the even later promise of v.34b and the forgiveness of sins Levin speaks in the strongest terms of the novelty of this announcement: 'the statement of forgiveness was practically non-existent' prior to its inclusion here.[100]

Levin's division of the text into its various strands rests on a reconstructed theological history of 'covenant' thought in Israelite religion. In some sense he is the best illustration of the power of a governing narrative to allow meaning: by isolating one or another aspect of the promise, stripping it of its current place and role, one can construct a coherent meaning for it by giving it a role in some newly constructed narrative context. But the approach begs far more questions than it answers and requires of the reader an agreement in Israelite theological development that is hard to garner—particularly when grounded in positing a confusion within that theological development. Further, there is very little reason to follow Levin's reading outside of the narrative that he constructs: he evidences his reading by the reconstruction and the reconstruction by the reading. A degree of circularity will always be operative in these discussions, but some circles are more vicious than others.

Norbert Lohfink and Erich Zenger have offered more influential discussions of the 'new covenant' as 'renewed', or as 'never revoked'—explicitly attempting to re-read the text in the light of contemporary Christian-Jewish rela-

---

98. Ibid., 141.

99. Ibid., 257. Thus after this shift, 'Der verheißene Bund, bei dem es bisher um die Wiederherstellung der heilsgeschichtlichen Kontinuität gegangen war, erhält hier nun eine auch inhaltlich neue Bestimmung.' Ibid.

100. 'Für den Bibelleser, der in der neutestamentlichen Tradition steht, ist kaum mehr zu erkenne, in welchem Maße die Botschaft der Vergebung damals als unerhört neues, befreiendes Evangelium gehört worden ist. Die Begriffsgeschichte zeigt, daß in den seinerzeit vorliegenden Texten des Alten Testaments von Vergebung so gut wie nie die Rede war. Selbst in der exilischen und späteren Literatur begegnet das Thema fast ausschließlich in der Bitte oder unter Bedingung oder in kultischer Verklausulierung, am deutlichsten in Bekenntnis, Dank und Lob. So ist die unbedingte Vergebungs-verheißung als freie Zusage Gottes weithin ohne Parallele.' Ibid., 134.

tions.[101] Lohfink acknowledges the difficulty in discussions of speaking of 'one' covenant with respect to the biblical data: there are clearly many covenants already in the Old Testament. But this does not mean we cannot speak of a unified 'something' for which we use the terminology of 'covenant':

> [W]e cannot speak of the 'covenant' in the field of the Old Testament. There is 'something' that is spoken about; there are images and ideas with which the biblical writers try to grasp what is meant by that 'something'; and they can change. This is where talk about 'covenant' belongs.[102]

Or, from elsewhere with Zenger:

> In the Hebrew Bible 'covenant' designates the relationship between YHWH and Israel not as something static, but as a dynamic event. 'Covenant' evokes the ever-changing history of God with God's people Israel. It is true that there is talk about a covenant in diverse contexts and eras. There are also differing conceptions of 'covenant,' and they occur in differing systems of discourse. Despite this, however, a 'canonical' discussion of covenant is also legitimate. Here, then, it is not a question of several 'covenants,' but of the one covenant from Sinai that unfolds and is actualized and becomes new (that is, is renewed by YHWH) again and again.[103]

The connections with earlier covenantal statements—especially of Oecolampadius—are evident, though naturally re-set into modern discourse. And such statements allow Lohfink to give a reading of Jer 31:31-34 as a renewal of the (one) covenant, without dismissing a development of 'covenants' and covenantal thinking. Lohfink makes a central issue of the continuity of content in the 'old' and 'new'—both the Torah and the covenant formula remaining constant and so both being, in fact, the same covenant:

---

101. See esp. Erich Zenger, "Thesen zu Hermeneutik des Ersten Testaments nach Auschwitz," in *Eine Bibel- zwei Testamente* (eds. Christoph Dohmen and Thomas Söding; Paderborn: Ferdinand Schöningh, 1995).

102. Norbert Lohfink, *The Covenant Never Revoked: Biblical Reflections on Christian-Jewish Dialogue* (Tr. by John J. Scullion. Mahwah, NJ: Paulist Press, 1991), 21. Cf. his "Ein Bund oder zwei Bünde in der Heiligen Schrift," in *L'interpretazione della Bibbia nella Chiesa* (Vatican City: Libreria Editrice Vaticana, 2001). This is not far at all from Eichrodt's position on 'covenant' or Vriezen's use of 'communion': Walther Eichrodt, *Theology of the Old Testament* (Tr. by John Baker. London: SCM Press, 1967), I.15; Th.C. Vriezen, *An Outline of Old Testament Theology* (Tr. by S. Neuijen. 2nd ed. Oxford: Blackwell, 1970), 153ff.

103. Norbert Lohfink and Erich Zenger, *The God of Israel and the Nations: Studies in Isaiah and the Psalms* (Tr. by Everett R. Kalin. Collegeville, MN: Liturgical Press, 2000), 191.

This very content at least is common alike to the broken 'covenant' and the promised 'new covenant': God institutes between himself and Israel that special God-people relationship which is expressed in the 'covenant formula,' and Israel takes over the torah. From the standpoint of this actual content, it is clearly a question of the same 'covenant.'[104]

The re-founding of a covenant after being broken, which had the same Torah and stemmed entirely on the grace of God, is by no means a novelty in the Old Testament: it is already embedded in the narrative of Exod 32-34.[105] Yet for all this Lohfink still does not move from the consensus of a new interiority: the 'newness' of the new covenant in Jeremiah lies in a promise of a great change of heart—an immediacy of obedience in freedom to the Torah set over against the way of learning before present in the Old Testament (e.g. Deuteronomy). Lohfink owes more to von Rad than a simple *leitmotif* here, as he phrases the whole previous 'way of learning' as a near summary of von Rad's approach:

> So the covenant in Israel had to be handed on from generation to generation through instruction. Each new generation (and each individual in Israel, again and again through the different phases of her or his life) had to try to know God ever anew and ever deeper. This took place as people continually instructed and assured one another about God's Torah. That was the only possible way for Israel to remain in this unique relationship, the covenant with the God of the Exodus from Egypt.
>
> But in the new covenant, according to the promise given us, it will be different. There each one already has God's Torah written on her or his heart, and thus each one already knows the whole from inside. That endlessly weary and in the end not entirely functional system of learning the Torah is no longer the ultimate recourse.[106]

---

104. Lohfink, *Covenant Never Revoked*, 47.

105. Zenger, *Erste Testament*, 116; Norbert Lohfink, *In the Shadow of Your Wings: New Readings of Great Texts from the Bible* (Tr. by Linda M. Maloney. Collegeville, MN: Liturgical Press, 2003), 51; Christoph Dohmen, "Sinaibund als neuer Bund nach Ex 19-34," in *Der neue Bund im Alten: Zur Bundestheologie der beiden Testamente* (ed. Erich Zenger; Freiburg: 1993). Lohfink explores the connections with Deuteronomy, but concludes against a parallel: Norbert Lohfink, "Der Neue Bund im Deuteronomium?," in *Studien zum Deuteronomium und zur deuteronomistischen Literatur V* (ed. Norbert Lohfink; Stuttgart: Katholisches Bibelwerk, 2005).

106. Lohfink, "Jeremiah and the Sacred Heart of Jesus. The 'New Covenant'," in Lohfink, *Shadow*, 49. Or, 'While the covenant with the ancestors was outwardly proclaimed, written on material substances, and had to be handed on through teaching, the same covenant will now be given as something internal, written on the heart, so that handing it on through teaching will be superfluous. This, then, is a renewed gift, a different kind of establishment, of the old relationship.' Idem, "Children of Abraham

Jeremiah's New Covenant

The consequences of this 'new covenant' include its inviolability: it will never be broken since the people will all have the Torah 'where human freedom has its true place, in the heart.'[107] What this means for Jewish-Christian dialogue is a movement away from language of 'supercessionism', in which the Christian covenant came and replaced the old way of things represented by the Old Testament. Indeed, Lohfink goes so far as to claim that the prayers of a 'new heart' (e.g. Ps. 51:12) show that 'God disposed to confer on Israel the very essence of the promised "new covenant," a heart stamped with the Torah.' The prayer and the prophecy of Jeremiah (with others) were bound together in the canon so that the prayer presumes the fulfillment of the prophecy.[108] The language is unabashedly theological at this point:

> As a sinner he [i.e. the Jew at prayer] was excluded from the community of those who proclaimed God's praise in community worship. When he prayed to God for the gifts he needed to enter again into this community, then he could ask that God would create for him what was of the essence of the statement of the promise of the new covenant: a heart renewed interiorly and completely attuned to the recognition of the will of God.[109]

Even more theological is Lohfink's claim that Jeremiah speaks here of the concept of 'justification' that runs throughout the whole of the Old Testament:

> This view of history... is one of the multiform figures within the Old Testament doctrine of justification.... That human beings in themselves are incapable of achieving a right situation before God, that all their attempts fail and that God alone, in divine forgiving grace, can effect the creative work of new love, is expressed here in the book of Jeremiah in the saying about the new covenant that consists of a Torah written on hearts.[110]

Links with the 'Augustinian' line are immense at this point: that the issue is justification is seemingly a 'salvific' concern, and Lohfink pointing to the possession of the new covenant in the ancient era is further evidence of this. But in spite of these links the emphasis on new immediacy over against earlier ex-

---

from Stones: Does the Old Testament Promise a New Covenant without Israel?" Ibid., 168.

107. Ibid., 49. Or, 'The earlier "covenant" was in fact broken. Hence, it must have been given to Israel in such a way that it could be broken. The "new covenant" will be given in a new way; it will be something within, with a torah written on the heart, it not being necessary to teach it from without.' Ibid., 168.

108. Lohfink, *Covenant Never Revoked*, 56.

109. Ibid.

110. Lohfink, *Shadow*, 51.

periences—beyond being unwarranted from the text—is distinct from the contrast as developed in Augustine's later works and from what I will argue.

Erich Zenger likewise puts forward a strong view of continuity in reading Jer 31:31-34, in a way even more obviously convergent with earlier Reformed positions:

> When we Christians admit, with the witness of the New Testament, that this renewed covenant with God was opened for us through the death and resurrection of Jesus so that we also live in his grace, then this is not a further covenant that will take the place of the renewed Sinai covenant. It is one and the same covenant of grace (*Gnadenbund*), to which the Jewish people and the people of the Church have a part in a different way. The covenant was made first of all with Israel, but the Church 'through Jesus Christ has been brought into the covenant of God with his people'.[111]

Once more Jer 31:31-34 is playing its role in discussions of a one or two-fold view of covenantal theology, and Lohfink and Zenger have offered significant proposals for seeing a one-covenant view and reading Jeremiah in this way even if surrounded by different constructions and interests than was present in the early modern period. The language of an 'unrevoked' covenant with Israel has by no means been universally adopted, even among Roman Catholic scholars.[112] And the notion of the 'one and the same' having apparently two different means of access (only one is through Jesus Christ?) would seem to be likely to garner even more criticism. But the significance of these proposals, and their similarities (and differences) to previous ways of thought—and to much of what will be proposed here—make an intriguing moment in the history of interpretation. The strong Augustinian insistence on the unity of the people of God rules out a blunt supercessionism. But for Lohfink especially, the contrast of Jer 31:31-34 is still between the deuteronomic teaching/learning and some more immediate work on the heart. The great contrast lies in the *means* of Yhwh's work, which suffers from the same deficiency as von Rad (i.e. argument from silence). We have inched closer to an Augustinian reading but we still have not seen the re-emergence of the contrast as absolute or salvific.

---

111. Zenger, *Erste Testament*, 118-19.

112. Prominent in exception is A. Vanhoye: see his "Salut universel par le Christ et validité de l'Ancienne Alliance," *Nouvelle Revue Théologique* 116 (1994); Idem, "Réaction à l'exposé du prof. Norbert Lohfink «Ein Bund oder zwei Bünde in der heiligen Schrift»," in *L'interpretazione della Bibbia nella Chiesa* (Vatican City: Libreria Editrice Vaticana, 2001). The most thorough response centred on Jer 31:31f is Groß, *Zukunft*.

6. An Augustinian Heritage

The differences between Jerome and Augustine in reading Jer 31:31-34 appear largely forgotten in modern interpretation.[113] But a handful of modern proposals, apparently unaware of the heritage, fall more directly in the 'Augustinian' line of understanding Jeremiah's new covenant as holding an absolute ('salvific') contrast of standing before God. In 1969 Wilber Wallis suggested that the oracle be read as an instance of irony. The reason for this is that every part of 31:33-34 'is but a repetition of some familiar aspect of salvation already known in the Old Testament.'[114] The solution, Wallis suggests, is to look at the audience to whom Jeremiah is (portrayed as) preaching: 'The open implication of the passage is that many in Jeremiah's day did not "know" the Lord, in contrast to the time when all would know him.'[115] By listing what was already assumed by the people in Jerusalem (that they had the law on the heart, were the people of Yhwh, knew Yhwh, and had forgiveness of sins), but placing them in terms of something that would have to be 'new', Jeremiah deconstructs the people's confidence:

> So in Jeremiah's prophecy the very commonplaceness, the familiarity, the banality of the oft-repeated words all become the leverage to drive home the stinging irony of the words "new covenant"—all this "new" to complacent sinners who thought it was theirs all the while![116]

Wallis's suggestion was taken up in two studies and given a better formulation. In an article in 1985, Fredrick Holmgren gave a sharper focus to the suggestion by framing the question, as new 'for whom'?[117] Holmgren raises the

---

113. The two still figure in the comments of one mid-19th century scholar, though in a very unconvincing manner: (explaining 31:31f) 'St. Augustine is more right than St. Jerome, since the first makes every law of the letter, and of Old Testament literalism, abolished in Christ, while the second abolishes only the ceremonial law; all which Luther and the Galatians well shows. Hence all that the nobler mystics and more reasoning Quakers have said from St. Paul in 2 Cor. 1 and 3 down to the purer neologians of our time, is justified; here is a charter which makes freedom of thought orthodox, so that without neology is no Christianity.' Williams, *Prophets*, 287.

114. Wilber B. Wallis, "Irony in Jeremiah's Prophecy of a New Covenant," *JETS* 12 (1969), 107.

115. Ibid., 108.

116. Ibid. Wallis also suggests this for the ways in which the contrast is used in the New Testament (109-110).

117. Frederick Holmgren, "A New Covenant? For Whom?," *The Covenant Quarterly* 43.1 (1985).

issue of the characterization of the people of Jeremiah's time, in words not entirely dissimilar to what is claimed by Bright and others:

> Yahweh wanted the Judeans of Jeremiah's time to be just, merciful, and loyal in the heart. But it is there—in the heart—that the problem lies. At the center, something is terribly wrong.[118]

But distinct from Bright, Holmgren remains at this level of contrast and reads the oracle as confronting this situation of infidelity:

> This "new" covenant would not be new to Moses, to the prophets, or to Yahweh. For whom, then, is this covenant a "new" covenant? It is "new" to those Judeans who are blind, but think they see; who are deaf, but believe they hear; who are hard of heart, but represent themselves as children of God. This covenant is "new" to a people who are supremely confident that they are Yahweh's people, when in truth their whole way of life is alien to Yahweh's teaching.[119]

Holmgren goes on to point out that what is required in having the 'law on the heart' is simple covenant fidelity, and what is at stake in 'knowing Yhwh' is 'to be kind to the weak, just to the poor' (22:16). The issue, Holmgren states, is about standing (or not) in the 'true covenant'.[120]

Two closely related differences from the dominant lines of interpretation should be pointed out in Wallis and Holmgren. First, they locate the oracle (its 'context') in the standard preaching of the prophet to a hard-hearted people, which at least has the advantage of simplicity over the reconstructions of the religious development of Jeremiah or Israelite religion. At the very least this is the literary presentation of the prophet's life and career in the book of Jeremiah. Further detail and psychological development becomes unnecessary as a 'key' for interpreting the oracle. Rather than looking for the 'true context' and historical narrative to form the background of meaning for the oracle, we simply remain content with the generalities as presented in the literary work of Jeremiah. Thus Wallis and Holmgren read the oracle as ironic—a disillusionment of the people's security. Related to this, the point of contrast is no longer Deuteronomy, a deuteronomic view of religion, or the reforms along those lines that (in

---

118. Ibid., 39.

119. Ibid., 40. Or elsewhere, 'If these people, who are "accustomed to do evil," could recognize the covenant for what it truly was, it would be a new teaching *for them.*' Frederick Holmgren, *The Old Testament and the Significance of Jesus* (Grand Rapids, MI: Wm. B. Eerdmans, 1999), 92. Emphasis his.

120. 'People who must be taught basic response to the poor and weak are those who stand outside the true covenant (that is, what Jeremiah calls the "new" covenant).' Holmgren, "New Covenant?", 42.

the reconstructed narratives) surrounded Jeremiah's career or the exilic and post-exilic communities. Instead the contrast is with the people as characterised in the book of Jeremiah. This second point I view as an immense step forward in the discussion, and will be taken up in the final chapters. The first point, however, insofar as it requires the oracle to be read as ironic, is more difficult to maintain. Irony in literature is always a possibility, but only provable with far more information than we possess. Interestingly, Cornill had already dismissed the option of irony here—though without argument—so the suggestion is not entirely unknown.[121] But it is also unlikely to garner much support.[122] Better, in my view, is to take the basic point of re-framing the context of the oracle and whether 'irony' is needed or not can be a matter of debate.

Wallis's suggestion was also taken up in a 1978 Ph.D. dissertation by Robert Rayburn. Rayburn offers the most thorough discussion from this line of interpretation. He shows some of the difficulties of modern readings typically by pointing either to the theological difficulty of denying any part of 31:33-34 to the faithful living before the new covenant,[123] or more often to the witness of the

---

121. He sees it as a possible application of Smend's view of irony in 4:4, but does not develop it and instead asserts that these words were spoken 'in heiligen Ernst.' Cornill, *Jeremia*, 351.

122. Though to have Jeremiah presented as undercutting established comforts would by no means be novel: 'the governing agenda of the first scroll [chs.1-25] is the tearing down of existing symbol systems and institutional supports. All sacred supports of the old world order are bravely deconstructed in the text. No temple, no covenant, no appeal to election or a Davidic ruler can deliver the community from imminent disaster.' Louis Stulman, *Order amid Chaos: Jeremiah as Symbolic Tapestry* (Sheffield: Sheffield Academic Press, 1998), 117.

123. E.g., 'it is impossible to maintain that Jeremiah regarded the Lord's writing of the law on the heart as a new feature of his relationship with his people because this would leave Jeremiah (and Ezekiel) without an explanation for the conversion and redemption and obedience of all the saints who lived before the new covenant including himself.' R. S. Rayburn, "The Contrast Between the Old and New Covenants in the New Testament" (Ph.D, Univ. of Aberdeen, 1978), 150. Or, 'according to Old Testament covenant thought, there is no place for a setting-aside of one covenant in favor of another. All the covenants were everlasting, even if broken. A "new" covenant could only be a final, complete, or perfect expression of the everlasting covenant (cf. Jer. 33:17ff).' Ibid., 163.

rest of the Old Testament.[124] The decisive point, however, comes in the analysis of the point of contrast for the two covenants:

> What then is the difference between the two covenants? The first was the relationship established by God with Israel which Israel in unbelief and disobedience broke. That posture of unbelief was maintained from the beginning through to Jeremiah's time (cf. 7:25ff) with, of course, many individual exceptions. For this unbelief and for Israel's hard-hearted response to God's appeal to her to repent and come back to him, God is now going to punish Israel and destroy many of the people. But in this time of judgment Jeremiah looks forward to a new act of salvation which God will perform in the future and which will have complete and unalterable success.[125]

The point of contrast for the 'new' is the covenant broken in unbelief: a contrast of standing before God.

The advance from Wallis is that the oracle is no longer tied to a particular moment in Jeremiah's ministry (though potential moments might easily be imagined for such a message). More importantly, in Rayburn the oracle is no longer considered 'irony', but a promise over against the realities of the judgment and its causes. Rayburn concludes in strong Augustinian language:

> We have already suggested that Jeremiah is not concerned with the contrasting of two objective economies or two consecutive religio-historical states of affairs. The contrast is of another sort entirely. It is the contrast of two subjective states of affairs: unbelief with faith, no peace with God with fellowship with him, and God's wrath and judgment with his salvation. The subject of Jer 31:31ff is subjective redemption, which redemption will come in its consummate fullness in a future act of God.[126]

I will argue that this line of discussion is exactly right by re-focusing the question of the nature of the contrast. Throughout the history of interpretation the defining of the point of contrast has been the central concern: the *vetus testamentum* (Augustine), the *vetus lex* (Thomas), *nuda lex* (Calvin), 'Mosaic covenant' (Ball), or more recently 'deuteronomic' thought. This, therefore, will

---

124. E.g. the Psalms (103, 119). In other words, two criteria that imply a unity of God and Scripture that are dismissed by examinations of the oracle as a part of the historical development of Israelite religion. This is not to say that the criteria are invalid (I happen to think they are very good), but they can be easily circumvented by claims regarding the chronology of the texts (e.g. Levin) or the incoherence of the theologies in the Old Testament.

125. Ibid., 158. My emphasis.

126. Ibid., 164-65.

be our first question: where do we turn to find the contrast to the 'new covenant' of Jer 31?

7. *Conclusions*

Modern readings of Jeremiah's 'new covenant' oracle span a number of planes. The many faces of the 'new covenant' oracle are held together, however, by the consistent emphasis in the majority of interpreters on some new form of *inwardness* in the new covenant. Exactly what such inwardness means or why it might be said to be new we find resolved by the various contexts in which the oracle (or its parts) are claimed to play their role in Israel's religious development. If nothing else, the 20th century has shown the 'overabundance' of meaning in the words of the oracle. Or to put it another way, it has demonstrated the underdeterminacy of semantics for any determinate meaning. The semantics of an utterance can be made to fit any number of varied circumstances, with its meaning (use) shifting accordingly.[127] The oracle has been read as jeremianic against the deuteronomist, as jeremianic in line with deuteronomic thought, as non-jeremianic and pro-deuteronomic, and as non-jeremianic and anti-deuteronomic. And one can arguably make any of these mutually contradictory views cohere with the semantics of Jer 31:31-34, so long as one constructs a fitting background for the semantics to play their role.

The main crux for Augustine's late readings of the 'new covenant' was defining and describing what was meant by this 'new' interiority and explaining what that meant for the contrast with the 'old'. In various ways this is picked up again in Thomas Aquinas, in Melanchthon, Calvin, Vermigli, Ball, and many others. But with the falling from grace of dogmatic theology the intricacies of this definition was lost. Modern biblical scholars became 'historians' *rather than* theologians, and their successors showed little eagerness to look back on what was lost in the bargain.

In what follows I will offer an exegetical study of Jeremiah's new covenant oracle in the light of the role that it plays within the book of Jeremiah. As will be plain the 'inwardness' of the new covenant which is the central facet of most modern treatments, is in fact right at the centre of the oracle's function. But the question why this is 'new' in the book of Jeremiah will lead us to a different line of suggestion for understanding the contrast in place. In fact, it will lead us directly back into the richness of theological interpretations in the Augustinian line.

---

127. A strong version of this philosophical position (perhaps too strong) is put forward by John R. Searle, "The Background of Meaning," in *Speech Act Theory and Pragmatics* (eds. John R. Searle et al.; Dordrecht: D. Reidel, 1980).

7

The Context of the New Covenant

In the last chapter I painted a scene in which 20th century readings of Jeremiah's new covenant were concerned largely with finding a context—a narrative—in which the oracle can play its role. The study was not exhaustive and would not account for many dogmatic discussions that have circled around this text—such as that by Barth or von Balthasar. Yet in biblical studies the burden of the thesis on that note is, I think, well-established. One looks at the oracle as a self-contained utterance (or a series of even smaller units or utterances) and then the oracle is placed into some reconstructed narrative of the development of Israelite religious thought. The reader's role as a 'historian' is to find where the oracle fits as a piece in the narrative puzzle of ancient Israel. The question of a determining context is unavoidable—it's a part of how language works. But where should we look for a determining context? That will be the first question of this chapter, though treated briefly (hermeneutics can be a swamp from which one might never emerge). I will argue that the controlling context for our purposes ought to be the edited form of the book of Jeremiah. That being stated we can turn to outline what this means for the function of the oracle in the book: first the function of the restoration oracles generally and then the context of the 'broken' covenant to which the 'new' is contrasted.

1. *The Oracle in the Book*

The remainder of this study will assume that the first point of context for determining the significance or function of the 'new covenant' oracle is the edited form of the book of Jeremiah. This should not be taken as an embrace of ahistoricism—I do not view the oracle (or the book, for that matter) as a contextless literary artifact or a 'world of the text' that floats through history. The aspect of truth in this view is obvious: we have seen different appropriations throughout the history of interpretation, accompanied by different standards of exegesis, different philosophical or theological commitments, and resulting in different ways of reading and appropriating the text. And the reading offered here is simply one more attempt to do the same—an attempt that is within the history of interpretation. But the mistake of the floating 'world of the text' lies elsewhere, in denying interpretive primacy to the initial act of communication. I have already pointed briefly to the underdeterminacy of semantics, a fact that holds true no matter the size of the semantic utterance (whether the oracle by itself or the book of Jeremiah by itself). The edited book of Jeremiah stands in all its complexity as an act or set of acts of communication.

In an article in 1994, H. van dyke Parunak offered a chart of the levels of communication he saw operative in the oracles of Jeremiah. In the chart, the three rounded boxes are three acts of communication while the squared boxes represent the content of that communication:[1]

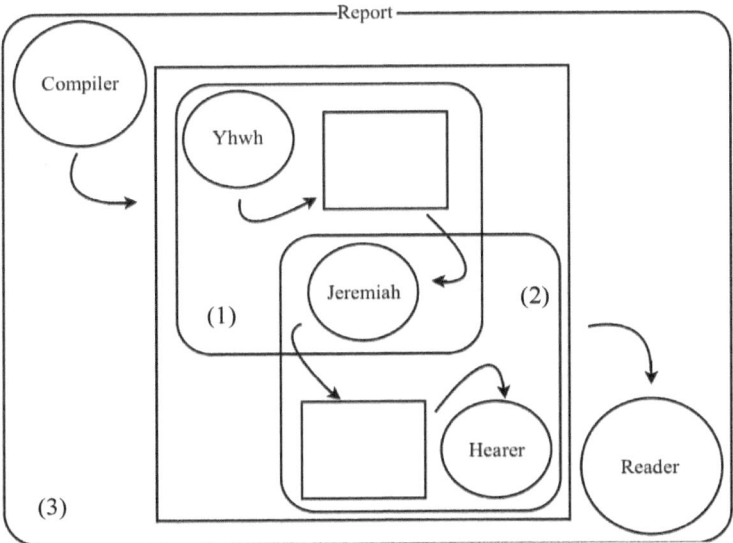

The three distinct communicative acts are: (1) Yhwh's communication to Jeremiah; (2) Jeremiah's communication to an audience/hearer (at least sometimes reported in the book)[2]; and (3) the (canonical) 'report' of one or both of

---

1. H. Van Dyke Parunak, "Some Discourse Functions of Prophetic Quotation Formulas in Jeremiah," in *Biblical Hebrew and Discourse Linguistics* (ed. Robert D. Bergen; Winona Lake: Eisenbrauns, 1994), 494. I have adapted some of the terminology.

2. If Jeremiah's words are made to 'count as' Yhwh's own, as in Wolterstorff's presentation, the schema still stands since the act of communication is distinct. Likewise for thinking that the recording, editing and preserving of the words are made to 'count as' God's own. The acts of communication are distinct (if inseparable) whatever further role they are made to play. See Nicholas Wolterstorff, *Divine Discourse: Philosophical Reflections on the Claim that God Speaks* (Cambridge: Cambridge Univ. Press, 1995).

these other embedded discourses which we confront when reading the book of Jeremiah—a communicative act that, for our purposes, can coincide with the inclusion of the oracle in the larger whole of the book.³

The chart is somewhat simplistic and operates only with respect to the surface presentation of certain oracles within the book.⁴ But the point at issue is the distinction between levels (2) and (3), so that level (3) ought to be treated as 'discourse.' The modern search outlined above has clearly been governed by level (2): a placement of the oracle in the role that it plays within a reconstructed religious history of Israel (or of Jeremiah's life and psychology). While such a mode of research continues unabated in many circles of Old Testament scholarship,⁵ a number of other studies have focused on the importance of the editing of Jeremiah for supplying 'meaning' to the oracles. Or, put another way, many recent readers focus in various ways (and for various reasons) on the use made of the oracles in their inclusion in the book of Jeremiah.⁶ Taking Jer 1 for an ex-

---

3. Thus bypassing the question of independent circulation of 'reported' oracles (as is possible for chs. 30-31, but could easily be included in the chart). I suppose the final inclusion does not have to be an 'act of communication', which I understand to be an intentional act. One might 'accidentally' include an oracle, or include it without any sort of independent reflection on its inclusion in the scroll (e.g. someone told me it was Jeremiah's, so I threw it somewhere in the middle of the scroll that said 'Jeremiah'). The former is not very believable, and the latter is stronger even than the skeptical account of the book's composition as a 'rolling corpus' by William McKane, *Jeremiah* (2 vols.; Edinburgh: T&T Clark, 1986), xlixf. But for strong skeptics, the following investigation can be taken as a hypothesis: 'If the oracle is included with some kind of intentionality, then how might we understand it?'

4. Thus Biddle's critique is correct, but not fatal: Mark E. Biddle, *Polyphony and Symphony in Prophetic Literature: Re-reading Jeremiah 7-20* (Macon, GA: Mercer Univ. Press, 1996), 65.

5. E.g. Terence Collins, "Deuteronomist Influence on the Prophetical Books," in *The Book of Jeremiah and its Reception* (eds. A.H.W. Curtis and T. Römer; Leuven: Leuven Univ. Press, 1997). Or the recent work, re-positing Jeremiah as a propagandist for Josiah's reforms, by Mark Leuchter, *Josiah's Reform and Jeremiah's Scroll: Historical Calamity and Prophetic Response* (Sheffield: Sheffield Phoenix, 2006).

6. Some of the more prominent or relevant readings include: Louis Stulman, "The Prose Sermons as Hermeneutical Guide to Jeremiah 1-25: The Deconstruction of Judah's Symbolic World," in *Troubling Jeremiah* (eds. A.R. Pete Diamond et al.; JSOTSup, 260; Sheffield: Sheffield Academic Press, 1999); Kathleen O'Connor, *The Confessions of Jeremiah: Their Interpretation and Role in Chapters 1-25* (SBLDS; Atlanta: Scholars Press, 1988); J. Gordon McConville, *Judgment and Promise: An Interpretation of the Book of Jeremiah* (Leicester/Winona Lake: Apollos/Eisenbrauns, 1993); Idem, "Jeremiah: Prophet and Book," *TynBul* 42 (1991).

ample, whatever one thinks of its formal history or its referentiality to the prophet himself, Brueggemann rightly claims that:

> the intent of this narrative is to affirm that the text which follows is not merely a human construction, but is in fact the purposeful governing assertion of Yahweh, who will have history move as Yahweh asserts it.[7]

This is neither an interest in the recesses of an unknown author's psyche (or motivation), nor a neglect of history: it is a claim concerning the role the text (utterance) is made to play in an historical act of communication. Whether or not one accepts the narrative provided by Jer 1 as reliable does not alter the role that it is made to play in the discourse.[8] The issue is clearly seen in Robert Carroll's complaint, speaking of himself in the third person:

> What is fundamental to Carroll's reading of the book of Jeremiah is the conviction that the editorial framework... especially the colophon of i 1-3, is a secondary but shaping feature of the book which has misdirected generations of readers into reading the book as if its utterances and events actually took place during that specified period.[9]

Carroll's complaint is (or ought to be) that people have *believed* the editorial framework, not that they have misunderstood its function in communication. So the 'misdirected generations of readers' may be reading the book correctly, even if Carroll thinks the book's presentation is wrong.

For the remainder of this study I will place the oracle of the new covenant (31:31-34) within the context of the book of Jeremiah: I will assume that it was included for a particular purpose (or set of purposes). Or, more precisely, I will explore the role(s) that it is made to play by the fact of its being included in the edited book. Naturally, this approach will not answer questions regarding the historical moment of its inclusion or utterance, the author, or many other (potentially valid) questions.[10] Rather than beginning within a reconstructed context of

---

7. Walter Brueggemann, *A Commentary on Jeremiah: Exile & Homecoming* (Grand Rapids, MI: Wm. B. Eerdmans, 1998), 25.

8. This is parallel to Alston's comment: 'Whether I told you that the dean is coming to dinner or asked you to bring me a towel does not hang on whether you heard or understood me. If you didn't my communicative purpose has been frustrated. But it doesn't follow that I didn't tell you or ask you.' William P. Alston, *Illocutionary Acts and Sentence Meaning* (Ithaca: Cornell Univ. Press, 2000), 24.

9. Carroll, *Chaos*, 52.

10. That I argue both (a) for a contextually-sensitive pragmatics of understanding an utterance, and (b) the unavailability (at least for the purposes of this study) of the precise location of the utterance (understood as the inclusion of the oracle in the larger collection) is, I think, unproblematic, contrary to what is implied by Dan R.

the oracle's 'original' location, I will begin with the 'report' of the oracle and its role in Jeremiah.[11] In other words, I will try to heed Wittgenstein's advice, applied to the paragraph: 'Let the use teach you the meaning.'[12] So our question: how is Jer 31:31-34 *used* in the book of Jeremiah (what is done by it)?

2. *The Broken Covenant*

The difference made by setting the oracle of Jer 31:31-34 back into the book of Jeremiah is illustrated on the negative side by Jože Krašovec when he

---

Stiver, *Theology after Ricoeur* (Louisville: Westminster John Knox, 2001), 132. My interest is not the psychological state or intention of the author—'He uttered x (Jer 31) because of p (he felt dissatisfied with the deuteronomists)', but rather communicative action—'He did y by uttering x'. There are different kinds of factors necessary to determine different kinds of communicative (Alston's 'illocutionary') actions: so I must know more contextually to understand the utterance 'Guilty!' as an act of judicial sentencing than I must know to understand 'These are the words of Jeremiah...' as an act of reported speech. For the former I must know (among other things) that the speaker is a judge, speaking in a court of law, at an appropriate time, about an appropriate person, and in English. But much less is necessary in a report.

So in a 'report that x', the speaker is assumed to have had access in some form to x. But I need not know (for instance) that he or she *has* that accessibility in order to understand what is done. One can offer a wrong report, a lying report, or an ill-grounded report. But it is still a report. Much less do I need to know the name or background of the speaker. Some contextual factors for Jer 31:31-34 are necessary (e.g. uses classical Hebrew normally), and sometimes more precise information is necessary (e.g. for metaphors: 'law on the heart'). These are, I think, better conceived in line with Paul Grice's or Kent Bach's 'conversational implicatures' that can shift upon context and desired communicative result. See H.P. Grice, *Studies in the Way of Words* (Cambridge, MA: Harvard Univ. Press, 1989); Kent Bach, "Minding the Gap," in *The Semantics/Pragmatics Distinction* (eds. Claudia Bianchi and Carlo Penco; CSLI, 2004); Idem, "Conversational Impliciture," *Mind and Language* 9 (1999); Idem, "Context ex Machina," in *Semantics vs. Pragmatics* (ed. Z. Szabó; Oxford: Oxford Univ. Press, 2005).

11. 'The received location of prophetic messages in descriptions (!) of speaking situations is primarily not a speaking situation that can be immediately reconstructed. Instead, the received location is a book. We only possess the book, and only the book is the ground upon which we can pose our questions.' O.H. Steck, *The Prophetic Books and their Theological Witness* (Tr. by James D. Nogalski. St. Louis, MO: Chalice Press, 2000), 9. Steck's assumption that this demands a source-critical analysis of the text *first* is, I think, unnecessary and unfortunate. But for an application of Steck's general position relevant to our text, see Schmid, *Buchgestalten*.

12. Ludwig Wittgenstein, *Philosophical Investigations* (Tr. by G.E.M. Anscombe. 3rd ed. Oxford: Blackwells, 2001), p.181.

begins his examination of the oracle by asking, 'what kind of covenant was the previous one, nowhere specifically described?'[13] By placing the oracle into the book we find numerous places where this 'previous' covenant was described with its most prominent aspects. One could even argue that the previous covenant is broadly the theme of chapters 1-25. Sigmund Böhmer's suggestion appears exactly right in maintaining that 'covenant' is simply one metaphor among many in Jeremiah, both in its positive and negative appearances.[14] The reader finds a mutiplicity of terms and metaphors in the book to refer to that 'relationship of obligation' between Yhwh and his people—that state of affairs in which Yhwh and Israel can expect faithfulness from one another.[15] And, if Böhmer is right, then the 'broken' covenant is one a variety of ways throughout the book to express the unfaithfulness of the people, a theme that forms the core of Jeremiah from the opening call narrative through the close of the book.

This brings in the first major point: the terminology used in the book for the 'previous' covenant. As Kraus points out, Jeremiah never in fact uses the language of 'old' to contrast to the 'new covenant'. But neither do we find it called a 'first covenant' as Kraus does,[16] or simply the 'covenant with the fathers' as Renaud—all of which might be taken as neutral terms.[17] Rather, the way in which that contrary covenant is presented is as a broken covenant.[18] An 'old'

13. Krašovec, *Reward*, 455. My emphasis.

14. Siegmund Böhmer, *Heimkehr und neuer Bund: Studien zu Jeremia 30-31* (Göttingen: Vandenhoek & Ruprecht, 1976), 75.

15. The phrase is from the excellent discussion of ברית in Gordon P. Hugenberger, *Marriage as a Covenant: Biblical Law and Ethics as Developed from Malachi* (VTSup 52; Leiden: Brill, 1994), 168-215. Kutsch's arguments (in *Verheissung und Gesetz*) for ברית as *Verpflichtung* without a notion of 'relationship' has found little support in more recent discussions of the term. Even Nicholson (*God and His People*, 216), who follows Kutsch to some extent, sees ברית here as including relationship (though concludes it must be therefore late). Likewise, Lalleman-de Winkel (*Jeremiah*, 203) points to the similarity between Hosea and Jeremiah in that ברית 'indicates a relationship' that demands loyalty. For full discussions interacting with Kutsch, see Hugenberger (op.cit.); P. J. Naylor, "The Language of Covenant: A Structural Analysis of the Semantic Field of ברית in Biblical Hebrew, with Special Reference to the Book of Genesis" (D.Phil, Oxford, 1980); D.J. McCarthy, *Treaty and Covenant: A Study in form in the Ancient Oriental Documents and in the Old Testament* (AnBib 21a; Rome: Biblical Institute, 1981); James Barr, "Some Semantic Notes on the Covenant," in *Beiträge zur alttestamentlischen Theologie* (eds. H. Donner et al.; Göttingen: Vandenhoeck & Ruprecht, 1977).

16. Kraus, "Der Erste," 63.

17. Renaud, "L'alliance éternelle," 41, et passim.

18. 'Die Eigenschaft des gebrochenen Bundes ist nach eindeutiger Aussage des

or 'first covenant' might be sound or helpful for certain ends, though perhaps imperfect (e.g. the 'old law' in Thomas). But because the contrast is with 'that covenant of mine which they broke', we can no longer read it as a neutral state of affairs. That state of affairs consisting of the covenant being broken is the point of contrast for the 'new covenant'. Or put simply, the contrast to the new covenant is infidelity.

Jer 11:1-13

We can establish the description of the 'broken' covenant rather simply around its central characteristic of infidelity. Two texts form the central burden of explaining this at length, though broadly speaking we could pull in almost any of the sermons or narratives as collateral support. And we will begin by examining 11:1-13, the most explicit text on the 'broken covenant'.[19] In addressing this text we must face the predominant concern in modern scholarship to associate (or disassociate) Jer 11 with the King Josiah's reforms in Jerusalem.[20] Interestingly, Bullinger already makes this connection and reads Jer 11 as a sermon regarding the failure of the people to follow through with Josiah's reforms (perhaps a connection too good to pass by for the Zurich Reformer).[21] Such historical connections are possible, naturally, but our concern is the role the text is made to play in the compiled work and that does not include a narrative of Josiah's reforms. As Carroll remarks:

> If the editors intended 11:1-13 to represent Jeremiah as the preacher of the covenant at Josiah's reform, then they have failed singularly to indicate that information in their presentation here. What they have done is to present him as a covenant preacher, but in such general terms that no precise historical setting can be established for his activity.[22]

Textes nicht, daß er alt oder anders, sondern daß er gebrochen ist. Deshalb und nur deshalb ist der Schluß eines neuen Bundes erfordert.' Levin, *Verheißung*, 141.

19. My decision to end the section at v.13 is somewhat arbitrary: Levin (as Duhm) includes v.14, while Maier, as Holladay, includes through v.17. Maier, *Jeremia*, 165ff. Neither decision makes an impact on the interpretation here.

20. See (e.g.) the two essays, now found together: Henri Cazelles, "Jeremiah and Deuteronomy," in *A Prophet to the Nations* (eds. Leo G. Perdue and B.W. Kovacs; Winona Lake: Eisenbrauns, 1984); J.P. Hyatt, "Jeremiah and Deuteronomy," in *A Prophet to the Nations* (eds. Leo G. Perdue and B.W. Kovacs; Winona Lake: Eisenbrauns, 1984).

21. Bullinger, *Ieremias*, 84b.

22. Carroll, *Jeremiah*, 269.

Jeremiah's New Covenant

Jeremiah stands as a covenant preacher, announcing in dramatic form the brokenness of the covenant between Yhwh and Israel. The section contains three interconnected parts. The first appears to be a kind of mock covenant ceremony, akin as an abbreviated cousin to the ritual in Deut 27:

> (1) The word that came to Jeremiah from Yhwh:
>
>> (2) 'Hear the words of this covenant, and speak them to the men of Judah and to the inhabitants[23] of Jerusalem.[24]
>>
>> (3) And you shall say to them:
>>
>>> "Thus said Yhwh, God of Israel:
>>>
>>>> 'Cursed be the one who does not hear the words of this covenant (4) that I commanded your fathers on the day when I brought them out of the land of Egypt, from the iron furnace, saying:
>>>>
>>>>> "Hear[25] my voice and do according to all that I command you, and you will be my people and I will be your God, (5) in order that I might perform the oath that I swore to your fathers, to give them a land flowing with milk and honey—as at this day."'

---

23. אֶל־אִישׁ ... וְעַל־יֹשְׁבֵי. The phrase could be translated 'to the men of Judah and *against* the inhabitants of Jerusalem' (cf. 18:11). But the overlap between the two prepositions makes a hard case for significance in divergence. The singular אִישׁ is common for this expression: e.g. 4:3, 4; 11:9; 17:25; 18:11; 32:32; etc.

24. The MT's plural in 2a (שִׁמְעוּ) and singular in 2b (דִּבַּרְתָּם)—both represented as such in the LXX—are deemed 'impossible' by Holladay (*Jeremiah* I.236). The whole is excised by Bright, and declared by Levin (*Verheißung*, 73) to be an 'unglaubichsten Konfusionen'. But this is not the only divine command to Jeremiah in the plural (cf. 5:20: 'Declare (הַגִּידוּ) this in the house of Jacob and make it heard (וְהַשְׁמִיעוּהָ) in Judah...'; also 5:1). The reversion to the singular in 2b would then be formulaic. Such may help establish it as an allowable construction, but one whose rhetorical import has been lost. Lundbom suggest that the normal order is being reversed here: the message is given prior to the messenger formula: Jack R. Lundbom, *Jeremiah 1-20* (The Anchor Bible; NY: Doubleday, 1999), 616-17. Calvin (*Jeremiah*, 2.70) saw the plurals as evidence of Jeremiah's having help, while some Jewish commentators (e.g. the Mezudath David) read them as commanding the prophets themselves to hear and understand the covenant: A.J. Rosenberg, *Jeremiah: A New English Translation of the Text, Rashi and a Commentary Digest* (New York: Judaica Press, 1985), I.99. The Targum and Vulgate have repointed 2b to the plural (דִּבַּרְתָּם) but this hardly resolves the difficulty.

25. I have translated שמע ב as 'hear' throughout rather than the standard 'obey' in order to draw attention to the repetitions of שמע.

And I answered and said, 'Amen, Yhwh.'

The central command of the covenant is clearly put forward: the curse associated with failure to 'hear' and then the command to 'hear my voice and do according to all that I command you.' The covenant formula is then presented, and the blessing of life in the land promised to the fathers.[26]

The middle unit (6-8) turns from a mock establishment of the covenant to the stance of a covenant preacher, repeating the central demand of the covenant ('hear') and now alluding to the curses rather than the blessings associated with it:

> (6) And Yhwh said to me:
>> 'Call out all these words in the cities of Judah and in the streets of Jerusalem:
>>> "Hear the words of this covenant and do them."
>>
>> (7) For I strongly warned your fathers—from the day I brought them up from the land of Egypt until this day, warning them persistently,[27] saying:
>>> 'Hear my voice.'
>>
>> (8) But they did not hear, and they did not incline their ear, and each man walked in the stubborness of his evil heart. So I brought upon them all the words of this covenant which I commanded them to do, but they did not.'[28]

---

26. The 'fathers' here are held by some to be distinct (patriarchal ancestors) from the unfaithful (wilderness) fathers in v. 7; this seems to make the most sense of the flow of argument. See Brueggemann, *Jeremiah*, 110; Lundbom, *Jeremiah 1-20*, 622; McKane, *Jeremiah*, I.238. They are seen as the same 'fathers' by Maier, *Jeremia*, 175. Her citation of כיום הזה as demanding this is unconvincing. The main difficulty is that the promise of the 'land flowing with milk and honey' only emerges in Exod 3, though that could be overcome by an anachronistic description of the promise to the patriarchs (as in 32:22).

27. הַשְׁכֵּם וְהָעֵד: For this translation see Carroll, *Chaos*, 88.

28. The LXX reduces the whole of vv. 7-8 to the simple negative: καὶ οὐκ ἐποίσαν. Most commentators prefer the MT on supposed stylistic grounds, but such preferences are hard to establish (includes Duhm, Holladay, Rudolph, Cornill, Hyatt, and Lundbom). Volz claims that 2-5 and 6-8 are doublets, and so excises the latter, but such a sentencing pays little attention to the details of the text. The best suggestion for the absence in the LXX is that of haplography from the formulaic 6b: as Gerald J. Janzen, *Studies in the Text of Jeremiah* (Cambridge, MA: Harvard Univ. Press, 1973), 39. For suggestions of deliberate abridgment, see Winfried Thiel, *Die deuteronomistische Redaktion von Jeremia 1-25* (Neukirchen-Vluyn: Neukirchener Verlag, 1973), 148-50.

Jeremiah's New Covenant

Again we see central call to covenant fidelity in the twin commands, 'Hear the words of this covenant,' and then 'Hear my voice.' The first is a call to the present generation, but the second is set within a brief historical narrative that is, as well, apparently part of what Jeremiah is to call out to the present. Jerusalem knows that it is hearing the same command as was given to the fathers, but the fathers were unfaithful in responding to the call. As McKane notes:

> [T]he function of vv.7-8 is to establish that from the time of the Exodus up to the present Yahweh, through his (prophetic) spokesmen, has unremittingly and urgently laid on his people the necessity of obedience to the terms of the covenant. Despite these solemn representations they have a record of unrelieved apostasy.[29]

The effect is a uniting of all the children of Israel into one familial line of those called to 'hear,' and whose fathers were unfaithful. And so the judgment of v. 8—however one understands it—stands as the pronouncement of a standard covenant curse.[30] The rhetorical effect establishes a pattern of rebellion and judgment that has been the defining characteristic of the people from the very beginning—from the birth of the promise until now—rhetorically presenting a 'record of unrelieved apostasy'.

The third movement of the text (vv.9-13) now carries the indictment forward directly to the apostasy or infidelity of the present generation:

> (9) And Yhwh said to me:
>
>> 'A conspiracy is found among the men of Judah and among the inhabitants of Jerusalem:
>>
>>> (10) They turned to the iniquities of their forefathers who refused to hear my words; and they went after other gods to serve them.
>>>
>>> The house of Israel and the house of Judah broke my covenant which I made with their fathers.'
>
> (11) Therefore thus said Yhwh:
>
>> 'Behold, I am bringing disaster upon them, from which they cannot escape. And they will cry to me, and I will not hear them.

---

29. McKane, *Jeremiah*, I.238.

30. McKane (*Jeremiah*, I.238-39) and Skinner (*Prophecy*, 102) object to the past tense of the judgment. But as Lundbom points out, the ones receiving the judgment is clearly the 'fathers'. Perhaps we are meant to understand the judgment in the wilderness (as Lundbom, *Jeremiah 1-20*, 623; Brueggeman, *Jeremiah*, 111); or the judgment on the Northern kingdom (Cornill, *Jeremia*, 146); or a more broad and extended bringing of curses of which the Northern exile is the most prominent (Graf, *Jeremia*, 179). Any would fit the context and too little is offered to judge between them.

(12) And the cities of Judah and the inhabitants of Jerusalem will go and cry to the gods to whom they burn incense, but they will surely not deliver them in their time of disaster. (13) For the number of your cities is the number of your gods, O Judah. And the number of the streets of Jerusalem is the number of altars you have set up to Shame—altars to burn incense to Baal.'

The link is forged again between Jerusalem and Judah and the 'fathers' but now to condemn the present Jerusalem. The summary statement at the close of v.10 is the centre of the whole: 'The house of Israel and the house of Judah broke my covenant which I made with their fathers.' The statement brings together the fathers of the past and the people of the present as having been unfaithful: a summary of the whole covenant indictment. The punishments that follow are then standard prophetic pronouncements of the punishment fitting the crime: they did not hear, now I will not hear.[31]

Lohfink points out that we often find the phrase שמע בקול in covenantal clauses of blessing and curse.[32] So while its imperatival form in 11:4, 7 (and 7:23) may be somewhat unique, the meaning is still transparent. And we find the parallel of the 'voice of Yhwh' to Yhwh's תורה or even the prophet's message—a rather straightforward use of the imagery—in (e.g.) 9:12 (MT); 10:13; 25:30; 32:23 and 44:23. So the central command to 'hear the voice of Yhwh' or to 'hear (obey) the words of the covenant' is standard to the point of being formulaic—but loses none of its rhetorical force for that. And despite the concern of some commentators to give a precision to the content of the 'words of the covenant' in 11:4 and 6, its open-ended nature appears deliberate. The explicit concern is the fundamental infidelity of the people, and the command to 'hear my voice' is likely (as Skinner) the general concern for 'obedience to the will of Yahwe [sic] in whatever way it may be revealed.'[33] In fact, few more basic structural ways of speaking of covenantal fidelity exist than the simple command to 'hear/listen' (as parents know for their children). So rather than a condemnation for having broken certain particular precepts, the condemnation re-

---

31. Thus the link to 11:14-17. See the classic study on the correspondences of sin and Yhwh's judgment by Patrick D. Miller, *Sin and Judgment in the Prophets* (SBLMS; Chico, CA: Scholars Press, 1982).

32. Norbert Lohfink, *Das Hauptgebot: Eine Untersuchung literarischer Einleitungsfragen zu Dtn 5-11* (AnBib 20; Rome: Pontifical Biblical Institute, 1963), 65. Cf. Deut 4:30; 8:20; etc.

33. Skinner, *Prophecy*, 100. The parallel to Exod 19:1-8 is relevant, with the people's accepting of the covenant's 'words' (even described as 'hear my voice and keep my covenant', v.5), *prior* to their being spelled out.

gards the whole construct of (dis)obedience to Yhwh: they have refused to 'hear,' the first and foundational duty for covenantal faithfulness.

So if the first characteristic of the covenant in 11:1-13 is the basic command to 'hear', then the second is the universal infidelity of the people: they were called to hear and refused to do so. Here we begin to find more direct links to the 'new covenant' of 31:31f. and in particular the reference to 'the day I brought them up out of Egypt'. We find two nearly identical ways of phrasing the clause in 11:4 and 7, apparently for stylistic variation:[34]

(v.4) בְּיוֹם הוֹצִיאִי אוֹתָם מֵאֶרֶץ מִצְרַיִם

(v.7) בְּיוֹם הַעֲלוֹתִי אוֹתָם מֵאֶרֶץ מִצְרַיִם

The deliverance from Egypt stands as the constitutive event for Israel as the people of Yhwh: it is Yhwh's action by which he laid claim to Israel, in accordance with the promise to the fathers. The deliverance from Egypt as Yhwh's claiming his people finds clear expression in the narrative of Exodus,[35] and comes clearly into focus throughout much of the deuteronomic literature:

> Deut 4:20 But Yhwh took you and brought you out (וַיּוֹצֵא) of the iron furnace, from Egypt, in order to be a people of his inheritance, as at this day.

Or more famously:

> Deut 5:6 I am Yhwh your God who brought you up (הוֹצֵאתִיךָ) from the land of Egypt, from the house of slavery.

The phrase points to the moment of birth for the people of God, or perhaps better the formal moment at which they were brought into the covenant relationship with Yhwh:

---

34. Levin (*Verheißung*, 136f.) makes much of the difference as a means of dating the texts, but that is much too wooden an approach: surely we cannot expect someone to be unable or unwilling to vary a formulaic phrase on occasion. Better is von Rad: 'for the most part the expression is already of the nature of a formula—in many cases it is clearly simply already taken over from hymnody. On the other hand, another of its characteristics is its great variability and elasticity, as the very different length in which it is formulated make apparent. This confession could be summed up in the juxtaposition of three words, but it could also find expression in a long hymn.' von Rad, *OT Theology*, I.176.

35. 'As [Exodus] xix 4 and xx 2 make clear, the covenant at Sinai is grounded in the redemption from Egypt.' J. Gerald Janzen, "On the Most Important Word in the Shema (Deuteronomy VI 4-5)," *VT* 37 (1987), 282.

> Deut 29:25: [the judgment came upon Israel] because they abandoned the covenant of Yhwh, God of their fathers, which he made with them when he brought them up out of the land of Egypt.

Thus, Yhwh's action in bringing the people from Egypt offers the ground for Yhwh's claim upon them (e.g. Deut 6:20-25; 8:14f; I Sam 10:18-19), or the act that 'established Israel's identity'.[36] As Patrick Miller notes:

> The single ground for identifying the Lord and *explaining why* that one claims to be "your God" is the clause "who brought you out of Egypt, out of the house of bondage".[37]

In line with this common position, the references to the exodus in Jer 11:4, 7 (as in 7:22, 25—and 31:32!) points us to the 'birth' of Israel as Yhwh's people through that great constitutive act. The phrase gives a concrete way of Yhwh saying, 'On the day when I claimed you as mine'. The phrase (in its variety) emerges with this role universally in Jeremiah:

> 2:6 [Your fathers] did not say, 'Where is Yhwh who brought us up (עלה) from the land of Egypt...?'

Here the reference is clearly to Yhwh's claim on the people and the ground upon which they owed him their allegiance. In 32:20-23 we have a near repetition of the main themes of 11:1-13 in which the reference to Yhwh's bringing up from Egypt clearly plays this same role: Yhwh has done this great work, according to his promise of the land, and so demands obedience (hearing his voice).

> 32:20-23 You offered signs and wonders in the land of Egypt until this day in Israel and among humankind, and you have made for yourself a name, as at this day. (21) And you brought your people Israel up (יצא) from the land of Egypt with signs and wonders and by a strong hand and outstretched arm, and by great terror. (22) And you gave to them this land, which you swore to their fathers to give to them—a land flowing with milk and honey, (23) and they entered and possessed it.
>
> But they did not hear your voice, and in your law [*Qere*] they did not walk. All that you commanded them to do, they did not. And so you have caused all these disasters to occur against them.

Likewise in 34:13-14, with more content given to the 'covenant':

---

36. Brevard S. Childs, *Biblical Theology of the Old and New Testaments: Theological Reflection on the Christian Bible* (Minneapolis: Fortress, 1992), 131. 'Israel became the people of God, not by a natural bond, but by its experience of redemption from Egypt which it understood as an act of divine favour (138).'

37. Patrick D. Miller, "The Most Important Word: The Yoke of the Kingdom," *Iliff Review* 41 (1984): , 20.

34:13 Thus said Yhwh, the God of Israel: 'I myself made a covenant with your fathers in the day I brought them up (יצא) from the land of Egypt, from the house of bondage, saying:

(14) "After seven years you are to release the Hebrew brother who was sold to you..."

And your fathers did not hear me, and they did not incline their ears.'

Incidentally, the reference here to the slave-laws underwrites that the 'words' throughout most of Jeremiah (as in ch.11) are some form of the Torah. But the reference to the deliverance from Egypt plays the same role as elsewhere: to point to that time when Yhwh's claim on the people began—i.e. when the (broken) covenant began.

Finally, the same reading should be seen in the (nearly identical) references of 16:14-15 and 23:7-8, where we find a climax of sorts regarding these statements:

16:14-15 Therefore, behold, the days are coming—oracle of Yhwh—and it will no longer be said 'As Yhwh lives who brought the people of Israel up (יצא) out of the land of Egypt', (15) rather, 'As Yhwh lives who brought the people of Israel up (עלה) out of the north country and all the countries where he had driven them.'

That great act by which Yhwh claimed the people for his own, out of the promise to the fathers, will be eclipsed by another act of Yhwh claiming the people for his own. Where the exodus grounded the covenantal obligations of Israel, now the return from exile will function in the same way. Importantly we ought not see here a 'replacement' or 'substitution' theology (and much less von Rad's 'rejection' of the 'older basis of salvation'). Better is Calvin:

[Jeremiah] does not mean that the memory of God's favour towards the Israelites, when he brought them from Egypt, was to be abolished; but he reasons here from the less to the greater, as though he had said that it was an evidence of God's favour that could not be sufficiently praised, when he delivered his people from the land of Egypt, that if it were taken by itself, it was worthy of being forever remembered; but that when compared with the second deliverance it would appear almost as nothing.[38]

We do not move along lines of rejection or replacement, but of eclipsing of the one great constitutive saving act by another even greater: as if to say, the exodus

---

38. Calvin, *Jeremiah*, III.148. Interestingly, Calvin claims for 16:14-15 a different function, intimating the exile as even more painful than the slavery in Egypt. This appears to be owing to לכן opening 16:14, which gives his reading some credence.

was when I first claimed you as mine by a great act; but I will do another greater act to claim you anew.

Our first firm point for reading 31:31-34 can now be established: the reference to 'the day when I brought them up out of Egypt' (whether at 31:32 or 11:4 and 7) is not used to identify 'which covenant' is made the point of contrast (e.g. Mosaic rather than Josianic). Nor does the phrase give justification for our leaping out of Jeremiah into a state of affairs described in the book of Exodus or Deuteronomy. Rather the phrase points us to the start of the relationship between Yhwh and his people, the great act by which Yhwh claimed them as his own. In other words, from ch.11 we learn that the infidelity of the people to Yhwh—the broken covenant—has been broken from the very start, from the time in which Yhwh acted to call and bring them to himself.

Such a single-stroke manner of characterizing Israel's history is prominent in the poetry and prose of Jeremiah. The universal failure is seen, e.g., in 5:1-5—and tied to the language of 'knowing', which will come back in 31:34:

> (1) 'Run throughout the streets of Jerusalem and look and know (ידע) and search her squares:
>
>> if you can find a person,
>>
>> if there exists one who does justice, who seeks faithfulness,
>>
>>> in order that I might forgive (סלח) her.' ...
>
> (4) And I said,
>
>> 'They are only the poor—
>>
>> they act foolishly because they do not know
>>
>>> the way of Yhwh, the justice of their God.
>
> (5) I will go to the great and speak to them,[39] because they know
>
>> the way of Yhwh, the justice of their God.'
>
> Yet they together had 'broken the yoke', they had 'torn apart the bonds'.[40]

The whole community is painted with the same brush as not 'knowing' the way of Yhwh. So Brueggemann: 'The city has refused in all parts of the citizenry to accept its proper vocation as Yahweh's covenant partner destined for submission

---

39. MT reads וַאֲדַבְּרָה אוֹתָם but there is no obvious reference for the object. The LXX has the above, αὐτοῖς.

40. The statements should perhaps be taken as ironic citations of the 'great', parallel to 2:31. The parallel of 5:1 to Gen. 18, with the even less stringent demand for Jeremiah, is already noted by Jerome (*Hieremiam*, §I.xcii.1), and mentioned by most modern commentators.

and obedience.'⁴¹ The universality of unfaithfulness to the covenant reaches backwards through the whole life of Israel as well as throughout all levels of society.

We find the same again in 9:1-6, structured by the parallel conclusions, 'and they do not know me—oracle of Yhwh (v.3)... they refuse to know me—oracle of Yhwh (v.6).' Lundbom speaks of this oracle as 'a sweeping condemnation...of the entire society.'⁴² Or in 6:13 and with the same encapsulating phraseology as 31:34:

> 6:13 'For from the least of them to the greatest (מִקְּטַנָּה וְעַד גְּדוֹלָם), everyone is greedily pursuing profit, and from prophet to priest, everyone commits falsehood.'⁴³

Throughout Jeremiah the universality of covenant infidelity runs deep as well as wide: through the generations of Israel from the moment of her 'birth' in the deliverance out of Egypt and into every level of her society. The generational depth is the clear point in 11:7-8. McKane's comment is worth citing again:

> [T]he function of vv.7-8 is to establish that from the time of the Exodus up to the present Yahweh, through his (prophetic) spokesmen, has unremittingly and urgently laid on his people the necessity of obedience to the terms of the covenant. Despite these solemn representations they have a record of unrelieved apostasy.⁴⁴

---

41. Brueggemann, *Jeremiah*, 63. For 'know' as having covenantal overtones, see below on 31:34a.

42. Lundbom, *Jeremiah 1-20*, 378.

43. Cornill's translation (*Jeremia*, 76) of 'jeder Einzelne' for כֹּל makes the point even stronger. Cf. also 7:18: 'the children gather the wood, the fathers kindle the fire, and the wives knead the dough to make cakes for the Queen of heaven.' Or, 25:1ff: 'The word that came to Jeremiah... which Jeremiah the prophet spoke to *all the people of Judah and all the inhabitants of Jerusalem*: From the thirteenth year of Josiah son of Amon king of Judah to this day, these twenty-three years, the word of Yhwh has come to me, and I have spoken to you—constantly speaking—but you have not heard. And Yhwh sent to you all his servants, the prophets—constantly sending—but you have not heard, and you have not inclined your ears to hear'.

44. McKane, *Jeremiah*, I.238. Or Calvin: 'Here the Prophet does not accuse a few men of perversenesss, but says that, from the time they had been redeemed, they had been rebellious against God'. Calvin, *Jeremiah*, II.82. Painting the history of Israel in this way is not unique here: in narrative form, see Deut 1:26-46, as well as much of the Numbers and Exodus narratives. More closely to the diction and themes of Jer 11, see the protracted apology for the exile in 2 Kgs 17:7-40; 21:15 ('they have done what is evil in my sight and have provoked me to anger from the day their fathers came out of Egypt,

So from the first to the last, from the least to the greatest, all have lived in unfaithfulness to Yhwh. The broken covenant refers us to that state of affairs of universal infidelity to the covenant.[45]

This is rather clear in the MT of 11:1-13. But what of the LXX? Adrian Schenker has posited a difference on this matter between the two texts, drawing from the reduction of 11:7-8 in the LXX as noted above. In the MT, he claims, we have a narrative that points to God's 'long patience' with the people, a point drawn from seeing the same covenant existing even after being broken by the 'fathers'. In the LXX, however, he finds two different covenants: in 11:1-7 we have no concern for the gap between the Exodus and the 'present' generation. Jeremiah simply re-presents the same covenant as was presented in Egypt, but it again failed (11:8, 'but they did not'). So while the MT has the same covenant continually presented, the LXX has the same covenant needing to be presented twice. So, he concludes, by assuming the need for a new covenant after one is broken, the LXX presents a state of affairs where 'Judah and Jerusalem are now without a covenant.'[46] Thus, ultimately, the MT sees the 'new covenant' as a renewal of the same covenant, while the LXX presents grounds for seeing the 'new' as different.

But his argument is difficult to maintain. The silence on the breaking of the covenant by the 'fathers' in the LXX cannot sustain such a weighty theological difference. We find the broken covenant clearly in v.10 where it is the fathers who 'refused to hear my words.'[47] So far the same substance exists in the MT and LXX. Now, Schenker is right to claim that the MT of 11:1-13 does not in itself necessarily entail the ending of the covenant. But neither does the LXX (and the point is rather benign: the MT does speak this way elsewhere—see below). And Schenker assumes that the repetition of the covenant in 11:1-5 (LXX) entails that the previous had ended—the 'new proclamation' is itself a 'new covenant'. But why? Why is its representation in the LXX significantly different from its representation continually in the MT? In the LXX we find the covenant broken, then the re-proclamation of the same covenant showing the same pattern

---

even to this day.'). Cf. Deut 9:7, 24; Jer 2:6f; 32:23; 34:13; and below. Such a description is represented in second-temple literature at (e.g.) Baruch 1:19.

45. Cp. the similar text of 16:11-13.

46. Adrian Schenker, *Das Neue am Neuen und das Alte am alten: Jer 31 in der hebräischen und griechischen Bibel, von der Textgeschichte zu Theologie, Synagoge und Kirche* (Göttingen: Vandenhoeck & Ruprecht, 2006), 38. His emphasis. See pp.35ff for discussion.

47. ἐπεστράφησαν ἐπὶ τὰς ἀδικίας τῶν πατέπων αὐτῶν τῶν πρότερον, οἳ οὐκ ἤθελον εἰσακοῦσαι τῶν λόγων μου.

of rebellion and infidelity (11:10).⁴⁸ And that is what we find in the MT as well. But the more important problem is that Schenker seems to be asking the wrong question. The issue is not whether or not the covenant will continue, whether regarding the MT or LXX. That is one step beyond the text's role. The more simple point is that the covenant has been broken time and again from the moment of its being made until the present. So now the people will reap its curses: God's 'long patience' has run out.

So when Kraus asks, 'When did the covenant-breaking begin?', we can give a clear answer: from the day the covenant began.⁴⁹ The absoluteness and universality of the infidelity so strongly painted in the book of Jeremiah ought to be striking. That such a painting ought not be taken quite literally is probably true. But we must not replace the hyperbolic (rhetorical) world with one of our own construction until we see the whole of the picture—for 31:31-34 plays its contrast within this rhetorical world rather than a (de-hyperbolized) reconstruction.

Jer 7:21-28

In 11:1-13 the broken covenant has two central aspect: its central demand ('hearing' as an expression of fidelity) and the universal failure to keep the demand. When we turn to 7:21-28 we find the same two aspects:⁵⁰

> (21) Thus said Yhwh of hosts, the God of Israel:
>> 'Add your burnt offerings to your sacrifices—and eat the meat! (22) For I did not speak to your fathers, nor did I command them in the day when I brought them out of the land of Egypt concerning burnt offerings and sacrifices. (23) Rather, this command I gave them:
>>> "Hear my voice, and I will be your God and you will be my people. And walk in all the way as I command you, that it may go well with you."⁵¹

---

48. This beyond the simple point that the text of 7:25 (below) is the same in both LXX and MT. Schenker makes too much out of too little by isolating the one case.

49. Kraus, "Der Erste," 64. Not, as Kraus holds, *after* the entry into the land. How this theme in Jeremiah sits with 2:2 is another matter, though quite simply one could say that the rhetorical device in each case is just that: a rhetorical device. Thus to expect them to fit *as such* an ostensive world of reference is misguided.

50. The similarities of the texts are shown in a table in Thiel, *Jeremia 1-25*, 149.

51. וְהָלַכְתֶּם בְּכָל הַדֶּרֶךְ: Note the similarity to Deut 5:33 (the only other occasion of 'walk in all the way'): 'In all the way which Yhwh your God commanded

198 The Context of the New Covenant

(24) But they did not hear or incline their ear. And they walked in their own counsels and in the stubbornness of their evil heart, and they turned backward rather than forward.[52] (25) From the day that your fathers came out of the land of Egypt to this day I sent—I repeatedly sent—all my servants the prophets to them—daily. (26) But they did not hear me or incline their ear. They stiffened their neck and did more evil than their fathers.

(27) And you will speak all these words to them,

    but they will not hear you,

And you will call to them,

    but they will not answer.

(28) And you will say to them:

"This is the nation (גוי) that did not hear the voice of Yhwh their God and did not accept discipline. Truth perished, it was severed from their mouth.'"[53]

The central themes are clear: the repetition of שמע (hear) and the universal failure to do so from the moment of their coming out of Egypt to the present. The emphasis on the constant work of the prophets to make the people 'hear' multiplies their guilt.

The most controversial text in this passage is the mocking irony of v.21 and the statement of v.22. In classic modern commentaries this was taken as a model of the prophet standing over against the cultic activities: the prophetic view of religion over against the 'popular' or cultic. Indeed, Hyatt goes so far as to declare this is the 'plain meaning.... [I]t is best to take Jeremiah's words here at their face value and see in them his belief that the sacrificial system was man-made and not willed by Yahweh.'[54] More recently and in a similar vein, v.22 has been read as a later perspective of a 'cult-less' foundation to the relationship between Yhwh and the people, compensating for the loss of the temple.[55] But such readings are not necessary. Lundbom suggests bypassing the wooden readings of, e.g., Hyatt by pointing to the 'idiom of exaggerated contrast' seen in other Hebrew and Semitic texts: the idiom backgrounds something by negating

---

you, you shall walk.'

52. וַיִּהְיוּ לְאָחוֹר וְלֹא לְפָנִים: This unique phrase is somewhat difficult, though the idea is clear. I have followed Holladay, *Jeremiah*, I.257.

53. Whether v.29 should be included here or as an introduction to 7:30f is unclear, and for our purposes immaterial.

54. J.P. Hyatt, "The Book of Jeremiah," in *The Interpreters Bible* (New York: Abingdon, 1956), 875; cf. Duhm, *Jeremia*, 81f; Skinner, *Prophecy*, 178f.

55. Maier, *Jeremia*, 107-09. In another way, Jerome, *In Hieremiam*, §II.xl.2.

it to make the point at issue unmistakeable, or to make the negated aspect false outside of the asserted one.[56] Nor does the backgrounding of the cultic activities speak necessarily of a 'cult-less' view of religion. The backgrounding simply makes clear that the issue is the more fundamental one of fidelity to Yhwh. In the setting in which the text plays its role within ch.7, the issue surrounding it on both sides (as in 11:13) is Israel's idolatry. Jeremiah is initially portrayed (7:1ff.) as condemning the presumption of trust in the temple apart from adherence to the 'ways' of Yhwh, the heart of which is seen in vv.9-10:

> Will you steal, murder, commit adultery, swear deceitfully, and offer incense to Baal, and walk after other gods whom you did not know, and come and stand in my presence, in this house which is called by my name, and say 'We are delivered'?

The absurdity of the proposition leads into a description of the cult of the Queen of Heaven, the judgment that results, and then the sarcasm of v.21. Again, on the other side of this section v.30f picks up on the theme of idolatry within 'the house that is called by name' and the 'high places of Topheth.' By placing the idolatrous activities in the foreground before and after this unit, and backgrounding any reference to a proper cultic alternative, the discourse clearly focuses the failure of the people on covenantal infidelity: violations of the Decalogue (7:9) and above all the infidelity to Yhwh by the service of foreign gods. So the issue is not whether proper religious service is cultic but rather the cultic infidelity of the people—setting the cultic service of Yhwh apart from the broader covenantal requirements.

Rashi, reading 7:22 more literally, still avoids Hyatt's conclusion by appeal to the narrative of Exodus where the very first recorded incident after the Exodus is the 'trial' at Marah (well before the commands at Sinai), in which lies this—the first—command:

> Exod 15:26 If you will diligently *hear the voice* (תִּשְׁמוֹעַ לְקוֹל) of Yhwh your God, and do what is right in his eyes, and give ear to his commandments and keep all his statutes, I will place on you none of the diseases I placed on the Egyptians, for I am Yhwh your healer.[57]

---

56. E.g. Deut 5:3; cf. the similar rhetorical device at 7:19, 'Is it me they are provoking to anger? (oracle of Yhwh) Is it not themselves to the shame of their own faces?'. See Lundbom, *Jeremiah 1-20*, 488-89. The terminology comes from James G. Carleton, "The Idiom of Exaggerated Contrast," *The Expositor* 4th Series, 6 (1892). For other options and discussion of the text, see Ernest C. Lucas, "Sacrifice in the Prophets," in *Sacrifice in the Bible* (eds. Roger T. Beckwith and Martin J. Selman; Carlisle/Grand Rapids: Paternoster/Baker, 1995), 62-63.

57. Rashi himself points to Exod 19:4-5 ('As for you, you saw what I did to the

Whatever option we take we find the same principle: the primary command is that of 'hearing the voice of Yhwh, which is covenantal loyalty and fidelity. As Carroll states it:

> Obedience, not sacrifice, was the original command, and by that standard the nation's history has been one of complete and continual rebellion against Yahweh. Hence its destruction is warranted.[58]

One obvious implication for our purposes lies in the challenge the text presents to the traditional definition of the contrast of the new covenant as a change of sacraments (*mutatio sacramentorum*).[59] At least as far as the book of Jeremiah is concerned, any definition of the 'old covenant' as Israelite cultic activities (*accidentalia*) in the Mosaic era is mistaken. In one form or another this represents the greatest bulk of pre-modern interpreters, from Jerome to Bullinger to Olevianus. Yet here in Jeremiah we find the covenant explicitly distanced from commanded cultic activities so that all of the focus lies on the central act of 'hearing,' which is simply covenantal fidelity. So when we come to the contrast in Jer 31:31-34, we have no reason to think of the broken covenant as the cultic activities of Israel or a particularly cultic 'view of religion.' If we are guided by the movements within the book of Jeremiah then the 'broken covenant' (seen in Jer 7 and 11) is concerned solely with covenant infidelity to Yhwh, emphatically *not* a set of cultic norms that Yhwh had established. And the result in 7:28 is an implicit judgment of the people (made explicit in v.30f) as simply one of the גוי.[60] The infidelity of the people to Yhwh results in an ending of the relationship between Yhwh and the people.

This sketch from chs. 7 and 11, however brief, is sufficient to show the main characteristics of the 'broken covenant': its requirement of fidelity, and the universal breaking of the requirement (i.e. infidelity). The payoff for our invest-

---

Egyptians, and how I carried you on eagles' wings and brought you to me. So now, if you will indeed hear my voice and keep my covenant, then you will be to me a treasured possession...'), which plays the same purpose *prior* to the Sinaitic laws. Rosenberg, *Jeremiah*, 70. So also, citing Kimchi, C.F. Keil, *The Prophecies of Jeremiah* (Tr. by David Patrick and James Kennedy. Edinburgh: T&T Clark, 1866), 102.

58. Carroll, *Jeremiah*, 216.
59. This point is already made in Cornill, *Jeremia*, 349.
60. So already, Jerome: 'Pulchre, ut ante iam dixi, nequaquam populum suum, sed gentem vocat.' Jerome, *In Hieremiam*, II.xliii.2. Or Abarbanel's explanation: 'Then you shall say to them that this nation is not of the children of Israel who heard the voice of the Lord their God on Mount Sinai, but they are like another nation, who did not hear His voice on Sinai and who has not received correction.' Rosenberg, *Jeremiah*, 71-72. More recently, see Aelred Cody, "When is the Chosen People called a gôy?", *VT* 14.1 (1964), 2.

igation is obvious: the new covenant does not stand in contrast to a neutral or simply imperfect (in the Thomistic sense) state of affairs. The new covenant stands in contrast to the universal infidelity of Israel, within the rhetorical world of Jeremiah: 'This has been your way from your youth, that you have not heard my voice (22:21).' The new covenant is 'not like' (31:32a) this universal state of infidelity—that is the state of affairs referred to as 'my covenant which they broke'.

Before moving on to the next step of the argument we must ask one more question: is it the case that (as von Rad) 'the old covenant is broken, and in Jeremiah's view Israel is altogether without one'?[61] Given the recent work of Lohfink and Zenger we might find such a claim suspect. But their concerns can be met if we distinguish between the cause of the relationship, and the relationship itself (covenant being a metaphor for the latter). Thus we can and should say with von Rad that there is a very real ending to the relationship in Jeremiah. The people can no longer claim Yhwh as their God, and he will no longer claim them for his people:

> 5:10 'Go up through her vine rows and destroy, but make not a full end; strip away her branches, for they are not Yhwh's.'
>
> 12:7-8 'I have forsaken my house, I have abandoned my heritage. I have given the beloved of my soul into the hands of her enemies... she has lifted up her voice against me; therefore I hate her.'
>
> 15:6-7 'You have rejected me... so I have stretched out my hand against you and destroyed you.... I have destroyed my people.'
>
> 23:39 'I will surely lift you up and cast you out of my presence, you and the city that I gave to you and to your fathers.'

The people are uncircumcised of heart (4:4) and so are considered simply as one from among the nations (9:24-25 MT). This is the language of 'cast out', 'uprooted', 'torn down', or 'divorced' that governs so much of the book. The relationship—the covenant—is truly at an end. Yet the language of 'unrevoked' is right nonetheless, for there is something more fundamental than the metaphors of relationship—the whole point, as we will see, of 31:35-37.

---

61. von Rad, *OT Theology*, 2.212. See Thomas M Raitt, *A Theology of Exile: Judgment/Deliverance in Jeremiah and Ezekiel* (Philadelphia: Fortress, 1977), 64, 81. Nicholson: 'The presupposition of the declaration which stands at the centre of the "new covenant"—"I will be their God, and they shall be my people" (v.33)—is "I am not your God, and you are not my people" (cf. Hos. 1:9).' Nicholson, *God and His People*, 212. Buis: 'la première est rompue de façon irrémédiable.' Pierre Buis, "La nouvelle alliance," *VT* 15 (1968), 6.

Can a covenant bond be broken—and at the same time persist? Can God sever a relationship as a result of covenant violations—and nevertheless maintain it in perpetuity? The Bible seems to answer in the affirmative.[62]

The tension between these two things—the ending of the covenant and its perpetuity—are resolved in one consistent theme: the 'mercy' or 'love' of Yhwh. And this, the cause of the covenant and its continuation through its own death, leads us directly to the oracles of restoration.

3. *The Oracles of Restoration: chs. 30-31*

The naming of chs. 30-33 as a 'book of consolation' in modern scholarship stems from two main facets: their character as 'consolatory' and their similarity in this regard to Isa. 40f (two observations already made by Bullinger).[63] My goal in this section is to support the claim that the oracles of restoration play a particular role in the book of Jeremiah: overturning the state of affairs in the oracles of judgment. This is by no means a novel claim, though little has been done to explore the idea throughout the whole of the book (which lies beyond my own scope as well).[64]

---

62. David Noel Freedman, "Divine Commitment and Human Obligation: The Covenant Theme," in *Divine Commitment and Human Obligation: Selected Writings of David Noel Freedman* (ed. John R. Huddlestun; Grand Rapids, MI: Eerdmans, 1997), 177.

63. 'The speech is clearly consolatory, written in imitation of Isaiah, who handles this very argument in chapter 40 and also in chapter 49.' Or, 'He proceeds with words bursting with consolation, and in imitation of Isaiah, that the captives and those afflicted on account of their goodness (*pietas*) are consoled.' Bullinger, *Ieremias*, 177b, 178b.

64. The relationship of the judgment and salvation preaching as relates to the prophet Jeremiah (rather than their relationship in the book) has been a significant source of dispute: see the skeptical remarks denying salvation oracles to Jeremiah by Carroll, *Chaos*, 200. The most thorough discussions in opposition to Carroll's view with regard to the career of the prophet are Nelson Kilpp, *Niederreißen und aufbauen: Das Verhältnis von Heilsverheißung und Unheilsverkündigung bei Jeremia und im Jeremiabuch* (BThSt 13; Neukirchen-Vluyn: Neukirchener Verlag, 1990); Unterman, *Repentance to Redemption.* Cf. Raitt's view that the salvation preaching 'opened an authentic and dramatic new episode' in Jeremiah's career: Raitt, *Theology of Exile*, 107. Similar resolution by appeal to changing experiences of the prophet is given by Otto Eissfeldt, "Unheils- und Heilsweissagungen Jeremias als Vergeltung für ihm erwiesene Weh- und Wohltaten," in *Kleine Schriften* (vol.4; Tübingen: J.C.B. Mohr (Paul Siebeck), 1968). See the summary of positions in J. Applegate, "'Peace, Peace, when there is no Peace': Redactional Integration of Prophecy of Peace into the Judgement of Jeremiah," in *The Book of Jeremiah and its Reception* (eds. A.H.W. Curtis and T. Römer; Leuven: Leuven

As I develop the claim I am consciously building on the work of John Bracke in his claims along these lines:

> In the context of the Book of Jeremiah, Yahweh's promise to restore the fortunes of his people (*šûb šebût*) of Israel and Judah becomes clear. It describes the reversal of Yahweh's judgments. That which God's people lost because of their sin is restored to them. The initial relationship between Yahweh and Israel and Judah is reestablished: Yahweh's care for his people is once more to be matched by their faithfulness and obedience. Yahweh will be God to all the families of Israel, and they will be his people.[65]

Bracke does not offer a unique reading of chs. 30-31 but his is the most thorough explication of this view from the 'present form' of Jeremiah.[66] And, indeed, the pattern is commonly recognized in much of the prophetic corpus.[67] That chs. 30-31 stand in a close relationship with the rest of the book has been emphasized in a number of ways: Fischer has compiled an impressive list of verbal and thematic links and characterizes the whole as 'reversal' (*Umkehrung*) of the previous state,[68] while McConville has gone as far as claiming that 'the relationship between the "Book of Consolation" and the rest of Jeremiah constitutes the distinctive theological contribution of the work'—a contribution

---

Univ. Press, 1997), 51-71.

65. J. M. Bracke, "The Coherence and Theology of Jeremiah 30-31" (Ph.D, Union Theological Seminary, 1983), 107.

66. See, e.g., Patrick Miller: 'These chapters look back to earlier parts of the book, using language and imagery—incurable pain, lovers who have forgotten—that occurs elsewhere and responding to issues and questions, to laments and woes expressed by Jeremiah or the people elsewhere. The judgment that has been announced so thoroughly in the first half of the book is clearly kept in mind, alluded to, and interpreted further. But judgment becomes the stepping-stone for speaking about restoration.' Patrick D. Miller, "The Book of Jeremiah," in *New Interpreters Bible* (Nashville: Abingdon, 2001), 804. Or, 'The intention of the editor in 30.4 is to contrast oracles of weal to Israel (30-31) with those of doom addressed to Judah (1-25) and the nations (46-51).' McKane, *Jeremiah*, II.756.

67. "Messages that dismantle the old, followed by those that build up the new age , characterize the preexilic literature." Bruce K. Waltke, *A Commentary on Micah* (Grand Rapids, MI: Eerdmans, 2007), 204. More broadly, see R.E. Clements, "Patterns in the Prophet Canon," in *Canon and Authority* (eds. G.W. Coats and B.O. Long; Philadelphia: Fortress, 1977).

68. Georg Fischer, *Das Trostbüchlein: Text, Komposition und Theologie von Jer 30-31* (Stuttgart: Verlag Katholisches Bibelwerk, 1993), 141-55, 157. Cf. Louis Stulman, *Jeremiah* (Abingdon Old Testament Commentaries; Nashville: Abingdon, 2005), 260-61.

centred on the 'illogical' overcoming of judgment.[69] My own claim among such company is relatively modest: that at least many of the oracles of salvation in Jer 30-31 play the role of reversing the state of affairs painted as the judgment. If this can be established then the pieces of the argument will be sufficiently in place to argue the main point: that Jer 31:31-34, as an oracle of salvation (or restoration), plays the rule of overturning a part of the state of affairs in the judgment (the universal infidelity of the broken covenant). And that conclusion will be the topic of the next chapter.

Jer 30:12-17

The thematic unity of 30-31 has long been admitted by critical scholarship to one degree or another, and some recent studies have pointed firmly away from the parsing out of the various oracles to different authors and periods.[70] One could point to various literary or verbal forms for this coherence, but for interpretation the more important unity lies in the movement embodied in one way or another throughout these poems: a move from a state of judgment to its reversal. The paradigmatic oracle in this regard is 30:12-17:

> (12) For thus said Yhwh:
> Incurable is your hurt, Grievous is your wound.
> (13) There is none to discern a diagnosis for your injury,
> there are no healing medicines for you.[71]

---

69. McConville, *Judgment*, 92. See his discussions of similarities to the rest of the book (p.94).

70. For the coherency of the chapters, see esp. Bracke, op cit.; Barbara A. Bozak, *Life 'Anew': A Literary-Theological Study of Jer. 30-31* (AnBib 122; Rome: Editrice Pontificio Istituto Biblico, 1991); Becking, *Fear and Freedom*, 49-134. Even Böhmer, who takes apart the bits of the oracles throughout his work, nonetheless admits that the chapters 'eine relative Einheit bilden'. Böhmer, *Heimkehr*, 88.

71. אֵין דָּן דִּינֵךְ לְמָזוֹר / רְפֻאוֹת תְּעָלָה אֵין לָךְ: This odd statement has caused significant difficulty and is omitted or emended by many (Bright, Holladay, Duhm). The difficulty is the abrupt move from an apparently legal metaphor to a medicinal one, but this appears simply an extension of the basic use of דִּין. Carroll and Becking read three different phrases here: 'There is none who procures you justice. For a suppurating wound there are medicines, but for you there is no healing with new flesh.' (Becking's translation, *Fear and Freedom*, 165; Carroll includes the negative in the middle clauses). There is little to choose between this and the above (though the MT would have the above, as the accents show). The use of similar terminology in 46:11 breaks the accent at רְפֻאוֹת, but to do so in this case would help very little: either we have לְמָזוֹר רְפֻאוֹת together in an odd way (as Carroll and Becking) or רְפֻאוֹת תְּעָלָה, of which the latter is

(14) All your lovers have forgotten you,
    For you they care nothing.
   For with the blow of an enemy I have struck you,
      with the punishment of a cruel foe:
   On account of the greatness of your iniquity,
      The great number of your sins.

(15) Why do you cry out over your wound?
   Your pain is incurable:
      On account of the greatness of your iniquity,
      The great number of your sins, I did these to you.

(16) That being the case (לָכֵן),
   All who devour you will be devoured,
   And all your foes—everyone of them—will go into captivity.[72]
   Those who plunder you shall be plundered,
   And all who prey on you I will make a prey.

(17) For I will bring health to you,
    and your wounds I will heal—oracle of Yhwh.
   For 'Banished One', they call you: 'She is Zion, for whom no one cares.'

The imagery of the 'wound' is common in Jeremiah for Zion's situation, and is put to particularly poignant use here.[73] The female Zion sits stranded with an incurable wound, deserted to her death, crying desperately but without any purpose. But the strong break in the oracle with לָכֵן in v.16 signals the great reversal. The disjunction, a clear *non sequitur*, has led some to parse out the oracle to two different authors, set 'illogically' together here.[74] Or, some

---

easiest by appeal to a double predicate ('no medicines, no healing/scarring') or a genitival relationship ('medicines that bring healing', as above). The precise meaning of רְפֻאוֹת is hard to determine, but some form of healing is clearly envisioned.

72. Dahood's suggested revocalisation from כֻּלָּם to כֹּלָם is unnecessary and demands the subject for יֵלֵכוּ to be the plunderers out of the next line, which then destroys the parallel word play to 16a. Mitchell Dahood, "The Word Pair *'AKAL*///*KALAH* in Jeremiah XXX 16," *VT* 27.4 (1977).

73. Cf. 6:14; 8:11, 21; 14:17. In 10:19 the lament of the 'wound' is taken by some to be Jeremiah over his own situation (e.g. Brueggemann, Lundbom), but probably ought to be read as a personification of Zion or Jerusalem, as is certainly the case in v.20: see Stulman, *Jeremiah*, 108.

74. Bright (*Jeremiah*, 271) calls it 'logically unsuitable' and 'may originally

have taken לָכֵן as an adversative conjunction.⁷⁵ Whether or not לָכֵן ever clearly appears as an adversative is open for discussion, but in Jeremiah the only other text that might support a reading is the structurally similar 16:14 in its context (and what one decides for one ought to determine the other).⁷⁶ Of course we could simply dismiss 30:16-17 to another contextual setting (interpreting our own constructed texts can be much easier). But such a move still fails to address why they were included in this way here, and I doubt very much that it was an accidental inclusion. More recent commentators have focused on the rhetorical

---

have been uttered in another context'. Or Hyatt ("Jeremiah", 1025): 'The two parts of this poem do not fit well together. In the first part, vss. 12-15, it is said that Zion's wound or hurt is incurable, and that God has brought upon the city deserved punishment. But in the second part, vss. 16-17, Zion is promised health and healing, with punishment to be visited upon its enemies.... [T]he connection is awkward and illogical.' Similarly, see Böhmer, *Heimkehr*, 62; Duhm, *Jeremia*, 241; Volz, *Jeremia*, 278. Even Lundbom (*Jeremiah 21-36*, 401), normally sensitive to such plays, attributes לָכֵן to the verses being originally independent.

75. Bozak, *Life 'Anew,'* 54; Becking, *Fear and Freedom*, 183; McKane, *Jeremiah*, II.769. Rudolph (*Jeremia*, 176) suggests an emendation to וְכֹל, and Holladay (*Jeremiah* 2.151) suggests an original לְכִי (a supposed archaic form of לָךְ), but neither have any reason beyond the supposed illogicality. Cornill (*Jeremia*, 327) rearranges the oracle under the same impulse, placing v.17 (with 'aber' for כִּי) prior to v.16. Calvin (*Jeremiah*, IV.32-33) appears to read it as drawing on 30:8-11, while Graf looks the other direction and treats it as anticipating v.17 (*Jeremia*, 375). Weiser reconciles the parts by claiming that 'die Bestrafung Israels den Heilsabsichten Gottes mit seinem Volke dient' (*Jeremia*, 280); but this would only resolve the use of לָכֵן if giving a reason for the punishment, not the restoration.

76. In the examples cited by the above scholars (Jer 2:33; I Sam 28:2; Mic 2:5) לָכֵן can be understood without difficulty as 'therefore' (or 'thus', 'for') or the broadened form, 'that being the case'. Other questionable texts that could be cited include Jdg 11:8 and 8:7. (Though in these the LXX translators apparently read לֹא כֵן; making the textual question important). Both Bozak and Becking appeal to Israel Eitan, "Hebrew and Semitic Particles: Comparative Studies in Semitic Philology," *American Journal of Semitic Literature and Languages* 44 (1928), 200. But Eitan there is speaking of the function of פֶּן, strangely misread in its many instances by both (!) Becking and Bozak as כֵּן. Indeed, the only place in which לָכֵן emerges in Eitan's discussion is a side-reference in a later article, explaining יַעַן as 'a motivating particle. It introduces a causal clause, wherefore it is often correlative with a לָכֵן starting the principal clause that presents the effect supposed to result'—the precise opposite of Bozak and Becking. Idem, "Hebrew and Semitic Particles (Continued): Comparative Studies in Semitic Philology," *American Journal of Semitic Literature and Languages* 46 (1929), 39. More in-depth, but with too little precision to be of help grammatically, is W.E. March, "*Laken*: Its Functions and Meanings," in *Rhetorical Criticism* (eds. J.J. Jackson and M. Kessler; Pittsburgh: Pickwick, 1974).

function of לָכֵן as deliberately establishing the non sequitur in the text. So Brueggemann:

> We discover... that the 'therefore' of v.16 is a verbal trick. The term prepares us for one more message of judgment, but in fact the following lines offer exactly the opposite message—a word of God's powerful, healing intervention.[77]

Whether לָכֵן is deliberately provocative, simply a formulaic opening, or a striking way to join the oracles, the tension between the parts is still maintained in the reversal of the people's present state from having Yhwh as enemy to Yhwh as healer and protector.[78] The point of the inclusion of 30:16-17 in this opening poem is precisely to create the movement of overturning the state of judgment.

After the non sequitur, just one reason for the overturning is offered. That is found in the last clause as lady Zion becomes a mockery among the nations.[79] The only means of this explanation functioning is the assertion of a pathos in Yhwh undergirding the whole movement: the jealousy that moves Yhwh to strike as an enemy and the love that moves Yhwh to heal and avenge. Here we find the answer to our question at the close of the previous chapter and the 'more fundamental reality' undergirding the metaphors of relationship between Yhwh and the people. The poem presents Yhwh's devotion to his people as the ground for overturning the state of affairs at the judgment. And his movement to restoration comes as the direct counterpoint to the judgment. What ought to have always been the case—Yhwh as the protector of his people—is brought about.

---

77. Brueggemann, *Jeremiah*, 276. Similarly, Clements (*Jeremiah*, 182): 'There can be no doubt that this sharp contrast is a deliberate and carefully constructed pattern.'

78. Kilpp's complaint ('Die Selbigkeit Gottes in Unheil und Heil bedeutet nicht, daß ein Prophet zur selben Zeit denselben Menschen ein doppeltes, in sich widersprüchliches Handeln Jahwes zu verkündigen vermag': *Niederreißen*, 123) betrays a simplistic view of rhetorical possibilities and misreads this movement of Yhwh as 'contradictory'—which is only the case if God promises to judge and not-judge (p and not-p) the same people at the same time in the same way. But there is no reason to think this is what is occurring: the judgment clearly precedes the movement to deliverance.

79. Jacobson's suggestion that this is a play on words (with צִיּוֹן 'a wasteland') makes good sense of understanding the taunt: Howard Jacobson, "Jeremiah XXX 17: צִיּוֹן הִיא," *VT* 54.3 (2004).

Jer 30:4-11

As McConville terms it, we have in these poems a 'theology of illogical grace.'[80] We could try and work our way through all of chs. 30-31 with this theme in mind but I will only pursue it in a selection of the poems. The goal, after all, is simply to set the pattern as an expected norm in which 31:31-34 finds a natural home. But the theme is already set in the opening poem of 30:4-11:

> (4) These are the words that Yhwh spoke to Israel and to Judah:
>
> (5)　For thus Yhwh said:
>
> > A voice of trembling, we have heard:[81]
> >
> > of dread, and there is no peace.
>
> (6)　Ask now, and see, whether a male gives birth?
>
> > Why then have I seen all the men,
> >
> > > their hands on their loins like a woman giving birth,
> > >
> > > and every face turned pale?
>
> (7)　Woe! For great is that day—there is none like it![82]
>
> > And a time of distress, it will be for Jacob,
> >
> > and from this he will be saved.
>
> (8)　And it will be on that day—oracle of Yhwh of hosts:
>
> > I will break his yoke from upon your neck,
> >
> > and your bonds I will tear apart.
> >
> > And they will no longer serve strangers in it,[83]

---

80. McConville, *Judgment*, 95.

81. The subject of 5b (שָׁמָעְנוּ) has been a matter of some dispute, being typically attributed to Yhwh or Jeremiah quoting the people (Calvin, *Jeremiah*, IV.9; Bozak, *Life 'Anew'*, 35; Holladay, *Jeremiah*, II.171; Keil, *Jeremiah*, 262), or to Jeremiah by emendation with Volz to שָׁמַעְתִּי (Volz, *Jeremia*, 285; Rudolph, *Jeremia*, 172; Böhmer, *Heimkehr*, 57; Kilpp, *Niederreißen*, 107, n.2). Better, however, is the analogy with 31:15 where the voice heard is a passive: the subject who hears is not the point. The inclusiveness of 'we' (30:5) or a passive (31:15) allows the audience to be included in the 'hearing' (cp. 25:36). Thus the plural imperative of 6a could be construed as an involving term, and the question of 6b is posed to the audience.

82. Repointing מֵאַיִן to מֵאִין, with Jack R. Lundbom, *Jeremiah 21-36* (The Anchor Bible; NY: Doubleday, 2004), 385. See 10:6-7.

83. The construction עָבַד בְּ is not overly common. Becking calls it a 'בְּ-pretii'

(9) but they will serve Yhwh their God,
and David their king whom I will raise up for them.

(10) And you, do not fear, my servant Jacob—oracle of Yhwh.
And you shall not be dismayed, Israel.
For behold, I will deliver you from afar,
and your seed from the land of captivity.
And Jacob will turn and have quiet, and ease, and there will be no trembling.

(11) For I am with you—oracle of Yhwh—to save you.[84]
For I will make a complete end of all the nations where I have scattered you,
though with you I will not make a complete end
And I will discipline you according to justice,
and I will certainly not acquit you.

(of price): 'they shall no longer serve strangers for it' (for the cost of getting it), but he fails to say to what this 'it' might refer (*Fear and Freedom*, 140). Typically the construction it is used to indicate means of service: 'serve Yhwh with all your heart' (לְעָבְדוֹ בְּכָל לְבַבְכֶם; see Deut 11:13; 10:12; cf. 28:47; Josh 22:5; 24:14a; 1 Sam 12:20; 1 Sam 12:24; 1 Chr 28:9; Ps 2:11; 100:2. For locative uses ['serve me *in the wilderness*']: Exod 7:16; Num 4:23, 37, 41; 8:19, 21; Josh 24:14b; Jer 5:19. Uses of בְּ for specificity: Gen 29:18 ['I will serve you...*for Rachel* your daughter']; 30:26; 31:41). Extended, then, is the suggestion of the construction signifying 'to work by means of another, to use another as a slave' (BDB, followed by Bozak, *Life 'Anew'*, 41). So עבד takes the broader meaning of 'to do one's work', and בְּ indicates the means by which it is done. This is similar to Lundbom's suggestion that the construction takes a causative meaning, which appears clear in a number of instances (e.g. Exod 1:14; 34:27; Lev 25:39; Deut 15:19; cf. Jer 25:14; 27:7; 34:9; Lundbom, *Jeremiah 21-36*, 282). If this is the case, then one must render the phrase, 'And strangers will no longer make him serve'—and the problem of pronoun agreement is even more pronounced ('will no longer make *him* serve, but *they* will serve Yhwh...'). The syntactic choice for 'they' in the latter line would be the strangers, but pragmatically this is unlikely unless shifts from singular to plural are not as disjunctive in Hebrew rhetoric, as is more common in shifts in second person shifts in number, as in Timothy A. Lenchak, *'Choose Life!': A Rhetorical-Critical Investigation of Deuteronomy 28,69-30,20* (AnBib 129; Rome: Editrice Pontificio Istituto Biblico, 1993), 12-16.

84. Many commentators (Volz, Rudolph, Bright, et al) insert וְאַתָּה אַל תִּירָא עַבְדִּי יַעֲקֹב prior to this colon, as in 46:28; but the MT and Targum do not have the phrase and its addition is unnecessary.

Two main textual details are significant for interpretation. The first is the proposal of some to change 7c, the hinge between the picture of destruction and that of restoration, to a question: 'And will he be saved from it?'[85] But this is grounded only in the conviction that the 'lament cannot end by announcing a miraculous deliverance.'[86] Precisely why this 'cannot' be—even granted some uniqueness—is unclear. Becking puts a grammatical justification in the form of a rule: 'The sequence adverb-verb with a *yiqtol*-form indicates that the clause is an interrogative sentence.'[87] Yet I can find no other instance of מָן followed by a *yiqtol* form that is in fact an interrogative sentence, which argues strongly against his suggestion.[88]

The second interpretive question arises from the articles of v.8.[89] Becking offers an explanation for the MT by positing two different speakers: v.8 is the oracle of Yhwh proper, and in v.9 'the prophetic author describes its effect.'[90] The two parts would then make some of the pronouns clearer:

> (Yhwh:) And it will be on that day—oracle of Yhwh of hosts:
>> I will break his yoke from upon your neck,
>> and your bonds I will tear apart.
> (Prophet:) And they will no longer serve strangers in it (יַעַבְדוּ בוֹ),
>> but they will serve Yhwh their God,
>> and David their king whom I will raise up for them.

As rendered above, the phrase יַעַבְדוּ בוֹ takes a standard locative use of בְּ: thus 'serving in' the 'yoke' of the above line. A drawback here is that it does not take into account the construct elsewhere. But the main difficulty with the above is the oddity of Jeremiah claiming to be the one to raise up David—an un-

---

85. First suggested by William L. Holladay, "Style, Irony and Authenticity in Jeremiah," *JBL* 81 (1962), 54-55.

86. Lundbom, *Jeremiah 21-36*, 385. Lundbom assumes that the saving must refer to the events of 586 BC, but there is no reason that this must be the case.

87. Becking, *Fear and Freedom*, 139.

88. So, e.g., Gen 17:6 (cp. 17:16): 'and I will make you into nations, and kings will come from you (וּמְלָכִים מִמְּךָ יֵצֵאוּ).' See, with varying degrees of similarity: Exod 10:26; Jdg 7:17; Job 28:5; Isa 49:17; 66:21; Ezek 5:4; Dan 11:31; Zech 10:4. The lone exception is Jer 32:27, where מָן is preceded by the interrogative הֲ (which, if Becking's rule held, would be unnecesssary).

89. The LXX eases the problem by changing to the 3rd person throughout: συντρίψω τὸν ζυγὸν ἀπὸ τοῦ τραχήλου αὐτῶν καὶ τοὺς δεσμοὺς αὐαὐτῶν διαρρήξω, καὶ οὐκ ἐργῶνται αὐτοὶ ἔτι ἀλλοτρίοις.

90. Ibid., 150. Also Bozak, *Life 'Anew,'* 41.

likely prospect. If the MT is to be retained, then the above rendition can be used and divided not with respect to speaker (as Becking), but with respect to audience. Yhwh speaks directly to Jacob in the first stanza, and then to Jeremiah (or the reader) in the second. Or it may be that the LXX has the better text here.

Rudolph heads his comments on 30:5-7 'durch Nacht zum Licht', a fitting scheme for the whole of 30:5-11.[91] The imagery of dread and destruction in 5-7b is overturned from 7c-11. 'Dread, trembling and no peace' becomes 'quiet, ease, and no trembling.' The similarity of 5-7b to an oracle of judgment has led some to interpret it as such, divorced from the reversal of 8-11.[92] But this similarity is precisely what is played on in the role of the oracle in chs. 30-31:

> Verses 5-7bα could have constituted one of those oracles which were common in the earliest chapters of *Jeremiah*, a message of doom. Here, however, it is completed, quite unexpectedly, with the little phrase: *ûmimmennâ yiwwāšēa'*... Salvation does not follow from what the body of the oracle prepares the hearer for; yet this is what will come.[93]

In fact, the tension is not initially in 7c, but in the judgment of 5-7b after the expectations given in 1-4.

> One would expect the opening lines of the first poem to develop the hope of salvation which was raised in a general way in the introductory verses (30:1-4).... However the opening stanza of Poem I (30:5-7) does not speak of the anticipated peace and security in the land, but rather portrays the opposite: the sights and sounds of distress.... This divergence in tone between the two stanzas (the first accenting distress, the second salvation) is of the same type as that found between the prose introduction and the opening line of Poem I. Such contrast, with its attention-drawing effect, plays an important role in this first poem as well as in the poetic cycle as a whole.[94]

To cooperate with the rhetoric is to see 'that day' (8a) as the greatest moment of punishment and pain. A number of commentators have sought after particular points of historical reference in this, or perhaps an appeal to an apoca-

---

91. Wilhelm Rudolph, *Jeremia* (2nd ed. Tübingen: J.C.B. Mohr (Paul Siebeck), 1958), 173.

92. E.g. Böhmer, *Heimkehr*, 57f. Schmid (*Buchgestalten*, 113f) treats 5-7, 8-9, and 10-11 as separate units.

93. McConville, *Judgment*, 94. Kilpp's reads 5-7 as originally Jeremianic and a judgment oracle, later re-worked into a salvation oracle: 'Der Verfasser... nimmt eine Unheilsverkündigung Jeremias auf und verarbeitet sie in einer außerordentlichen theologischen Leistung zu einer Heilsverheißung.' Kilpp, *Niederreißen*, 118.

94. Bozak, *Life 'Anew,'* 34.

lyptic setting.⁹⁵ But above all this is a rhetorical point to jar the reader by the disjunction: 'and from this he will be saved.' Again, the oracle hinges on a moment of disjunction and movement. So however we explain the change in pronoun the reversal is carried through clearly in vv. 8-9: what came about in judgment is overturned.

Or we could keep in mind other texts from the book of Jeremiah where we find the overturned state of 30:8-9:

> 5:19 [As] you have served foreign gods in your land, so you will serve strangers in a land (תעבדו זרים בארץ) that is not yours.

This is now entirely reversed so that none will make Israel serve—he will serve Yhwh his God and David the king, as he ought. Again, what always ought to have been the case is brought about, in counterpoint to the state of affairs at the judgment.

Or, perhaps more of a stretch, we could bring into the discussion 2:20 where divine deliverance had failed to lead to service to Yhwh:

> 2:20 For from long ago (מֵעוֹלָם) I broke your yoke
>
> I tore apart your bonds
>
> But you said, 'I will not serve.'

In 30:9 the result is what it always ought to have been, with the people responding to Yhwh's liberation by serving Yhwh and 'David their king'—who stands as the rightful and paradigmatic king over the people, with all of the political overtones of a re-unified nation.⁹⁶

The absence of 30:10-11 in the LXX, its repetition in 46:27-28 (MT), and its similarities to parts of a typically earlier-dated Deutero-Isaiah, have led

---

95. Already in Rashi and Kimchi, but more recently in Carroll (*Jeremiah*). The assumption that this is the 'Day of Yhwh' used more technically in other prophetic books (e.g. Carroll, Lundbom, et al.) is unnecessary, given that we find only one occurrence of 'day' in this manner in Jeremiah (46:10). More often it is a general term: e.g. 4:9; 12:3; 16:19; 17:16f; 18:17; 25:33; 39:16f; 44:6. But in either case the point here is unaffected.

96. Lundbom claims, 'This king will not simply be like David or be a king in the Davidic line; he will be a David *redivivus*.' Lundbom, *Jeremiah 21-36*, 390. I'm not entirely sure what this means—though the text is surely Messianic to some degree. Perhaps Lundbom is concerned to state this over against the bland remarks of Carroll (*Jeremiah*, 576; likewise Brueggemann, *Jeremiah*, 271) reducing the claim to a belief in the 'restoration of the deposed dynasty of David'. Rather, the reference is to 'David' as the ideal king, in contrast to those who brought about judgment (as in 23:5).

some to dismiss the verses as out of place here.⁹⁷ But these similarities are easily overstated and literarily and conceptually the verses fit well here.⁹⁸ The use of 'Jacob' may be important in emphasizing the unity of the restored people—or more precisely, the unity of the people as Yhwh sees them in his promises of restoration. The closure in 10-11b to the opening distress of v.5 completes the movement of a restored people, now made the way that they ought to be if Yhwh is their God.

But this leaves 11c-d with little to do, seemingly out of place as a statement of warning to close the movement of hope:

> I will discipline you according to justice,⁹⁹
>
> and I will certainly not acquit you.

While the statement holds much 'gravitas' it must not be taken (as any of these) apart from the book of Jeremiah. What it brings to the poem is a reminder of the unchanged nature of Yhwh. Yhwh still stands as the jealous one. The appeals to 'divine changeability' with reference to the movements from judgement to restoration are unconvincing, and in part for this reason.¹⁰⁰ Yhwh's promise of restoration is not inconsistent with his promise of judgment, a point drawn from the future orientation of both in 10-11 and the use of the formulaic לֹא נַקֵּה.¹⁰¹ In fact, what we see here is the opposite of divine changeability: the one who will act in mercy is the same as the one bringing judgment. Yhwh is holy and jealous

---

97. E.g. Böhmer, *Heimkehr*, 60; Johan Lust, "'Gathering and Return' in Jeremiah and Ezekiel," in *Le Livre de Jérémie* (Leuven: Leuven Univ. Press, 1981), 131-32.

98. See Becking, *Fear and Freedom*, 155. Kilpp attempts a mediating position: 'In Jer 30,10f kommt ein selbständiger Verfasser zum Vorschein, der auf der einen Seite aus der Gedanken- und Sprachwelt Jeremias schöpft, auf der anderen eine gewisse Verwandtschaft mit Dtjes aufweist.' Kilpp, *Niederreißen*, 117. Lundbom (*Jeremiah 21-36*, 387f.) sees 8-9 and 10-11 as originally independent oracles, placed here (in presumably their original shape) as deliberately overturning 5-7—which would explain some of the obscurities.

99. The similarity to 10:24 is only superficial: Jeremiah asks to be punished בְּמִשְׁפָּט rather than בְּאַף, but the function of the prepositions are important. Jeremiah's request in 10:24 has to do with the way in which Yhwh comes to him, while the point in 30:11 is the necessity of discipline on account of justice (לְמִשְׁפָּט).

100. Walter Brueggemann, "The 'Uncared for' Now Cared for (Jer 30:12-17): A Methodological Consideration," *JBL* 104 (1985); Becking, *Fear and Freedom*, 165ff.

101. Most formatively, Exod 34:7; cf. Exod 20:7; Num 14:18; Deut 5:11; Jer 46:28; Nah 1:3.

and abounding in steadfast love: none of these are set aside in the demand for judgment or the demand for restoration.

In 30:4-11 we see once more the role played by the restoration oracles as overturning the state of affairs at the judgment. The statements of deliverance stand in deliberate counterpoint to the causes and effects of the judgment. And in the end everything is made the way it ought to be: Jacob moves from suffering pain and torment at the service of foreigners to enjoying peace and security as the servant of Yhwh.

Jer 30:18-22

Throughout the remainder of chs. 30-31 this 'turning of fortunes' for the people of Yhwh dominates the nature of the oracles. So in 30:18-22 we read of the express reversal of the destruction of the city and the people, so often a theme throughout the book:

(18b) The city will be rebuilt on its mound,

and the fortified place[102] will stand where planned.[103]

(19) Thanksgiving will go out from them,

and the voice of the merrymakers.

I will make them many, and they will not be few;

I will make them glorious (כבד), and they will not be small.

(20) And his sons will be as formerly,

and his congregation will be established in my presence.

(21) His prince will be one of their own,

his ruler (משל) will come out from his midst.

I will make him draw near and he will approach me -

for who is the one that pledged his heart to approach me?

oracle of Yhwh.

(22) And you will be my people, and I will be your God.

Where the earlier poems work the reversal into the structure itself, here we find the assumption—justified only in the rest of the book—that these things are not the case. So Carroll concludes that with these promises, 'things will become the

---

102. אַרְמוֹן: Understood as 'temple' in Targum and LXX, but the term is more general; this would be the sole reference for the rebuilding of the temple in Jeremiah (though it is implied in a number of places).

103. עַל מִשְׁפָּטוֹ: See the extended use of משפט at Exod 26:30; I Kgs 6:38.

way they used to be.'¹⁰⁴ We are given an idyllic picture: things will become the way they ought to have been and remained. So the structures are restored, the people restored, and all stand in a state of honour and joy. The reversal of the previous state of affairs is clearly stated by Hutchinson:

> Given that 25:9-11 binds together the disappearance of joyful voices, the devastation of the country and the domination of Babylon, it comes as no surprise that the renewed sound of joyful voices goes hand in hand with a restoration of the conditions that prevailed prior to the exile.¹⁰⁵

And further, as in 30:8-9, rather than having a foreign ruler (or a puppet ruler), their ruler will be one of their own—'a clear contrast to foreign reign'.¹⁰⁶

A slight puzzle exists in the language of 21b (וְהִקְרַבְתִּיו וְנִגַּשׁ) which is often claimed to be cultic. If so, then it might lead away from understanding משל as functionally equivalent to a king (מלך).¹⁰⁷ Or, as Duhm, it might lead to a model like the Maccabean political high priest.¹⁰⁸ The cultic orientation is supported by the way in which the Targum takes the text, though without any hesitation of joining it to the Messianic figure seen as the משל.¹⁰⁹ But the verbs of 21b are very common and we should not always view them as technical terms for cultic activity.¹¹⁰ We especially don't need to take them here in the strong

---

104. Carroll, *Jeremiah*, 584.

105. J.H. Hutchinson, "A New-covenant slogan in the Old Testament," in *The God of Covenant* (eds. Jamie I. Grant and Alistair Wilson; Leicester: Apollos, 2005), 104. Cp. 33:10-11, 'In this place of which you say "It is a waste...", there will be heard again the voice of rejoicing and the voice of mirth, the voice of the bridegroom and the voice of the bride, the voices of those who sing... for I will return the fortunes of the land as in its original state.' For the contrast, see 7:34.

106. Cornill, *Jeremia*, 329. The link to Deut 17:15 ('from the midst of your brothers you shall set up over yourself a king') is helpfully made by (among others) Holladay, *Jeremiah*, II.179.

107. So suggests McKane, *Jeremiah*, II.774; Carroll, *Jeremiah*, 584. Though we also do not have any text in which a משל has cultic responsibilities. The LXX curiously uses a plural, followed by a singular, perhaps seeing a difference between the two figures: καὶ ἔσονται ἰσχυρότεροι αὐτοῦ ἐπ᾿ αὐτούς καὶ ὁ ἄρχων αὐτοῦ ἐξελεύσεται. The characterization of the future leader as משל is also found in Mic 5:1 (MT).

108. Duhm, *Jeremia*, 242.

109. 'Their king (מלך) will be anointed/raised up (וְיִתְרַבָּא) from them, and their anointed one (וּמְשִׁיחֲהוֹן) revealed from among them.' The translation (as throughout) is adapted from Robert Hayward, *The Targum of Jeremiah: Translated, with a Critical Introduction, Apparatus, and Notes* (Edinburgh: T&T Clark, 1987).

110. For קרב, see Deut 1:17, 22; 2:19, 37; 5:23; 20:2; etc. Further, unless 'cultic' simply means approaching Yhwh (which is then cultic here by definition!), see

sense of a 'right of access to the altar.'[111] The LXX does not take the terms to be cultic: 'I will gather them, and they will return to me, for who is he who sets his heart to return to me?'[112] Thus the referent for the final clause becomes Jacob—the referent of the singular pronouns in 21a—rather than the מֹשֵׁל.[113] The focus never turns to a description of the ruler for his own sake, but only with reference to the restoration of the people (as in 18-20). The thrust of the text becomes Yhwh's prerogative in drawing Israel back when Israel's history (עָרַב, qatal) is so clearly marked by not pledging their 'heart' to Yhwh.[114]

In using the covenant formula (22) to close the poem we find the climax to the people's movement back to Yhwh, addressed directly to the people.[115] The function of the formula here is to '[spell] out the implications of the great restoration of the nation's fortunes.'[116] The whole movement is one of restoration to Yhwh as a counterpoint to what was the case. As in the earlier poems, the judgment of Yhwh is overturned—both in effects and cause—and Yhwh makes everything to be the way it always ought to have been. The covenant formula thus fits quite happily as the final word: 'And you will be my people, and I will be their God.'

Exod 3:5; 16:9; 22:7 or Deut 4:11—none of which is approaching Yhwh for cultic activity. For נָגַשׁ, see (e.g.) Gen 18:3; 27:21; Deut 25:1, 9; etc. For the two together without cultic activity, see Deut 20:2 or Isa 41:1.

111. S.R. Driver, *The Book of the Prophet Jeremiah* (London: Hodder & Stoughton, 1906), 182. Among modern commentators, Volz (*Jeremia*, 291) protests against a cultic implication.

112. καὶ συνάξω αὐτούς, καὶ ἀποστρέψοθσιν πρός με. ὅτι τίς ἐστιν οὗτος, ὃς ἔδωκεν τὴν καρδίαν αὐτοῦ ἀποστρέψαι πρός με; Followed also by the Vulgate: 'quis enim iste est qui adplicet cor suum ut adpropinquet mihi.'

113. This is entertained (with the added support of the Chaldee text) and dismissed by Keil, *Jeremiah*, 266. But his sole reason is 'the context evidently requires us to refer the words to the king, with regard to whom one here looks for a further statement.' But the focus of 18-20 is the people, and 21a appears to be the same focus by virtue of the pronouns. So why one need look for a further statement on the ruler is unclear.

114. Thus Calvin's aside (following the Vulgate) on the issue of 'free-will' here (*Jeremiah*, IV.46); an understandable concern even in modern interpretations: '[30:21] closes by emphasizing the distance between an individual... and Yhwh, a distance unbridgeable by any human action yet bridgeable by the action and initiative of Yhwh alone.' Bozak, *Life 'Anew,'* 65.

115. The verse is deleted in the LXX.

116. Carroll, *Jeremiah*, 584.

Jer 31

The theme of restoration standing in counterpoint to or overturning judgment continues in ch. 31, to which a series of glances is sufficient for our purposes. The poem of 31:2-6 explicitly dwells on the theme of restoration (שוב) in the climactic repetition of 4-5a:

> (4) Again (שוב) I will build you,
>> and you will be built, O virgin Israel.
>
> Again (שוב) you will adorn yourself with your drums,
>> and go out in the dance of merrymakers.
>
> (5) Again (שוב) you will plant vineyards on the mountains of Samaria.

The imagery of 31:7-9 is of return from exile—an obvious overturning of the judgment, and in 31:9 the reason given is similar to that of 30:3 and 30:17—Yhwh's persistent love.

> 31:9 For I am a father to Israel, and Ephraim is my firstborn.[117]

Likewise, the declaration to the 'nations' in 31:10-14 speaks of the reversal of the judgment:

> (10c) The scatterer of Israel will gather him,
>> and will keep him as a shepherd (does) his flock.
>
> (11) For Yhwh has ransomed Jacob
>> and redeemed him from a hand stronger than him.
>
> (12) And they will come and sing on the height of Zion,
>> and they will shine for Yhwh's goodness
>>> on the grain and on the wine
>>> and on the oil and on the sons of the sheep and the cattle.
>
> And their souls will be as a watered garden,
>> and they will languish no more.
>
> (13) Then the virgins will rejoice in the dance—young men and old together.[118]
>
> And I will turn their mourning to rejoicing,
> And I will comfort them

---

117. So Graf's gloss: 'ihn liebe ich am innigsten.' Graf, *Jeremia*, 382.

118. Or 'young men and elders will be merry', if repointing to יַחְדּוּ (so Holladay) to match the LXX χαρήσονται.

>   And I will gladden them from their sorrow.
> (14) And I will feast the soul of the priests with fat,
>   And my people will be satisfied with my goodness
>   oracle of Yhwh.

The explicit notes of overturning and reversal of judgment (10c-11, 13b-c) combine with the return of rejoicing (as in 30:19; 31:4) to present an idyllic picture of the life in Zion—with possible overtones of a cultic celebration ('the height of Zion').[119] The judgment of the priests so heavy throughout the book is overturned, and the people are finally satisfied with Yhwh's 'goodness'—expressed in the bountiful produce of the land.[120] The clear contrast, as in 30:19, is the state of judgment:

> 7:34 I will silence in the cities of Judah and the streets of Jerusalem the voice of mirth and the voice of gladness, the voice of the bridegroom and the voice of the bride, for the land will become desolate.

Yhwh overturns his own judgment by restoring the people's delight and rejoicing in the goodness of Yhwh's care over the people.

The empathetic poem of 31:15-20[121] is structured more like 30:5-11 and 12-17, with both the scenes of judgment and restoration painted into the text. In v.15 we see Rachel weeping because her sons 'are no more' (אֵינֶנּוּ). This lament echoes through the judgments of the book:

> 10:20 My tent is destroyed, and all my cords are broken.
>
>   My sons have gone from me, and they are no more (וְאֵינָם).

---

119. So, already, Calvin, *Jeremiah*, IV.81. See the Targum, v.12: 'And they shall come and praise on the mountain of the house of the sanctuary which shall be built on Zion.' This may also explain the LXX use of συναγωγη for 'dance' (מָחוֹל) in v.13.

120. See, e.g., Holladay, *Jeremiah*, II.186. Cocceius reads 31:14 and 25 as the contrast between redemptive-historical eras: 'it was a time of ἐλπις, of thirst, of the expectation of righteousness and the Gospel, and that thirst was not assuaged.' Johannes Cocceius, *Disputationes selectae* (Opera 6; Amsterdam: 1673), 19, §69. The product is a consistent model (more than most) for reading the contrasts of judgment and hope in the book, but rather less than convincing.

121. Formally, the section may include vv.21-22 (as Bozak, Becking, et al.). But the idiom of 22b is nearly indecipherable, and its exploration is unnecessary for our purposes. For a reading that finds in 21-22 a reversal of judgment fitting well with the present proposals, see Bernhard W. Anderson, "'The Lord Has Created Something New': A Stylistic Study of Jer 31:15-22," *CBQ* 40.4 (1978).

This ending of the people of Yhwh—which we have already had reason to note in discussing the broken covenant—stands out in stark terms. But now we find that ending of the people repeated as a contrast with their restoration:

> (16) Restrain your voice from weeping, and your eyes from tears:
>
> for there is a wage for your work—oracle of Yhwh.
>
> And they will return from the land of the enemy,
>
> And there is hope for your posterity—oracle of Yhwh.
>
> And the sons will return to their country.

As in 30:5-11 and 12-17, there is some measure of 'illogicality' here: the sons who 'are not' will return. The tension of the ending of the covenant and yet its preservation is painted in terms of the life and death of the sons of Rachel. And the fundamental reason for the overturning of judgment, once more, is Yhwh's persisting love:

> 31:20 Is Ephraim my dear son?
>
> Is he a child of delights?
>
> For as often as I speak against him, yet surely I remember him.[122]
>
> Therefore my inmost parts (מעה) yearn for him.
>
> I will surely have compassion on him.

The fatherly love of 31:9 is complemented here with deep pathos—some have suggested the imagery as the motherly love of Yhwh.[123] Once again, the fundamental reality that undergirds the movement from judgment to restoration is attributed to nothing beyond or outside of Yhwh's love for his people—more fundamental than the covenant metaphor itself and surviving the latter's collapse. Yhwh's inexplicable love reverses the state of affairs deserving and resulting from his judgment, and makes things the way that they always ought to have been.

---

122. The translation is from Phyllis Trible, *God and the Rhetoric of Sexuality* (Philadelphia: Fortress, 1978), 44.

123. Unterman, *Repentance to Redemption*, 49; Trible, *Rhetoric*, 45. The issue depends in part upon one's translation of מעה, which can be taken as 'womb' in some circumstances (though in others it refers to the innards of males). Unterman's other two reasons for this choice are inconsequential: (a) that there is no explicitly fatherly imagery (an argument from silence); and (b) that the verbal form שעע ('delight, consolation') is used in Isa 66:12 in the context of playing on a mother's knee. But in Isaiah it is clearly the context, not the word itself, that conveys this. Nonetheless there is precedent for Yhwh as expressing motherly affection in Isa 66:13 and 49:14-15.

The Wider Book

One can easily find this pattern of the restoration overturning the state of affairs at the judgment in any number of points in Jeremiah. One of the more explicit is Jer 23:1-4:

> (1) Woe to the shepherds, the destroyers and scatterers of the sheep of my pasture—oracle of Yhwh. (2) Therefore, thus Yhwh the God of Israel said concerning the shepherds shepherding my people:
>
> As for you, you scattered my sheep and thrust them away,
>
> and you did not attend to them.
>
> Behold, I am attending to you, to your evil practices
>
> oracle of Yhwh.
>
> (3) As for me, I will gather the remnant of my sheep from all the lands where I thrust them away.[124]
>
> And I will return them to their fold,
>
> and they will be fruitful and multiply.
>
> (4) And I will appoint shepherds over them
>
> and they will shepherd them.
>
> And they will no longer fear, nor be dismayed, nor be missing[125]
>
> oracle of Yhwh.

The reversal at the heart of the restoration is clear: the shepherds are replaced by shepherds who will do as they ought to do (i.e. protect, keep from going astray, provide). Yhwh will overturn the state of affairs causing the judgment, and will bring about what always ought to have been the case.

---

124. The shift from the evil shepherds thrusting away to Yhwh thrusting away is often either emended or seen as (clumsy) editing: e.g. Volz, Holladay. But this is simply the standard way of Yhwh claiming responsibility for the exile: 'Within this pericope, then, the shepherds' failures are identified as the cause of their own exile and of that of their flock. The agent of that exile, theologically speaking, is not the Babylonians or their king Nebuchadnezzar. The executioner or judge is Yahweh himself.' Ralph W. Klein, "Jeremiah 23:1-8," *Int* 34 (1980), 168. There may be a subtle shift involved: the shepherds thrust the people out of the fold of Yhwh (i.e. another metaphor with 'covenant'), and Yhwh thrusts them out of the land.

125. As Klein points out, this is the same term as 'attend' in v.2, and implies the deliverance of the people (see 29:10): Ibid., 169.

In the larger literary context in which this oracle is made to play a role, even more can be said. Jer 23:5-8 and the promise of the ideal king in the line of David stands in direct contrast to the censures of Shallum and Jehoiakim in ch.22. What ought to have been the case is promised: a king in David's line who is 'righteous', and 'does justice and righteousness' (explicitly absent under Shallum and Jehoiakim, 22:13-17), and who brings deliverance and safety (23:6) — standing in contrast to the state under these kings (22:26). The issue is not a presentation of a new kingship *in se*, but something that would certainly be 'new' relative to that state of affairs: all is made as it always ought to have been.

Thematically, the centrality of the 'land' in both the judgment and restoration oracles produces a similar pattern. The theological dimension of the land in the Old Testament has been repeatedly emphasized since von Rad pointed to the lacuna on the topic.[126] The first point at issue is that the land is Yhwh's land, which is given to the people with certain obligations: life within Yhwh's land must be lived in proper cultic and moral relationship to him—a common way of viewing the matter in the Ancient Near East.[127] Disobedience to Yhwh pollutes the land and demands that the people be cast out (2:7), so the judgment is often linked directly to the land:

> 3:2 You have polluted the land in your whoring and in your wickedness. So the showers are withheld and the spring rain has not come.
>
> 12:10-11 Many shepherds have spoiled my vineyard, trampled my portion, made my delightful portion into a barren wilderness. They have made it a desolation—desolate she mourned to me. All the land is desolate.
>
> 16:18 I will repay two-fold their iniquity and sin, for they have polluted my land.

---

126. "The Promised Land and Yahweh's Land in the Hexateuch," in Gerhard von Rad, *The Problem of the Hexateuch and Other Essays* (New York: McGraw-Hill, 1966). For a critical discussion of von Rad's proposals see Christopher J.H. Wright, *God's People in God's Land: Family, Land, and Property in the Old Testament* (Grand Rapids, MI: Eerdmans, 1990), 5ff.

127. 'Since they [i.e. the people in ANE societies] had received their territory as a grant from the deity (at least in Israel), and since their occupation of his land was subject to his pleasure, they were charged with keeping the divine patron happy. This meant loyal devotion, demonstrated in careful attention to the cult and the observance of the ethical and moral expectations of the divine sovereign.' Daniel I. Block, *The Gods of the Nations: Studies in Ancient Near Eastern National Theology* (2nd ed. Grand Rapids, MI: Baker Academic, 2000), 109-10.

> 17:4 You will loosen your hand from your portion (נחלה)[128] that I gave to you, and I will make you to serve your enemies in a land you do not know.

The examples could be expanded *ad nauseam* within Jeremiah, especially if combined with the implicit loss of land in the 'war poems' and the narratives in the book.[129] As is the case in Deuteronomy, the loss of the land is not simply a loss in national terms or a simple by-product of divine judgment. The land is at the heart of the judgment as a central consequence of the end of the covenant:

> [L]and loss in the Book of Jeremiah is not a description of Israel's geopolitical fate. The significance of land, its loss and its restoration, is finally a theological issue having to do with the relationship between God and his people.[130]

Indeed, the relationship between Yhwh, the land, and the people is tied so closely together that Peter Diepold concludes that it would be simply unthinkable to have the covenant without the land or the land without the covenant.[131] The expulsion from the land is a 'sign and seal,' as it were, of the ending of the covenant between Yhwh and the people. Given the theme of an overturning of the state of affairs at the judgment, we should not be surprised to find return to the land at the heart of the restoration oracles in Jeremiah. Indeed, the very first component of restoration in chs. 30-31 is just this promise of return to the land:

> 30:3 For behold, the days are coming—oracle of Yhwh,
>
> And I will return the fortunes of my people Israel and Judah,
>
> Yhwh said.
>
> And I will cause them to return to the land which I gave to their fathers, and they will possess it.[132]

---

128. Or 'your inheritance': the latter is defended by Wright, *God's People*, 19, n.29. But 'portion' is defended by Block, *Gods of the Nations*, 78-79; Norman C. Habel, *The Land is Mine: Six Biblical Land Ideologies* (Minneapolis: Fortress, 1995), 33-35.

129. More explicit illustrations: 4:7, 20-26; 5:18; 7:34; 8:16; 24:10; 25:11; et al. See J. M. Bracke, "Coherence," 72f. The implicit loss of land is pointed out by Walter Brueggemann, *The Land: Place as Gift, Promise, and Challenge in Biblical Faith* (Philadelphia: Fortress, 1977), 111-13.

130. J. M. Bracke, "Coherence," 70. For discussion of the theme in Deuteronomy, see Habel, *Land*, 36-53; Patrick D. Miller, "The Gift of God: The Deuteronomic Theology of the Land," *Int* 23 (1969).

131. Peter Diepold, *Israels Land* (Stuttgart: Kohlhammer, 1972), 187-88.

132. See also 3:16-18; 12:15 (broadened to include a return for the 'nations' as well); 16:15; 23:8; 24:6; 29:14; 32:15, 37, 42-44. Cf. 25:5 for the promise: 'Turn now... and dwell upon the land that Yhwh has given to you and your fathers from of old and

But, as is the common pattern, the return to the land is an idyllic return: things are not just reversed, but made the way they always ought to have been. Thus the descriptions in 31:5, 12, and 24-25 of the abundance of the land's produce.[133] This is simply the way things always ought to have been if the people had been faithful in Yhwh's land. In a similar strain, the judged city is turned into its ideal: the destruction of the city is overturned so that it is again rebuilt (31:21, 24, and esp. 38-40—'It will not be uprooted and it will not be overthrown any longer, forever'), and Jerusalem—so roundly condemned for unfaithfulness and wickedness throughout the book—becomes the 'habitation of righteousness' (31:23).

4. Conclusions

In many ways the argument of this chapter ought to come as no surprise. Within the prophets (e.g. Hosea 1-2) we often find the 'new' state of affairs painted as an idyllic overturning of the state of affairs painted in judgment. And this is plainly the case in at least many of the oracles of salvation in Jeremiah. In each case the text or poem plays the role of standing in counterpoint to the oracles of judgment, overturning both the causes and effects of Yhwh's judgment. The pattern is set in Jeremiah's call (1:10) 'to pluck up and break down, destroy and overthrow, *and to build and plant*'—the judgment and its counterpoint. Brueggemann comments on this seminal call:

> It may be suggested that this range of six verbs [in 1:10] provides the essential shape of the book of Jeremiah in its present form.... The book of Jeremiah in its main thrust concerns *the ending of beloved Jerusalem... and the formation of a new beloved Jerusalem.*[134]

But the 'new beloved Jerusalem' is again and again simply Jerusalem as she always ought to have been. That same pattern runs throughout the book finding special emphasis in the collection of restoration oracles in 30-31. The pattern is not simply a negative overturning of the punishment. In overturning the *causes* and *effects* of the judgment Yhwh makes everything the way it always ought to have been between himself and his people. This pattern is explicit in a number of poems throughout 30-31 and is identifiable both in other texts and thematically in the book of Jeremiah.

From this vantage point we can see the culmination of the import of Jeremiah's 'new covenant' oracle. By and large the oracles of salvation in 30-31

---

forever.'

133. The motif is from the standard covenantal curses and blessings with respect to the land: see Deut 28.

134. Brueggemann, *Jeremiah*, 25-26. His emphasis.

play the role of overturning the state of affairs at the judgment. And 31:31-34 fits perfectly within these oracles of salvation. So we ought to expect the oracle to play the role of overturning the state of affairs at the judgment, making everything the way it always ought to have been. In particular, the role of 31:31-34 is overturning the state of affairs in the 'broken covenant'—the state of universal infidelity painted so often and so boldly throughout the book. The 'new covenant' plays its part in these chapters by overturning this state of affairs and making the relationship between Yhwh and his people what it always ought to have been.

7

Jeremiah's New Covenant: *Restitutio ad Integrum*

In Augustine's reading of the oracle of the 'new covenant' in Jer 31:31-34 he maintained an absolute kind of contrast between the 'old' and the 'new': a state of infidelity (old) and a state of faithfulness (new). The theological results included the work of the Spirit in the lives of the believers in the ancient era and the inclusion of all the saints of any era within the same (new) covenant. This did not entail a complete lack of development or deny some differences between eras in the church—Augustine is clear in some of those matters. But he did see 31:31-34 as a unifying covenant for all the faithful over all time. In the last chapters I have begun my attempt to revive a reading that fits in this 'Augustinian' line, and in this chapter I will make the direct case. The point of contrast for the new covenant in 31:31 is not some 'old' or 'first' covenant that remains a mystery to the reader of the book. The point of contrast, at least in the literary presentation (which is the only presentation we have), is the broken covenant—the universal state of infidelity given shape and discussion throughout the book of Jeremiah, and especially in chs. 7 and 11.

But standing over against the oracles of judgment—oracles tied directly to indictments such as we find in the broken covenant—are the oracles of restoration. In these oracles, especially in chs. 30-31, we find a counterpoint to the state of affairs at the judgment. All that caused and resulted from Yhwh's judgment is overturned in an idyllic world where everything is made the way it always ought to have been. These two points—the broken covenant and the oracles of restoration—have given the background and backbone of the argument in this chapter. And, helping the case somewhat, neither is overly controversial in modern readings of Jeremiah and both have been recognized to some degree by many scholars. In this chapter we can draw these two points toward a direct understanding of Jer 31:31-34.

The 'new covenant' oracle plays the role within the book of Jeremiah of overturning the state of affairs at the judgment, especially regarding the brokenness of that covenant which has come to an end. In this sense, Römer is right to see 31:31-34 as the 'response' to 11:1-13.[1] The role of 31:31-34 is one

---

1. Thomas Römer, "Les "anciens" pères (Jér 11,10) et la "nouvelle" alliance

part of making everything the way that it always ought to have been between Yhwh and his people: universal infidelity is overturned into universal fidelity, a hatred and ignorance of the law is overturned into the law placed on the heart, the ending of the covenant between Yhwh and his people is overturned into a re-assertion of the covenant formula, and the judgment for sins is overturned into forgiveness.

1. *The Broken Covenant: 31:31-32*

Behold, the days are coming—oracle of Yhwh -

> And I will make a new covenant with the house of Israel and with the house of Judah: not like the covenant which I made with their fathers in the day I took them by their hand to lead them out of the land of Egypt—
>
> which as for them, they broke my covenant,
> and as for me, I was their husband/lord (בָּעַלְתִּי)[2]
>
> oracle of Yhwh.

The structure of v.32 appears to play off the contrast emphasized in the MT between המה and אנכי—perhaps a play on a typical presentation of the obligations of the covenant, first 'as for me...' (אנכי/אני) and then 'as for you' (אתה).[3] The general point of the text is clear enough, with the main question for our purposes looming as a question of *which* or *what* covenant the new one is 'not like'. But a few further textual details are important. Most commentators take ואת יהודה in v.31 as a late interpolation on the ground of v.33 using 'Is-

---

(Jér 31,31)," *BN* 59 (1991), 26. Similar is Holladay (though I would phrase it differently): 'The passage 11:1-17... depicts the call to obey the old covenant, to which the people failed to respond, so that a new covenant becomes necessary.' William L. Holladay, *The Architecture of Jeremiah 1-20* (Lewisburg, PA: Bucknell Univ. Press, 1976), 162.

2. The discussions between translating 'lord' or 'husband' here seem intractable, and generally beside the point. The central concern in each would be the expectation of loyalty and faithfulness, and while the latter appears more in line with the familial overtones in its only other use in Jeremiah—Jer 3:14 (cf. 3:1ff)—neither one can be said to be the obvious choice for the translator. 'Lord' sounds overly impersonal in our usage but gains the advantage of authority used with בעל, but 'husband' has the advantage of being more personal, while losing the tones of authority in present-day English.

3. This pattern is laid out clearly in each instance of the 'eternal' covenants in the Pentateuch: see Mason, *Eternal Covenant,* passim. Groß structures the verse around the two occurrences of אֲשֶׁר, using בְּרִית as an inclusio (against the contrast of המה and אנכי), but this is less helpful. Groß, *Zukunft*, 136.

rael' to denote the whole of the people.[4] However, we have already seen this phrase in 11:10:

> 11:10 The house of Israel *and the house of Judah* have broken my covenant that I made with their fathers.

But that statement is surrounded by context (11:9, 12) in which the addressees are 'the men of Judah and the inhabitants of Jerusalem.' The phrase in both cases is likely formulaic, perhaps emphasizing the totality of the breaking of the covenant. So we find 31:31 standing precisely against this state of affairs of the covenant broken by 'the house of Israel and the house of Judah'. That the rhetoric reverts to 'Israel' afterwards, then, is unsurprising. And that we find the same rhetorical constructions here as in the discussion of the covenant 'they broke' in ch.11 is, from the standpoint of the present argument, likewise unsurprising.

In v.32 we have the only significant difference in the oracle's presentation in the LXX and the MT. The former reads:

> 38:32 (LXX) Not like the covenant, which I made with their fathers on the day I took them by the hand to lead them out of the land of Egypt, for they did not remain in the covenant (ὅτι αὐτοὶ οὐκ ἐνέμειναν ἐν τῇ διαθήκῃ), and I disregarded them (καὶ ἐγὼ ἠμέλησα αὐτῶν).

Adrian Schenker has made most of the differences between these texts, suggesting that the LXX draws an end to the covenant, while the MT leaves the matter open.[5] Some rhetorical difference does exist: the MT focuses on the people and their action ('as for them, *they* broke my covenant'). Even the structure of the MT appears to emphasize the people's failure. But on that matter the LXX is rather similar 31:32a (MT), saying in the negative what is stated in the positive in the MT: μένω taken to express covenant fidelity, as we see in later Johannine literature (e.g. John 15).[6] So this clause is functionally equivalent, stating in the negative ('they did not remain') what the MT says in the positive ('they broke').

But the clause in 32b (MT) finds the difference. In the MT saying, 'and I was their בעל,' serves to heighten the crime yet one more step. In the LXX, however, the rhetoric seems to emphasize Yhwh's action: '*I* disregarded them.'

---

4. See Rudolph, *Jeremia*, 184 (who edited the BHS of Jeremiah); Cornill, *Jeremia*, 353.

5. Schenker, *Das Neue*, 20f.

6. See Deut 27:26; Isa 28:18; Jer 51:25 (LXX); 1 Macc 10:26. For a brief discussion of μένω in John, see Rekha M. Chennattu, *Johannine Discipleship as Covenant Relationship* (Peabody, MA: Hendrickson, 2006), 112-15.

Some have suggested that the LXX read גָעֲלתִי (cf. 14:9) instead of בָעַלְתִי.⁷ And that would explain the LXX without imputing to the text (or its author) such a difference as Schenker suggests, though the textual justification lies only in the LXX translation. But in any case, to make too much of this rhetorical emphasis in the LXX on Yhwh's action is to neglect that Yhwh's leaving (or 'abhorring', etc.) is repeatedly present in the MT at other points—we have seen a number of them above. Nor is it a novelty in the MT to assert that in the exile Yhwh sent the people away or cast them off.⁸ Thus, though the rhetoric is different in the two texts at this point, there is no reason to think of the two as offering significantly divergent teachings as Schenker suggests. Little reason is left to find the LXX offering a definitive break in the covenant and the MT offering only a potential break. One can find such a teaching only in apart from the role the oracle plays in the book. The contrast for the new covenant is the 'broken covenant.' And the broken covenant is that state of universal infidelity described within the rhetoric of Jeremiah. The substance of the LXX and MT on that note remains the same.

Above we looked at length at the 'broken covenant' in its larger context in the book of Jeremiah. The 'covenant which they broke,' and made when Yhwh 'took them by the hand to lead them out of Egypt,' represents the consistent and universal infidelity of the people since the moment when they were constituted the people of God. As the rest of chs. 30-31 re-uses various metaphors exploited elsewhere in the book to paint the picture of exile, here we see the explicit re-use of the metaphor of 'covenant'. As a reader of Jeremiah, we have no need to bring in ideas and re-constructions from Exodus or Deuteronomy to interpret what is meant by the broken covenant: in the book of Jeremiah we are left in no doubt what that is and what is meant (how it is used). What we need to know, as readers of the book, is what Yhwh will do in response to the people's universal infidelity and the consequences of it. We know the fact of the universal infidelity and breaking of the covenant (rhetorically), and we know the reasons for it. But is that the close of Yhwh's dealings with this people? Is that the last of the 'covenant' he made with them? The 'new covenant' is first of all a statement of hope that plays its role within this world of divine judgment brought justly upon the people of Yhwh.

---

7. So Rudolph (cf. BHS apparatus), Groß, *Zukunft*, 143; Becking, *Fear and Freedom*, 38; et al. Schenker sees ἀμελεῖν as translating מאס or שלח in a different *vorlage*, rather than a misreading of בָעַלְתִי. Schenker, *Das Neue*, 23.

8. E.g., 6:30: 'Rejected silver they are called, because Yhwh has rejected (MT: מאס; LXX: ἀποδοκιμάζω) them.'

2. *The 'New' Covenant*

As we turn to the promise of the new covenant itself, it is worth remembering that a rendering of חֲדָשָׁה as 'new' or 'renewed' was already broached above in the discussion of Levin's proposals. The difficulty with following Levin to interpret the word as 'renewed' is that the lexical data can be used to go either way: the term clearly sometimes means 'fresh' ('new moon') and other times means some kind of ontological novelty, or even replacement of the old (e.g. 'new king').[9] Given this evidence, too much has been made of the rendering of this term. The weight of the argument must be on the kind of contrast at stake in any given use of the term—which is found only by examining its use in any individual case. The English term 'new' is sufficiently vague for our purposes and functions well in the semantic role taken up by חֲדָשָׁה.

31:33a-b: The Law on the Heart

In the survey of modern scholarship above one can easily find a consensus from the last century holding that here, in the placement of the law on the heart, one finds the true 'novelty' of the state of affairs Jeremiah pictures in contra-distinction to the 'old covenant'. Unfortunately, this was often a rather vague statement. And in the place of earlier worries about denying the law on the heart to the 'fathers' of the ancient era, we find (at best) shallow reflections on the difficulty justified by a supposed 'historical view of religion'. The full text of 31:33a-b is as follows:

> For this is the covenant which I will make with the house of Israel after these days:
>
> oracle of Yhwh
>
> I will place my law in their inward parts,
>
> And on their hearts I will write it.

As is now almost universally recognized, we have in the text and context no reason to imagine the תּוֹרָה (law) here as something 'new' or novel—a

---

9. See R. North, "חדשׁ," in *Theological Dictionary of the Old Testament* (eds. G.Johannes Botterweck and Helmer Ringgren; vol. 4; Grand Rapids, MI: Eerdmans, 1980). Groß suggests that if the author wanted to say 'renewed', he might have used a passive participle form or made 'renew' the verb ('will renew the covenant').'Entsprechend kann das Hebräische nicht zwischen "ganz neu" und "ein wenig neu" lexikalisch differenzieren.' Groß, *Zukunft*, 148. But this does not seal the case either: that he *might* have said it one way to be more clear does not mean that he *must* say it in the more clear manner.

point we saw already in Calvin.[10] The term תּוֹרָה functions here as a general term for covenantal stipulations, standing in close connection to the 'knowledge of Yhwh' in v.34 (below).[11] Whatever the precise 'contents' of the Torah in this case, the issue is clearly that of covenantal fidelity. The necessity of having the תּוֹרָה on the heart runs deep in deuteronomic thought (thus Duhm's criticisms)

---

10. Put well by Rolf Rendtorff: 'Jeremiah does not envisage a new covenant without Torah, without the "burden of the law"... what he has in mind is a covenant in which the Torah is even more firmly anchored'. *Canon and Theology: Overtures to an Old Testament Theology* (Tr. by Margaret Kohl. Philadelphia: Fortress, 1993), 197. The argument of Adeyẹmi (*New Covenant*, 59-63) for a 'new Torah' here is unconvincing. His argument proceeds by the following form:

(a) 'covenant' and 'law' are inextricably bound together;
(b) the 'covenant' is new (i.e. different);
(c) therefore, the 'law' is new (i.e. different).

But this is a *non sequitur*. To get to his conclusion, we would have to add a premise:

(a) Any covenant is such that it has a law;
(b) No two covenants can have the same law;
(c) The Mosaic covenant is other than the new covenant;
(d) Therefore, the new covenant has another law than the Mosaic covenant.

Clearly (b) is untenable but I have no idea how to get from (a) to (d) without it. And this beyond the questionable (or at least overly vague) assumption of (c).

11. As evidenced in Adrian Schenker, "Die Tafel des Herzens," in *Text und Sinn im Alten Testament: Textgeschichtliche und Bibeltheologische Studien* (ed. Adrian Schenker; Göttingen: Vandenhoeck & Ruprecht, 1991). Likewise Weippert: 'doch sollte der Ausdruck hier wegen seines sachlichen Bezuges zur Jahweerkenntnis in V.34 nicht nur als Sammelbegriff für eine Vielzahl von Einzelgesetzen aufgefaßt werden, sondern umfassender auch als Willenskundgebung Jahwes.' Helga Weippert, "Das Wort vom neuen Bund in Jeremia XXXI 31-34," *VT* 29.3 (1979), 338. See (e.g) the parallelism of Hos 4:6. Thus Lundbom's concern (perhaps from reading Duhm) is somewhat beside the point: 'Jeremiah does not specify what this law will consist of, but it is only reasonable to assume that it will be the law at the heart of the Sinai covenant..., which at minumim [sic] would be the Ten Commandments, but doubtless something more.' Lundbom, *Jeremiah 21-36*, 467-68. The particulars are almost never spelled out except in the most general terms in the book of Jeremiah: it is an assumed reality, a basic principle at stake: 'whatever it is that God has required in the covenant' (see above on 'words' in ch.11). So Zenger: 'sein Inhalt ist die Tora als Weg-Weisung für das Leben.' Zenger, *Erste Testament*, 116. Why the plural of the LXX (νόμους) might be different in this regard, suggested by Davies and followed by Adeyẹmi, is unclear: W.D. Davies, *Torah in the Messianic Age and/or the Age to Come* (Philadelphia: Society of Bib. Lit, 1952), 25, n.24.

and finds negative expression throughout Jeremiah's condemnations of the people:

> 3:10 Judah... did not turn to me with all her heart.
>
> 3:17 At that time... the nations will no longer follow stubbornly after their evil heart.
>
> 4:14 Wash your heart from evil, O Jerusalem!
>
> 5:23-24a And this people has a stubborn and rebellious heart, they have turned aside and walked (away). And they did not say in their hearts, 'Let us fear Yhwh our God...'
>
> 22:17 For your eyes and your heart are for nothing but unjust gain.[12]

Throughout the book the emphasis falls time and again on the heart (לֵב) following the commands of Yhwh, a point in full continuity with Deuteronomy (e.g. 6:4-5).

That לֵב cannot function as 'memory' in 31:33b, as has been proposed,[13] should be clear from the ways in which לֵב functions in the above instances. While I might have sympathy with those bemoaning a stubborn and rebellious memory, that seems rather far from the thrust in Jeremiah. A similar emphasis on the law on the heart being a *memorizing* of the individual laws (so that they not be 'forgotten') runs deep into Jewish interpretive tradition on Jer 31:33-34.[14] But that too is inadequate if reduced to a cognitive remembrance.

---

12. Cf. 4:18, 19; 5:21; 7:24; 8:18; 9:13; 11:8; 13:10; 16:12; 17:5, 9; 23:17; et al.

13. Ego, "Zur Rezeption," 280. This is a possible translation at Jer 3:16 (וְלֹא יַעֲלֶה עַל לֵב), but 'mind' is still a better term than 'memory' (as 7:31; 14:14; 23:16); and this line of use (and construction) is distinct from the themes here. The expressions in Prov 3:3 and 7:3 are likewise distinct constructions (כָּתְבֵם עַל לוּחַ לִבֶּךָ) and issues, and cannot be used as parallels (contra Ego). Again, experience might prove (especially as one gets older) that the memory can be 'deceitful above all things' (17:9), but that is likely not the point there.

14. 'R. Judah said: When Israel heard the words, *I am the Lord thy God*, the knowledge of the Torah was fixed in their heart and they learnt and forgot not. They came to Moses and said, "Our master, Moses, do thou become an intermediary between us, as it says, *Speak thou with us, and we will hear... now therefore why should we die* (Exod 20:16; Deut 5:22). What profit is there in our perishing?" They then became liable to forget what they learnt.... Forthwith they cam a second time to Moses and said: "Our master, Moses, would that God might be revealed to us a second time! Would that He would kiss us "with the kisses of his lips"! Would that He would fix the knowledge of the Torah in our hearts as it was!" He replied to them: "This cannot be now, but it will be in the days to come," as it says, *I will put My law in their inward parts and in their heart will I write it.*' Song of Songs Rabba, 1.2.4, to Son 1:2 [c. 4th-5th c. CE]; cited in Richard

The problem is not that the people keep forgetting some of the 613 commandments (or however many they had at the time), but that they have an 'organic failure'.[15] There is no reason to think any place in the book of Jeremiah refers to a forgetfulness of the Torah, as though the people would have acted according to it if only they had remembered what to do! The problem runs significantly deeper, as does the cure: 'The issue is focused on whether Israel is willing to obey the law that God has so graciously given.'[16]

As Herrmann rightly points out (contrary to most modern commentators), having the law on stone tablets is *not* the contrast to having the law on the heart.[17] Rather the contrast to the law on the heart is having a 'stubborn and rebellious heart' (or we might say, as Augustine, to have the law *only* on stone tablets). The heart is the center of the person's life and thought: not to have

---

S. Sarason, "The Interpretation of Jeremiah 31:31-34 in Judaism," in *When Jews and Christians Meet* (ed. Jakob J. Petuchowski; Albany, NY: State Univ. of New York Press, 1988), 102. For possible—though still debatable—reasons to take the 'law on the heart' this way in some parts of Deuteronomy (e.g. 6:7, as in Prov 3:3; 7:3; Ps 119:11), see F. Fischer and Norbert Lohfink, "'Diese Worte sollst du summen': Dtn 6,7 *wedibbartā bām*—ein verlorener Schlüssel zur meditativen Kultur in Israel," *TP* 62 (1987). But these ought not be compared to its use here in Jeremiah (contra Fischer/Lohfink, p.63). After all, that memorization might be envisioned as *necessary* without being *sufficient*.

15. 'Die Menschen in Juda und Israel hätten die Möglichkeit und die Fähigkeit, JHWH zu verstehen, aber da ist etwas, was diese Fähigkeit blockiert in der Weise eines organischen Fehlers, der das ganze Organ sinnlos macht, weil er es um seine normale Funktion bringt.' Schenker, "Die Tafel," 4.

16. Clements, *Jeremiah*, 191. My emphasis. This view is strengthened if Zenger's suggestion linking 'heart' and 'hearing' (e.g. 1 Kings 3:9) is sustained: 'Vor allem aber gilt—in Israel und in Ägypten—das Herz als das Organ, durch das Gott "gehört" wird und durch das Gott dem Menschen "einwohnt".' Quoting H. Brunner, *Das hörende Herz: Kleine Schriften zur Religions- und Geistesgeschichte Ägyptens* (Göttingen, 1988): 'die zentrale Stelle im Menschen ist, der alle Sinne ihre Eindrücke "melden" und das dann die Lage erkennt und Entschlüsse faßt. Es hat also auf das, was von außen zum Menschen kommt... zu hören.' Thus, one Egyptian text (cited from Brunner): 'Es ist das Herz, das einen Mann zu einem Hörenden werden läßt oder zu einem, der nicht hört. Leben, Heil und Wohlergehen eines Menschen bedeutet sein Herz.' Erich Zenger, *Am Fuss des Sinai* (2nd ed. Düsseldorf: Patmos Verlag, 1994), 101. Thus the connection to chs. 7,11 becomes even closer and the overturning of the state of affairs at judgment clearer.

17. '"steinerne Tafeln" als Gegensatz zum menschlichen Herzen werden hier nicht erwähnt.' Siegfried Herrmann, *Jeremia: Der Prophet und das Buch* (Darmstadt: Wissenschaftliche Buchgesellschaft, 1990), 197.

Yhwh's law there is a matter of infidelity, to 'walk according to the stubbornness of one's own heart.'

Many have pointed out the parallel imagery between having the law on the heart and having a 'circumcised heart'. But in the same way, the opposite of a circumcised heart is not a circumcision in the flesh *per se*.[18] One could have both a circumcision of the flesh and of the heart (and that lack seems to be the great problem). For Yhwh to speak of his people as not having a circumcised 'heart' is to say that they are not the true people of Yhwh, as is clearly the point of Jer 9:24-25 (MT).[19] Given the recognized deuteronomic view of the law on the heart as a requirement of the covenant, to lack the law on the heart is a matter of covenantal infidelity. They ought to be guided in the 'heart' (mind, will, desires) by the law of Yhwh. One can do that (or not do that) regardless of having the law on stone tablets.

Again, this is seen in the parallel texts in Jeremiah where the change of heart is explicitly concerned with fidelity and loyalty to Yhwh:

> 24:7 I will give to them a heart to know me, that I am Yhwh. And they will be my people and I will be their God, for they will turn to me with their whole heart [contrast 3:10].

> 32:39 I will give them one heart and one way, so they will fear me forever... I will put the fear of me in their hearts, they they will not turn from me.

And we also see the logic in the common acknowledgement that 31:33 stands over against 17:1, where the issue is clearly infidelity:

> 17:1-3a The sin of Judah is written with a pen of iron, with the point of a diamond engraved on the tablets of the heart and on the horns of their altars as their children remember their altars and their Asherim upon every fresh [tree], upon the lofty heights, the hills in the field.[20]

---

18. Contra what appears to be stated in Weinfeld, "Spiritual Metamophosis," 34.

19. 'The result is that the chosen people are as ritually unacceptable and disqualified as any other *goy*. It is not only a judgment on both Israel and the *goyim*, but an argument that there is no distinction.' Brueggemann, *Jeremiah*, 101. See also above on the 'broken covenant'.

20. 'Jer 31,33 steht... in einem Verweiszusammenhang zu Jer 17,1.' Lohfink, "Der Neue Bund?", 27. Nearly all the commentaries make a similar connection. Groß is hesitant (*Zukunft*, 145), but my claim is not one of semantic or literary dependence but rather of the two standing in counterpoint, as Weippert: 'Die Gemeinsamkeiten beider Texte beschränken sich nicht auf terminologische Punkte wie *lēb* und *ktb*; auch gedanklich sind sie eng miteinander verflochten.' Weippert, "Neuen Bund," 346.

When Yhwh promises to place the law on the heart, he is promising to overturn the current state of affairs: a people whose very core is 'uncircumcised', 'stubborn', 'rebellious', 'evil', 'engraved with sin' (idolatry above all), and 'sick beyond healing', will be healed. What was never the case (in the rhetoric of Jeremiah) will finally come about: the true fidelity of the people to Yhwh and his תּוֹרָה. We might certainly characterize this as a 'radical anthropological renewal of the people of God.'[21] But the contrast is not with the state of affairs instituted by Yhwh at Sinai or the teaching of Deuteronomy. We are not taking a step in the development of religious thought from those teachings or that state of affairs. We are, rather, finding what always ought to have been the case brought about. The state of affairs between Yhwh and his people at the judgment—their infidelity springing from the heart—is overturned and the people are made what they ought to have been. The people of Yhwh will be guided by and faithful to the word of Yhwh. As Holmgren states, '[t]he change that a "new covenant" calls for is the one ever on Jeremiah's mind: a genuine return to the Torah of the God of Sinai.'[22] Or another scholar, in language more similar to Augustine:

> [T]he contrast in fact is the familiar one between a genuine obedience and dedication from the heart (circumcision of the heart) and a *merely* outward, formalistic obedience.[23]

Whether or not we find even formalistic obedience in Jeremiah, the principle is exactly right. The contrast is between genuine obedience and rebellious disobedience.

One final note must be made regarding the first colon of this promise. A strong argument has recently been made by Adrian Schenker against the standard understanding of נָתַתִּי as functioning as a future—either as a kind of 'prophetic perfect'[24] or 'future perfect',[25] or as a scribal error that ought to read

---

21. Horst Seebass, "Erstes oder Altes Testament?," in *Die Einheit der Schrift und die Vielfalt des Kanons* (eds. John Barton and Michael Wolter; Berlin: Walter de Gruyter, 2003), 33.

22. Holmgren, *Old Testament*, 79.

23. James D.G. Dunn, *The Parting of the Ways: Between Christianity and Judaism and their Significance for the Character of Christianity* (2nd ed. London: SCM Press, 2006), 59-60. His emphasis.

24. Renaud, *Nouvelle ou Éternelle?*, 35; Schmid, *Buchgestalten*, 79.

25. As Lundbom (*Jeremiah 21-36*, 469) following Weinfeld, "Spiritual Metamorphosis," 27. See Schenker, *Das Neue*, 30, n.29. Becking claims that Tita (who argues the same view as Schmidt) 'overlooks the fact that the asyndetical *qatal*-form נתתי functions as the introduction of the divine direct speech.' Becking, *Fear and Freedom*, 249. But why this is a 'fact' is hard to see (he gives no evidence), and precisely why this answers the use of the *qatal* is unclear—presumably one can open divine direct

וּנְתַתִּי.²⁶ The tense ought to be taken as a standard past tense: 'I gave'. Schenker's argument consists in three basic points: first, all of the 'good and determining' Hebrew textual witnesses have the perfect. This is given solid support by Hubert Tita, effectively rendering appeals to וּנְתַתִּי inadequate.²⁷ Second, Schenker states that the rendering of the two different temporal forms is unproblematic, as there are other examples of parallelism make use of this same construction (e.g. Ps 63:8; 110:4). Lastly, good sense can be made of the perfect here in opposition to the future in the second line, and thus appeal to a future sense is unnecessary and, so, undesirable.²⁸ קרב would then take on a corporate sense, so that the basic meaning according to Schenker is:

> I had given my Torah in your midst, but I will now write it on your hearts.²⁹

In Jeremiah the opening clause would parallel the use of נתן in, e.g., 9:12:

> And Yhwh said: Because they left my law which I set before them (אֲשֶׁר נָתַתִּי לִפְנֵיהֶם), and did not hear my voice and did not walk according to it...³⁰

Though my own arguments do not necessarily depend on the matter, there are reasons for disputing Schenker's reading. First, the other parallels he cites that operate with a *qatal* form in one line and an imperfect (or *weqatal*) in the next do not support his view of a contrast in 31:33. He cites:

> Ps 89:36 Once I swore in my holiness
>
> I will not be deceitful with David. (cp. 110:4)
>
> Ps 63:8 For you were a help to me
>
> And in the shadow of your wings I will rejoice.³¹

---

speech with an imperfect. I find no parallel that satisfies Becking's position in the discussion of asyndesis in Paul Joüon and T. Muraoka, *A Grammar of Biblical Hebrew* (2 vols.; Rome: Editrice Pontificio Istituto Biblico, 2000), §177.

26. Rudolph, *Jeremia*, 184 (cf. BHS apparatus); Holladay, *Jeremiah*, II.154.

27. Hubert Tita, "'Ich hatte meine Tora in ihre Mitte gegeben': Das Gewicht einer nicht berücksichtigten Perfektform in Jer. XXXI 33," *VT* 52 (2002).

28. This is in line with his 'hermeneutical rule': 'Es jedoch eine hermeneutische Regel, für zwei verschiedene sprachliche Formen oder Ausdrucksweisen auch zwei verschiedene Bedeutungen anzunehmen.' Schenker, *Das Neue*, 28, see 27-31.

29. 'Ich hatte meine Tora in eure Mitte gegeben, aber ich werde (oder will) sie nunmehr auf euer Herz schreiben.' Ibid., 29-30. Understanding קרב this way alleviates somewhat the concern of Schmid, *Buchgestalten*, 79.

30. So Renaud, *Nouvelle ou Éternelle?*, 56.

31. His other examples (Jer 3:14; 31:29) are misleading because they represent

In these cases a previous action is declared with a *qatal* as the ground or evidence for the second, future-oriented colon. And that is the rhetorical opposite of a contrast. So even if one agrees to a perfect tense for 33b this by no means entails a contrast with 33c, as Schenker states. In fact, if we are to translate according to Schenker's parallels, then a better translation would be:

> I gave my law in your midst, and (so) I will write it on your hearts.

There are a number of other poetic texts that make use of a parallelism with a *qatal* in one colon and an imperfect in the next. Most are akin to the above illustrations and the grounding of the future event in the past.[32] But some are either clearly concerned with temporally identical events in both colons (either past, present or future), or at least ambiguous. A handful of examples make this clear:

> Ps 139:13 For you formed my inner parts (קָנִיתָ כִלְיֹתָי), you knitted me together (תְּסֻכֵּנִי) in my mother's womb.
>
> Isa 33:7 Behold, their heroes cry (צָעֲקוּ) in the streets, the messengers of peace weep (יִבְכָּיֻן) bitterly.
>
> Isa 29:20 For the ruthless one will cease (אָפֵס) and the mocker come to a complete end (וְכָלָה), and all who watch for evil will be cut off (שֹׁקְדֵי).
>
> Isa 52:8 Your watchmen lift up (נָשְׂאוּ) their voice, their voice together they shout for joy (יְרַנֵּנוּ).[33]
>
> Ps 18:5 The cords of death encompassed me (אֲפָפוּנִי), and the torrents of destruction terrified me (יְבַעֲתוּנִי).
>
> Ps 6:7 I grow weary (יָגַעְתִּי) with my groaning, I make my bed swim (אַשְׂחֶה) every night...

---

two different thoughts entirely rather than two thoughts in parallel.

    32. Jer 2:25 ('I have loved foreign things, and after them I will go.'); 2:37 ('Yhwh has rejected those in whom you trust, and you will not prosper by them'); 4:30 ('Your lovers have rejected you, they seek your soul.'); 20:11; 31:11-12 ('Yhwh has ransomed Jacob and redeemed him... they will come and sing aloud on the height of Zion'). Elsewhere, see (e.g.) Ps 3:6; 4:4; 6:10; 10:17; 16:8; 17:6; 108:8; 119:11, 73. This discussion has been shaped trying to do justice to those who minimize the qatal as used in a non-past sense (e.g. a 'prophetic perfect'): the best recent discussion is M.F. Rogland, *Alleged Non-Past Uses of Qatal in Classical Hebrew* (Assen: Van Gorcum, 2003), esp. §3.

    33. The syntax here is somewhat odd, but does not impact the point here: קוֹל צֹפַיִךְ נָשְׂאוּ קוֹל יַחְדָּו יְרַנֵּנוּ.

Ps 24:2 For upon the waters he has founded it (יְסָדָהּ), and upon the rivers he has established it (יְכוֹנְנֶהָ).[34]

These make little sense if we understand the colons as temporally distinct—and even less sense if they are contrasting temporally (e.g. 'You formed my inner parts, but you will (in the future) knit me together in my mother's womb'?). In many of these instances the different verbal tenses appear to function as an envelope around the event(s), expressing a kind of completeness. So in the first example (Ps 139:13) the completeness of the divine action is portrayed by the verbal tenses used. This seems to be the best solution for some texts in Jeremiah as well:

4:30c: Your lovers despise you (מָאֲסוּ),

They seek after (יְבַקְשׁוּ) your life.

5:6 Therefore a lion from the woods will strike them down (הִכָּם)

A wolf from the desert will destroy them (יְשָׁדְדֵם).

The events of both colons should be taken as temporally identical, but the use of the different tenses—moving from qatal to the imperfect—brings out the completeness of Judah's being devoured (5:6) or her now reversed relationship with her previous lovers (4:30c).[35] Naturally, suppositions for rhetorical uses are always somewhat tenuous given our lack of access to native speakers.[36] But if the above argument is feasible, then it offers a simple way to understand the change of tense in 31:33.

Further, the dismissal of other textual witnesses weakens Schenker's case. As mentioned above, Tita helpfully corrects the ambiguity of the BHS note: 'mlt MSS ונתתי'. In fact, the main textual witnesses (Leningrad, Cairo and Petropolitanus) read נתתי, so there is little reason to think the Hebrew ought to be anything other than this.[37] But Schenker dismisses too quickly the translation history—especially the Peshitta and Targum, but also the LXX—which understood the activity of 'placing' as future.[38] That none of these texts have a conjun-

---

34. A number of other texts could be cited with varying certainty, esp. from the Pslms: 7:14; 16:9; 17:11; 18:9; 26:4-5; 34:6; 38:5; 39:4; 50:19; 56:2; 57:4; 59:4; 63:7; 73:9; 81:7; 93:3; 102:25; 104:6; 105:40; 114:3; 116:3; 138:3; 143:5.

35. Other possible examples: Jer 5:8, 26, 31; 6:10; 8:13c; 12:2 (ילכו); 15:6.

36. Ibid., 82-83.

37. The Aleppo codex is missing this portion. The only significant text differentiation is 'Berlin Or fol 1-4', used by Kennicott in the late 18th century. See Tita, "Perkeftform."

38. He claims the Peshitta and Targum (as well as the Vulgate) were, like modern translators, too affected by the 'Dynamik der Hauptaussage in die Zukunft'.

ction argues against their having ונתתי in their Vorlage, and so in each case the action of the first colon is understood as temporally future, in spite of the *qatal* form.

Finally, the use of קרב in parallel to לב also occurs elsewhere in Jeremiah and cannot be said to be 'sociological' though that would seem necessary for Schenker's suggestion:

> 4:14 Wash your *hearts* from evil, O Jerusalem, that you might be saved.
>
> How long will your evil thoughts lodge in your *inner parts* (בְּקִרְבֵּךְ)?
>
> 23:9 Broken is my *heart*, my *inner parts* (בְקִרְבִּי) collapse.

Indeed, in every instance throughout the Hebrew Bible with only one possible exception, the parallelism of the two words assumes קרב to be 'inner parts' rather than 'sociological'.[39] But if קרב means 'inner parts' then we are much more inclined to understand נָתַתִּי as temporally future.

Thus both colons of 31:33b ought to be read as referring to the same future-oriented event, the different verbal tenses perhaps used to envelop the event to stress its completion. But if one follows Schenker and takes נָתַתִּי as a past-oriented *qatal*, there is still no reason to think this establishes a contrast with deuteronomic thought. It would have been no surprise to anyone that Yhwh had given his Torah to the people. The writing on the hearts is still the divine activity of a necessary but absent reality. The point of the polemic is not the deuteronomists and their 'theology of teachers and learners,'[40] but Yhwh's people as painted in the book of Jeremiah—people who had the Torah in their midst but did not have it on their heart. Thus in either case the function of the second colon remains unchanged: what ought to have been the case between Yhwh and the people (but universally was not, in the rhetorical world) is brought about. All is made the way that it always ought to have been.

Schenker, *Das Neue*, 31. He brackets out the LXX entirely.

39. See Lam 1:20, Ps 51:12; 64:7 and the famous verses of Ezek 11:19; 36:26. The two terms are in construct in Ps 36:2 ('the heart of my inner parts'); 39:4. Similar (though not in construct) is Ps 55:5; 109:22. Both occur in Jer 30:21, but as parts of two different thoughts. The only instance potentially lending support to Schenker's reading is Prov 14:33, 'In the heart of a discerning person lies wisdom, and in the inner parts/midst of fools it is known.' But this too appears more likely to be the 'inner parts' rather than sociological.

40. Groß, *Zukunft*, 145.

31:33c: The Covenant Formula

31:33c: I will be their God and they will be my people.

Helga Weippert rightly comments that with this statement the 'horizon of the new covenant is defined.'[41] And, in fact, the inclusion of this formula offers the clearest statement of an Augustinian view of the matter. Common as the formula is to the Old Testament, it represents nothing more than that desired relationship between Yhwh and the people: what always ought to have been the case, but came to an end in some real way in the judgment in the book of Jeremiah (cf. above on the broken covenant). Contrary to the impression from some readers, the reason for the inclusion of the covenant formula here is not simply to show some continuity with the 'old'. This covenant formula lies directly at the centre of the 'newness' of the new covenant. As William Strong framed this promise many years ago:

> '[This promise] Musculus calls *caput foederis*, the head of the Covenant: the chief and the bottom promise, on which the Covenant stands, is this, I will be thy God: and Pareus calls it *anima foederis*, the soul of the Covenant, for it's the principal promise of the Second Covenant [i.e. the covenant of grace].[42]

Right here at the heart of the oracle we see what is 'new' in the new covenant, but it is only new given the situation at the judgment. What we find in 31:33c is that Yhwh will restore things to what they always ought to have been. And at the center of that restoration lies the (old) formula that frames the core of the covenant between Yhwh and his people.

31:34a: Knowledge of Yhwh

> 31:34a: And no longer will a person teach his neighbour, or a person his brother saying, 'Know Yhwh'—for they will all know me, from the least to the greatest of them—oracle of Yhwh.

As Coppens states, this verse does not simply claim that there will be no more religious teaching generally, but that there will no longer be a *need* for instruction in the knowledge of Yhwh.[43] This knowledge of Yhwh, once again,

---

41. Weippert, "Neuen Bund," 338.
42. Strong, *Discourse of the Two Covenants*, 259.
43. 'Au verset 34, qui se réfère à l'instruction religieuse, ou plus exactement à l'absence de tout besoin d'instruction qui caractérisera l'ère de l'alliance nouvelle'. Whether this renders future divine intervention 'superfluous' by virtue of the law being in the heart (as he suggests), is another matter. Coppens, "Nouvelle alliance," 18.

concerns the fidelity of the people to Yhwh. Commenting on 4:22, Brueggemann states:

> Covenantal acknowledgement of Yahweh and covenantal obedience are intimately linked. Israel knows about neither, and therefore Israel knows nothing about its own identity and proper role in history.[44]

But Israel's lack of covenantal acknowledgement/obedience is exactly what we find overturned in the restoration. Just such 'covenantal obedience' is clearly the issue in what Moberly calls the 'quasi-definition'[45] of the phrase 'know Yhwh' at 22:15-16:

> (15) Are you a king because you compete in cedar? Your father—did he not eat and drink and do justice and righteousness? Then it was well with him. (16) He judged the case of the poor and needy. Then it was well. Is that not to know me?—oracle of Yhwh.

Josiah's obedience to the requirements of kingship counted as 'knowledge of Yhwh', and a failure to do so would be a failure to 'know Yhwh'. We find the link of knowing Yhwh and obedience (or their opposites) consistently throughout the book:

> 2:8 The priests did not say, 'Where is Yhwh?' Those dealing with the law did not know me. The shepherds transgressed against me. The prophets prophesied by Baal. And they (all) went after things that do not profit.[46]

> 9:3 They proceed from evil to evil, and me they do not know—oracle of Yhwh.

---

44. Brueggemann, *Jeremiah*, 58-59. Cp. R.W.L. Moberly, *Prophecy and Discernment* (Cambridge: Cambridge Univ. Press, 2006), 64-70: 'the practice of oppression, falsehood, and evil in one form or other is a disqualification from knowing YHWH (68).' Or Lundbom: 'When Jeremiah talks... about the knowledge of Yahweh, he is talking about compliance with covenant stipulations.' Jack R. Lundbom, "Jeremiah, Book of," in *Anchor Bible Dictionary* (ed. D.N. Freedman; 3; New York: Doubleday, 1992), 718b. For discussion with reference to broader covenant- and treaty-forms, see Herbert B. Huffmon, "The Treaty Background of *Yāda'*," *BASOR* 181 (1966).

45. Moberly, *Prophecy*, 66. Cornill (*Jeremia*, 352) refers to it as a 'formal definition,' though Moberly's more careful term is preferable. Cornill states, 'Demnach ist nach jeremianischen Sprachgebrauche Jahve erkennen so viel als fromm und sittlich leben, also das thun, was wir als den Inhalt des in unser Herz geschriebenen göttlichen Gebots erkannt haben:'—then, less helpfully (if predictably)—'nicht Befolgung des Ceremonialgesetzes, sondern Befolgung des Sittengesetzes.'

46. For the last phrase as encapsulating all the previous groups, see Holladay, *Jeremiah*, I.88.

> 9:23 And let him who boasts boast in this: that he is prudent and knows me—that I am Yhwh, practicing steadfast-love, justice and righteousness in the land. For in these I delight.

Thus, insofar as the prophetic task is a call to obedience to Yhwh, Lundbom is right to say 'that Jeremiah envisions a day when people the likes of himself will be out of a job.'[47] What ought to be the case is that all the people of Yhwh 'know Yhwh' and no longer (לֹא עוֹד) need exhortations to obedience. This is obvious in an idyllic state: the people will not, as before, need those who call the people back to covenantal fidelity because they will already 'know Yhwh'. What we see, once again, is the overturning of the situation of judgment with an idyllic statement of the way things always ought to have been.

31:34b: For I Will Forgive Their Iniquities

> 31:34b: For I will forgive (אֶסְלַח) their iniquities,
> And their sins I will remember no longer.

The final line of the oracle opens, as 30:17, with an explanatory כִּי and here we find the *sine qua non* for the new covenant: that without which the earlier parts of the promise would be unthinkable—at least for 'the house of Israel and the house of Judah.'[48] As Calvin insisted, the issue here is not the abstract notion of forgiveness as a way of God's dealing with his people, but of the forgiveness of *this* people who sit under divine judgment—it is the same use of לֹא...עוֹד as 34a.[49] One need not look far to find the point of contrast to this state of affairs. The very fact of the judgment is the claim that their sins are not forgiven. Yet we find a striking statement of that fact in 14:10:

> 14:10 Yhwh does not accept them:
> Now he will remember their iniquity (יִזְכֹּר עֲוֺנָם),
> and will punish their sins (וְיִפְקֹד חַטֹּאתָם).

With the new covenant the precise opposite becomes the case. If the other parts of the oracle are an overturning of the cause of the judgment, making the people what they always ought to have been (thus no longer deserving judgment), the promise of 34b moves the focus to Yhwh's overturning of his own actions in or-

---

47. Lundbom, *Jeremiah 21-36*, 470. Thus we can include the teaching of 5:1-6 on the universal failure to 'know the way of Yhwh, the justice of our God'.
48. 'Dieser Schluß gibt an, wie es möglich ist, daß nach dem "Bundesbruch" ein neuer "Bund" geschlossen wird. Jahwes Sündenvergebung eröffnet den Weg in die Zukunft.' Böhmer, *Heimkehr*, 77. Cf. Rudolph, *Jeremia*, 185; Weippert, "Neuen Bund," 338; Krašovec, *Reward*, 457.
49. Calvin, *Jeremiah*, IV.138-39.

der to restore his people to that state. Eichrodt put the matter in a way perfectly suited for Jeremiah:

> Now [for the prophets] forgiveness was acknowledged as the central act of succour without which all other goods lost their value. Without it the change from doom to salvation, in which God would turn back to his people, was unthinkable. Thus the prophets, when they depict the contrite conversion of their people, and their prayer to be readmitted to fellowship with God, put in their mouths first and foremost an entreaty for forgiveness.... Correspondingly, God's promise of salvation gives the place of honour to the gift of pardon; this forms the threshold of the new age in which the creation returns to its original state [citing Jer 31:34].[50]

The regaining of what Eichrodt calls an 'original state'—at least in an idyllic form—is precisely the issue in Jer 31:31-34. And the promise of forgiveness grounds the possibility of this hope.

The necessity of forgiveness further affirms that the 'new covenant' will be with the 'house of Israel and the house of Judah' rather than a new people (*contra* Jerome). Forgiveness is a prerequisite to the new relationship only because of the state of the present people. If Yhwh had been starting over with a new people then the clause would be unnecessary. But as it stands the forgiveness of the people grounds the whole of 31:31-34 and leads directly into the dual expression of the permanence of Yhwh's care for this people in vv.35-37:

> (35) Thus Yhwh said -
>> who gives the sun for light by day
>>> and the statute of the moon and stars for light at night,
>> who stirs up the sea so its waves growl
> - Yhwh of hosts is his name:
>> (36) If these statutes are removed from my presence—oracle of Yhwh—then also the seed of Israel will cease from being a nation in my presence forever.
> (37) Thus Yhwh said:
>> If the heavens above can be measured,
>>> and the foundations of the earth explored below,
>> then will I, for my part, reject all the seed of Israel for all that they have done
>>> oracle of Yhwh.

---

50. Eichrodt, *Theology*, II.458-59. Emphasis removed.

Unterman is right to say that these verses 'play a substantial role in the prophecy of the new covenant'. But not, as he says, to show 'the eternality of the ideal relationship which will be established'.[51] Rather, these lines show the eternality of Yhwh's care for Israel that undergirds the *making* of that ideal relationship.[52] Here we find the reason for what seems the absurdity of forgiving this people and making all things as they ought to be. As 31:9 and 31:20 ground the restorative act of Yhwh in his persistent devotion to Ephraim—and as 30:17 implies the same to Lady Zion—so 31:35-37 offers a theological ground for the act of restoration in the unceasing devotion of Yhwh. Whether or not we speak of a covenant that is 'unrevoked,' we certainly here have warrant for speaking of Yhwh's devotion to his people as unrevoked and 'unrevokable'.

3. *Conclusions*

In this chapter I have put forward a reading of the 'new covenant' in Jer 31:31-34 (or 31:31-37) in line with the Augustinian tradition. Fredrick Holmgren changes the nature of the discourse on this subject by asking: 'new for whom?' and in many ways this chapter is simply following his lead. Rather than asking simply 'what is new?', I have consistently asked *why* each part of the oracle is called 'new'. And the answer, once asked, is found on nearly every page of the book: because this people have broken the covenant; because this people are unfaithful—do not have Yhwh's law on their heart; because this people do not know Yhwh; and because this people are reaping Yhwh's judgment upon their sins.

In the book of Jeremiah the covenant which the people broke was nothing other than the infidelity of the people of Israel and Judah, at every point, to the covenant established between them and Yhwh. From the time they were constituted the people of Yhwh (the time when 'the Lord took them by the hand and

---

51. Unterman, *Repentance to Redemption*, 106. Against the common separation of the two (whatever their 'original' setting) as most commentators, following Graf, *Jeremia*, 366. The meaning in that case becomes akin to Böhmer: 'Dieser Spruch will wie Deuterojesaja anscheinend eine Antwort auf die Zweifel geben, die in der Exilszeit an der Treue Jahwes wach geworden sind: Jahwe hat uns verworfen, wir sind nicht mehr sein Volk.' Böhmer, *Heimkehr*, 79. But this could be said of the whole of chs. 30-31.

52. Thus, better, is Lohfink (immediately prior to citing the text): 'That Israel is Yhwh's people, and that Yhwh is Israel's God, that this situation drives history from within itself and ever onward, that even when this history one day will encompass the world of the nations, Zion will remain at the center—all this is omnipresent in Israel's narrative writings... Nowhere is there any hint of a definitive cancellation of this prerogative of Israel at any time in the future.' "Children of Abraham," in Lohfink, *Shadow*, 153.

led them out of Egypt') the people have been unfaithful. And so they are, in the book, receiving the punishment for that infidelity. The broken covenant is that current state of affairs of which we read in the oracles of judgment throughout the book of Jeremiah. And, as in the various other oracles of restoration in the book of Jeremiah, the oracle of 31:31-34 plays the role of overturning that state of affairs in the judgment. At every point the 'new' covenant confronts the realities of the 'broken' covenant. Rather than a people with hearts that are stubborn, rebellious, evil, or hearts that are engraved with sin, we find hearts that have the Law of Yhwh inscribed upon them. They move from infidelity to faithfulness. Rather than the present situation of being (or appearing) disowned by Yhwh in an ending to the covenant, Yhwh reasserts the covenant formula. In the place of a universal lack of knowledge (obedience) to Yhwh, the people will universally possess that knowledge and obedience. At every point the judgment, in its causes and effects, is overturned and Yhwh makes things the way they always ought to have been. And all is grounded upon the unexplained grace of the forgiveness of sins and devotion of Yhwh to his people. The hope and the promise is of a *restitutio ad integrum*: a return to a state of integrity.[53] The people of Yhwh will stand before Yhwh, standing restored as his true and faithful people.

---

53. Levin, *Verheißung*, 140.

8

Conclusions and Theological Directions

At the heart of an Augustinian reading of Jeremiah's new covenant, as developed in this work, lies the view that Jer 31:31-34 does not contrast two successive eras in redemptive history, but rather two standings before God. So Augustine states concerning the *vetus testamentum*:

> But those belong to the *vetus testamentum*, 'which generates from Mount Sinai to slavery, which is Hagar', who, after receiving the holy and just and good law, think that the letter can suffice for their life, and therefore, insofar as they become observers of the law, they do not inquire after divine mercy. Rather, 'ignoring the righteousness of God and wanting to establish their own righteousness, they are not subjects of the righteousness of God.' Of this kind were that multitude who murmured against God in the wilderness and made idols, and those who even in the promised land itself fornicated after foreign gods.[1]

And likewise, concerning the *novum testamentum* of which Jeremiah speaks:

> These [who follow the Law in faith and the Spirit] belong to the *novum testamentum*, are the children of promise, and are regenerated by God the Father and a free mother. Of this kind were all the righteous ones of old – even Moses himself, minister of the *vetus testamentum*, heir of the *novum*.[2]

Augustine's absolute contrast of old/new as two mutually exclusive standings before God—what Lössl calls a contrast is between salvation and judgment ('*Heil und Nicht-Heil*')[3]—can be traced throughout the history of Christian interpretation, though it is often muted or even drowned by the other leading view in which the 'new covenant' is a picture of a future era of God's dealing with his people, unknown to those of old. In the more dominant reading the 'old covenant' is that state of affairs instituted by Yhwh at Sinai, and the

---

1. Augustine, *Contra epp. Pel*, §3.9.
2. Ibid., §3.11.
3. Lössl, *Intellectus Gratiae*, 192.

'new covenant' is that new state of affairs instituted by the coming of the Messiah. In this latter reading the contrast is necessarily chronological, two eras succeeding one another within redemptive history; in the former the contrast is non-chronological. In what I have called the Augustinian line of reading the contrast concerns two mutually exclusive states before God: one faithful (the 'new covenant') and one unfaithful (the 'old' or broken covenant).

Augustine's reading is rather poorly represented in the modern period, and even prior to that is rarely presented with full consistency. John Ball or Caspar Olevianus or John Calvin each offer aspects of the reading, as we find also in Thomas Aquinas and others. And in nearly every case Augustine is cited as the authority for the reading. With modern scholarship the interests and concerns shifted away from the overtly theological questions that led to Augustine's re-addressing what he seemed to read in Jer 31:31-34 prior to the interaction with Julian of Aeclanum. The search moved away from theological significance (at least within Old Testament studies) and into the historical questions surrounding the rise of the utterance in the development of Israelite religion—either within the life of Jeremiah or later developments. But too often not only were the legitimate concerns and insights of pre-modern theologians lost, but the role of the oracle as it stands in the book was set aside. But 'reading the Bible with the dead,' as one recent work calls it, can invigorate contemporary exegesis and contemporary theology.[4]

Jeremiah's 'new covenant' has played a significant role in Christian theology. For Augustine the text was central in the Pelagian controversy as a re-statement of the necessity of the grace of the Spirit to live a faithful Christian life. In the medieval church the text stood in the midst of negotiating the place of the law in dialogue with the Passaginis and Cathars. For Reformed theologians and their interlocutors, the text became important for negotiating the relationship of God and his people throughout history—whether we find in the Bible a single covenant of grace that covers both 'old testament' and 'new testament' eras with two separate 'administrations', or two distinct covenants. And to this day Jer 31:31-34 sits at the heart of many discussions regarding the practice of infant baptism. But to turn from the above discussion of Jeremiah's 'new covenant' into any of these discussions would open avenues and questions that cannot be fully covered here. In fact, the above would be something of a preliminary or first step of many in a fuller discussion—and is offered in hope that further questions will be asked and a better way of reading Jer 31:31-34 might be enter-

---

4. John L. Thompson, *Reading the Bible with the Dead: What You Can Learn from the History of Exegesis that You Can't Learn from Exegesis Alone* (Grand Rapids, MI: Eerdmans, 2007).

tained in theological discussions. In this context, I can do no more than hint at some possible directions or implications for Christian theology. Some will find more of these suggestions likelier than others, but in each case it is hoped simply to open some of the discussions in light of the above proposal for Jer 31:31-34.

1. *Unity of the Covenant*

The New and Eternal Covenant (of Grace)

The Reformed tradition has long spoken of the notion of 'one covenant of grace' and 'two administrations'. The model is only one manner of expressing the unity of the people of God and the unity of God's dealings with his people throughout redemptive history—not far, in fact, from Augustine's notion of the (one) 'City of God'. But the particular construal in Reformed theology has come under criticism (and is largely set aside in contemporary discourse) due to the 'covenant of grace' becoming divorced from any of the actual instances of 'covenant(s)' in Scripture. So John Stek writes:

> It must be duly noted that in this [Reformed] tradition 'covenant' had become a theological *concept* utilized to *construe* the *nature* of the God-humanity relationship, and was necessitated by the ontic distance between Creator and creature. As such, it had been abstracted from and cut loose from the narrative (and historical) specificity of the biblical covenants.[5]

Yet there may be more to be said. On the one hand, to state that the 'covenant of grace' is a theological construction, based on a 'concept' of covenant, is not to say it is therefore invalid. It is merely to say that it is a theological construction and ought not, necessarily, be confused with 'covenant' as used in some other sense. But I think much more could potentially be said from the standpoint of what Stek calls the 'biblical covenants'. In fact, the above argument of Jer 31:31-34 may be able to contribute to a new re-statement of the traditional language set more firmly in an exegetical framework.

Steven Mason recently offered an illuminating study of the use of the phrase 'eternal covenant' in the Pentateuch. Among his various conclusions, he states:

> The survey of scholarship reveals that an eternal covenant is generally assumed to be an unbreakable, unconditional, and unilateral covenant which primarily reflects the gracious promises of God... [However] my study

---

5. John H. Stek, "'Covenant' Overload in Reformed Theology," *Calvin Theological Journal* 29 (1994), 15. His emphasis. See the response by Craig R. Bartholomew, "Covenant and Creation: Covenant Overload or Covenantal Deconstruction," *Calvin Theological Journal* 30 (1995).

shows that ברית עולם is a *bilateral, conditional, and breakable* covenant involving the obligations of God and humans.[6]

He supports the claim with (largely persuasive) engagement with Gen 9, 17; Exod 31; Lev 24; and Num 18 and 25. What makes the covenant 'eternal' is not that it has the properties of being unbreakable or unconditional, but rather that the covenant is rooted in the promise of God who continually offers the covenant anew to his people:

> while eternal covenants are broken, they are also continually re-offered, not only to succeeding generations, but also to different people of various eras and scope of influence.[7]

The offering of the 'new covenant' in Jer 31, grounded in the devotion of Yhwh to his people (31:35-37) would fit very closely with the same idea. The covenant is 'renewed' but in a stronger sense than sometimes given to it: it is re-offered to the people of Israel and Judah in defiance of their having broken the covenant. An exploration of the same notion in other instances may provide similar conclusions: the covenant with David, called an 'eternal covenant' (2 Sam 23:5), or the promise of the land also called an 'eternal covenant' (1 Chr 16:17/ Psa 105:10), and yet with the exile both land and kingship are in some way brought to an end. Such caused at least some reflection on the faithfulness of God to his covenant(s) (e.g. Lamentations, or Psa 89). But, according to Mason's thesis, in each case the covenant is 'eternal' by virtue of being continually re-offered, even if offered to 'different people of various eras and scope of influence'. We could cite Freedman's statement here in the same way it was cited in the study of the new covenant above:

> Can a covenant bond be broken—and at the same time persist? Can God sever a relationship as a result of covenant violations—and nevertheless maintain it in perpetuity? The Bible seems to answer in the affirmative.[8]

That is what we see in the 'new covenant' and, according to Mason, in the use of 'eternal covenant' in the Pentateuch.

What does not change is Yhwh's determination to have a people for himself, who live and act in a way fitting the covenant: whether a davidic king fitting his calling, or a people who are fit to live in Yhwh's land. That determ-

---

6. Mason, *Eternal Covenant*, 226. His emphasis.

7. Ibid. We see reference to a broken 'eternal covenant' in Isa 24:5, and in a manner parallel to the 'broken covenant' of Jer 11: "The land lies defiled under the inhabitants, for they have transgressed the laws, violated the statutes, broken the eternal covenant."

8. Freedman, "Divine Commitment," 177.

ination of Yhwh grounds both the eternal covenant(s) and is the explicit ground of the 'new covenant' in Jer 31. In fact, the connection of the 'new' and 'eternal' covenant(s) grows very close in Jeremiah—so much so that both seem to play a very similar function. So, echoing 31:31-34 is 32:36-41:

> (36) Now therefore thus said Yhwh, God of Israel, concerning this city of which you say, 'It is given into the hand of the king of Babylon by sword, by famine, and by pestilence':
>
> (37) Behold, I will gather them from all the countries to which I drove them in my anger and my wrath and in great indignation.
>
> > I will bring them back to this place, and I will make them dwell in safety.
>
> (38) And they shall be my people, and I will be their God.
>
> > (39) I will give them one heart and one way,
> >
> > > that they may fear me forever,
> > >
> > > > for their own good and the good of their children after them.
>
> (40) I will make with them an eternal covenant,
>
> > that I will not turn away from doing good to them.
> >
> > And I will put the fear of me in their hearts,
> >
> > > that they may not turn from me.
>
> (41) I will rejoice in doing them good,
>
> > and I will plant them in this land in faithfulness,
> >
> > > with all my heart and all my soul.

The 'eternal covenant' consists of many of the same parts of the 'new covenant': statement of the covenant formula; a heart that fears Yhwh (as an expression of covenant fidelity), and does not turn away; and a renewed determination on Yhwh's part to bless and 'do good to them.' As with the new covenant each part of the above takes its place in the rhetorical world of Jeremiah by contrasting with the state of affairs under divine judgment. Yhwh has exiled them, but will return them to the land; they have lived under wrath, now they will dwell in safety; the covenant was broken, and is now restored—and the people will be what they always ought to have been. The overturning of judgment continues in 32:42-44, with the closing phrase returning to that which opened ch.30: 'for I will restore their fortunes (שוב שבות), oracle of Yhwh.'

It is tempting, then, to see the 'new covenant' and the 'eternal covenant' as functionally playing the same role in Jeremiah, even if carrying distinct nuances.⁹ The new covenant becomes the re-offering of the 'eternal' covenant, centred around the covenant formula as promised first to Abraham and to his offspring 'forever'. (A similar exercise could come from engagement with Jer 50:4-5.) The unity of the covenant then stands grounded in the desire and devotion of Yhwh to have a people for himself, regardless of its need to be continually re-offered and re-appropriated by his people. The 'eternal covenant' continues to be re-offered to the people of God, by grace, centered in the covenant formula that Yhwh is their God and they are his people. The eternal covenant in such light can be straightforwardly adapted into the language of the covenant of grace—not, now, as a mere 'concept' or theological construction, but as a central theme of the Scriptures in which God is working to bring a people to himself.

Such approaches as Mason's study of the 'eternal covenant' and this study of the 'new covenant' may prove fruitful for finding increased points of convergence between the construct of classical Reformed theology while avoiding Stek's criticism of constructs divorced from 'biblical covenants.' Whatever one might think of the usefulness of the Reformed construct, the assertion of a unified covenant grounded in the devotion of God to have a people for himself, whose climax is in the work of Jesus Christ (below), is not far from the first developments of covenant theology (e.g. Bullinger). There the concern was far more the covenantal framework that arose from the biblical material than a constructive system based upon an *a priori* concept of 'covenant'. One covenant with potentially varied 'administrations' would not fall far from what is suggested by this study. But can such a suggestion survive the manner in which Jer 31:31-34 is used in the New Testament?

Qumran and the New Covenant

The most formative use of Jer 31:31-34 for Christian theology lies in the letters of Paul and Hebrews. But prior to arriving at the reception and use of Jeremiah in those texts, the use of 'new covenant' by the Qumran community is of particular interest for the present thesis. The community is well known for its staunch emphasis on fidelity to the covenant over against its being broken (in their view) among the larger Jewish community.¹⁰ And so it seems, in that re-

---

9. The attempt to build entirely distinct theological 'schools' underneath the two phrases by Renaud (*Nouvelle ou Éternelle?*) is more than a little tenuous: see the discussion in Mason, *Eternal Covenant*, 35-38, et passim.

10. For an introduction to the manuscripts see Charlotte Hempel, *The Damascus Texts* (Sheffield: Sheffield Academic, 2000). See also the recent intriguing work, starkly different from Hempel and most critical scholarship on the document, by Ben Zion Wacholder, *The New Damascus Document: The Midrash on the Eschatological*

gard, unsurprising to find in the *Damascus Document* the use of the expression 'new covenant' far more suited to the 'salvific' reading here defended than with a reading pronouncing the end of deuteronomic thought or 'methods', or with a reading that looks forward to an era freed from the 'Mosaic' covenant. In the Qumran community the 'new covenant' clearly did not mean 'the end of all learning and teaching'.[11] Nor did the community see the 'new covenant' as entailing an 'instinctive' obedience that (hence) 'can no longer be broken.'[12] Rather the contrast appears between those who reject God's precepts with a stubborn heart, and those who enter the 'new covenant' which is the embrace of faithfulness. And those who enter the new covenant and then leave it (so it *can* be broken) are worthy of judgment themselves:

> CD 19:32-35: And like this judgment will be all who reject God's precepts... and forsake them and move aside in the stubbornness of their heart. [...] Thus all the men who entered the new covenant in the land of Damascus and turned and betrayed and departed from the well of living waters, shall not be counted in the assembly of the people, they shall not be inscribed in their lists, from the day of the gathering in {of the teacher}.[13]

To be a member of the 'new covenant in the land of Damascus' was to pursue fidelity to the covenant: 'the new covenant substantially had to do with observation of the *torah*.'[14] Or, as Jerome Murphy-O'Connor states: 'To enter

---

Torah of the Dead Sea Scrolls: Reconstruction, Translation and Commentary (STDJ; Leiden: Brill, 2007).

11. As commonly asserted regarding Jer 31:31-34—e.g., Ego, "Zur Rezeption," 288. For the continuation of teaching, the existence of the document itself would appear ample evidence! But see, e.g., CD 15:14-15: if the one who has entered the covenant 'inadvertently fails, the Inspector should tea[ch] [h]im and give orders concerning him, and he should le[arn] for a full year.' Translations are from Florentino García Martínez and Eibert J.C. Tigchelaar, eds. *The Dead Sea Scrolls Study Edition* (2 vols. Leiden/ Grand Rapids: Brill/Eerdmans, 2000).

12. 'nicht mehr brechen *konnen*': Schmid, *Buchgestalten*, 68-69. His emphasis.

13. This reading of a new 'instinctive' obedience (found in Weippert, "Neuen Bund") is also made within discussion of Qumran: Jer 31:31-34 entailed 'the inner transformation of every individual Jew, for whom the will of God was to become, as it were, second nature.' Geza Vermes, *An Introduction to the Complete Dead Sea Scrolls* (Minneapolis: Fortress, 1999), 146. The question of CD 19:32-35 as a later stratum of the document (as most, though cf. Wacholder) need not mitigate against this point: it simply postpones the issue for a few years.

14. Hermann Lichtenberger and Stefan Schreiner, "Der neue Bund in jüdischer Überlieferung," *TQ* 176.4 (1996), 277.

the new covenant is to commit oneself totally to the law of Moses.'[15] That Jeremiah's oracle might most properly refer to a final, pure community did not mean either that one could not be a member of it until then, nor that being a member of it (now) entailed some instinctive or necessary fidelity, or some leap into a future era of redemptive-history. But such a reading sits very awkwardly with most modern readings of the 'new covenant' in Jer 31—where so many have found a displacement of the covenant at Sinai nowhere imagined when the phrase is used at Qumran. Some have noted these differences and suggested on that ground that Jer 31 is not in fact sitting behind the use of the phrase at Qumran.[16] Others have gone even further and posit that the reading at Qumran, if having to do with Jer 31, stands as deliberately antithetical to the oracle.[17]

But surely it is better to question the accepted reading of Jer 31:31-34, for the use of the phrase 'new covenant' at Qumran would fit rather easily with the general thesis put forward here with no need to construct such a difficult posture. Entrance into the 'new covenant' meant a devotion to fidelity rather than apostasy, fitting well the sectarian atmosphere of the Qumran community. It may be that no deliberate interpretation of Jer 31:31-34 stands behind the *Damascus Document*, but the easy use of the phrase certainly need not stand opposed to the oracle of the 'new covenant' in Jeremiah. It would rather be just one application of the projected-world of Jer 31:31-34 into a situation within second temple Judaism. One enters a 'new covenant' not in order to have something *different* from the covenant made with Abraham or Israel, but in order to be faithful to that same covenant.

---

15.   Jerome Murphy-O'Connor, "The New Covenant in the Letters of Paul and the Essene Documents," in *To Touch the Text* (eds. Maurya P. Horgan and Paul J. Kobelski; New York: Crossroad, 1989), 199. Similarly, Markus Bockmuehl: 'Even the *Damascus Document's* notion of a "new" covenant... merely fulfils and validates, but does not displace, the old.' Markus Bockmuehl, "1QS and Salvation at Qumran," in *The Complexities of Second Temple Judaism* (eds. D.A. Carson et al.; Grand Rapids, MI: Baker, 2001), 391. Or cf. E.P. Sanders, *Paul and Palestinian Judaism* (Philadelphia: Fortress, 1977), 241.

16.   E.g. Raymond F. Collins, "The Berith-Notion of the Cairo Damascus Document and Its Comparison with the New Testament," *ETL* 39 (1963). Collins is followed by Michael D. Morrison, *Who Needs a New Covenant? Rhetorical Function of the Covenant Motif in the Argument of Hebrews* (Eugene, OR: Pickwick, 2008), 122-23.

17.   a 'selbständige antithetische Formulierung': Christian Wolff, *Jeremia im Frühjudentum und Urchristentum* (Texte und Unteersuchungen; Berlin: Akademie Verlag, 1976), 124-25. Better is Dunn, *Parting of Ways*, 60, n.32.

The Climax of the Covenant

For Christian theology this moves rather easily into discussions from New Testament scholarship regarding 'the climax of the covenant.' N.T. Wright, though not without his critics, has been the most influential advocate for a construction of Paul's thought in which covenant takes a central role, with Christ at the center as its climax.[18] But such a general approach could be taken in any number of directions. At the center of the unity of Yhwh's work to bring a people to himself (the unity of the covenant) stands the person and work of Jesus Christ (the climax of the covenant). Very little can be said here with regard to the New Testament material on the subject—any venture into Pauline studies alone would take a further volume. But at the least I think many of the assumptions brought to bear on the New Testament uses of 'new covenant' ought to be revisited. And reasons exist for seeing the language of the 'new covenant' in the NT as in line with the salvific contrast from Augustine or as outlined above—an announcement of *fidelity* to God in the covenant, rather than announcing a break with respect to two successive eras of God's dealings with his people. (After all, it was Paul's discussion of 'new covenant' that grounded Augustine's first explorations of the contast as salvific or absolute.) Paul in 2 Cor 3 speaks of the ministry of the 'old covenant' as bringing *condemnation* before God, rather than 'life'; a contrast between those whose 'minds were hardened' and those who have the Spirit. Attempts to describe these as differences of 'accidents'—or to explain the old covenant here as primarily an *era* both run aground on the uncompromising nature of the contrast. Each state describe a position before God: of salvation or judgment (*Heil und Nicht-Heil*). We move close to Augustine's position and language when Scott Hafemann states regarding 2 Cor 3:

> [T]he letter/Spirit contrast is between *the Law itself without the Spirit*, as it was (and is! cf. 3:14-15) experienced by the majority of Israelites under the Sinai covenant, and *the Law with the Spirit*, as it is now being experienced by those who are under the new covenant in Christ.[19]

To emerge with Augustine's position we could simply add a phrase to the final clause: 'the Law with the Spirit, as it is now being experienced (*and was always experienced*) by those who are under the new covenant in Christ.' The issue is not a simple contrast of two 'eras' of God's dealings, but the infidelity of those who reject Jesus Christ as the climax of the covenant—those Jews who hear the

---

18. N.T. Wright, *The Climax of the Covenant: Christ and the Law in Pauline Theology* (Philadelphia: Fortress, 1993).

19. Scott Hafemann, *Paul, Moses, and the History of Israel* (Tubingen: J.C.B. Mohr (Paul Siebeck), 1995), 171. His emphasis.

narrative of the hardened hearts in the wilderness and continue just like their fathers in unbelief. Moses becomes a minister of condemnation so long as the 'veil' remains, unmoved by the Spirit; i.e. so long as one lives apart from faith in Jesus Christ. Fidelity to the covenant and membership in the new covenant are co-referential. As with Jeremiah's 'broken covenant' the point of contrast for Paul's new covenant ministry is that state of rejection of God's covenant, or an apostasy that brings condemnation. As with Augustine and as in Jeremiah, the old covenant ministry was death, the new covenant is that state of life and fidelity.

The general thesis of the new covenant as regarding fidelity to God seems to hold up as well when reading the 'Last Supper' narrative of Luke 22:14-20 (if we accept the longer text).[20] But here we can see the shift from the use at Qumran. It is fine to assert that membership in the 'new covenant' has to do with fidelity to the covenant with Yhwh. But at the heart of much of the so-called 'parting of the ways' in early Judaism/Christianity concerned what such fidelity meant. What does it mean to participate in the 'new covenant'—to pursue fidelity to the covenant? At Qumran it meant merely a re-devotion of one's self to the Torah, as interpreted by the Teacher. It seems possible, at least, to find the use of 'new covenant' in Luke's narrative of the Last Supper to be an implicit answer to this question: to be a member of the 'new covenant' (to be faithful to the covenant with Yhwh) is to identify with and participate in the sacrifice of Jesus Christ. Fidelity to God and his covenant is now accomplished by participation in or sanctification by the blood of Christ that is poured out.

The newness in Luke 22:20 lies not in a *different* covenant being established—at least not necessarily. Many commentators appear to leap from the mention of 'new covenant' to an assertion that we have here the 'inauguration' of a covenant.[21] But at issue in the narrative of the Supper is not a breaking from

---

20. The longer text exists in P75, ℵ, A, B, et al., though occasionally in different order. The shorter text (without v.19b-20) exists only in D and some Old Latin texts. For a rather full bibliography on this pericope, see François Bovon, *Das Evangelium nach Lukas (Lk 19,28-24,53)* (Neukirchener-Vluyn/Düsseldorf: Neukirchener/Patmos, 2009), 231-36.

21. E.g. Ibid., 246-47; or Darrell L. Bock, *Luke* (vol. 2; Grand Rapids, MI: Baker, 1996), 1727: 'The new covenant is inaugurated in his blood, that is, by his death.... With Jesus' death, salvific benefits can be distributed.' Though Bock is not entirely clear, it seems that this is something chronologically 'new' in which case we can ask the question we have seen throughout this study: if 'salvific benefits' come only *after* Jesus' death, then what of all those who came before Jesus? That 'salvific benefits' come on the *ground* of Jesus' death would be a more classical theological position. But that the *ground* must have been played out within history prior to any form of the enjoyment of

a previous era of God's actions with his people, but a participation in the sacrifice and work of Jesus. The newness may reasonably be said to lie in recognizing and celebrating the 'climax of the covenant' between Yhwh and his people, and participating faithfully in that climax. Entrance into or participation in the 'new covenant'—which is fidelity to God's covenant—becomes tied to a participation in the sacrifice of Jesus Christ. This is not to say that no change of sacraments (*mutatio sacramentorum*) may be implicit by the instituting of the meal, but that this change of sacraments (if it is found in the text) is *because* of what it means to faithfully participate in the covenant. The climax of the covenant has come, and fidelity to that covenant now centers on the sacrifice of Jesus Christ.

The use of Jer 31:31-34 in Hebrews likewise would be a rather larger discussion. One reading generally in line with the above thesis was put forward at length by Rayburn some years ago, though possibly needing revisiting and updating.[22] A view of the new covenant as concerning fidelity to God over against apostasy would, at least on the surface, fit much of the purpose of the 'word of exhortation' in Hebrews as this contrast of fidelity/apostasy emerges time and again. But more particularly, one potential home (among several options) within modern discussion of Hebrews would place this view of the 'new covenant' in the contrast of 'ontological' rather than merely economical states of affairs.[23] The argument in Hebrews against the 'earthly' cultic activities, or the 'first covenant' considered only with respect to its earthly cultic activities, becomes relativized over against the 'heavenly' cultic activity of the greater high priest. All this would stand over against those, real or imagined, who thought the cultic activities were sufficient for the perfecting of conscience (9:9, 14), the forgiveness of sins (10:4), or the attainment of the 'better promises' (8:16). Jesus Christ is not only the climax of the covenant, but his high priestly work is heavenly and so able to accomplish what the merely 'earthly' priestly work could not do. Jesus' blood is the blood of the 'eternal covenant' (!—13:22). At the least, this study should demonstrate that many of the assumptions too often taken into these New Testament texts is worth further examination.

At the end, this work can only hint towards such possibilities. The central impulse arises from the potential unifying of the covenant idea in Jeremiah,

---

'salvific benefits' would be a further claim, and one already disputed by Augustine.

22. Rayburn, "Contrast."

23. 'Nicht um theologische Polemik gegen das Jüdische geht es dem Hebr, sondern um ontologische Relativierung des Irdischen. Der Gegenbegriff zum neuen Bund ist daher nicht "alter Bund" im heilsgeschichtlichen, sondern "irdischer Kult" im metaphysischen Sinne.' Knut Backhaus, "Gottes nicht bereuter Bund: Alter und neuer Bund in der Sicht des Frühchristentums," in *Ekklesiologie des Neuen Testaments* (eds. Rainer Kampling and Thomas Söding; Freiburg: Herder, 1996), 44.

so that the 'new covenant' is simply the way things always ought to have been: the covenant ('I will be your God, you will be my people') engaged with fidelity from the people. Far from dividing the life and experience of the people of God into two successive religio-historical eras, the oracle of the new covenant unites the people of God around its center, the climax of the covenant in Jesus Christ.

Judaizing of Christianity?

Such a summary will perhaps seem rather bold with the little amount of work done above regarding the apostolic and New Testament uses of Jeremiah's new covenant (or the 'eternal covenant'). Nonetheless, a salvific or absolute contrast of fidelity and apostasy in Jer 31:31-34 carries at least a strong implication of greater unity in the covenant than often posited. At least one negative impulse towards this approach, however, is framed by Francis Watson, who summarizes a perceived weakness of Brevard Childs's work in the following way. With Childs's approach, he says:

> Scriptural 'authority' is, as it were, spread evenly across this flat surface, and the church is no less obliged to confess God as Yahweh, the God of our fathers who delivered us from slavery in Egypt, than it is to confess him as the God and Father of our Lord Jesus Christ. The Old Testament confession of God retains its place alongside the New Testament one, for the Old Testament itself coexists with the New in a state of pure, dehistoricized textuality.[24]

The great danger of this, Watson holds, would be a 'radical judaizing of Christianity':

> characterized, for example, by the expansion of the creeds to include the great events of Old Testament *Heilsgeschichte* and by the incorporation of the Jewish feasts within the Christian liturgical calendar. Male circumcision would have to be reintroduced: for, according to the scripture that the church acknowledges as authoritative, the God of Abraham, Isaac and Jacob is the God who has established circumcision as the unsubstitutable sign of his everlasting covenant. There can be no appeal to the New Testament treatment of these matters; on the contrary, we must resist 'the Christian temptation to identify Biblical Theology with the New Testament's interpretation of the Old, as if the Old Testament's witness were limited to how it was once heard and appropriated by the early church'. Indeed, the dangerous adjectives 'Old' and 'New', suggestive both of diachronicity and displacement, would presumably have to be replaced by a more neutral

---

24. Francis Watson, *Text and Truth: Redefining BIblical Theology* (Grand Rapids, MI: Eerdmans, 1997), 214-15; quoting Brevard Childs, *Biblical Theology*, 77.

terminology that does not compromise the enduring, 'vertical' authority of the so-called 'Old' Testament.'[25]

Watson seems to join together a number of fears and seems, likewise, not to have become as familiar as he might have with the Reformed tradition out of which Childs does much of his work. In any case, Watson raises a key question for the present suggestions: Does an assertion of the unity of the covenant, or a disputing of the terminology 'old' and 'new' (especially in the sense Watson takes those terms) mean a return to circumcision? Or a return to the Jewish feasts for Christian communities? Traditional Reformed thought, following medieval distinctions, would appeal here to a distinction between the ceremonial and moral aspects of the covenant as it is administered—an admittedly difficult distinction to establish within the biblical texts. But we need not go so far to answer Watson's concern. A simple principial solution exists. Developments in religious thought, theological conviction, knowledge, and experience of God all occur in and through history, both in individual and corporate life. And since God interacts with his people in and through history we do not need to be surprised if the particulars of what it means to be faithful to God (the content) might change while the subjective determination of faith, loyalty and faithfulness remains consistent. So we need not, in principle, be surprised to see circumcision a faithful expression of loyalty to Yhwh by Abraham and Moses, and yet no longer a faithful expression of loyalty to Yhwh by others. At every point in one's individual life and the corporate life of the people of God, fidelity is relative to what God has revealed of himself and his Torah. So as a matter of principle, Watson's objection can be addressed without great difficulty in a manner that can be applied any number of ways within Christian theology and need not stand in the way of the present proposal. Exactly how one might address the objection in practice, of course, would return to the debates of Catharism, Passaginis, and much of the history of Christian theology.

In summary, the theological direction of the above reading of Jeremiah's 'new covenant' offers a strong emphasis on the unity of covenant considered either in terms of the 'new' or 'eternal' covenant in which all the faithful stand before God. The climax of that covenant towards which it always pressed and from which it then flows is the saving work of God in Jesus Christ. One can frame this larger devotion of Yhwh to have a people for himself as a single 'covenant of grace' with various 'administrations' as in classical Reformed thought (as well as Karl Barth or, differently, Erich Zenger). Or one might simply speak of the unity of the person of God who has always determined to have a people for himself—the restoration of rightful humanity by the work of God (grace restoring nature). But at the heart of either would be the 'steadfast love' of God,

---

25. Ibid., 215.

which is the fountain and ground of the new covenant that unifies all of his redeeming work centred on the Christ, the climax of that one gracious covenant.

2. *Unity of the People of God*

In the same vein we can see a potential implication of the above reading of Jer 31:31-34 with respect to the unity of the people of God (offered, again, with all due qualifications that much more work would need be done). Such a unity was a crucial matter, though in various ways, for many throughout Christian theological history—from Augustine's single 'city of God' to Calvin's construction of the unity of the 'covenant'. At the heart of each stands the unity of God ('the same yesterday, today, and forever') and the consequent unity of those who are saved. A strong statement of that unity with respect to the contrast of old/new covenants was made by Rayburn in his conclusions:

> The one covenant is made with a people who do not believe and are not being saved, the other is made with the called, those who are being saved. The distinction between these two covenants thus has no more to do with time B.C. and A.D. than do any other of the great issues of eternal salvation. The gospel has always been the same, the condition always the same, the blessings always the same. Some have accepted that gospel and some have not. This is the difference between the old covenant and the new.[26]

One need not conclude that, therefore, no distance or difference exists for those prior to and following the work of Jesus Christ—a kind of 'flattening' of redemptive-history. To the contrary, redemptive-history would become entirely centred upon that work of Christ as the ground and climax of the whole: all flows from that work in every direction, past and future, throughout the history of the people of God. Whatever differences exist, the centre remains with Christ and fidelity to God in his covenant. There is one City of God for all the faithful, with Christ at its head and center.

But, again, Watson's statement can be cited as a warning against such an approach. Watson fears a claim of too strong a unity between the ancient era of the people of God and the era after Christ, because in that case:

> [T]he church is no less obliged to confess God as Yahweh, the God of our fathers who delivered us from slavery in Egypt, than it is to confess him as the God and Father of our Lord Jesus Christ. The Old Testament confession of God retains its place alongside the New Testament one, for the Old Testament itself coexists with the New in a state of pure, dehistoricized textuality.

---

26. Rayburn, "Contrast," 507-08.

We could dispute the *non sequitur* of the final clause, as if a granting of authority becomes necessarily a belief in the Scriptures as existing 'in a state of pure, dehistoricized textuality.'[27] But I cannot help but think Christian theology ought to find some joy and satisfaction in confessing God as Yhwh, the God of our fathers who delivered us from slavery in Egypt. This seems to be a part of Paul's emphasis in 1 Cor 10 when he declares to the largely Gentile church, 'I want you to know brothers that *our fathers* were all under the cloud, and all passed through the sea....' Each part of redemptive-history can legitimately be said to become a part of one's own history when one becomes engrafted into the people of God. By being engrafted into the same tree (which is almost opposite from any notion of *replacement* theology; rather, Gentiles are granted that great privilege once confined largely to Israel), the faithful Christian does call Abraham his father, and looks upon Yhwh's saving acts as done for the people of God— of whom the Christian has become a part. Watson seems to think it some kind of opprobrium to be so associated with Yhwh, or to hold to the 'Old Testament confession of God' (whatever exactly that becomes). But it appears strange to question whether not the church ought to confess God as Yhwh, or view itself as united to the faithful before Christ and the work of God on their behalf becoming our own. So the early historian Eusebius could say:

> All these, whose righteousness won them commendation, going back from Abraham himself to the first man, might be described as Christians in fact (*tamen rebus*) if not in name, without departing far from the truth... Obviously we must regard the religion proclaimed in recent years to all nations through Christ's teaching as none other than the first, most ancient, and most primitive of all religions, discovered by Abraham and his followers, God's beloved.... What then is to prevent us from admitting that we, Christ's followers, share one and the same life and form of religion with those who were dear to God so long ago? Thus the practice of religion as communicated to us by Christ's teaching is shown to be not modern and strange but, in all conscience, primitive, unique, and true. There we will leave the matter.[28]

---

27. Cf. Berkouwer's contrary statement: 'The Word of God, Scripture in the form of a servant, is not known to us in the outlines of a supernatural miracle lifted out of time and human weakness, excluding all questions *ipso facto*, but in the human form of word and writing.' G.C. Berkouwer, *Holy Scripture* (Grand Rapids, MI: Eerdmans, 1975), 207. Or the more recent study by John Webster, *Holy Scripture: A Dogmatic Sketch* (Cambridge: Cambridge Univ. Press, 2003).

28. Eusebius, *The History of the Church* (Tr. by G.A. Wiliamson, rev. A. Louth. London: Penguin, 1989), I.4.

A more poetic expression of this unity emerges in the lines of a hymn by St. Ephrem of Syria:

> The sound form of our faith is from Abraham,
>
> And our repentance is from Nineveh and the house of Rahab,
>
> And ours are the expectations of the Prophets,
>
> Ours of the Apostles.[29]

The above reading of Jer 31:31-34 allows the Christian church to bring itself into the entirety of the story of God's dealings with his people throughout all generations. It does not establish the unity around the climax of the covenant, but at the least it suggests such ideas. It may be that the use to which the 'new covenant' oracle is put in the apostolic writings diverges significantly from the role it plays in the book of Jeremiah, or from the use of the phrase at Qumran. My tendency, however, would be to re-question the assumptions that have informed those readings regarding what the 'new covenant' must mean. And in my view, Christian theology will only deepen with a fuller appreciation of the unity of those who have faithfully embraced that great central promise: 'I will be your God, and you will be my people.' Many have argued that the oracle of the new covenant is 'eschatological,' and in one sense that must be right: it describes the world as the way it ought to be, and announces that it *will* be like that one day.[30] The people of God will *all* love and fear as they ought (and as the faithful desire) and the promise of the covenant will be known and experienced as it always ought to have been known and experienced. The oracle is one of hope for exiled Israel and Judah, and with the coming of the Messiah the climax of the covenant and sureness of that hope arrived. And so the people of God stand gathered around that climax, the person and work of Jesus Christ, looking and longing for the final and full completion of Jeremiah's new covenant now guaranteed, as it were, by the resurrection: that all things will be the way they always ought to have been.

---

29. Ephrem the Syrian, "Hymn 7," in *The Pearl* (NPNF 2.13; Peabody, MA: Hendrickson, 1994), 299.

30. Cp. Peter Vogt's statement on Deuteronomy: 'Deuteronomy is, in a sense, "eschatological" in its outlook. That is, it *envisages a society as it ought to be.*' Peter T. Vogt, *Deuteronomic Theology and the Significance of Torah: A Reappraisal* (Winona Lake, IN: Eisenbrauns, 2006), 231. My emphasis.

Works Cited

Pre-18th Century

Alcuin of York. *Expositio in Epistolam Pauli Apostoli ad Hebraeos*. PL 100. Edited by J.-P. Migne. Paris: 1863.

Augustine. "Epistula 138." Pages 525-35 in volume 33 of *S. Aurelii Augustini Opera Omnia*. Edited by J.-P. Migne. PL. Paris: 1861.

_____. *De Gratia novi testamenti liber (Epistola 140)*. PL 33. Edited by J.-P. Migne. Paris: 1861.

_____. *Contra Faustum Manichaeum*. CSEL 25. Vienna: 1891.

_____. *De spiritu et littera*. CSEL 60. Vienna: 1913.

_____. "In Answer to the Jews." Pages 391-414 in *Treatises on Marriage and other Subjects*. FC. Washington DC: CUA Press, 1955.

_____. *De dono perseverantiae*. Œuv. de S.Aug. 24. Paris: Desclée de Brouwer, 1962.

_____. *Quaestionum in Heptateuchum*. CCL 33. Tournholt: Brepols, 1963.

_____. *De baptismo*. Œuv. de S.Aug. 29. Paris: Desclée de Brouwer, 1964.

_____. *De libero arbitrio*. CCL 29. Tournholt: Brepols, 1970.

_____. *Contra duas epistulas Pelegianorum*. Œuv. de S.Aug., 23. Paris: Desclée de Brouwer, 1974.

_____. *Enchiridion de fide spe et caritate*. Œuv. de S.Aug. 9. Paris: Desclée de Brouwer, 1988.

_____. *De catechizandis rudibus*. Œuv. de S.Aug. 11/1. Paris: Desclée de Brouwer, 1991.

_____. *De gestis Pelagii*. Œuv. de S.Aug 21. Paris: Desclée de Brouwer, 1994.

_____. "Letter 28." Pages 251-53 *The Confessions and Letters of St. Augustine*. NPNF 1.1. Grand Rapids, MI: Eerdmans, 1994.

_____. "Letter 40." Pages 272-75 in *The Confessions and Letters of St. Augustine*. NPNF 1.1. Grand Rapids, MI: Eerdmans, 1994.

_____. "Letter 55." Pages 303-16 in *The Confessions and Letters of St. Augustine*. NPNF 1.1. Grand Rapids, MI: Eerdmans, 1994.

_____. *On Christian Teaching*. Translated by R.P.H. Green. Oxford Univ. Press, 1997.

_____. *The City of God*. Translated by R.W. Dyson. Cambridge Univ. Press, 1998.

_____. *Unfinished Work in Answer to Julian*. Works of St. Augustine. Translated by Roland J. Teske. New City Press: NY, 1999.

Ball, John. *A Short Treatise: Containing all the principall grounds of Christian Religion*. London: 1617.

_____. *A Treatise of the Covenant of Grace wherein The graduall breakings out of Gospel grace from Adam to Christ are clearly discovered*. London: 1645.

The [Geneva] Bible: That is, the Holy Scriptures, contained in the Olde and Newe Testament. with most profitable Annotations upon all the hard places, and other things of great importance. London: 1595.

Blake, Thomas. *Vindiciae Foederis: or, A Treatise of the Covenant of God entered with Man-Kinde, in the several Kindes and Degrees of it*. 2nd ed. London: 1658.

Bolton, Samuel. *The True Bounds of Christian Freedom*. Edited by S.M. Houghton. Carlisle, PA: Banner of Truth, 1964.

À Brakel, Wilhelmus. *The Christian's Reasonable Service*. 4 vols. Translated by Bartel Elshout. Grand Rapids, MI: Reformation Heritage Books, 1992.

Bucer, Martin. *In sacra quatuor Euangelia, enarrationes perpetuae, secundum & postremum recognitae*. Geneva: 1553.

_____. *Dialogi oder Gesprech von der gemainsame und den Kirchenübungen der Christen und was yeder Oberkait von ampts wegen auß Göttlichen befelch an denselbigen züversehen und zü besserteb gebüre*. Martin Bucers Deutsche Schriften 6.2. Edited by Robert Stupperich. Gütersloh: Verlagshaus Gerd Mohn, 1984.

Bullinger, Heinrich. *De testamento seu foedere Dei unico & aeterno*. Zürich: 1534.

_____. *Ieremias fidelissimus et laboriosissimus Dei propheta, expositus per Heinrychum Bullingerum*. Zürich: 1575.

_____. *Looke from Adam, And behold the Protestant's Faith and Religion*. Translated by Miles Coverdale. London: 1624.

_____. *The Decades*. 5 vols. Translated by Thomas Harding. Cambridge: Cambridge Univ. Press, 1849.

_____. "Vorlesung über den Hebräerbrief." Pages 135-268 in volume III.1 of *Heinrich Bullinger Werke*. Edited by Hans-Georg vom Berg and Susanna Hausammann. Zurich: Theologischer Verlag, 1983.

_____. *Studiorum Ratio: Text und Übersetzung*. Edited by Peter Stotz. Zürich: Theologischer Verlag, 1987.

_____. "A Brief Exposition of the One and Eternal Testament or Covenant of God." Pages 100-38 in *Fountainhead of Federalism*. Edited by Charles S. McCoy and J. Wayne Baker. Louisville, KY: Westminster John Knox, 1991.

_____. "Antwort an Burchard." Pages 140-72 in volume III.2 of *Heinrich Bullinger Werke*. Edited by Hans-Georg vom Berg and Bernhard Schneider. Zurich: Theologischer Verlag, 1991.

_____. "Von dem Touff." Pages 66-85 in volume III.2 of *Heinrich Bullingers Werke*. Edited by Hans-Georg vom Berg. Zurich: Theologischer Verlag, 1991.

_____. "De scripturae negotio." Pages 12-31 in volume III.2 of *Heinrich Bullingers Werke*. Edited by Hans-Georg vom Berg. Zurich: Theologischer Verlag, 1991.

Burgess, Anthony. *Vindiciae Legis: or, A Vindication of the Morall Law and the Covenants*. London: 1646.

Calamy, Edmund. *Two Solemne Covenants Made between God and Man*. London: 1646.

Calvin, John. *The Sermons of M. Iohn Calvin upon the Fifth Booke of Moses called Deuteronomie*. Translated by Arthur Golding. London: 1583.

_____. *Ioannes Calvinus caesaribus, regibus, principibus, gentibusque omnibus Christ imperio subditis salutem*. Ioannes Calvini Opera 9. Edited by J.W. Baum, A.E. Cunitz and E. Reuss. Brunswick: 1870.

_____. *A tous amateurs de Iesus Christ, et de son S. Evangile, salut*. Ioannes Calvini Opera 9. Brunsfield: 1870.

_____. "Preface to Olivétan's New Testament." Pages 58-73 in *Calvin: Commentaries*. Edited by Joseph Haroutunian. LCC. Philadelphia: Westminster Press, 1958.

_____. *Institutes of the Christian Religion*. 2 vols. LCC. Edited by John T. Mcneill. Translated by Ford Lewis Battles. Philadelphia: Westminster Press, 1960.

_____. *Commentaries on the Book of the Prophet Jeremiah and the Lamentations*. 5

vols. Translated by John Owen. Grand Rapids, MI: Baker, 1979.

_____. *Commentaries on the Epistle of Paul the Apostle to the Romans*. Translated by John Owen. Grand Rapids, MI: Baker, 1979.

_____. *Commentary on a Harmony of the Evangelists, Matthew, Mark and Luke*. 3 vols. Translated by William Pringle. Grand Rapids, MI: Baker, 1979.

_____. *Commentary on the Book of the Prophet Isaiah*. Translated by William Pringle. Grand Rapids, MI: Baker, 1979.

_____. *Commentary on the Book of the Psalms*. 5 vols. Translated by James Anderson. Grand Rapids, MI: Baker, 1979.

_____. *Iohannes Calvini Commentarius in Epistolam Pauli ad Romanos*. Edited by T.H.L. Parker. Leiden: E.J. Brill, 1981.

_____. *Commentaries on the Epistle of Paul the Apostle to the Hebrews*. Translated by John Owen. Grand Rapids, MI: Baker, 1998.

Cameron, John. "*De triplici Dei cum homine foedere theses.*" Pages 544-51 in *Ioannis Cameronis Scoto-Britanni Theologi Examii TA ΣΩZOMENA siue Opera Partim ab auctore ipse edita*. Geneva: 1642.

Chrysostom, John. *Commentaire sur Isaïe*. SC 304. Paris: Les Éditions du Cerf, 1983.

_____. *Homilies on Hebrews*. NPNF I.14. Translated by F. Gardiner. Grand Rapids, MI: Eerdmans, 1996.

Clarke, Samuel. "The Lives of Thirty-two English divines." in *A General Martyrologie, containing a collection of all the greatest persecutions which have befallen the Church of Christ*. London: 1677.

Cocceius, Johannes. *De ultimis Mosis considerationes*. Opera 1. Amsterdam: 1673.

_____. *Summa Theologiae ex Scripturis Repetita*. Opera 6. Amsterdam: 1673.

_____. *Summa doctrinae de foedere et testamento Dei*. Opera 6. Amsterdam: 1673.

_____. *Disputationes selectae*. Opera 6. Amsterdam: 1673.

Cyprian. *Ad Quirinum*. CCL 3. Tournholt: Brepols, 1972.

Descartes, René. *The Correspondence of René Descartes: 1643*. Edited by Theo Verbeeck, Erik-Jan Bos and Jeroen Van De Ven. Utrecht: Utrecht University, 2004.

Ephrem the Syrian. *The Pearl*. NPNF 2.13. Peabody, MA: Hendrickson, 1994.

Eusebius. *The History of the Church*. Translated by Rev. A. Louth G.A. Wiliamson. London: Penguin, 1989.

Fenner, Dudley. *Sacra Theologia, sive Veritas quae est secundum Pietatem*. n.a.: 1585.

Ferrandus. "*The Life of the Blessed Bishop Fulgentius.*" Pages 1-56 in *Fulgentius: Selected Works*. Washington, D.C.: CUA Press, 1997.

Fulgentius. "Epistula 17." Pages 563-615 in volume 91A of *Fulgentius Ruspensis: Opera*. Edited by J. Fraipont. CCL. Tournhout: Brepols, 1968.

_____. *Selected Works*. FC. Washington, D.C.: CUA Press, 1997.

_____. "Letter 14 to Ferrandus." Pages 499-565 in *Selected Works*. FC. Washington, D.C.: CUA Press, 1997.

Gillespie, George. *The Ark of the Testament Opened*. London: 1661.

_____. *The Ark of the Covenant Opened*. London: 1677.

Hugh of St. Victor. *Summa sententiarum septem tractatibus*. PL 176. Edited by J.-P. Migne. Paris: 1884.

_____. *On the Sacraments of the Christian Faith (De Sacramentis)*. Translated by Roy

J. Deferrari. Cambridge, MA: Mediaeval Academy of America, 1951.

Glossa Ordinaria: Prophetia Jeremiae. PL 114. Edited by J.-P. Migne. Paris: 1879.

Glossa Ordinaria: Epistola ad Hebraeos. PL 114. Edited by J.-P. Migne. Paris: 1879.

Jerome. *In Hieremiam Prophetam libri VI.* CCL 74. Tournholt: Brepols, 1960.

——. *Commentarium in Osee prophetam.* Corpus Christianorum Series Latina 76. Turnhout: Brepols, 1969.

——. *Commentariorum in Malachiam prophetam.* CCL 76a. Tournholt: Brepols, 1970.

——. "Letter 75." Pages 13-18 in volume I.1 of *The Confessions and Letters of St. Augustine.* NPNF. Grand Rapids, MI: Eerdmans, 1994.

——. *Against Jovinianus.* NPNF II.6. Translated by W.H. Fremantle. Grand Rapids, MI: Eerdmans, 1996.

——. "Letter 14." Pages 13-18 in volume II.6 of *The Principle Works of St. Jerome.* NPNF. Grand Rapids, MI: Eerdmans, 1996.

——. "Letter 22." Pages 22-41 in volume II.6 of *The Principal Works of St. Jerome.* NPNF. Grand Rapids, MI: Eerdmans, 1996.

Julian Of Toledo (?). *Responsio.* PL 96. Edited by J.-P. Migne. Paris: 1862.

Justin Martyr. *Dialogue with Trypho, a Jew.* ANF 1. Translated by Alexander Roberts And James Donaldson. Grand Rapids, MI: Wm. B. Eerdmans, 1996.

Kant, Immanuel. "Groundwork for the Metaphysics of Morals." Pages 43-117 in *Practical Philosophy.* Edited by Mary J. Giger. The Cambridge Edition of the Works of Immanuel Kant. Cambridge: Cambrige Univ. Press, 1996.

——. "An Answer to the Question: What is Enlightenment?" Pages 11-22 in *Practical Philosophy.* Edited by Mary J. Giger. Cambridge: Cambridge Univ. Press, 1996.

Luther, Martin. *The Babylonian Captivity of the Church.* Luther's Works 36. Translated by A.T.W. Steinhäuser, F.C. Ahrens and A.R. Wentz. Philadelphia: Fortress Press, 1959.

——. *The Misuse of the Mass.* Luther's Works 36. Translated by F.C. Ahrens. Philadelphia: Fortress, 1959.

——. *Lectures on Deuteronomy.* Luther's Works 9. Translated by R.R. Caemmerer. St. Louis, MO: Concordia, 1960.

Maccovius, Johannes. *Loci communes theologici.* Amsterdam: 1658.

Melanchthon, Philip. *Loci communes von 1521.* Melanchthons Werke II.1. Edited by Hans Engelland. Gütersloh: Bertelsmann Verlag, 1952.

——. *On Christian Doctrine: Loci Communes 1555.* Translated by Clyde L. Manschreck. Oxford: Oxford Univ. Press, 1965.

——. "*Loci Communes Theologici (1521).*" in *Melanchthon and Bucer.* Edited by Wilhelm Pauck. London: SCM Press, 1969.

Musculus, Wolfgang. *Loci communes theologicae sacrae.* Ultima ed. Basel: 1599.

Oecolampadius, Johannes. *In Hieremiam prophetam commentariorum libri tres Ioannis Oecolampadii.* Argentinae: 1533.

——. *In Jesaiam Prophetam Hypomnematon.* Basel: 1525.

——. *In Ezechielem: Prophetam Commentarii Ioannis Oecolampadii.* Geneva: 1583.

Olevianus, Caspar. *An Exposition of the Symbole of the Apostles, or rather of the Articles of Faith. In which the chiefe points of the everlasting and free covenant betweene God and the faithfull is briefly and plainly handled.* Translated by John Fielde. London: 1581.

_____. *De substantia foederis gratuiti inter deum et electos, itemque De mediis, quibus ea ipsa substantia nobis communicatur.* Geneva: 1585.

_____. *A Firm Foundation: An Aid to Interpreting the Heidelberg Catechism.* Translated by Lyle D. Bierma. Grand Rapids, MI: Baker, 1995.

Origen. *Commentaire sur Saint Jean II.* SC 157. Paris: Les Éditions du Cerf, 1970.

_____. *Commentaire sur Saint Jean I.* SC 120. Paris: Les Éditions du Cerf, 1996.

_____. *Homilies on Jeremiah.* FC 97. Translated by John Clark Smith. Washington DC: CUA Press, 1998.

Paulus Alvarus Cordubensis. *Epistle 18: Epistola Alvari transgressori directa.* PL 121. Edited by J.-P. Migne. Paris: 1880.

Pelagius. *Pelagius's Commentary on St. Paul's Epistle to the Romans.* Translated and Edited by Theodore De Bruyn. Oxford: Clarendon, 1993.

Pemble, William. *Vindiciae Fidei, or A Treatise of Justification by Faith.* Oxford: 1625.

Perkins, William. *A Golden Chaine.* Cambridge: 1591.

Peter Lombard. *Sententiae in IV libris distinctae.* PL 192. Edited by J.-P. Migne.

Polyander, Johannes, Andreas Rivetus, Antonius Walaeus and Antonius Thysius. *Synopsis Purioris Theologiae.* Edited by Herman Bavinck. Leiden: D. Donner, 1881.

Possidius. "Life of Augustine." Pages 71-124 in *Early Christian Biographies.* Washington DC: CUA Press, 1952.

Prepositinus (?). *Summa Contra Haereticos: Ascribed to Praepositinus of Cremona.* Edited by Joseph N. Garvin and James A. Corbett. Notre Dame: Univ. of Notre Dame Press, 1958.

Preston, John. *The New Covenant, or The Saints Portion.* London: 1629.

_____. *The Law Out-Lawed or, The Charter of the Gospel shewing the priviledge and prerogative of the Saints by vertue of the Covenant.* Edinburgh: 1631.

Rabanus Maurus. *Enarrationum in epistolas beati pauli.* PL 112. Edited by J.-P. Migne. Paris: 1852.

Rollock, Robert. *Quaestiones et responsiones aliquot de foedere Dei.* Edinburgh: 1596.

_____. *A Treatise of God's Effectual Calling.* Translated by Henry Holland. London: 1603.

_____. *Analysis Logica in Epistolam ad Hebraeos.* Edinburgh: 1605.

Rupert of Deutz. *Liber de divinis officiis.* CCL 7. Edited by Hrabanus Haacke. Tournholt: Brepols, 1967.

Rutherford, Samuel. *A Survey of the Spirituall Antichrist.* London: 1648.

_____. *The Covenant of Life Opened: or, a Treatise of the Covenant of Grace.* Edinburgh: 1654.

_____. *The Trial and Triumph of Faith.* Edinburgh: Banner of Truth, 2001.

Servetus, Michael. *The Two Treatises of Servetus on the Trinity.* HTS 16. Translated by Earl Morse Wilbur. Cambridge, MA: Harvard Univ. Press, 1932.

Strong, William. *A Discourse of the Two Covenants: wherein the Nature, Differences, and Effects of the Covenant of Works and of Grace are distinctly, rationally, spiritually and practically discussed; together with a considerable quantity of Practical Cases dependent thereon.* London: 1678.

Thomas Aquinas. *Scriptum super sententiis.* Sancti Thomae Aquinatis Doctoris angelici. Opera Omnia 6-7. Parma: 1858.

_____. *In Jeremiam prophetam expositio.* Sancti Thomae Aquinatis Doctoris angelici.

Opera Omnia 14. Parma: 1863.

_____. *Super II Epistolam B.Pauli ad Corinthios lectura*. Sancti Thomae Aquinatis Doctoris angelici. Opera Omnia 13. Parma: 1863.

_____. *In psalmos Davidis expositio*. Sancti Thomae Aquinatis Doctoris angelici. Opera Omnia 14. Parma: 1863.

_____. *Summa Theologiae*. 5 vols. Ottawa: Studii Generalis, 1949.

_____. *Commentary on Saint Paul's Epistle to the Galatians*. Translated by F.R. Larcher. Albany, NY: Magi Books, 1966.

_____. "De decem preceptis." in *Recherches Thomasiennes*. Edited by Jean-Pierre Torrell. Recherches Thomasiennes. Paris: Librairie Philosophique J.Vrin, 2000.

_____. *Commentary on the Epistle to the Hebrews*. Translated by Chrysostom Baer. South Bend: St. Augustine's Press, 2006.

Turretin, Francis. *Institutes of Elenctic Theology*. 4 vols. Edited by James T. Dennison Jr. Translated by George Musgrave Giger. Phillipsburg, NJ: P&R Publishing, 1994.

Ursinus, Zacharius. *Commentary of Dr. Zacharius Ursinus on the Heidelberg Catechism*. Translated by G.W. Williard. Cincinnati, OH: 1852.

Vermigli, Peter Martyr. *In Mosis Genesim. Commentarii*. Basel: 1554.

_____. *The Most fruitfull & learned Commentaries of Doctor Peter Martir Vermil [on Judges]*. Translated by John Day. London: 1564.

_____. *In Epistolam S. Pauli Apostoli ad Romanos*. 3rd ed. Basel: 1568.

_____. *Loci Communes D. Petri Martyris Vermilii. ex varis ipsius authoris scriptis in unum librum collecti & in quatuor Classes distributi*. London: 1583.

_____. *The Life, Early Letters & Eucharistic Writings of Peter Martyr*. Courtenay Library of Reformation Classics. Edited by J.C. Mclelland and G.E. Duffield. Oxford: Sutton Courtenay Press, 1989.

Voetius, Gispertus. *Selectarum Disputationum Theologicarum*. 5 vols. Utrecht: 1648.

Witsius, Herman. *The Economy of the Covenants between God and Man*. Translated by William Crookshank. London: 1822.

_____. *Sacred Dissertations, on what is commonly called the Apostles' Creed*. 2 vols. Translated by Donald Fraser. Edinburgh: 1823.

Zwingli, Ulrich. *Jeremia-Erklärungen: Complanationis Ieremiae prophetae foetura prima*. Huldrych Zwingli Sämtliche Werke 14. Edited by Emil Egli. Zurich: Verlag Berichthaus, 1959.

_____. "Refutation of the tricks of the Baptists." Pages 123-258 in *Ulrich Zwingli (1484-1531): Selected Works*. Philadelphia: Univ. of Pennsylvania Press, 1972.

Post-18th Century

Adeyẹmi, Fẹmi. *The New Covenant Torah in Jeremiah and the Law of Christ in Paul*. Studies in Biblical Literature 94. New York: Peter Lang, 2007.

Allert, Craig D. *Revelation, Truth, Canon, and Interpretation: Studies in Justin Martyr's Dialogue with Trypho*. VCSup 64. Leiden: Brill, 2002.

Alston, William P. *Illocutionary Acts and Sentence Meaning*. Ithaca: Cornell Univ. Press, 2000.

Anderson, Bernhard W. "'The Lord Has Created Something New': A Stylistic Study of

Jer 31:15-22." *Catholic Biblical Quarterly* 40.4 (1978): 463-78.

Anderson, Marvin Walter. *Peter Martyr, A Reformer in Exile (1542-1562): A chronology of biblical writings in England & Europe*. Nieuwkoop: B. de Graaf, 1975.

Andrée, Alexander. *Gilbertus Universalis: Glossa Ordinaria in Lamentationes Ieremie Prophete. Prothemata et Liber I. A Critical Edition with an Introduction and a Translation*. Studia Latina Stockholmiensia. Stockholm: Almquist & Wiksell Intl, 2005.

Applegate, J. "'Peace, Peace, when there is no Peace': Redactional Integration of Prophecy of Peace into the Judgement of Jeremiah." Pages 51-89 in *The Book of Jeremiah and its Reception*. Edited by A.H.W. Curtis and T. Römer. Leuven: Leuven Univ. Press, 1997.

Archilla, Aurelio A. Garcia. *The Theology of History and Apologetic Historiography in Heinrich Bullinger*. San Fransisco: Mellen Research Univ. Press, 1992.

van Asselt, Willem J. "The Doctrine of the Abrogations in the Federal Theology of Johannes Cocceius (1603-1669)." *Calvin Theological Journal* 29 (1994): 101-16.

_____. "*Amicitia Dei* as Ultimate Reality: An Outline of the Covenant Theology of Johannes Cocceius (1603-1669)." *Ultimate Reality and Meaning. Interdisciplinary Studies in the Philosophy of Understanding* 21.1 (1998): 35-47.

_____. *The Federal Theology of Johannes Cocceius (1603-1669)*. Studies in the History of Christian Thought. Translated by Raymond A. Blacketer. Leiden: Brill, 2001.

Aubert, Jean-Marie. "L'analogie entre Lex nova et la loi naturelle." Pages 248-53 in *Lex et Libertas*. Edited by L.J. Elders and K. Hedwig. Studi Tomisitici. Vatican City: Libreria Editrice Vaticana, 1987.

Bach, Kent. "Conversational Impliciture." *Mind and Language* 9 (1999): 124-62.

_____. "Minding the Gap." Pages 27-43 in *The Semantics/Pragmatics Distinction*. Edited by Claudia Bianchi and Carlo Penco. CSLI, 2004.

_____. "Context ex Machina." Pages 15-44 in *Semantics vs. Pragmatics*. Edited by Z. Szabó. Oxford: Oxford Univ. Press, 2005.

Backhaus, Knut. "Gottes nicht bereuter Bund: Alter und neuer Bund in der Sicht des Frühchristentums." Pages 33-55 in *Ekklesiologie des Neuen Testaments*. Edited by Rainer Kampling and Thomas Söding. Freiburg: Herder, 1996.

_____. "Das Bundesmotiv in der frühchristlichen Schwellenzeit: Hebräerbrief, Barnabasbrief, Dialogus cum Tryphone." Pages 211-31 in *Der ungekündigte Bund? Antworten des Neuen Testaments*. Edited by Hubert Frankenmölle. QD. Freiburg: Herder, 1998.

Backus, Irena. *Historical Method and Confessional Identity in the Era of the Reformation (1378-1615)*. Studies in Medieval and Reformation Thought 94. Leiden: Brill, 2003.

Backus, Irena and Claire Chimelli, eds. *La Vraie Piété: Divers traités de Jean Calvin et Confession de foi de Guillaume Farel*. Geneva: 1986.

Baker, J. Wayne. "Das Datum von Bullingers 'Antwort an Johannes Burchard'." *Zwingliana* 14 (1976): 274-75.

_____. *Heinrich Bullinger and the Covenant*. Athens: Ohio Univ. Press, 1980.

_____. "*Sola Fide, Sola Gratia*: The Battle for Luther in Seventeenth-Century England." *The Sixteenth Century Journal* 16.1 (1985): 115-33.

_____. "Heinrich Bullinger, the Covenant, and the Reformed Tradition in Retrospect." *The Sixteenth Century Journal* 29 (1988): 359-76.

Balke, Willem. *Calvin and the Anabaptist Radicals*. Translated by William J. Heynen.

Grand Rapids, MI: Wm. B. Eerdmans, 1981.
Barr, James. "Some Semantic Notes on the Covenant." Pages 23-38 in *Beiträge zur alttestamentlischen Theologie*. Edited by H. Donner, R. Hanhart and R. Smend. Göttingen: Vandenhoeck & Ruprecht, 1977.
Bartholomew, Craig R. "Covenant and Creation: Covenant Overload or Covenantal Deconstruction." *Calvin Theological Journal* 30 (1995): 11-33.
Bavinck, Herman. *Reformed Dogmatics*. 4 vols. Edited by John Bolt. Translated by John Vriend. Grand Rapids, MI: Baker, 2003.
Bebbington, David. "Evangelicals and Eschatology in Britain." Unpublished paper presented at the University of St Andrews, 2007.
Beck, Andreas J. "Zur Rezeption Melancthons bei Gisbertus Voetius (1589-1676), namentlich in seiner Gotteslehre." Pages 317-42 in *Melanchthon und der Calvinismus*. Edited by Günter Frank and Herman J. Selderhuis. Stuttgart: Friedrich Frommann Verlag, 2005.
Becking, Bob. *Between Fear and Freedom: Essays on the Interpretation of Jeremiah 30-31*. Leiden: Brill, 2004.
Beeke, Joel R. "The Dutch Second Reformation (Nadere Reformatie)." Pages lxxxv-cxi in *Christian's Reasonable Service*. Grand Rapids, MI: Reformation Heritage Books, 1992.
Berkouwer, G.C. *Holy Scripture*. Grand Rapids, MI: Eerdmans, 1975.
Biddle, Mark E. *Polyphony and Symphony in Prophetic Literature: Re-reading Jeremiah 7-20*. Macon, GA: Mercer Univ. Press, 1996.
Bierma, Lyle D. "Olevianus and the Authorship of the Heidelberg Catechism: Another Look." *The Sixteenth Century Journal* 13.4 (1982): 17-27.
_____. "Federal Theology in the Sixteenth Century: Two Traditions?" *Westminster Theological Journal* 45 (1983): 304-21.
_____. "The Role of Covenant Theology in Early Reformed Orthodoxy." *The Sixteenth Century Journal* 21, no.3 (1990): 453-62.
_____. *German Calvinism in the Confessional Age: The Covenant Theology of Caspar Olevianus*. Grand Rapids, MI: Baker, 1996.
_____. "What Hath Wittenberg to do with Heidelberg? Philip Melanchthon and the Heidelberg Catechism." in *Melanchthon in Europe: His Work and Influence beyond Wittenberg*. Edited by Karin Maag. Grand Rapids, MI: Baker, 1999.
Blocher, Henri. "Old Covenant, New Covenant." Pages 240-70 in *Always Reforming: Explorations in Systematic Theology*. Edited by A.T.B. McGowan. Leicester, England: Apollos, 2006.
Block, Daniel I. *The Gods of the Nations: Studies in Ancient Near Eastern National Theology*. 2nd ed. Grand Rapids, MI: Baker Academic, 2000.
Blumenkranz, Bernhard. *Die Judenpredigt Augustins: ein Beitrag zur Geschichte der jüdisch-christlichen Beziehungen in den ersten Jahrhunderten*. Basel: Helbing & Lichtenhahn, 1946.
Bock, Darrell L. *Luke*. vol. 2. Grand Rapids, MI: Baker, 1996.
Bockmuehl, Markus. "1QS and Salvation at Qumran." Pages 381-414 in *The Complexities of Second Temple Judaism*. Edited by D.A. Carson, P.T. O'Brien and M.A. Seifrid. Grand Rapids, MI: Baker, 2001.
Böhmer, Siegmund. *Heimkehr und neuer Bund: Studien zu Jeremia 30-31*. Göttingen: Vandenhoek & Ruprecht, 1976.
Bonnardière, A.-M. La. *Le Livre de Jérémie*. Biblia Augustiniana. Paris: Études

Augustiniennes, 1972.

Bonner, Gerald. *St Augustine of Hippo: Life and Controversies*. Rev. ed. Norwich: Canterbury Press, 1986.

Bornkamm, Heinrich. *Luther and the Old Testament*. Translated by Eric W. And Ruth C. Gritsch. Philadelphia: Fortress Press, 1969.

Bovon, François. *Das Evangelium nach Lukas (Lk 19,28-24,53)*. Evangelisch-Kothlischer Kommentar zum neuen Testament. Neukirchener-Vluyn/Düsseldorf: Neukirchener/Patmos, 2009.

Boyle, Leonard E. "The Setting of the Summa Theologiae of St. Thomas—Revisited." Pages 1-16 in *The Ethics of Aquinas*. Edited by Stephen J. Pope. Washington D.C.: Georgetown Univ. Press, 2002.

Bozak, Barbara A. *Life 'Anew': A Literary-Theological Study of Jer. 30-31*. AnBib 122. Rome: Editrice Pontificio Istituto Biblico, 1991.

Bracke, John M. "The Coherence and Theology of Jeremiah 30-31." Ph.D. Diss, Union Theologial Seminary. 1983.

Bright, John. *Jeremiah*. The Anchor Bible 21. New York: Doubleday, 1965.

_____. "An Exercise in Hermeneutics: Jeremiah 31:31-34." *Interpretation* 20.2 (1966): 188-210.

_____. *Covenant and Promise*. London: SCM Press, 1977.

Brown, Dennis. *Vir Trilinguis: A study in the biblical exegesis of Saint Jerome*. Kampen: Kok Pharos, 1992.

Brown, Peter. *Augustine of Hippo: A Biography*. Rev. ed. University of California Press, 2000.

Brueggemann, Walter. *The Land: Place as Gift, Promise, and Challenge in Biblical Faith*. Philadelphia: Fortress, 1977.

_____. "The 'Uncared for' Now Cared for (Jer 30:12-17): A Methodological Consideration." *Journal of Biblical Literature* 104 (1985): 419-28.

_____. *A Commentary on Jeremiah: Exile & Homecoming*. Grand Rapids, MI: Wm. B. Eerdmans, 1998.

Buis, Pierre. "La nouvelle alliance." *Vetus Testamentum* 15 (1968): 1-15.

Büßer, F. "Calvin und Bullinger." Pages 107-26 in *Calvinus Servus Christi*. Edited by Wilhelm H. Neuser. Budapest: 1988.

Buswell, J. Oliver, Jr. *A Systematic Theology of the Christian Religion*. 2 vols. Grand Rapids, MI: Zondervan, 1962.

Caponetto, Salvatore. *The Protestant Reformation in Sixteenth-Century Italy*. Sixteenth Century Essays and Studies. Translated by Anne C. Tedeschi and John Tedeschi. Kirksville, MO: Thomas Jefferson Univ. Press, 1999.

Carleton, James G. "The Idiom of Exaggerated Contrast." *The Expositor* 4th Series, 6 (1892): 365-72.

Carroll, Robert P. *From Chaos to Covenant*. London: SCM Press, 1981.

_____. *Jeremiah*. OTL. London: SCM Press, 1986.

Cazelles, Henri. "Jeremiah and Deuteronomy." Pages 89-112 in *A Prophet to the Nations*. Edited by Leo G. Perdue and B.W. Kovacs. Winona Lake: Eisenbrauns, 1984.

Cessario, Romanus. *The Moral Virtues and Theological Ethics*. Notre Dame: Univ. of Notre Dame, 1991.

Chennattu, Rekha M. *Johannine Discipleship as Covenant Relationship*. Peabody, MA:

Hendrickson, 2006.

Childs, Brevard S. *Biblical Theology of the Old and New Testaments: Theological Reflection on the Christian Bible.* Minneapolis: Fortress, 1992.

Clark, R. Scott. *Caspar Olevianus and the Substance of the Covenant: The Double Benefit of Christ.* Rutherford Studies in Historical Theology. Edinburgh: Rutherford House, 2005.

Clements, R.E. *Prophecy and Covenant.* London: SCM Press, 1965.

_____. *A Century of Old Testament Study.* London: Lutterworth Press, 1976.

_____. "Patterns in the Prophet Canon." Pages 42-55 in *Canon and Authority.* Edited by G.W. Coats and B.O. Long. Philadelphia: Fortress, 1977.

_____. *Jeremiah.* Atlanta: John Knox Press, 1988.

Cobb, W.F. *The Book of Psalms.* London: Methuen, 1905.

Cody, Aelred. "When is the Chosen People called a gôy?" *VT* 14.1 (1964): 1-6.

Coggins, Richard. "What Does "Deuteronomistic" Mean?" Pages 22-35 in *Those Elusive Deuteronomists.* Edited by Linda S. Schearing and Steven L. McKenzie. Sheffield: Sheffield Academic Press, 1999.

Collins, Raymond F. "The Berith-Notion of the Cairo Damascus Document and Its Comparison with the New Testament." *Ephemerides theologicae lovanienses* 39 (1963): 555-94.

Collins, Terence. "Deuteronomist Influence on the Prophetical Books." Pages 15-26 in *The Book of Jeremiah and its Reception.* Edited by A.H.W. Curtis and T. Römer. Leuven: Leuven Univ. Press, 1997.

Cooper, Tim. "The Antinomians Redeemed: Removing Some of the "Radical" from Mid-Seventeenth-Century English Religion." *Journal of Religious History* 24.3 (2000): 247-62.

Coppens, J. "La nouvelle alliance en Jer 31,31-34." *Catholic Biblical Quarterly* 25.1 (1963): 12-21.

Cornill, C.H. *The Prophets of Israel.* Translated by Sutton F. Corkran. 4th ed. Chicago: The Open Court, 1899.

_____. *Das Buch Jeremia.* Leipzig: Chr. Herm. Tauchnitz, 1905.

Courtenay, W.J. *Schools and Scholars in Fourteenth Century England.* Princeton: Princeton Univ, 1987.

Crüsemann, Frank. *The Torah: Theology and Social History of Old Testament Law.* Translated by Allan W. Mahnke. Edinburgh: T&T Clark, 1996.

Dabney, Robert L. *Lectures in Systematic Theology.* Grand Rapids, MI: Zondervan, 1972.

Dahood, Mitchell. "The Word Pair 'AKAL//KALAH in Jeremiah XXX 16." *Vetus Testamentum* 27.4 (1977): 482.

Daniell, David. "Review of *Translating the Bible. From the 7th to the 17th century.* By Lynne Long." *Journal of Ecclesiastical History* 54.4 (2003): 765-67.

Danner, D.G. "The Contribution of the Geneva Bible of 1560 to the English Protestant Tradition." *The Sixteenth Century Journal* 12.3 (1981): 5-18.

Davies, W.D. *Torah in the Messianic Age and/or the Age to Come.* JBL Monograph Series 7. Philadelphia: Society of Bib. Lit, 1952.

De Reuver, Arie. *Sweet Communion: Trajectories of Spirituality from the Middle Ages through the Further Reformation.* Translated by James A. De Jong. Grand Rapids,

MI: Baker, 2007.
Delhaye, Philippe. "La Loi nouvelle comme dynamisme de l'Esprit-Saint." Pages 265-80 in *Lex et Libertas*. Edited by L.J. Elders and K. Hedwig. Studi Tomisitici. Vatican City: Libreria Editrice Vaticana, 1987.
Dent, C.M. *Protestant Reformers in Elizabethan Oxford*. Oxford Univ. Press, 1983.
Diepold, Peter. *Israels Land*. Stuttgart: Kohlhammer, 1972.
Dohmen, Christoph. "Sinaibund als neuer Bund nach Ex 19-34." Pages 51-83 in *Der neue Bund im Alten: Zur Bundestheologie der beiden Testamente*. Edited by Erich Zenger. QD. Freiburg: 1993.
Donnelly, John Patrick. *Calvinism and Scholasticism in Vermigli's Doctrine of Man and Grace*. Leiden: E.J. Brill, 1976.
Driver, S.R. *The Book of the Prophet Jeremiah*. London: Hodder & Stoughton, 1906.
_____. *The Ideals of the Prophets*. Edinburgh: T&T Clark, 1915.
Duhm, Bernhard. *Die Theologie der Propheten als Grundlage für die innere Entwicklungsgeschichte der israelitischen Religion*. Bonn: Verlag von Adolph Marcus, 1875.
_____. *Über Ziel und Methode der theologischen Wissenschaft*. Basel: Benno Schwabe, 1889.
_____. *Jeremia*. Tubingen: J.C.B. Mohr (Paul Siebeck), 1901.
_____. *Israels Propheten*. 2nd ed. Tubingen: J.C.B. Mohr (Paul Siebeck), 1922.
Duke, Alastair. *Reformation and Revolt in the Low Countries*. London: Hambledon Press, 1990.
Dumbrell, W.J. *Covenant and Creation: A Theology of the Old Testament Covenants*. Exeter: Paternoster, 1984.
Dunn, James D.G. *The Parting of the Ways: Between Christianity and Judaism and their Significance for the Character of Christianity*. 2nd ed. London: SCM Press, 2006.
Sanders, E.P. *Paul and Palestinian Judaism*. Philadelphia: Fortress, 1977.
Ebeling, Gerhard. "Die Anfänge von Luthers Hermeneutik." *Zeitschrift für Theologie und Kirche* 48 (1951): 172-230.
Ego, Beate. "'In meinem Herzen berge ich dein Wort': Zur Rezeption von Jer 31,33 in der Torafrömmigkeit der Psalmen." *Jahrbuch für Biblische Theologie* 12 (1997): 277-89.
Eichrodt, Walther. *Theology of the Old Testament*. 2 vols. The Old Testament Library. Translated by John Baker. London: SCM Press, 1967.
Eissfeldt, Otto. "Unheils- und Heilsweissagungen Jeremias als Vergeltung für ihm erwiesene Weh- und Wohltaten." Pages 181-92 in volume 4 of *Kleine Schriften*. Tübingen: J.C.B. Mohr (Paul Siebeck), 1968.
Eitan, Israel. "Hebrew and Semitic Particles: Comparative Studies in Semitic Philology." *American Journal of Semitic Literature and Languages* 44 (1928): 177-205.
_____. "Hebrew and Semitic Particles (Continued): Comparative Studies in Semitic Philology." *American Journal of Semitic Literature and Languages* 46 (1929): 22-51.
Elders, Leo J. "La relation entre l'ancienne et la nouvelle Alliance, selon saint Thomas d'Aquin." *Revue thomiste* 100 (2000): 580-602.
Elliott, Mark W. "Oecolampadius." Pages 403-04 in *The Dictionary of Historical Theology*. Edited by Trevor A. Hart. Grand Rapids, MI: Wm. B. Eerdmans, 2000.
Étiene, Jacques. "Loi et grâce: Le concept de loi nouvelle dans la Somme théòlogique de

S. Thomas d'Aquin." *Revue théologique de Louvain* 16 (1985): 5-22.

Ewald, Heinrich. *Commentary on the Prophets of the Old Testament*. 5 vols. Translated by John Frederick Smith. London: Williams and Norgate, 1875.

Faber, Riemer. "The Humanism of Melanchthon and of Calvin." Pages 11-28 in *Melanchthon und der Calvinismus*. Edited by Günter Frank and Herman J. Selderhuis. Stuttgart: Friedrich Frommann Verlag, 2005.

Farthing, John L. "*Foedus Evangelicum*: Jerome Zanchi on the Covenant." *Calvin Theological Journal* 29 (1994): 149-67.

Fast, Heinold and John H. Yoder. "How to Deal with Anabaptists: An Unpublished Letter of Heinrich Bullinger." *The Mennonite Quarterly Review* 33 (1959): 83-95.

Fieret, W. "Wilhelmus à Brakel." Pages xxxi-lxxxi in *Christian's Reasonable Service*. Grand Rapids, MI: Reformation Heritage Books, 1992.

Fischer, F. and Norbert Lohfink. "'Diese Worte sollst du summen': Dtn 6,7 wedibbartā bām—ein verlorener Schlüssel zur meditativen Kultur in Israel." *Theologie und Philosophie* 62 (1987): 59-72.

Fischer, Georg. *Das Trostbüchlein: Text, Komposition und Theologie von Jer 30-31*. Stuttgart: Verlag Katholisches Bibelwerk, 1993.

Freedman, David Noel. "Divine Commitment and Human Obligation: The Covenant Theme." Pages 168-78 in *Divine Commitment and Human Obligation: Selected Writings of David Noel Freedman*. Edited by John R. Huddlestun. Grand Rapids, MI: Eerdmans, 1997.

Fudge, Thomas A. "Icarus of Basel? Oecolampadius and the Early Swiss Reformation." *Journal of Religious History* 21.3 (1997): 268-84.

Ganoczy, Alexandre. *The Young Calvin*. Translated by David Foxgrover and Wade Provo. Edinburgh: T&T Clark, 1987.

Geisler, Jonathan Neil. *The Thousand Generation Covenant: Dutch Reformed Covenant Theology and Group Identity in Colonial South Africa, 1652-1814*. Studies in the History of Christian Thought. Leiden: E.J. Brill, 1991.

Gordon, A.R. "A Study of Jeremiah." *The Biblical World* 22.2 (1903): 98-106.

Gordon, Bruce. "Calvin and the Swiss Reformed Churches." Pages 64-81 in *Calvinism in Europe, 1540-1620*. Edited by Andrew Pettegree, Alastair Duke and Gillian Lewis. Cambridge: Cambridge Univ. Press, 1994.

_____. *The Swiss Reformation*. Manchester: Manchester Univ. Press, 2002.

_____. "Introduction: Architect of Reformation." Pages 17-32 in *Architect of Reformation: An Introduction to Heinrich Bullinger, 1504-1575*. Edited by Bruce Gordon and Emidio Campi. Grand Rapids, MI: Baker, 2004.

_____. *Calvin*. New Haven: Yale Univ. Press, 2009.

Gordon, Robert P. "A Story of Two Paradigm Shifts." Pages 3-26 in *"The Place Is Too Small for Us": The Israelite Prophets in Recent Scholarship*. Edited by Robert P. Gordon. Sources for Biblical and Theological Study. Winona Lake: Eisenbrauns, 1995.

Goudriaan, Aza. *Reformed Orthodoxy and Philosophy, 1625-1750: Gisbertus Voetius, Petrus van Mastricht, and Anthonius Driessen*. Brill's Series in Church History. Leiden: E.J. Brill, 2006.

Graafland, Cornelis. "Alter und neuer Bund: Calvins Auslegung von Jeremia 31,31-34 und Hebräer 8,8-13." *Zwingliana* 19.2 (1993): 127-45.

Gräbe, Petrus J. *New Covenant, New Community: The Significance of Biblical and Patristic Covenant Theology for Contemporary Understanding*. Carlisle:

Paternoster, 2006.
Graf, Karl Heinrich. *Der Prophet Jeremia*. Leipzig: T.O. Weigel, 1862.
Grice, H.P. *Studies in the Way of Words*. Cambridge, MA: Harvard Univ. Press, 1989.
Groß, Walter. *Zukunft für Israel: Alttestamentliche Bundeskonzepte und die aktuelle Debatte um den neuen Bund*. Stuttgart: Verlag Katholisches Bibelwerk GmbH, 1998.
Grudem, Wayne. *Systematic Theology: An Introduction to Biblical Doctrine*. Grand Rapids, MI: Zondervan, 1994.
Gunkel, Hermann. "The Secret Experiences of the Prophets." *Expositor* 9.1, 9.2 (1924): 356-66, 427-35; 23-32.
Habel, Norman C. *The Land is Mine: Six Biblical Land Ideologies*. Minneapolis: Fortress, 1995.
Hafemann, Scott. *Paul, Moses, and the History of Israel*. Tubingen: J.C.B. Mohr (Paul Siebeck), 1995.
Hagen, Kenneth. *A Theology of Testament in the Young Luther: The Lectures on Hebrews*. Studies in Medieval and Reformation Thought. Leiden: E.J. Brill, 1974.
Hall, Pamela M. *Narrative and the Natural Law: An Interpretation of Thomistic Ethics*. Notre Dame: Univ. of Notre Dame, 1994.
_____. "The Old Law and the New Law." Pages 194-206 in *The Ethics of Aquinas*. Edited by Stephen J. Pope. Washington D.C.: Georgetown Univ. Press, 2002.
Hammer, Karl. "Der Reformater Oekolampad (1482-1531)." *Zwingliana* 19.1 (1992): 157-70.
Hayward, Robert. *The Targum of Jeremiah: Translated, with a Critical Introduction, Apparatus, and Notes*. ArBib. Edinburgh: T&T Clark, 1987.
Healy, Nicholas. "Introduction." Pages 1-20 in *Aquinas on Scripture*. Edinburgh: T&T Clark, 2005.
Hempel, Charlotte. *The Damascus Texts*. Sheffield: Sheffield Academic, 2000.
Hennings, Ralph. *Der Briefwechsel zwischen Augustinus und Hieronymus und ihr Streit um den Kanon des Alten Testaments und die Auslegung von Gal. 2,11-14*. VCSup 21. Leiden: E.J. Brill, 1994.
Herrmann, Siegfried. *Jeremia: Der Prophet und das Buch*. Darmstadt: Wissenschaftliche Buchgesellschaft, 1990.
Hibbs, Thomas S. "Divine Irony and the Natural Law: Speculation and Edification in Aquinas." *International Philosophical Quarterly* 30.4 (1990): 419-29.
_____. "Interpretations of Aquinas's Ethics since Vatican II." Pages 412-25 in *The Ethics of Aquinas*. Edited by Stephen J. Pope. Washington D.C.: Georgetown Univ. Press, 2002.
Hoekema, Anthony A. "The Covenant of Grace in Calvin's Teaching." *Calvin Theological Journal* 2 (1967): 133-61.
Holladay, William L. "Style, Irony and Authenticity in Jeremiah." *Journal of Biblical Literature* 81 (1962): 44-54.
_____. *The Architecture of Jeremiah 1-20*. Lewisburg, PA: Bucknell Univ. Press, 1976.
_____. *Jeremiah*. 2 vols. Hermeneia. Minneapolis: Fortress, 1986.
_____. "Elusive Deuteronomists, Jeremiah, and Proto-Deuteronomy." *Catholic Biblical Quarterly* 66.1 (2004): 55-77.
Holmgren, Frederick. "A New Covenant? For Whom?" *The Covenant Quarterly* 43.1 (1985): 39-44.

_____. *The Old Testament and the Significance of Jesus.* Grand Rapids, MI: Wm. B. Eerdmans, 1999.

Horton, Michael S. *Covenant and Eschatology: The Divine Drama.* Louisville: Westminster John Knox, 2002.

Huffmon, Herbert B. "The Treaty Background of *Yāda'*." *Bulletin of the American Schools of Oriental Research* 181 (1966): 31-37.

Hugenberger, Gordon P. *Marriage as a Covenant: Biblical Law and Ethics as Developed from Malachi.* VTSup 52. Leiden: Brill, 1994.

Hutchinson, J.H. "A New-covenant slogan in the Old Testament." Pages 100-21 in *The God of Covenant.* Edited by Jamie I. Grant and Alistair Wilson. Leicester: Apollos, 2005.

Hyatt, J.P. *Prophetic Religion.* NY: Abingdon Cokesbury, 1947.

_____. "The Book of Jeremiah." Pages 775-1142 in *The Interpreters Bible.* New York: Abingdon, 1956.

_____. "Jeremiah and Deuteronomy." Pages 113-27 in *A Prophet to the Nations.* Edited by Leo G. Perdue and B.W. Kovacs. Winona Lake: Eisenbrauns, 1984.

Israel, Jonathan. *The Dutch Republic: Its Rise, Greatness, and Fall 1477-1806.* Oxford History of Early Modern Europe. Oxford: Clarendon Press, 1995.

Jacobson, Howard. "Jeremiah XXX 17: ציון היא." *Vetus Testamentum* 54.3 (2004): 398-99.

James, Frank A. III. *Peter Martyr Vermigli and Predestination: The Augustinian Inheritance of an Italian Reformer.* Oxford: Oxford Univ. Press, 1998.

Janzen, Gerald J. *Studies in the Text of Jeremiah.* Cambridge, MA: Harvard Univ. Press, 1973.

Janzen, J. Gerald. "On the Most Important Word in the Shema (Deuteronomy VI 4-5)." *Vetus Testamentum* 37 (1987): 280-300.

Joüon, Paul and T. Muraoka. *A Grammar of Biblical Hebrew.* 2 vols. Rome: Editrice Pontificio Istituto Biblico, 2000.

Karlberg, Mark W. "Reformed Interpretation of the Mosaic Covenant." *Westminster Theological Journal* 43.1 (1980): 1-57.

_____. "The Mosaic Covenant and the Concept of Works in Reformed Hermeneutics: A Historical-Critical Analysis with Particular Attention to Early Covenant Eschatology." 1980.

Keil, C.F. *The Prophecies of Jeremiah.* Translated by David Patrick And James Kennedy. Edinburgh: T&T Clark, 1866.

Kelly, J.N.D. *Jerome: His Life, Writings, and Controversies.* London: Duckworth, 1975.

Keown, G.L., P.J. Scalise and T.G. Smothers. *Jeremiah 26-52.* WBC. Dallas: Word, 1995.

Kerr, Fergus. "Aquinas and Analytic Philosophy: Natural Allies?" Pages 119-36 in *Aquinas in Dialogue: Thomas for the Twenty-First Century.* Edited by Jim Fodor and F.C. Bauerschmidt. Oxford: Blackwell, 2004.

Kevan, Ernest F. *The Grace of Law: A Study of Puritan Theology.* Grand Rapids, MI: Baker, 1976.

Kieffer, René. "Jerome: His Exegesis and Hermeneutics." Pages 663-81 in volume 1.1 of *Hebrew Bible/Old Testament: The History of its Interpretation.* Edited by Magne Saebo. Göttingen: Vandenhoeck & Ruprecht, 1996.

Kilpp, Nelson. *Niederreißen und aufbauen: Das Verhältnis von Heilsverheißung und*

Unheilsverkündigung bei Jeremia und im Jeremiabuch. BThSt 13. Neukirchen-Vluyn: Neukirchener Verlag, 1990.

Klauber, Martin I. "Continuity and Discontinuity in Post-Reformation Reformed Theology: An Evaluation of the Muller Thesis." *Journal of the Evangelical Theological Society* 33.4 (1990): 467-75.

Klein, Ralph W. "Jeremiah 23:1-8." *Interpretation* 34 (1980): 167-72.

Koch, Klaus. *The Prophets.* 2: The Babylonian and Persian Periods. London: SCM Press, 1983.

Krašovec, Jože. *Reward, Punishment, and Forgiveness: The Thinking and Beliefs of Ancient Israel in the Light of Greek and Modern Views.* VTSup 78. Leiden: Brill, 1999.

Kraus, Hans-Joachim. *Biblisch-theologisches Aufsätze.* Neukirchen-Vluyn: Neukirchener Verlag, 1972.

———. "Der Erste und der Neue Bund." Pages 59-69 in *Eine Bibel—zwei Testamente.* Edited by Christoph Dohmen and Thomas Söding. Paderborn: Ferdinand Schöningh, 1995.

Kuenen, A. *The Prophets and Prophecy in Israel.* Translated by Adam Milroy. London: Longmans, Green, & Co, 1877.

Kühn, Ulrich. *Via Caritatis: Theologie des Gesetzes bei Thomas von Aquin.* Göttingen: Vandenhoeck & Ruprecht, 1965.

———. "Nova Lex. Die Eigenart der christlichen Ethik nach Thomas von Aquin." Pages 243-47 in *Lex et Libertas.* Edited by L.J. Elders and K. Hedwig. Studi Tomisitici. Vatican City: Libreria Editrice Vaticana, 1987.

Kunz, Marcus. "Sending Words into Battle: Reformation Understandings and Uses of Letter and Spirit." 2002.

Kutsch, Ernst. *Verheissung und Gesetz.* Berlin: Walter de Gruyter, 1973.

Lacombe, Georges. *La Vie et les Oeuvres de Prévostin.* Bibliothèque Thomiste 11. Le Saulchoir: 1927.

Lalleman-De Winkel, H. *Jeremiah in Prophetic Tradition: An Examination of the Book of Jeremiah in the Light of Israel's Prophetic Traditions.* Leuven: Peeters, 1997.

Lambert, Malcolm. *The Cathars.* Oxford: Blackwell, 1998.

———. *Medieval Heresy: Popular Movements from the Gregorian Reform to the Reformation.* 3rd ed. Oxford: Blackwell, 2002.

Lancel, Serge. *St. Augustine.* Translated by Antonia Nevill. London: SCM Press, 2002.

Landgraf, A.M. *Dogmengeschichte der Frühscholastik.* Regensburg: Verlag Friedrich Pustet, 1954.

Leblanc, Marie. "Le péché originel dans la pensée de S. Thomas." *Revue thomiste* 93 (1993): 567-600.

Lee, Brian J. *Johannes Cocceius and the Exegetical Roots of Federal Theology: Reformation Developments in the Interpretation of Hebrews 7-10* (Göttingen: Vandenhoeck & Ruprecht, 2009).

Lehne, Susanne. *The New Covenant in Hebrews.* JSNTSup 44. Sheffield: Sheffield Academic Press, 1990.

Lemke, Werner E. "Jeremiah 31:31-34." *Interpretation* 37.2 (1983): 183-87.

Lenchak, Timothy A. *'Choose Life!': A Rhetorical-Critical Investigation of Deuteronomy 28,69-30,20.* AnBib 129. Rome: Editrice Pontificio Istituto Biblico, 1993.

Letham, Robert. "The Foedus Operum: Some Factors Accounting for Its Development."

Sixteenth Century Journal 14.4 (1983): 457-67.

Leuchter, Mark. *Josiah's Reform and Jeremiah's Scroll: Historical Calamity and Prophetic Response*. Sheffield: Sheffield Phoenix, 2006.

Levering, Matthew. *Christ's Fulfillment of Torah and Temple: Salvation according to Thomas Aquinas*. Notre Dame: Univ. of Notre Dame, 2002.

Levin, Christoph. *Die Verheißung des neuen Bundes: in ihrem theologiegeschichtlichen Zusammenhang ausgelegt*. Göttingen: Vandenhoeck & Ruprecht, 1985.

Lichtenberger, Hermann and Stefan Schreiner. "Der neue Bund in jüdischer Überlieferung." *Theologische Quartalschrift* 176.4 (1996): 272-90.

Lillback, Peter A. "Ursinus' Development of the Covenant of Creation: A Debt to Melanchthon or Calvin?" *Westminster Theological Journal* 43 (1981): 247-88.

———. *The Binding of God: Calvin's Role in the Development of Covenant Theology*. Grand Rapids, MI: Baker, 2001.

———. "The Early Reformed Covenant Paradigm: Vermigli in the Context of Bullinger, Luther and Calvin." Pages 70-96 in *Peter Martyr Vermigli and the European Reformations: Semper Reformanda*. Edited by Frank A. III James. Leiden: Brill, 2004.

Lohfink, Norbert. *Das Hauptgebot: Eine Untersuchung literarischer Einleitungsfragen zu Dtn 5-11*. AnBib 20. Rome: Pontifical Biblical Institute, 1963.

———. *The Covenant Never Revoked: Biblical Reflections on Christian-Jewish Dialogue*. Translated by John J. Scullion. Mahwah, NJ: Paulist Press, 1991.

———. "Was There a Deuteronomistic Movement?" Pages 36-66 in *Those Elusive Deuteronomists*. Edited by Linda S. Schearing and Steven L. McKenzie. Sheffield: Sheffield Academic, 1999.

———. "Ein Bund oder zwei Bünde in der Heiligen Schrift." Pages 272-97 in *L'interpretazione della Bibbia nella Chiesa*. Vatican City: Libreria Editrice Vaticana, 2001.

———. *In the Shadow of Your Wings: New Readings of Great Texts from the Bible*. Translated by Linda M. Maloney. Collegeville, MN: Liturgical Press, 2003.

———. "Der Neue Bund im Deuteronomium?" Pages 9-36 in *Studien zum Deuteronomium und zur deuteronomistischen Litereatur V*. Edited by Norbert Lohfink. Stuttgart: Katholisches Bibelwerk, 2005.

Lohfink, Norbert and Erich Zenger. *The God of Israel and the Nations: Studies in Isaiah and the Psalms*. Translated by Everett R. Kalin. Collegeville, MN: Liturgical Press, 2000.

Loofs, Friedrich. "Pelagius und der pelagianische Streit." Pages 747-74 in volume 15 of *Realencyklopädie für protestantische Theologie und Kirche*. Edited by Albert Haurk. Leipzig: 1904.

Lössl, Josef. *Intellectus Gratiae: Die erkenntnistheoretische und hermeneutische Dimension der Gnadenlehre Augustins von Hippo*. Leiden: E.J. Brill, 1997.

———. *Julian von Aeclanum: Studien zu seinem Leben, seinem Werk, seiner Lehre und ihrer Überlieferung*. VCSup 60. Leiden: E.J. Brill, 2001.

Lubac, Henri de. *Medieval Exegesis*. 2 vols. Translated by Mark Sebanc. Edinburgh: T&T Clark, 1998.

Lucas, Ernest C. "Sacrifice in the Prophets." Pages 59-74 in *Sacrifice in the Bible*. Edited by Roger T. Beckwith and Martin J. Selman. Carlisle/Grand Rapids: Paternoster/Baker, 1995.

Lundbom, Jack R. "Jeremiah, Book of." Pages 706-21 in volume 3 of *Anchor Bible*

Dictionary. Edited by D.N. Freedman. New York: Doubleday, 1992.

———. *Jeremiah 1-20*. The Anchor Bible. NY: Doubleday, 1999.

———. *Jeremiah 21-36*. The Anchor Bible. NY: Doubleday, 2004.

Lust, Johan. "'Gathering and Return' in Jeremiah and Ezekiel." Pages 119-42 in *Le Livre de Jérémie*. Leuven: Leuven Univ. Press, 1981.

MacCulloch, Diarmaid. "Peter Martyr and Thomas Cranmer." Pages 173-201 in *Peter Martyr Vermigli: Humanism, Republicanism, Reformation*. Edited by Emidio Campi. Geneva: Libraririe Droz, 2002.

Maier, Christl. *Jeremia als Lehrer der Tora: Soziale Gebote des Deuteronomiums in Fortschreibungen des Jeremiabuches*. Gottingen: Vandenhoeck & Ruprecht, 2002.

Marafioti, Domenico. *Sant'Agostino e la Nuova Alleanze: L'Interpetazione agostiniana di Geremia 31,31-34 nell'ambito dell'esegesi patristica*. Rome: Gregorian Univ. Press, 1995.

March, W.E. "*Laken*: Its Functions and Meanings." Pages 256-84 in *Rhetorical Criticism*. Edited by J.J. Jackson and M. Kessler. Pittsburgh: Pickwick, 1974.

Martínez, Florentino García and Eibert J.C. Tigchelaar, eds. *The Dead Sea Scrolls Study Edition*. 2 vols. Leiden/Grand Rapids: Brill/Eerdmans, 2000.

Mason, Steven D. *"Eternal Covenant" in the Pentateuch: The Contours of an Elusive Phrase*. Library of Hebrew Bible/Old Testament Studies. Edinburgh: T&T Clark, 2008.

Maurer, Wilhelm. "Melanchthons Loci communes von 1521 als wissenschaftliche Programmschrift." *Luther-Jahrbuch* 27 (1960): 1-50.

Maurus, Rabanus. *Expositionis super Jeremiam prophetam, libri viginti*. PL 111. Edited by J.-P. Migne. Paris: n.d.

McCarthy, D.J. *Treaty and Covenant: A Study in form in the Ancient Oriental Documents and in the Old Testament*. AnBib 21a. Rome: Biblical Institute, 1981.

McConville, J.G. "Jeremiah: Prophet and Book." *Tyndale Bulletin* 42 (1991): 80-95.

———. *Judgment and Promise: An Interpretation of the Book of Jeremiah*. Leicester/Winona Lake: Apollos/Eisenbrauns, 1993.

McCoy, Charles S. and J. Wayne Baker. *Fountainhead of Federalism: Heinrich Bullinger and the Covenantal Tradition*. Louisville, KY: Westminster John Knox Press, 1991.

McGiffert, Michael. "Grace and Works: The Rise and Division of Covenant Divinity in Elizabethan Puritanism." *Harvard Theological Review* 75.4 (1982): 463-502.

———. "From Moses to Adam: The Making of the Covenant of Works." *Sixteenth Century Journal* 19.2 (1988): 131-55.

McKane, William. *Jeremiah*. 2 vols. ICC. Edinburgh: T&T Clark, 1986.

McNair, Philip. *Peter Martyr in Italy: An Anatomy of Apostasy*. Oxford: Clarendon, 1967.

Miller, Patrick D. "The Gift of God: The Deuteronomic Theology of the Land." *Interpretation* 23 (1969): 451-65.

———. *Sin and Judgment in the Prophets*. SBLMS. Chico, CA: Scholars Press, 1982.

———. "The Most Important Word: The Yoke of the Kingdom." *Iliff Review* 41 (1984): 17-29.

———. "The Book of Jeremiah." Pages 553-926 in volume 6 of *New Interpreters Bible*. Nashville: Abingdon, 2001.

Miyatami, Y. "Theologia conversionis in St. Augustine." *Congresso Internazionale su S. Agostino Nel XVI Centenario della Conversione* 1 (1987): 49-60.

Moberly, R.W.L. *Prophecy and Discernment.* Cambridge: Cambridge Univ. Press, 2006.

Morrison, Michael D. *Who Needs a New Covenant? Rhetorical Function of the Covenant Motif in the Argument of Hebrews.* Princeton Theological Monograph Series. Eugene, OR: Pickwick, 2008.

Moulton, W.J. "The New Covenant in Jeremiah." *The Expositor, 7th Series* 1 (1906): 370-82.

Movers, F.C. *De utriusque recensionis vaticiniorum Ieremiae, Graecae Alexandrinae et Hebraicae marorethicae, indole et origine commentatio critica.* Hamburg: 1837.

Mowinckel, Sigmund. *Zur Komposition des Buches Jeremia.* Dybwad: Kristiania, 1914.

Mullan, David George. *Scottish Puritanism 1590-1638.* Oxford: Oxford Univ. Press, 2000.

Muller, Richard A. "The Covenant of Works and the Stability of Divine Law in Seventeenth-Century Reformed Orthodoxy: A Study in the Theology of Herman Witsius and Wilhelmus à Brakel." *Calvin Theological Journal* 29 (1994): 75-101.

_____. "Ordo Docendi: Melanchthon and the Organization of Calvin's Institutes." Pages 123-40 in *Melanchthon in Europe: His Work and Influence beyond Wittenberg.* Edited by Karin Maag. Grand Rapids, MI: Baker, 1999.

_____. *The Unaccomodated Calvin: Studies in the Foundation of a Theological Tradition.* Oxford Univ. Press, 2000.

_____. "Reformed Confessions and Catechisms." Pages 466-85 in *Dictionary of Historical Theology.* Edited by Trevor A. Hart. Grand Rapids, MI: Wm. B. Eerdmans, 2000.

_____. *Post-Reformation Reformed Dogmatics.* 4 vols. Grand Rapids, MI: Baker, 2003.

Murphy-O'Connor, Jerome. "The New Covenant in the Letters of Paul and the Essene Documents." Pages 195-204 in *To Touch the Text.* Edited by Maurya P. Horgan and Paul J. Kobelski. New York: Crossroad, 1989.

Naylor, Peter J. "The Language of Covenant: A Structural Analysis of the Semantic Field of ברית in Biblical Hebrew, with Special Reference to the Book of Genesis." D.Phil. Diss, Oxford University. 1980.

Neumann, Peter H.A. "Prophetenforschung seit Heinrich Ewald." Pages 1-51 in *Das Prophetenverständnis in der deutschsprachigen Forschung seit Heinrich Ewald.* Edited by Peter H.A. Neumann. Darmstadt: Wissenschaftliche Buchgesellschaft, 1979.

Nicholson, Ernest W. *Preaching to the Exiles: A Study of the Prose Tradition in the Book of Jeremiah.* Oxford: Blackwell, 1970.

_____. *God and His People: Covenant and Theology in the Old Testament.* Oxford: Clarendon Press, 1986.

North, R. "חָדָשׁ." Pages 225-44 in volume 4 of *Theological Dictionary of the Old Testament.* Edited by G.Johannes Botterweck and Helmer Ringgren. Grand Rapids, MI: Eerdmans, 1980.

O'Connor, Kathleen. *The Confessions of Jeremiah: Their Interpretation and Role in Chapters 1-25.* SBLDS. Atlanta: Scholars Press, 1988.

O'Donnell, James J. "Augustine: his time and lives." Pages 8-25 in *Cambridge Companion to Augustine.* Edited by Eleanore Stump and Norman Kretzmann. Cambridge Univ. Press, 2001.

_____. *Augustine, Sinner and Saint: A New Biography.* London: Profile Books, 2005.
O'Neill, Colman E. "St. Thomas on the Membership of the Church." *Thomist* 27 (1963): 88-140.
Opitz, Peter. *Heinrich Bullinger als Theologe: Eine Studie zu den "Dekaden".* Zurich: Theologischer Verlag, 2004.
_____. "Bullinger's *Decades*: Instruction in Faith and Conduct." Pages 101-16 in *Architect of Reformation: An Introduction to Heinrich Bullinger, 1504-1575.* Edited by Bruce Gordon and Emidio Campi. Grand Rapids, MI: Baker, 2004.
Osterhaven, M. Eugene. "The Experiential Theology of Early Dutch Calvinism." *Reformed Review* 27.3 (1974): 180-89.
_____. "Calvin on the Covenant." Pages 89-106 in *Readings in Calvin's Theology.* Edited by Donald K. McKim. Grand Rapids, MI: Baker, 1984.
Parker, T.H.L. *Calvin's Old Testament Commentaries.* Edinburgh: T&T Clark, 1986.
_____. *Calvin's New Testament Commentaries.* Louisville, KY: Westminster John Knox Press, 1993.
Parunak, H. Van Dyke. "Some Discourse Functions of Prophetic Quotation Formulas in Jeremiah." Pages 489-519 in *Biblical Hebrew and Discourse Linguistics.* Edited by Robert D. Bergen. Winona Lake: Eisenbrauns, 1994.
Pelikan, Jaroslav. *The Emergence of the Catholic Tradition (100-600).* The Christian Tradition 1. Chicago: Univ. of Chicago Press, 1971.
Perlitt, Lothar. *Vatke und Wellhausen: Geschichtsphilosophische Voraussetzungen und historiographische Motive für die Darstellung der Religion und Geschichte Israels durch Wilhelm Vatke und Julius Wellhausen.* Berlin: Verlag Alfred Töpelmann, 1965.
_____. *Bundestheologie im Alten Testament.* Neukirchen-Vluyn: Neukirchener Verlag, 1969.
Pesch, O.H. *Die Theologie der Rechtfertigung bei Martin Luther und Thomas von Aquin: Versuch eines systematisch-theologischen Dialogs.* Mainz: Matthias-Grünewald-Verlag, 1985.
Pettegree, Andrew. "Coming to terms with victory: the upbuilding of a Calvinist church in Holland, 1572-1590." Pages 160-80 in *Calvinism in Europe, 1540-1620.* Edited by Andrew Pettegree, Alastair Duke and Gillian Lewis. Cambridge: Cambridge Univ. Press, 1994.
Pollmann, Karla. "Augustine's Hermeneutics as a Universal Principle!" Pages 206-31 in *Augustine and the Disciplines: From Cassiacum to Confessions.* Oxford Univ. Press, 2005.
Porter, Jean. "Desire for God: Ground of the Moral Life in Aquinas." *Theological Studies* 47 (1986): 48-68.
_____. *Natural & Divine Law: Reclaiming the Tradition for Christian Ethics.* Grand Rapids, MI: Eerdmans, 1999.
Potter, H.D. "The New Covenant in Jeremiah XXXI 31-34." *Vetus Testamentum* 33.3 (1983): 347-57.
Preus, James Samuel. *From Shadow to Promise: Old Testament Interpretation from Augustine to the Young Luther.* Cambridge, MA: Harvard Univ. Press, 1969.
Puckett, David L. *John Calvin's Exegesis of the Old Testament.* Louisville, KY: Westminster John Knox Press, 1995.
von Rad, Gerhard. *Old Testament Theology.* 2 vols. Translated by D.G.M. Stalker. Edinburgh: Oliver and Boyd, 1962.

———. *The Problem of the Hexateuch and Other Essays.* New York: McGraw-Hill, 1966.

Raitt, Thomas M. *A Theology of Exile: Judgment/Deliverance in Jeremiah and Ezekiel.* Philadelphia: Fortress, 1977.

Rayburn, Robert S. "The Contrast Between the Old and New Covenants in the New Testament." Ph.D. Diss, University of Aberdeen. 1978.

Rees, B.R. *Pelagius: A Reluctant Heretic.* Woodbridge: Boydell Press, 1988.

Renaud, Bernard. "L'alliance éternelle d'Ez 16,59-63 et l'alliance nouvelle de Jr 31,31-34." Pages 335-59 in *Ezekiel and his Book*. Edited by J. Lust. Leuven: Univ. of Leuven, 1986.

———. *Nouvelle ou Éternelle Alliance? Le message des prophètes.* Paris: Les Éditions du Cerf, 2002.

Rendtorff, Rolf. *Canon and Theology: Overtures to an Old Testament Theology.* Translated by Margaret Kohl. Philadelphia: Fortress, 1993.

Rendtorff, Rolf and H.H. Henrix, eds. *Die Kirchen und das Judentum. Dokumente von 1945-1985.* 2nd ed. Munich: Paderborn, 1989.

Reta, José Oroz. "L'homme nouveau selon saint Augustin." *Augustinian Studies* 17 (1986): 161-67.

Reventlow, Henning Graf. *The Authority of the Bible and the Rise of the Modern World.* Translated by John Bowden. London: SCM Press, 1984.

Robinson, Bernard P. "Jeremiah's New Covenant: Jer 31,31-34." *Scandinavian Journal of the Old Testament* 15.2 (2001): 182-204.

Robinson, H. Wheeler. "Hebrew Psychology." Pages 353-82 in *The People and the Book*. Edited by A.S. Peake. Oxford: Clarendon Press, 1925.

———. *The Cross of Jeremiah.* London: SCM Press, 1925.

Rogers, Eugene F., Jr. "Thomas and Barth in Convergence on Romans 1?" *Modern Theology* 12.1 (1996): 57-84.

———. "The Narrative of Natural Law in Aquinas's Commentary on Romans 1." *Theological Studies* 59.2 (1998): 254-76.

Rogland, M.F. *Alleged Non-Past Uses of Qatal in Classical Hebrew.* SSN. Assen: Van Gorcum, 2003.

Römer, Thomas. "Les "anciens" pères (Jér 11,10) et la "nouvelle" alliance (Jér 31,31)." *Biblische Notizen* 59 (1991): 23-27.

Van Rooden, Peter T. *Theology, Biblical Scholarship and Rabbinical Studies in the Seventeenth Century: Constantijn L'Empereur (1591-1648) Professor of Hebrew and Theology at Leiden.* Leiden: E.J. Brill, 1989.

Rosenberg, A.J. *Jeremiah: A New English Translation of the Text, Rashi and a Commentary Digest.* New York: Judaica Press, 1985.

Roth, John D. "Harmonizing the Scriptures: Swiss Brethren understandings of the relationship between the Old and New Testament during the last half of the sixteenth century." Pages 35-52 in *Radical Reformation Studies: Essays presented to James M. Stayer*. Edited by Werner O. Packull and Geoffrey L. Dipple. St. Andrews Studies in Reformation History. Aldershot: Ashgate, 1999.

Rudolph, Wilhelm. *Jeremia.* 2nd ed. Tübingen: J.C.B. Mohr (Paul Siebeck), 1958.

van Ruler, J.A. *The Crisis of Causality: Voetius and Descartes on God, Nature and Change.* Brill's Studies in Intellectual History. Leiden: E.J. Brill, 1995.

Sarason, Richard S. "The Interpretation of Jeremiah 31:31-34 in Judaism." Pages 99-123 in *When Jews and Christians Meet*. Edited by Jakob J. Petuchowski. Albany, NY:

State Univ. of New York Press, 1988.
Schenker, Adrian. "Unwiderrufliche Umkehr und neuer Bund: Vergleich zwischen der Wiederherstellung Israels in Dt 4,25-31; 30,1-14 und dem neuen Bund in Jer 31,31-34." *Freiburger Zeitschrift für Philosophie und Theologie* 27 (1980): 93-106.

———. "Die Tafel des Herzens." Pages 1-14 in *Text und Sinn im Alten Testament: Textgeschichtliche und Bibeltheologische Studien*. Edited by Adrian Schenker. Göttingen: Vandenhoeck & Ruprecht, 1991.

———. *Das Neue am Neuen und das Alte am alten: Jer 31 in der hebräischen und griechischen Bibel, von der Textgeschichte zu Theologie, Synagoge und Kirche*. Göttingen: Vandenhoeck & Ruprecht, 2006.

Schindler, Alfred. "Vermigli und die Kirchenväter." Pages 37-43 in *Peter Martyr Vermigli: Humanism, Republicanism, Reformation*. Edited by Emidio Campi. Geneva: Librairie Droz, 2002.

Schmid, Konrad. *Buchgestalten des Jeremiabuches: Untersuchungen zur Redaktions- und Rezeptionsgeschichte von Jer 30-33 im Kontext des Buches*. WMANT 72. Neukirchen-Vluyn: Neukirchener Verlag, 1996.

Schmidt, Nathaniel. "Covenant." Pages I.928b-37a in *Encyclopaedia Biblical*. Edited by T.K. Cheyne and J. Sutherland Black. London: Adam & Charles Black, 1899.

———. "Jeremiah (Book)." Pages 2372b-95a in *Encyclopaedia Biblica*, vol. 2. Edited by T.K. Cheyne and J. Sutherland Black. London: Adam & Charles Black, 1901.

Schofield, John. *Philip Melanchthon and the English Reformation*. St. Andrews Studies in Reformation History. Ashgate: Aldershot, 2006.

Scholl, Hans. "Calvin und die Schweiz—Die Schweiz und Calvin." Pages 303-28 in *Calvin im Kontext der Schweizer Reformation*. Edited by Peter Opitz. Zurich: Theologische Verlag, 2003.

Schrenk, Gottlieb. *Gottesreich und Bund im älteren Protestantismus vornhemlich bei Johannes Coccejus*. Giessen: Brunnen Verlag, 1985.

Searle, John R. "The Background of Meaning." Pages 221-32 in *Speech Act Theory and Pragmatics*. Edited by John R. Searle, F. Kiefer and M. Bierwisch. Dordrecht: D. Reidel, 1980.

Sedgwick, John. *Antinomianism Atomized*. London: 1643.

Seebass, Horst. "Erstes oder Altes Testament?" Pages 27-43 in *Die Einheit der Schrift und die Vielfalt des Kanons*. Edited by John Barton and Michael Wolter. Berlin: Walter de Gruyter, 2003.

Selderhuis, Herman J. "Ille Phoenix: Melanchton und der Heidelberger Calvinismus 1583-1622." Pages 45-59 in *Melanchthon und der Calvinismus*. Edited by Günter Frank and Herman J. Selderhuis. Stuttgart: Friedrich Frommann Verlag, 2005.

Skinner, John. *Prophecy and Religion: Studies in the Life of Jeremiah*. Cambridge: Cambridge Univ. Press, 1961.

Smalley, Beryl. "William of Auvergne, John of La Rochelle and St. Thomas Aquinas on the Old Law." Pages 11-71 in volume 2 of *St. Thomas Aquinas: Commemorative Studies*. Edited by Armand A. Maurer. Toronto: Pontifical Institute of Medieval Studies, 1974.

Smend, Rudolf. *Lehrbuch der alttestamentlichen Religionsgeschichte*. Leipzig: J.C.B. Mohr (Paul Siebeck), 1893.

———. *From Astruc to Zimmerli: Old Testament Scholarship in Three Centuries*. Translated by Margaret Kohl. Tübingen: Mohr Siebeck, 2007.

Smith, George Adam. *Jeremiah*. London: Hodder & Stoughton, 1923.

Sprunger, Keith L. *Dutch Puritanism: A History of English and Scottish Churches of the Netherlands in the Sixteenth and Seventeenth Centuries*. Studies in the History of Christian Thought. Leiden: E.J. Brill, 1982.

Staehelin, Ernst. *Briefe und Akten zum Leben Oekolampads*. 2 vols. Quellen und Forschungen zur Reformationsgeschichte 10. Leipzig: 1934.

_____. *Das theologische Lebenswerk Johannes Oekolampads*. Quellen und Forschungen zur Reformationsgeschichte 21. Leipzig: M. Heinsius, 1939.

Steck, O.H. *The Prophetic Books and their Theological Witness*. Translated by James D. Nogalski. St. Louis, MO: Chalice Press, 2000.

Stek, John H. "'Covenant' Overload in Reformed Theology." *Calvin Theological Journal* 29 (1994): 12-41.

Stiver, Dan R. *Theology after Ricoeur*. Louisville: Westminster John Knox, 2001.

Stöhr, Johannes. "Bewahrt das Sittengesetz des alten Bundes seine Geltung im neuen Bund?" Pages 219-40 in *Lex et Libertas*. Edited by L.J. Elders and K. Hedwig. Studi Tomisitici. Vatican City: Libreria Editrice Vaticana, 1987.

Story, Joanna. *Carolingian Connections: Anglo-Saxon England and Carolingian Francia, c.750-870*. Studies in Early Medieval Britian. Aldershot/Burlington: Ashgate, 2003.

Strehle, Stephen. *Calvinism, Federalism, and Scholasticism: A Study of the Reformed Doctrine of Covenant*. Bern: Peter Lang, 1988.

Strohm, Christoph. "Bullingers *Dekaden* und Calvins *Institutio*. Gemeinsamkeiten und Eigenarten." Pages 215-48 in *Calvin im Kontext der Schweizer Reformation*. Edited by Peter Opitz. Zurich: Theologischer Verlag, 2003.

Stulman, Louis. *Order amid Chaos: Jeremiah as Symbolic Tapestry*. Sheffield: Sheffield Academic Press, 1998.

_____. "The Prose Sermons as Hermeneutical Guide to Jeremiah 1-25: The Deconstruction of Judah's Symbolic World." Pages 34-63 in volume 260 of *Troubling Jeremiah*. Edited by A.R. Pete Diamond, Kathleen O'Connor and Louis Stulman. JSOTSup. Sheffield: Sheffield Academic Press, 1999.

_____. *Jeremiah*. Abingdon Old Testament Commentaries. Nashville: Abingdon, 2005.

Swetnam, J. "Why was Jeremiah's New Covenant New?" Pages 111-15 in *Studies on Prophecy*. Edited by J.A. Emerton. VTSup. Leiden: Brill, 1974.

Thiel, Winfried. *Die deuteronomistische Redaktion von Jeremia 1-25*. Neukirchen-Vluyn: Neukirchener Verlag, 1973.

_____. *Die deuteronomistische Redaktion von Jeremia 26-45*. Neukirchen-Vluyn: Neukirchener Verlag, 1981.

Thompson, John L. *Reading the Bible with the Dead: What You Can Learn from the History of Exegesis that You Can't Learn from Exegesis Alone*. Grand Rapids, MI: Eerdmans, 2007.

Tita, Hubert. "'Ich hatte meine Tora in ihre Mitte gegeben': Das Gewicht einer nicht berücksichtigten Perfektform in Jer. XXXI 33." *Vetus Testamentum* 52 (2002): 551-56.

Torrell, Jean-Pierre. *Saint Thomas Aquinas: The Person and His Work*. Translated by Robert Royal. Washington D.C.: Catholic Univ. of America, 2003.

Trible, Phyllis. *God and the Rhetoric of Sexuality*. Philadelphia: Fortress, 1978.

Tyacke, Nicholas. *Aspects of English Protestantism c.1530-1700*. Manchester: Manchester Univ. Press, 2001.

Unterman, Jeremiah. *From Repentance to Redemption: Jeremiah's Thought in Transition*.

JSOTSup 54. Sheffield: Sheffield Academic Press, 1987.

Vanhoye, A. "Salut universel par le Christ et validité de l'Ancienne Alliance." *Nouvelle Revue Théologique* 116 (1994): 815-35.

———. "Réaction à l'exposé du prof. Norbert Lohfink «Ein Bund oder zwei Bünde in der heiligen Schrift»." Pages 298-303 in *L'interpretazione della Bibbia nella Chiesa*. Vatican City: Libreria Editrice Vaticana, 2001.

Venema, Cornelis P. *Heinrich Bullinger and the Doctrine of Predestination: Author of "the other Reformed Tradition"?* Grand Rapids, MI: Baker, 2002.

Vermes, Geza. *An Introduction to the Complete Dead Sea Scrolls*. Minneapolis: Fortress, 1999.

Vermeylen, J. "L'alliance renouvellée (Jr 31,31-34). L'histoire littéraire d'un text célèbre." Pages 57-84 in *Lectures et relectures de la Bible*. Edited by J.-M. Auwers and A. Wénin. Leuven: Leuven Univ. Press, 1999.

Visser, Derk. *Zachary Ursinus: The Reluctant Reformer, His Life and Times*. New York: UCC Press, 1983.

Vogt, Peter T. *Deuteronomic Theology and the Significance of Torah: A Reappraisal*. Winona Lake, IN: Eisenbrauns, 2006.

Volz, D. Paul. *Der Prophet Jeremia*. 2nd ed. Leipzig: A. Deichertsche Verlagsbuchhandlung D. Werner Scholl, 1928.

Vos, Geerhardus. "The Doctrine of the Covenant in Reformed Theology." Pages 234-67 in *Redemptive History and Biblical Interpretation: the Shorter Writings of Geerhardus Vos*. Edited by Richard B. Gaffin. Phllipsburg, NJ: P&R, 1980.

Vriezen, Th.C. *An Outline of Old Testament Theology*. Translated by S. Neuijen. 2nd ed. Oxford: Blackwell, 1970.

Wacholder, Ben Zion. *The New Damascus Document: The Midrash on the Eschatological Torah of the Dead Sea Scrolls: Reconstruction, Translation and Commentary*. STDJ. Leiden: Brill, 2007.

Wakefield, Walter L. and Austin P. Evans, eds. *Heresies of the High Middle Ages: Translated with Notes*. New York: Columbia Univ. Press, 1991.

Wallis, Wilber B. "Irony in Jeremiah's Prophecy of a New Covenant." *Journal of the Evangelical Theological Society* 12 (1969): 107-10.

Waltke, Bruce K. *A Commentary on Micah*. Grand Rapids, MI: Eerdmans, 2007.

Watson, Francis. *Text and Truth: Redefining Biblical Theology*. Grand Rapids, MI: Eerdmans, 1997.

Weaver, Rebecca Harden. *Divine Grace and Human Agency: A Study of the Semi-Pelagian Controversy*. Patristic Monograph Series. Macon: Mercer Univ. Press, 1996.

Webster, John. *Holy Scripture: A Dogmatic Sketch*. Cambridge: Cambridge Univ. Press, 2003.

Webster, Tom. *Godly Clergy in Early Stuart England: the Caroline Puritan Movement c.1620-1643*. Cambridge: Cambridge Univ. Press, 1997.

Weinfeld, Moshe. "Jeremiah and the Spiritual Metamorphosis of Israel." *Zeitschrift für die alttestamentliche Wissenschaft* 88.1 (1976): 17-56.

Weippert, Helga. "Das Wort vom neuen Bund in Jeremia XXXI 31-34." *Vetus Testamentum* 29.3 (1979): 336-51.

Weir, David A. *The Origins of the Federal Theology in Sixteenth-Century Reformation Thought*. Oxford: Clarendon Press, 1990.

Weiser, Artur. *Der Prophet Jeremia 25,14-52,34*. Göttingen: Vandenhoeck & Ruprecht,

1955.

Wengert, Timothy J. *Law and Gospel: Philip Melanchthon's Debate with John Agricola of Eisleben over Poenitentia*. Grand Rapids, MI: Baker, 1997.

―――. "We will Feast Together in Heaven Forever: The Epistolary Friendship of John Calvin and Philip Melanchthon." Pages 19-44 in *Melanchthon in Europe: His Work and Influence beyond Wittenberg*. Edited by Karin Maag. Grand Rapids, MI: Baker, 1997.

Westberg, Daniel. *Right Practical Reason: Aristotle, Action and Prudence in Aquinas*. Oxford: Clarendon, 1994.

Wilcox, Pete. "Calvin as Commentator on the Prophets." Pages 107-30 in *Calvin and the Bible*. Edited by Donald K. McKim. Grand Rapids, MI: Baker, 1997.

Williams, Megan Hale. *The Monk and the Book: Jerome and the Making of Christian Scholarship*. Chicago/London: Univ. of Chicago, 2006.

Williams, Rowland. *The Hebrew Prophets*. 2. London: Williams and Norgate, 1871.

Wilson, Robert R. "Who Was the Deuteronomist? (Who Was Not the Deuteronomist?): Reflections on Pan-Deuteronomism." Pages 67-82 in *Those Elusive Deuteronomists*. Edited by Linda S. Schearing and Steven L. McKenzie. Sheffield: Sheffield Press, 1999.

Wittgenstein, Ludwig. *Philosophical Investigations*. Translated by G.E.M. Anscombe. 3rd ed. Oxford: Blackwells, 2001.

Wolf, Hans Heinrich. *Die Einheit des Bundes: Das Verhältnis von Altem und Neuem Testament bei Calvin*. Neukirchen: Verlag der Buchhandlung des Erziehungsvereins Neukirchen Kreis Moers, 1958.

Wolff, Christian. *Jeremia im Frühjudentum und Urchristentum*. Texte und Unteersuchungen. Berlin: Akademie Verlag, 1976.

Wolterstorff, Nicholas. *Divine Discourse: Philosophical Reflections on the Claim that God Speaks*. Cambridge: Cambridge Univ. Press, 1995.

Wright, Christopher J.H. *God's People in God's Land: Family, Land, and Property in the Old Testament*. Grand Rapids, MI: Eerdmans, 1990.

Wright, David F. "Augustine: His Exegesis and Hermeneutics." Pages 701-30 in volume 1.1 of *Hebrew Bible/Old Testament: The History of its Interpretation*. Edited by Magne Saebo. Göttingen: Vandenhoeck and Ruprecht, 1996.

Wright, N.T. *The Climax of the Covenant: Christ and the Law in Pauline Theology*. Philadelphia: Fortress, 1993.

Zenger, Erich. *Am Fuss des Sinai*. 2nd ed. Düsseldorf: Patmos Verlag, 1994.

―――. "Thesen zu Hermeneutik des Ersten Testaments nach Auschwitz." Pages 143-58 in *Eine Bibel- zwei Testamente*. Edited by Christoph Dohmen and Thomas Söding. Paderborn: Ferdinand Schöningh, 1995.

―――. *Das Erste Testament: Die jüdischen Bibel und die Christen*. 2nd ppb. ed. Düsseldorf: Patmos, 2004.

Index: Biblical Citations

Gen	3:15	84	Num	4:23, 37, 41	209
	9	248		8:19, 21	209
	15:6	38		14:18	213
	17	248		18	248
	17:6	210		25	248
	18	194			
	18:3	216	Deut	1:17	215
	27:21	216		1:22	215
	29:18	209		1:26-46	195
	30:26	209		2:19	215
	31:41	209		2:37	215
				4:10-14	94
Exod	1:14	209		4:11	216
	3:5	216		4:13	147
	7:16	209		4:20	191
	10:26	210		4:25-31	166
	15:26	199		4:30	190
	16:9	216		5:3	199
	19:1-8	190		5:6	191
	19:4	191		5:11	213
	19:4-5	199		5:22	158, 231
	20-23	147		5:23	215
	20:2	191		5:33	197
	20:7	213		6:4-5	231
	20:16	231		6:6-8	143
	22:7	216		6:20-25	192
	26:30	214		8:14f	192
	31	248		8:20	190
	31:18	146		9:7, 24	196
	34:7	213		9:15-21	94
	34:27	209		10:1-8	94
				10:12	209
Lev	5:10	38		11:13	209
	24	131, 248		17:15	215

Deut (cont.)

20:2	215, 216	33:3	130
25:1, 9	216	34:6	237
26:16-19	94	36:2	238
27	187	38:5	237
27:26	227	39:4	237, 238
28	223	46:2	130
28:47	209	50:19	237
29:25	192	51	52
30	118, 166	51:12	173, 238
30:6	128	55:5	238
30:11	90	56:2	237
30:1-14	166	57:4	237
30:6	128-29	59:4	237
30:11	143	63:7	237
32:44-47	94	63:8	235
		64:7	238

Josh
5:19	209	73:9	237
22:5	209	81:7	237
24:14	209	89	248
		89:36	235

Psalm
1	144, 162	93:3	237
2:11	209	100:2	209
3:6	236	102:25	237
4:4	236	103	178
4:7	130	104:6	237
6:7	236	105:10	248
6:10	236	105:40	237
7:14	237	108:8	236
10:17	236	109:22	238
16:9	237	110:4	235
16:18	236	114:3	237
17:6	236	116:1	130
17:11	237	116:3	237
18:1	130	119	144, 162, 178
18:5	236		
18:9	237	119:11	232, 236
18:15	8	119:13	90
19	144, 162	119:54	90
24:2	237	119:73	236
26:4-5	237		

Psalms (cont.)					
	138:3	237	2:33	206	
	139:13	236	2:37	236	
	143:5	237	3:2	221	
Prv	3:3	231-32	3:10	231	
	7:1	167	3:14	226, 235	
	7:3	231-32	3:16	231	
1 Sam	10:18-19	192	3:16-18	222	
	12:20, 24	209	3:17	231	
	28:2	206	4:3,4	187	
2 Sam	23:5	248	4:4	13, 201	
1 Kgs	3:9	232	4:7	222	
	6:38	214	4:9	212	
2 Kgs	17:7-40	195	4:14	231, 238	
	21:15	195	4:18-19	231	
1 Chr	16:17	248	4:20-26	222	
	28:9	209	4:22	240	
Isa	2:3	88	4:30	236-37	
	24:5	248	5:1-6	187, 194, 241	
	28:18	227			
	29:20	236	5:6	237	
	33:7	236	5:8	237	
	35:3-4	76	5:10	201	
	40f	202	5:12	32	
	41:1	216	5:18	222	
	49:14-15	219	5:19	209, 212	
	51:4	75	5:20	187	
	51:7	76	5:21	231	
	52:8	236	5:23-24	231	
	59:21	76	5:26	237	
	63:16	130	5:31	237	
	66:12-13	219	6:10	237	
			6:13	195	
Jer	1	82-83	6:14	205	
	1:10	223	6:30	228	
	2:6	192, 196	7:1f	199, 225	
	2:7	221	7:18	195	
	2:8		7:19	199	
	2:20	212	7:21-28	197-202	
	2:25	236	7:22-23	146, 192	
	2:31	194	7:23f	170	

Jer (cont.)

7:24	231	17:1-3	233
7:31	231	17:4	222
7:34	218, 222	17:5	231
8:11	205	17:9	162, 231
8:13	237	17:16f	212
8:16	222	17:25	187
8:18	231	18:11	187
8:21	205	18:17	212
9:1-6	195	20:11	236
9:3	240	22	221
9:12	190, 235	22:15-16	147, 176, 240
9:13	231		
9:23	241	22:17	231
9:24-25	201, 233	22:21	201
10:13	190	22:26	221
10:19	205	23:1-4	220
10:20	218	23:5	212
10:24	213	23:5-8	221
11	115	23:6	221
11:1-13	186-97, 225, 227	23:7-8	193
		23:8	222
11:8	231	23:9	238
11:14-17	190	23:16, 17	231
12:2	237	23:39	201
12:3	212	24:6	222
12:7-8	201	24:7	233
12:10-11	221	24:10	222
12:15	222	25:1f	195
13:10	231	25:5	222
14:9	228	25:9-11	215
14:10	241	25:11	222
14:14	231	25:30	190
14:17	205	25:33	212
15:6-7	201, 237	29:10	220
16:12	231	29:14	222
16:14-15	193	30:3	217, 222
16:15	222	30:4-11	208-14, 219
16:18	221		
16:19	212	30:8-11	206, 215
17:1	158		

Jer (cont.)

30:12-17	204-07, 219	34:13-14	192-93, 196
30:14	155	39:16f	212
30:17	217, 243	44:6	212
30:18-22	214-16, 218	44:23	190
		46:11	204
30:21	238	46:27-28	212
31:2-6	217	46:28	209, 213
31:4	218	50:4-5	250
31:5	223	Lam 1:20	238
31:9	217, 219, 243	Ezek 11:19	238
31:10-14	217	36:26	122, 238
31:11-12	236	40:28-37	78
31:12	223		
31:15-20	218-19	Hos 1-2	223
31:20	219, 243	Mic 2:5	206
31:21	223		
31:21-30	26	Nah 1:3	213
31:21-22	218		
31:23	223	Matt 5:17	91
31:24-25	223	15:24	8
31:27-30	36		
31:28	158	Luke 22:14-20	254
31:29	235		
31:30	144	John 1:17	89
31:35-37	201	15	227
31:38-40	223		
32:15	222	Acts 13:46	8
32:20-23	192	15	134
32:23	196	15:10	63-64
32:32	187		
32:33	190	Rom 3:31	13
32:37	222	8	134
32:39	233	10:5-10	89
32:36-41	249	11	122
32:42-44	222, 249	1 Cor 10	259
33:17f	177		

2 Cor	3	7, 119, 133, 139, 147, 253	Heb (cont.)
			9:1 134
			10:1 133
			10:4 255
Gal	4	134	13:22 255
Heb	7-8	139	Baruch 1:19 196
	7:12	37	
	8:6-7	122	1 Mac 10:26 228
	8:8-9	109, 119, 123	*Damascus Document*
	8:13	39, 134	15:14-15 251
	8:16	255	19:32-35 251
	9:9	38, 255	

Author and Subject

Adeyemi, F.	1, 230
Alcuin of York	32-33, 37, 80
Alston, W.	183-84
Anabaptists	67-69, 75-76, 85, 101, 126
Augustine	1, 3, 5-29, 30, 33-34, 36, 41-42, 46-47, 49-64, 66-68, 70, 72, 74, 78, 88, 90-91, 95-97, 99, 100-03, 117, 123, 133-34, 137-38, 140-42, 150, 155-56, 162, 174-75, 178-79, 225, 232, 234, 245-47, 253-55, 258
Ball	104, 110-23, 127, 132, 134, 138, 145, 178-79, 246
Bierma, L.	66, 83, 97, 105, 107-09, 112
Blake, T.	113, 117, 119-20, 123
Bolton, S.	111, 115, 138, 147
A Brakel, W.	125-26, 132, 136-38
Bright, J.	155-58, 164, 166, 176, 187, 204-05, 209
Bucer, M	59, 74, 87, 90, 98, 109-10
Bullinger	58, 67-82, 84-85, 87, 92, 96-99, 102-05, 109, 129, 135, 137,
Calamy, E.	111-12, 115, 123
Calvin, J.	1-2, 58, 66, 75, 82-98, 102-03, 105, 117-18, 121, 123, 138, 163, 178-79, 187, 193, 195,

Calvin (cont.) 206, 208, 216, 218, 230, 241, 246, 258
Cameron, J. 112, 138
Carroll, R. 157, 162, 164-66, 183, 186, 188, 200, 202, 204, 212, 214-16
Cathars 34-35, 53, 55, 67, 246, 257
Chrysostom, J. 9-10, 31, 33, 36
Clark, R.S. 104-05
Cocceius, J. 114, 124-31, 134, 136, 218
Cornill, C.H. 146-48, 157-58, 177, 188-89, 195, 200, 206, 215, 227, 240
Covenant
 and Abraham 32-33, 78-80, 82, 87-88, 107, 115-16, 121, 130-31, 250, 252
 Broken 4, 77, 115, 132, 135, 156, 169, 172-73, 178, 180, 184-202, 204, 218-19, 224-28, 233, 239, 243-44, 248-51, 254.
 Eternal 69, 94, 101, 121-23, 127, 132, 149, 160, 177, 226, 247-50, 255-58
 Formula 171, 188, 226, 239, 244, 249-50
 of Grace 101, 109, 111-17, 119, 121-38, 247, 250

Covenant (cont.)
 Mosaic 32, 80, 82, 101, 110-14, 126, 130, 151, 178, 194, 230, 251
 Renewed 80, 144, 156-57, 168-74, 229, 248
 of Works 32, 109-21, 126-27, 136
Cyprian 8, 10-11
Duhm, B. 4, 142-48, 150, 159-60, 164-66, 186, 188, 198, 204, 206, 215, 230
Groß, W. 166-68, 174, 226, 228-29, 233, 238
Holmgren, F. 175-76, 234, 243
Jerome 5-14, 16, 23-24, 27, 28, 30-31, 33, 35, 36-37, 74, 103, 140, 175, 194, 198, 200, 242
Julian of Aeclanum 14-15, 19, 21, 26, 31, 67, 155, 246
Kant, I. 141, 146-47
Kraus, H.-J. 162-63, 166, 185, 197
Law
 Ceremonial 38, 45-47, 49, 64, 68, 73, 93, 109, 118, 120, 175, 240, 257
 vs. Gospel 7, 11, 31-32, 37-38, 60-62, 64, 71, 75, 86-96, 100-102, 110-112, 117-119, 134

Law (cont.)
  Vetus/nova 9, 35, 38-39, 45-53, 57, 75, 111
Lillback, P. 83, 85, 89, 97-98
Lohfink, N. 160, 166, 168, 170-74, 190, 201, 232-33, 243
Lössl, Josef 14-17, 21-22, 27, 245
Luther, M. 1, 50, 59-64, 81, 95
Maccovius, J. 134-135, 138
Mason, S. 160, 226, 247-48, 250
Melanchthon 45, 58-67, 72, 81, 85, 90, 93, 95, 101-02, 105, 109, 179
Moulton, W.J. 147-48
Muller, R. 83, 85, 103, 110, 113, 126
Musculus, W. 80, 239
Oecolampadius 33, 58, 75-82, 85-86, 92, 95, 101-103, 109, 126, 130, 132, 138, 145, 154, 171
Olevianus, C. 104-110, 112, 119-20, 127, 131, 136, 138, 200, 246
Origen 6, 8, 10, 20
Paul Alvarez of Cordoba 31, 111
Pelagius 13-14, 16, 25
Pemble, W. 111
Perkins, W. 111, 113
Perlitt, L. 141, 161-62
Peter Lombard 35-37, 45-46, 55, 61
Polyander, J. 133-34
Prepositinus 35, 53-54
Preston, J. 112

Rabanus Maurus 5, 33
von Rad, G. 152-55, 157, 160, 162-63, 167, 172, 174, 191, 193, 201, 221
Rayburn, R.S. 2, 177-78, 255, 258
Renaud, B. 159-60, 165, 185, 234-35, 250
Rogland, M. 236
Rollock, R. 69, 109, 112, 138
Rutherford, S. 113, 116-17, 119, 123
Schenker, A. 166, 168, 196-97, 227-28, 230, 232, 235-38
Skinner, J. 142, 150, 157, 164, 189-90, 198
Servetus, M. 86-87
Strong, W. 113, 120-22, 239
Thomas Aquinas 1, 30, 33-58, 63, 77, 97, 179, 246
Turretin, F. 131-32
Ursinus, Z. 66, 104, 108
Vermigli 58, 97-105, 141, 179
Voetius, G. 124-27, 134
Volz, P. 149, 151, 156, 188, 206, 208-09, 216, 220
Watson, F. 256-59
Witsius, H. 2, 104, 124-32, 138
Zanchius, J. 135
Zenger, E. 166, 168-74, 201, 230, 232, 257
Zwingli, H. 67, 69, 77, 82, 87

www.ingramcontent.com/pod-product-compliance
Lightning Source LLC
Chambersburg PA
CBHW030306080526
44584CB00012B/465